PAUL IN HIS HELLENISTIC CONTEXT

PAUL IN HIS
HELLENISTIC CONTEXT

edited by

TROELS ENGBERG-PEDERSEN

T&T CLARK INTERNATIONAL
A Continuum imprint
LONDON • NEW YORK

Published by T&T Clark International
A Continuum imprint
The Tower Building, 11 York Road, London SE1 7NX
15 East 26th Street, Suite 1703, New York, NY 10010

www.tandtclark.com

British Library Cataloguing-in-Publication Data
A catalogue record for this book is available from the British Library

ISBN 0567084264 (paperback)

Typeset by Trinity Typesetting, Edinburgh
Printed on acid-free paper in Great Britain by The Bath Press, Bath

Contents

Contributors ix

Abbreviations xi

Introduction xv
Troels Engberg-Pedersen

1. Universalism in Judaism and Christianity 1
Alan F. Segal

2. 'Yes,' 'No,' 'How Far?': The Participation of Jews and Christians in Pagan Cults 30
Peder Borgen

3. Paul and the Hellenistic Schools: The Evidence of Galen 60
Loveday Alexander

4. Transferring a Ritual: Paul's Interpretation of Baptism in Romans 6 84
Hans Dieter Betz

5. Enthymemic Argumentation in Paul: The Case of Romans 6 119
David Hellholm

6. Romans 7.7–25 as a Speech-in-Character (προσωποποιία) 180
Stanley K. Stowers

7. The Quest for Honor and the Unity of the Community in Romans 12 and in the Orations of Dio Chrysostom 203
Halvor Moxnes

Contributors

Loveday Alexander
University of Sheffield
Sheffield, England

David E. Aune
Loyola University of Chicago
Chicago, Illinois

Hans Dieter Betz
University of Chicago
Chicago, Illinois

Peder Borgen
Trondheim University
Trondheim, Norway

Troels Engberg-Pedersen
Copenhagen University
Copenhagen, Denmark

David Hellholm
Oslo University
Oslo, Norway

Abraham J. Malherbe
Yale Divinity School
New Haven, Connecticut

Halvor Moxnes
Oslo University
Oslo, Norway

Alan F. Segal
Barnard College
New York, New York

Stanley K. Stowers
Brown University
Providence, Rhode Island

Abbreviations

The essays in this book employ the style of the *Journal of Biblical Literature* as set out in *JBL* 107, 3 (1988) 579–96. Abbreviations of Greco-Roman authors and texts in principle follow the *Oxford Classical Dictionary*, but where misunderstandings were excluded authors were allowed to retain their preferred abbreviations. The following list includes abbreviations of periodicals, reference works, and serials that either differ from those adopted by *JBL* or are not included in the *JBL* list.

AAWG.PH	Abhandlungen der Akademie der Wissenschaften in Göttingen. Philologisch-historische Klasse
ABSA	*Annual of the British School at Athens*
AGLB	Vetus latina. Aus der Geschichte der lateinischen Bibel
AlbR.PPh	Alber-*Reihe* Praktische Philosophie
ALW	*Archiv für Liturgiewissenschaft*
AnSoc	*Ancient Society*
AnSt	*Anatolian Studies*
ASNU	Acta Seminarii Neotestamentici Upsaliensis
AThANT	Abhandlungen zur Theologie des Alten und Neuen Testaments
AThD	*Acta Theologica Danica*
AthSL	Athenaion-Skripten Linguistik
AW	*Antike Welt*
BHM	*Bulleting of the History of Medicine*
BHTh	Beiträge zur historischen Theologie
CCSL	Corpus Christianorum. series latina
ClR	*The Classical Review*
CStL	Cambridge Studies in Linguistics
CTL	Cambridge Textbooks in Linguistics
dGL	de Gruyter Lehrbuch
EEvT	Einführung in die Evangelische Theologie

EKK	Evangelisch-Katholischer Kommentar zum Neuen Testament
HAW	Handbuch der Altertumswissenschaft
HUTh	Hermeneutische Untersuchungen zur Theologie
Hyp.	Hypomnemata
IstM	*Istanbul Mitteilungen*
JIdS	Jahrbuch des Instituts für deutsche Sprache
JSS	Jewish Social Studies
KAV	Kommentar zu den Apostolischen Vätern
LEC	Library of Early Christianity
LiLi	*Zeitschrift für Literaturwissenschaft und Linguistik*
MThS	Münchener Theologische Studien
MThZ	*Münchener Theologische Zeitschrift*
PRE	Pauly's Real-Encyclopädie der classischen Altertumswissenschaft
PT	Papiere zur Textlinguistik/Papers in Textlinguistics
QAL	*Quaderni del archeologia della Libia*
RQ	*Römische Quartalschrift*
RThR	*Reform Theological Review*
RVV	Religionsgeschichtliche Versuche und Vorarbeiten
Scriptor	Scriptor Taschenbücher
SHAW.PH	Sitzungsberichte der Heidelberger Akademie der Wissenschaften, philol.-hist. Klasse
SLKW	Schwerpunkte Linguistik und Kommunikationswissenschaft
SMB.Sb-e	Serie Monografica di "Benedictina" Sezione biblico-ecumenica
SNIA	Skrifter utgitt av Det Norske Institutt i Athen
Spud.	Spudasmata
StL	*Studia Liturgica*
StTh	*Studia Theologica*
stw	suhrkamp taschenbuch wissenschaft
SVF	*Stoicorum Veterum Fragmenta*, ed. H. von Arnim, 4 vols. (Leipzig: B.G. Teubner, 1903–24, repr. 1964)
TBL	Tübinger Beiträge zur Linguistik
TEH	Theologische Existenz heute
Tem	*Temenos*
ThV	*Theologia Viatorum*

UaLG	Untersuchungen zur antiken Literatur und Geschichte
UTB	Universitätstaschenbücher
VSII.HF	Videnskabsselskapets Skrifter II. Hist. filos. Klasse
WJA	*Würzburger Jahrbücher für die Altertumswissenschaft*
ZfS	*Zeitschrift für Sprachwissenschaft*
ZGL	*Zeitschrift für germanistische Linguistik*
ZPE	*Zeitschrift für Papyrologie und Epigraphik*

Introduction

Troels Engberg-Pedersen

This book owes its origin to a conference on Paul and his Hellenistic background held in June 1991 in Copenhagen, Denmark. The conference was attended by the following scholars and research students from the United States, Great Britain, and the Nordic countries: Loveday Alexander (Sheffield), David E. Aune (Chicago), Hans Dieter Betz (Chicago), Per Bilde (Aarhus), Peder Borgen (Trondheim), Samuel Byrskog (Lund), Trond Skard Dokka (Oslo), Troels Engberg-Pedersen (Copenhagen), Anders Eriksson (Lund), Lone Fatum (Copenhagen), Birger Gerhardsson (Lund), Clarence E. Glad (Reykjavik), Georg Graesholt (Copenhagen), Geert Hallbäck (Copenhagen), Lars Hartman (Uppsala), David Hellholm (Oslo), Bengt Holmberg (Lund), Niels Hyldahl (Copenhagen), René Kieffer (Uppsala), Timo Laato (Aabo), Bente Bagger Larsen (Aarhus), Eva Maria Lassen (Copenhagen), Inger Marie Lindboe (Oslo), Abraham J. Malherbe (Yale), Wayne A. Meeks (Yale), Halvor Moxnes (Oslo), Mogens Müller (Copenhagen), Johannes Nissen (Aarhus), Aage Pilgaard (Aarhus), John K. Riches (Glasgow), Lars Rydbeck (Lund), Heikki Räisänen (Helsinki), Alan F. Segal (Columbia), Turid Karlsen Seim (Oslo), Torrey Seland (Möre and Romsdal, Norway), Stanley K. Stowers (Brown), Henrik Tronier (Copenhagen), Walter Übelacker (Lund), Håkan Ulfgard (Lund/Copenhagen).

The essays in this volume, with the exception of that by Moxnes, began as papers read at the conference. (Moxnes's essay was presented on a later occasion in Denmark.) The authors wish to acknowledge the invaluable help they received from all participants in the discussion, including those who supplied written comments after the conference.

The conference was a happy occasion, with participants having a mounting sense that they were on to some important insights on an age-old scholarly issue. A sign of this is the change from the original title of the conference, which reflected the traditional idea of 'backgrounds', to that of the present volume. Paul was part and parcel of Hellenistic culture, a participant in it as opposed to an outside spectator to it. It is appropriate to develop the implications of this a little more fully with a view to highlighting the overall profile of the book.

The Hellenistic Context

From very early the study of Paul has been bound up with the more general debate on the relationship of Judaism and Hellenism. The last two decades, however, have seen some notable advances, which may end up by overcoming altogether the almost endemic presupposition that there is a Hellenistic Paul to be played out against a Jewish Paul, or vice versa. The crucial factor behind this development has been the determined effort of scholars either to leave on one side as completely as possible their own religious interests or else to put them up-front, rather than hiding them — and to scrutinize rigorously those readings of other scholars which do not manage to do this.

One very clear result of this is the trend on the part of Christian scholars to see Paul very much as a Jew — one who espoused what is no doubt a special form of Judaism, but still something that remains one recognizable form of Judaism among many others in the Hellenistic and Roman periods. At least since 1977,[1] this has meant that earlier readings of Paul by Jewish scholars have received renewed attention. Similarly, modern attempts by Jewish scholars to look more confidently at Paul as an important link in the history of Judaism in antiquity are accepted as potentially highly illuminating contributions to the historical understanding of Paul — even though they may not in the end capture the whole Paul.

Along with this development, the same period has witnessed a surge of interest in analyzing the Pauline texts in close comparison with phenomena that are traditionally taken to be specifically Hellenistic. These are phenomena that pertain to (1) the social setting of the Pauline texts; (2) their rhetorical structure, style, and argumentation; and (3) Paul's use of the *topoi* of popular moral philosophy. Since the Pauline

---

[1] With the publication of E. P. Sanders, *Paul and Palestinian Judaism: A Comparison of Patterns of Religion* (Philadelphia: Fortress Press, 1977).

letters were primarily addressed to Gentiles living in the Greek world, and since rhetoric and moral philosophy were distinctly, that is, originally, Greek contributions, with only very slight counterparts in originally Jewish culture, the three approaches that focus on these features of the Pauline texts treat Paul very much as a Greek, or at least as a Jew heavily influenced by originally Greek cultural elements.

The three approaches that focus on the Greek Paul represent a renewal of an interest that developed and gathered strength in Pauline scholarship about a hundred years ago, around 1890, only to be cut short by the new developments in German theology that resulted from the First World War. An excellent survey by Rudolf Knopf of work on 'Paul and Hellenism' in German scholarship, published in October 1914 (and hence written on the very eve of the war), bears witness to this.[2] Knopf is careful to avoid the specious contrasts between the Jewish and the Hellenistic Paul that have otherwise plagued scholarship. Thus he starts out emphasizing that 'Paul was a Jew': 'Paul grew up, and remained, within the rich religious tradition of his people,' and 'his religion is to be understood in the light of the theology and practice of later Judaism.' He goes on, however, to show, referring to an impressive line of contemporary scholars (Deissmann, Norden, J. Weiss, Bultmann, Bonhöffer, Wendland, Lietzmann, Dibelius, Reitzenstein, and others), how Paul was influenced by his Hellenistic surroundings in language, style, literary genre, philosophical ideas, and religious motifs. The close similarity of this with at least two of the three modern approaches identified above (the rhetorical and the moral philosophical one) is obvious.[3]

The analysis of Paul's handling of specifically religious motifs has undergone a complete change since the period of scholarship covered by Knopf. Then, as is well known, work done in the *Religionsgeschichtliche*

---

[2]   *AJT* 17, 4 (1914) 497–520. Note the following statement: 'The subject "Paul and Hellenism" seems to me beyond question to designate the field in which the chief problems of Pauline study for the future lie' (p. 497). Subsequent quotations are from pp. 499–500 and 514.

[3]   The situation is slightly different in the case of the social historical approach, which has no direct counterpart in Knopf's survey. However, this approach, too, has its antecedents in scholarship of the same period; cf. the introductory remarks in Wayne A. Meeks, *The First Urban Christians: The Social World of the Apostle Paul* (New Haven: Yale University Press, 1983) 3.

Schule had turned decisively towards the Hellenistic mystery religions in an attempt to elucidate the mystical elements in Paul's religion. Thus in spite of energetic criticism of this non-Jewish orientation, for example, by Schweitzer, Knopf could summarize this approach by claiming that 'mysticism [including the kind represented by Paul] did not grow upon Jewish soil'. With the discovery of the Qumran writings, however, with the more careful dating of Gnosticism that has followed upon the discovery of the Nag Hammadi library, and with more work having been done on early Jewish mysticism (by Scholem), the pendulum has rightly moved toward Judaism — to such an extent, however, that one may begin to wonder whether something is not again beginning to be lost here. It is certainly true that Paul the mystic constitutes an important link in Jewish religion in antiquity, but would an unprejudiced look at the many varieties of Judaism in the Hellenistic and Roman periods not show many more points of contact with one or the other type of non-Jewish, 'Hellenistic' religion proper (or with individual motifs therein) than scholars are at present prepared to allow for? A renewed, thorough analysis of this question seems long overdue. What has hindered its realization is presumably two facts. First, we are still in a period of reaction to the *Religionsgeschichtliche Schule* in the form it took in dialectical theology. And, second, in spite of the new developments, scholars (including Jewish ones) have been slow to shake off completely the old prejudices tied to the very terms Judaism and Hellenism, particularly in the area of specifically religious motifs.

This general topic lies outside the scope of the present volume, which concentrates instead on the three approaches that stand in direct continuation of the line of research initiated a hundred years ago: the social historical, the rhetorical and the moral philosophical one. In spite of this affiliation, however, there is a special emphasis in the kind of investigation undertaken in this volume. Since it is determined not to let any given theological interest color its comparison of Paul with phenomena in his cultural context, whether (originally) Jewish or (originally) Greek, it is entirely open to seeing Paul as a place of confluence of ideas, motifs, and practices of almost any provenance. Thus if a scholar succeeds in establishing important points of contact between Pauline Christianity and other Jewish religious groups, this is not to be taken as an argument for a specifically Jewish Paul, nor does it exclude the possibility that there may be equally important points of contact with non-Jewish, specifically Hellenistic groups, and vice versa. Paul was neither *specifically* Jewish nor *specifically* Hellenistic. Any one- or two-word categorization of him should be avoided.

The point is exceedingly simple and already familiar to anyone who has felt the severe inadequacy of '-ism-stereotypes. It was well formulated by Arnaldo Momigliano in his coy statement that a comparison of Hellenism and Judaism is a comparison of two unknown quantities.[4] But this point needs to be restated again and again due to the way these two '-isms have constantly been put to theological use — from antiquity to the present day.

This breaking down of boundaries between 'Hellenism' and 'Judaism' has been much helped by two recent developments in scholarship that have been occurring in complete independence of the Pauline issue — one in classical scholarship on the Hellenistic period in general and one in Jewish scholarship on the history of Judaism in the same period. First, in modern historiography on the Hellenistic period proper (from Alexander to the Roman political takeover, which occurred at different times in different places in the eastern Mediterranean area) there has been a decisive break away from understanding the history of the period in terms of the old, ideologically based monolithic contrast between the rationally superior out-going Greek or 'Western' culture and the justly submitting 'Oriental' cultures conquered by Alexander. Ancient historians have looked far more carefully at what happened in detail in the Seleucid and Ptolemaic kingdoms that resulted from Alexander's conquests. The result has been a picture that stresses both the initial insularity of the Greek conquerors in the conquered lands, in political as well as more broadly cultural terms, but also a continuance of the steady influence of Greek culture in the Near East and Egypt which had begun a long time before Alexander and was not decisively changed by the conquests. Conversely, people from the East who went as merchants to the old Greek heartland brought with them their own culture, which was made to fit into the originally Greek culture in

4 In Momigliano's review of *Judentum und Hellenismus* by Hengel, *JTS* 21 (1970) 149–53.

many different ways. The result of all these developments was 'Hellenistic culture', which, depending on the area and group of people one is talking about, should be understood as a term for the culture that results from mixing *originally* Greek cultural elements with *originally* non-Greek cultural elements. It is *the mixture* (in a given time and place) that constitutes Hellenistic culture proper (in that place).

As an important corollary of this, the term 'Hellenistic' itself should not be understood as signifying those elements in the Hellenistic cultural melting-pot that were specifically and originally Greek. Rather, it is a substantively empty term designating the mixture of cultural elements that one is likely to find when one considers a certain phenomenon in the Hellenistic period proper (as defined above in political terms) — and in the Roman period too as long as one is talking about the eastern Mediterranean area.[5] It is for this reason that the present volume of essays on Paul 'in his Hellenistic context' begins with two attempts to explore similarities and differences between Paul and other *Jewish* groups or patterns of thought in the Hellenistic world. Such issues too are part of Paul's 'Hellenistic' context.

The other recent development alluded to above is the determined effort of scholars working on Judaism in the Hellenistic and Roman periods not to make any big, generalizing claims about Diaspora Judaism versus Palestinian Judaism, but rather to sort out in patient, painstaking analysis the differences and similarities between different types within those two categories and the similarities across the categorical boundaries. Here too, what the present approach comes down to is a dedication to detailed precision rather than ideologically based overall generalizations.

There is one corollary of this whole understanding that should be made explicit. When the essays in the present volume reach out to

---

[5]   Two usages of the term 'Hellenistic' should be kept distinct. In one sense it designates a period of political dominance. This period ends in the eastern Mediterranean area at different times in different places with the Roman political takeover. According to this usage we should speak of the Hellenistic and Roman periods as two consecutive ones. In another sense the term designates the mixed culture that developed in the various parts of the eastern Mediterranean area before, during, and after the Hellenistic period proper. Thus we may continue to speak, in that area, of a 'Hellenistic' culture even during the Roman period – and so also of Paul's 'Hellenistic' context.

introduce various elements from Paul's cultural context that seem comparable to Pauline ones, the aim, as will already be clear, is not to tie Paul exclusively to one or the other cultural configuration in that context. But further, the primary aim of bringing in the parallels is not in fact at all to contribute to such historical, objective stock-taking from the outside. Rather, it is the more creative one of further elucidating, as it were from within, the meaning of individual passages in the Pauline text. It is this textual meaning that is in focus — what Paul was saying and doing through his text; what message he was trying to convey. Paul is not to be seen as some disembodied mind against the 'background' of his surrounding culture, and the Pauline texts are not analyzed merely as examples of general cultural phenomena. Rather, what the scholars represented in this volume wish to illuminate is *Paul* and the communities he addressed, and the texts are analyzed as unique acts of communication within the common and complex media of 'Hellenistic' culture.

Here too the present essays show their indebtedness to the period a hundred years ago when a critical historical consciousness was most forcefully alive in Pauline scholarship. What did Paul mean in this text, at this particular point in his address, to these particular people? What were the contextual connotations of the terms he used? And how do these connotations help determine his meaning? In short, the turn to parallels is not aimed at merely labelling Paul from the outside, nor are they simply being introduced as it were for their own sake (in a fit of parallelomania — which is always a risk). Rather, the aim is to elucidate the meaning of the Pauline text. And the exercise is only successful where the scholar manages to add to the understanding of that.

The Essays

The essays are presented in an order that blends thematic considerations with the aim of following the canonical sequence of the letters. Thus in a first group of three more broadly ranging essays that are basically social historical in orientation, Alan F. Segal ('Universalism in Judaism and Christianity') investigates the various Jewish models for the relationship between Gentiles and Jews in use in the first and second centuries C.E. and compares them both with the apostolic decree in Acts and with a number of theologoumena in the Pauline letters. The methodological assumption is that more can be learned about each early community by interleafing the traditions from both. Thus in Luke and Paul there are structural counterparts to the two different and somewhat contradictory models of coexistence in the Jewish tradition — the Noachian commandments and the laws of the sojourner. And Segal shows how both the rabbis and the church moved over time from the latter to the former in line with a late Hellenistic movement from particularism towards universalism. Paul's writings, he argues, are evidence for both communities.

Peder Borgen ("'Yes', 'No', 'How far?': The Participation of Jews and Christians in Pagan Cults") bases his essay on the same premise that there is a need to pay more attention to the complexity of Judaism both within Palestine and in the Diaspora — and also to the many different tendencies that existed within Christianity as it emerged from (and within) Judaism. On this basis he studies a wide variety of attitudes adopted by Jews in their encounter with their non-Jewish surroundings with regard to the special issue of participation in pagan cults. Borgen musters an array of literary and archaeological sources as evidence for the many different practical options that were apparently available to Jews. Finally, he inserts Paul into the same overall pattern, thereby in effect subscribing to the principle enunciated by Segal of seeing Paul's writing as evidence for both the developing Christian and Jewish communities.

Beginning from an altogether different angle, Loveday Alexander ('Paul and the Hellenistic Schools: The Evidence of Galen') compares the social structures of the Pauline mission with those of the Hellenistic medical and philosophical schools. She takes as her starting point the polemic of the second century Greek doctor Galen against the medical and philosophical schools of his own day and his comparison of them with the Christian groups and argues that the received distinction between 'school' and 'church' (or religious group, whether of the Christian or the Jewish type) may be another specious distinction derived from a later perspective, but with little or no basis in historical facts. Thus here too justice is done to the complexity of Hellenistic culture only when scholars are prepared to recognize similarities across accustomed boundaries, which may then serve to highlight any distinctive dissimilarities.

The essay by Hans Dieter Betz ('Transferring a Ritual: Paul's Interpretation of Baptism in Romans 6') provides a bridge to the following
essays, which focus more decisively on particular Pauline texts. Betz too
takes as his point of departure a comparison of Paul, viewed as a
'founder figure' who introduced a new cult in cities of the Greek
world, with other, non-Christian, cultic officials who did the same.
Thus Betz's strategy is the same as in the earlier essays; he starts out
from similarities in social practice across accustomed boundaries. On
this basis Betz further shows how Paul's handling of the ritual of baptism is best understood as a case of 'ritual transfer' (*Kultübertragung* —
a phenomenon well known from other Hellenistic religions) from its
Jewish origin to its final Pauline form as evidenced in Romans 6. But
Betz also shows how this transfer was a process of ever new recon-
ceptualizations in the Pauline letters arising out of the difficulties and
tensions with which it met. Thus it was only in Romans 6 that the
ritual of baptism and its interpretation were fully brought into agreement with its new context in the Gentile Christian church. Here, then,
is a case where contextualization is explicitly made to serve a deepened
understanding of a particular Pauline text.

The same strategy is adopted by David Hellholm ('Enthymemic
Argumentation in Paul: The Case of Romans 6'), though now no
longer on the basis of parallels of a social historical kind, that is, parallels of practice. Rather, Hellholm takes as his point of departure a body
of Hellenistic theory, namely, rhetoric, thereby exemplifying the second, rhetorical approach identified above. He even goes back to the
founding father of a fully developed, theoretical rhetorical analysis,
Aristotle, just before the Hellenistic period. Combining this whole ancient body of theory with insights from modern textlinguistics, he
proceeds to show how Paul's argumentation in Romans 6 becomes
clear when seen in light of this conceptual apparatus and how this
approach solves problems of interpretation that have hitherto kept scholars busy.

Continuing the rhetorical line, Stanley K. Stowers ('Romans 7.7–25
as a Speech-in-Character (προσωποποιία)') shows that Rom 7.7–25 is
best understood as an instance of an ancient, widely used rhetorical
technique of speech representing not the speaker or writer himself but
another person or type of character. Learning how to recognize and to

create speech-in-character was important, Stower argues, in the kind of education that Paul probably had, and the characteristics of the technique are apparent in Romans 7. Stowers combines this analysis with a novel claim about the specific character Paul is impersonating in Romans 7. If he is right, the understanding of Romans as a whole will be drastically altered. This too, then, is a clear case of putting the Hellenistic contextualization of Paul to use for further elucidation of a Pauline text.

Following on these attempts to draw on rhetorical theory, the essay by Halvor Moxnes ('The Quest for Honor and the Unity of the Community in Romans 12 and in the Orations of Dio Chrysostom') introduces the third approach identified above, that of developing the points of contact between Paul and Hellenistic moral philosophy. In Moxnes's case this strategy is combined with the social historical approach. Starting from certain speeches by Paul's near-contemporary, the Cynic-Stoic philosopher or sophist Dio Chrysostom, on the issue of unity in various individual cities in Asia Minor, Moxnes examines the social and political setting of Dio's ideas and shows how he used Stoic ideas of unity and cooperation to argue for a political culture within the city which would best secure a relative independence from the Roman rulers. Next Moxnes shows how Paul's argument in Romans 12–13 is understood better when it is seen as a similar attempt to establish a semi-independent political unit (the Christian congregation) within the Greco-Roman city, one characterized by internal harmony and non-competitiveness but external subservience to the dominant political powers.

Even more directly in the moral philosophical line, Abraham J. Malherbe ('Determinism and Free Will in Paul: The Argument of 1 Corinthians 8 and 9') contends that a fully coherent argument can only be discerned in 1 Corinthians 8 and 9 once it is realized that Paul here uses Stoic and Cynic reflections on determinism and free will. Starting from some Corinthians' claim that they had *exousia* to eat meat offered to idols, Paul develops in a paradoxical manner the Stoic notion of freedom of choice implicit in *exousia*. Like the Stoics, he believed himself entrusted with an *oikonomia*, and like them, he willingly aligned himself with God's will. But the way in which he exercized his freedom has more in common with some Cynics who placed a premium on voluntary, unconventional behavior regarded as servile in their society. These affinities, Malherbe further argues, are not merely due to the exigencies of the moment. 'To think of Paul as either Jewish or Greek is not only superficial but wrong. If one simply cannot work without labels, that of eclectic may be applied to him, but only if that label were not taken to describe him as though he indiscriminately collected thoughts from hither and yon.' Paul, in other words, *means* his Stoic and Cynic ways of arguing.

Moving from 1 Corinthians to Philippians, Troels Engberg-Pedersen ('Stoicism in Philippians') argues that the presence in the letter of a number of terms with a background in Stoic technical moral philosophy is not just to be explained by referring to the level of discourse usually designated as 'popular moral philosophy'. Rather, once the technical background to these terms is reintroduced, one can see that the whole picture of living contained in this pattern of thought serves to structure the message Paul intends to convey by his letter. It does this in close cooperation with a few other basic motifs of an altogether non-Stoic kind, but the claim is that these various groups of motifs work together completely in the thought structure of the letter. There is no friction between originally Greek, originally Jewish, and specifically Christian elements, but rather a total fusion. Finally, in a discussion of the role played in the letter by the notion of subordination, it is suggested that even though there is a certain tension to be diagnosed in Paul's thought, between subordination and a nonhierarchical sharing, the tension is not between the Stoic elements and the non-Stoic ones. Rather, where Paul is at his most Stoic, he is also at his most Christian.

In the concluding, more broadly ranging essay on the general philosophical context, David E. Aune ('Human Nature and Ethics in Hellenistic Philosophical Traditions and Paul: Some Issues and Problems') shows that Greek views of human nature were far more complex than New Testament scholars have usually recognized. Correspondingly, the views of human nature implied and occasionally expressed in Paul's letters are complex as well as inconsistent and incorporate specifically Greek as well as specifically Jewish anthropological traditions. In a special study of death as a metaphor for the morally transformed life, Aune argues that since this metaphor does not occur in Judaism, Paul's use of it is in part dependent on the *commentatio mortis* or 'practice of death' emphasized in various Hellenistic philosophical schools, in which the denial of concerns of the body is a proleptic experience of the liberation which can only be fully experienced following death.

Acknowledgements

It remains to thank a number of institutions and individuals who have contributed decisively to the realization both of the conference and of the present volume.

The Danish Research Council for the Humanities supported the conference very generously as did the Nordic Academy for Advanced Study (under the Nordic Council of Ministers). It is to the great credit of these two institutions that they helped bringing together a group of renowned Pauline scholars from the Northern Hemisphere. With the number of research students participating in the conference, one may feel confident that the international contacts that were established will bear fruit for many years to come.

Warm thanks are also due to four individuals, Hans Dieter Betz, Lars Hartman, Wayne A. Meeks, and John K. Riches, who willingly consented after the conference to act as an editorial board for the publication of the essays arising from the conference. In spite of their other commitments they have with unswerving readiness commented on the essays, to the great benefit of each individual author and of the volume as a whole.

1

Universalism in Judaism and Christianity
Alan F. Segal

Many fundamental rabbinic traditions can no longer be assumed to date to the time of Jesus although they purport to be even more ancient.[1] Although rabbinic Judaism claims the Pharisees as forebears, the differences between the rabbis and the Pharisees are great. The pharisaic movement was one among a variety of sects in the first century, while rabbinic Judaism matured beginning about 220 C.E. with the publication of the Mishnah.[2] The pharisaic traditions evidenced in the Mishnah are of uncertain date. Since they were preserved in oral form, they may have originated in the first two centuries or much earlier, as the traditions often claim. As in any oral literature, they may have been significantly altered in transmission and especially by their rabbinic editors in the middle and end of the second century. In any event, rabbinic documents unconsciously transform evidence of the Pharisees from their first-century position of shared power into statements of comfortable community leadership in the second, third, and fourth centuries.

The most famous handbook of Jewish background to the New Testament is the Strack-Billerbeck, *Kommentar zum Neuen Testament aus Talmud und Midrasch*,[3] which lists important midrashic and mishnaic

---

[1] I would like to thank Heikki Räisänen, Per Bilde, Peder Borgen, the editor, and the other members of the seminar for their kind suggestions about this paper.
[2] See the work of Jacob Neusner on this subject. Of his many publications, two of particular interest in this context (because they summarize his form critical approach) are *The Rabbinic Traditions about the Pharisees before 70* vol. 1–3 *The Masters, The Houses* and *Conclusions* (Leiden: Brill, 1971); and *Judaism: The Evidence of the Mishnah* (Chicago: University of Chicago Press, 1981).
[3] München: C. H. Beck, 1928.

traditions for each New Testament passage. In spite of its sometimes unappreciated erudition and sometimes egregious value judgments, its methodology rather than its scholarship is the difficulty. The real problem with the book is the methodological assumption that Talmud and Midrash which are, in their written form, documents from the second through sixth centuries can automatically elucidate the New Testament, a first-century document. Of course, Jews argue that they are oral traditions which go back much earlier. But the question is which traditions and when? One has to trace each tradition individually, making decisions case by case. In such a methodological world, the New Testament constitutes important evidence that some of the rabbinic material claimed to be ancient actually goes back to the first century — something that we cannot claim without the New Testament. In other words, the New Testament is better evidence for fixing the date of rabbinic documents than are the rabbinic texts for illuminating the New Testament. One should write a commentary to the Mishnah using the New Testament as *marginalia* that demonstrates its antiquity. What I am suggesting, therefore, is that we have been going about our study of the first century backwards.

The Salvation of the Gentiles: Luke, Paul, and the Rabbis

But there is much to be gained by interleafing the reading of Jewish literature and Christian documents. I can illustrate the benefits by asking the question, What was the Jewish view in the first century of the place of Gentiles in God's scheme?

There is not a single answer to the question. That is to say, Judaism did not have a single policy on the status of Gentiles; there was no single Judaism of the day. Jews did have opinions about Gentiles but that is not the same as policy. Various Jewish sects had policies or theologies that involved Gentiles in some way. And most Jews and Jewish sects had ambivalent opinions. This essay will attempt to address the ambivalence and show how various communities dealt with it.

A major point will be that the New Testament evinces the same ambivalence on the issue of the inclusion of Gentiles as do the other Jewish sects. Indeed, the history of early Christianity is a history of resolving that ambiguity after a great deal of conflict. So the easy

2

contrasts made between the New Testament and other varieties of Judaism do not work. It is not just a question of Jewish parochialism being replaced by Christian universalism. Each community discussed universalism and answered the question in a different but similar way, resolving that quandary in a similar but unique way. In both communities, the solution favors universalism. In both communities the path to universalism is an aspect of the intellectual climate of late Hellenism mediated by the special and differing historical circumstances of the nascent rabbinic Jewish and Christian communities. We shall see that Paul's writing provides an early intersection in the two different intellectual histories.

Let us consider the Christian community first, because its history on this issue is actually clearer than that of the rabbinic community. According to Acts 15 the issue originated at Antioch before the Jerusalem Council, because emissaries from Jerusalem maintained that one cannot be saved unless one is circumcised according to the custom of Moses (ἐὰν μὴ περιτμηθῆτε τῷ ἔθει τῷ Μωϋσέως, οὐ δύνασθε σωθῆναι, Acts 15.1). Sometimes the rejection of this principle is taken by a Christian readership to show the beginning of the process by which Christianity rid itself of painfully parochial ideas in Judaism. Yet, leaving aside the issue of dating in rabbinic Judaism, one puzzling aspect of this report is at odds with normative rabbinic thought of later centuries, which maintains that the righteous of all nations have a place in the world to come. There seem to be only two practical choices: (1) Luke was right and the accepted rabbinic doctrine is later and a complete innovation; (2) Luke was at least partly misinformed, if perhaps innocently (as seems to me to be the case). But what makes the problem infinitely more complicated is that both possibilities appear to be partly correct, resulting in a deep ambiguity. The ambiguity appears due to the time and distance that had elapsed between the actual issue and Luke's narrative, as I will try to show.

One does not take issue with an ancient historical source without some sense of also taking on the burden of proof. Almost all New Testament critics distrust Luke's chronology of the events of Paul's life for several reasons, not least of all that he is writing at least a generation after the fact. When it comes to issues of historical interpretation the situation is more subtle and less satisfying. As I will show, Luke appears correct in saying that there were Jews who refused to allow the possibility that some Gentiles could be saved as Gentiles, who even would not accept any Gentiles into the Israelite faith, or who imposed certain ritual requirements on them. So it is entirely possible that the conservative members of the church did not go along with the Jerusalem church's decision. (A new directive from Jerusalem is not likely to have changed their opinion either, since these positions are variously founded in Jewish law, which the conservative members of the church continued to observe.) The restrictive understanding of salvation is characteristic of some kinds of apocalyptic Judaism. But we shall see that it was certainly not uniformly accepted within the Jewish community. Paul partly helps us resolve this dilemma of unraveling the ancient Jewish positions and datings for this issue because he is the only Pharisee who has left us his personal writings.

In this thicket a few things are exceedingly clear and that is perhaps where we should start. Paul states clearly his opinion that Gentiles do not need to be circumcised to be saved. Whether Paul makes this statement before or after the Jerusalem conference is not important for the purposes of this paper. Instead I will try to show that Paul's statement is not uniquely characteristic of Pauline Christianity and is not likely to be Paul's innovation. It is characteristic of some pharisaic and later rabbinic Judaism but emphatically not true of apocalypticism. A stronger statement attributable to Paul — namely, that no one needs to be circumcised to be saved (which I believe he says; *pace* Gaston) — also appears to have some precedent within the Jewish community, but it is a very minority position, limited to that class of Jews represented by the 'radical allegorizers' mentioned by Philo (*Migr. Abr.* 89–94), who apparently identify as Jews but do not perform the rituals.[4] Thus, Luke and Paul witness to some of the rough spectrum of Jewish opinions as well as the early Christian opinions on that issue. What differs in the Jewish community is the relative weight to be given to the various positions, but the alternatives are roughly the same as those outlined in the writings of the early church.

---

[4]   Lloyd Gaston has made the case repeatedly that Paul was proclaiming an antinomian way for Gentiles only. Gaston believes that Jews can continue to be saved through the law. See *Paul and the Torah* (Vancouver: University of British Columbia Press, 1987).

Luke equates the idea that there is no salvation without circumcision with the position of the party of the Pharisees who say 'It is necessary to circumcise them, and to charge them to keep the law of Moses' (Acts 15.5). For Luke, writing from a comfortable historical distance, the questions appear to be part of the same single issue of the inclusion of Gentiles into the community of the saved. But for rabbinic Judaism the two questions Luke mentions in this passage are hardly identical. In the first instance (Acts 15.1), we are talking about justification and salvation; in the second (Acts 15.5), we need only be talking about proper conversion. Rabbinic Judaism (as evidenced by the Mishnah, which was redacted at the beginning of the third century) distinguishes radically between conversion and salvation. It does say all Israel will be saved. But it allows that some Gentiles can be saved without conversion although conversion is certainly admirable. The rabbis do not define as exclusive a club for salvation as does Christianity, and the reasons for it are not hard to find in the historical context, as will shortly become clear. On the other hand, rabbinic Judaism requires that all converts to Judaism be strictly charged to keep the law of Moses. No doubt this is what Paul had in mind when he says: 'Now I, Paul, say to you that if you receive circumcision, Christ will be of no advantage to you. I testify again to every man who receives circumcision that he is bound to keep the whole law' (Gal 5.2–3). Viewed in this way, Paul can tell us that the rabbinic notion that Gentiles can be saved without conversion is already in existence (on which see the brief discussion below of Romans 2).

Rabbinic writings debate the issue of the salvation of the Gentiles, as they debate almost every issue.

> Rabbi Eliezer said: 'All the nations will have no share in the world to come, even as it is said, "the wicked shall go into Sheol, and all the nations that forget God" (Ps 9.17). The wicked shall go into Sheol — these are the wicked among Israel.' Rabbi Joshua said to him: 'If the verse had said, "The wicked shall go into Sheol with all the nations," and had stopped there, I should have agreed with you, but as it goes on to say "who forget God", it means there are righteous men among the nations who have a share in the world to come.' (*t. Sanh.* 13.2)[5]

---

[5]   Cf. *m. Sanh.* 10, *b. Sanh.* 105a, *Sifra* 86b, *b. B. Qam.* 38a.

According to the rabbinic writings, Luke is half right. Some Pharisees (for argument's sake I identify Pharisees with Tannaim, even though the two are not exactly coterminous), represented by Rabbi Eliezer, said that only Israel will be saved. Others, represented by Rabbi Joshua, said that the righteous Gentiles would be saved as well. Would that we could trust that these were the actual positions of the rabbis! We cannot any more, given our natural skepticism about the value of oral reports. But we should not assume that the texts are deliberately misinforming us either. Like Luke, the Midrash is not necessarily totally at error; it has probably foreshortened and conflated in a way that seems justified from its own perspective.

The Mishnah and Midrash are at least consistent on this issue, which one can hardly claim about a number of other issues. The positions attributed to Rabbis Eliezer b. Hyrcanus and Joshua b. Hananiah, two Pharisees of the late first century, are typical of other remarks that rabbinic literature has attributed to them. Eliezer is a severe critic of Gentiles. Joshua b. Hananiah is more liberal. He removes all distinctions between Jew and Gentile in attaining salvation through the doing of good deeds. He says that everyone who walks in blamelessness before his Creator in this world will escape the judgment of hell in the world to come. He even disagrees with Gamaliel by maintaining that the blameless children of the wicked heathen will also have a share in the world to come. Though Joshua probably does not allow conversion without circumcision, he at least looks at the positive side of the issue by stating that baptism without circumcision makes one a *ger* (a proselyte, a convert) — that is, all the ritual has to be done, but if the circumcision is to be performed, the status of convert can be regarded as beginning with baptism from some points of view (see *b. Yebam.* 46a).

If the argument between Eliezer and Joshua were historical, they would be directly coterminous with the first generations of Christians. And they are to be found in early rabbinic sources — the Tosefta is as important as the Mishnah in terms of authority and dating. But if the early third century is our *ad quem*, the attribution to the first century is the very thing we must question unless we have evidence to establish it. Furthermore, the rabbinic discussions are certainly not *ipsissima verba* of the rabbis, just as Luke's statements are not the exact words of the conservative party of Jews within the Christian movement. But the Midrash does leave us with the impression that the same issues which were debated in the church were also being debated by the rabbis. It is possible that all the Christian Pharisees were of the most conservative persuasion, and some more liberal ones show up in rabbinic Jerusalem, but that seems statistically unlikely. Note too that this issue is crucial for understanding Paul's program for Christianity, to which I shall return at the end of this essay.

It is possible that the rabbis debated this issue because it was raised by the Christian community and that they take their cues from them. This has always been an unpopular hypothesis in the study of rabbinic texts but it should not be automatically excluded because Jews have perennially learned significantly from their friends and neighbors, creating throughout their history similar as well as contrasting formulations of issues which they absorbed from outside sources. But the questions in Luke and the rabbis are sufficiently different in formulation and logic to preclude direct borrowing. We seem to have two different but originally loosely related (and, as we shall see, probably contemporaneous) formulations of the issue of God's universal concern for humanity. The most satisfactory understanding of the problem appears to be that it was an issue of late Hellenistic Judaism exacerbated and interpreted by each community in terms of their increasingly separate historical predicaments.

Before we come to Paul directly we have to look at the wider context of these ideas in more detail. And the wider context includes some sociological observations about the nascent Christian and Jewish communities.

The Jewish Environment

The ambiguity of these traditions is furthered by the fact that there are two different models for Gentile inclusion in Jewish tradition. The status of the Gentiles is discussed in later rabbinic Judaism through both the rubric of the *resident sojourner* and the doctrine of the *Noachian commandments*. They conflict, in the first place by making different assumptions about the purpose and motivation of Gentile interest in Judaism. The conflicts had to be systematically worked out both in

Christianity and rabbinic Judaism. In both cases the ambiguity is resolved in the direction of universalism.

The issue of the resident sojourner derived from the biblical rules incumbent upon 'the stranger in your gates'. Resident sojourners were obliged to abstain from offering sacrifices to strange gods (Lev 17.7–9), from eating blood in any form (Lev 17.10ff.), from incest (Lev 18.6–26), from work on the Sabbath (Exod 20.10f.), and from eating leavened bread during the Passover (Exod 12.18f.).[7]

The second model is the rabbinic doctrine of the Noachian commandments. This rabbinic doctrine is derived from a sophisticated and theological formulation that some legal enactments were given before Sinai to all human beings. Furthermore, the sign of the Noachian covenant, the rainbow, symbolizes God's promise of safety for all humanity. And it is completely outside of the special covenant with Abraham and his descendants. The covenant with Noah is expanded to encompass all the revealed commandments preceding Sinai. The Noachian commandments (e.g., *t. Abod. Zar.* 8.4 and more fully in *b. Sanh.* 56b) function somewhat like a concept of 'natural law', which any just person can be expected to follow by observation and reason. In more Christian theological language, it is available by God's grace to all humanity. Following is the earliest rabbinic version, as stated in the Tosefta to *Abodah Zarah*:

> Seven commandments were the sons of Noah commanded: (1) concerning adjudication (*dinim*), (2) and concerning idolatry (*abodah zarah*), (3) and concerning blasphemy (*qilelat ha-shem*), (4) and concerning sexual immorality (*giluy arayot*), (5) and con-

---

6   Here the work of David Novak (*The Image of the Non-Jew in Judaism: An Historical and Constructive Study of the Noahide Laws* [Toronto: Edwin Mellen, 1983]) is right on the mark. But Christian scholarship has preceded him. For bibliography, see John Coolidge Hurd, *The Origin of 1 Corinthians* (2nd ed.; Macon, GA: Mercer University Press, 1983). See also Peter Richardson, *Israel in the Apostolic Church* (Cambridge: Cambridge University Press, 1969) and Nils A. Dahl, *Das Volk Gottes: Eine Untersuchung zum Kirchenbewusstein des Urchristentums* (Det Norske Videnskaps-Akademi i Oslo, II. Hist.-filos. Klasse, 1941 no. 2, Oslo; Jacob Dybwad, 1941; reprinted Darmstadt: Wissenschaftliche Buchgesellschaft, 1963).

7   See Steven Wilson, *The Gentiles and the Gentile Mission in Luke-Acts* (Cambridge: Cambridge University Press, 1974). My interpretation softens Wilson's argument a bit but agrees with it in principle.

cerning bloodshed (*shefikhut damim*), (6) and concerning robbery (*ha-gezel*), (7) and concerning a limb torn from a living animal (*eber min ha-hayy*).[8]

In the basic version, nothing is mentioned that crosses into the purview of the special ordinances encumbent upon Jews in Jewish law. The rabbis immediately bring up more questionable ordinances, presumably asking whether a particular rule is specifically Jewish or should apply to all humanity. For instance, the rabbis mention cross-breeding (*kilayim*), castration (*sirus*), eating blood from a living animal (*dam min ha-hayy*), and witchcraft (*kishuf*). To these, in later discussions, is sometimes added the recognition that YHWH, the God of Israel, is the one true God. Other Tannaim limit the Noachian commandments to the prohibition of idolatry, or prohibitions concerning blasphemy and adjudication (see *y. Kil.* 2.7). As David Novak says in his discussion of the Noachian commandments: 'What emerges from all of this discussion is that in the tannaitic period, there was a debate over the number and content of the Noahide laws. We have no record, however, that any authority in that period rejected the doctrine *per se*.'[9]

Of course, the minute we mention a rabbinic doctrine from a third-century text we risk anachronism in assuming that it comes from the first century. To find out what was practiced in first-century Judaism, one must consult other varieties of Judaism, including Christianity. But first, in order to avoid circular logic, let us look at a pre-Christian document. Once it can be ascertained that the ideas are prevalent in pre-Christian Judaism, we can safely use Christianity as another variation on a preexistent theme.

Another close parallel to the Noachian commandments can be found in *Jubilees* 7.20–21, which is pre-Christian:[10]

---

[8] The technical terminology of these sections is so commonly transliterated into English that I forego the more scientific notation for clarity's sake.

[9] Novak, *The Image of the Non-Jew in Judaism*, 6.

[10] See Novak, *The Image of the Non-Jew in Judaism*, 3–35. Novak dates the laws to Maccabean times, albeit with no textual support, because it seems to him to be appropriate to the time of forced conversions. Then he discounts the witness of *Jubilees*. Neither hypothesis convinces me. But Novak's main emphasis is on the later discussion of these rules in talmudic and post-talmudic times, which is more convincing.

> And in the twenty-eight jubilee Noah began to command his grandson with ordinances and commandments and all of the judgments which he knew. And he bore witness to his sons so that they might do justice and cover the shame of their flesh and bless the one who created them and honor father and mother, and each one love his neighbor and preserve themselves from fornication and pollution and from all injustice.

The particular ordinances thought to be universally humane by *Jubilees* are establishing justice, eschewing incest, honoring parents, loving neighbors, and prohibiting adultery, promiscuity, and pollution from injustice.[11] In *Jubilees* this short law code forms the basis of the judgment against the giants, which brings on the flood and sets the scene for the myths contained in the book of *Enoch*.

It would be unwise, however, to assume that *Jubilees* is promulgating such ideas in order to find a basis for humane universalism — which is more or less what the rabbis and Christians do with it. Quite the contrary, *Jubilees* has a strictly dualistic view of the world, on both the divine and human level, in consonance with the ideas of Qumran sectarians, in whose library it figured prominently. Israel is identified as a good kingdom. God selected it as special and above all other peoples (2.21) to be marked by circumcision (15.11). It alone can participate in the Sabbath and the other God ordained festivals. The other nations are condemned and God has placed spirits in authority over them to lead them astray. *Jub* 22.16 warns Jews not to eat with a Gentile. *Jubilees* forcefully says that there is no salvation without circumcision on the eighth day (15.26–27). That virtually means that conversion of the Gentiles is impossible. Even a charitable reading supposes that only the children of converts can enter the community:

> And anyone who is born whose own flesh is not circumcised on the eighth day is not from the sons of the covenant which the Lord made for Abraham, since (he is) from the children of destruction. And there is therefore no sign upon him so that he might belong to the Lord because (he is destined) to be destroyed

[11] As in Paul's writing and parallel with the other Judaisms of the day, *Jubilees* here uses pollution as a metaphor for unrighteousness.

and annihilated from the earth and to be uprooted from the earth because he has broken the covenant of the Lord our God. Because the nature of all the angels of the presence and all of the angels of sanctification was thus from the day of their creation. And in the presence of the angels of the presence and the angels of sanctification he sanctified Israel so that they might be with him and with his holy angels.[12]

The obvious reason for the inclusion of the Noachian commandments at this place is to provide *Jubilees* with a legal warrant for condemning the Gentiles. God would not consign most of humanity to destruction without reason; the Gentiles know his law and have spurned it. This is entirely appropriate to a sectarian position, where all the Gentiles and but a saving remnant of Israel are scheduled for destruction. We know from this evidence that there were sects within Judaism which did not subscribe to any liberal ideas about the capabilities of Gentiles.[13]

This issue had already surfaced in the lives of sectarian Jews, as *Jubilees* makes clear. In contrast to this, the Jewish *Sibylline Oracles* specify those rules incumbent upon righteous Gentiles:

> Happy will be those of mankind of earth
> who will love the great God, blessing him
> before drinking and eating, putting their trust in piety.
> They will reject all temples when they see them,
> altars too, useless foundations of dumb stones
> (and stone statues and handmade images)
> defiled with blood of animate creatures, and sacrifices
> of four-footed animals.[14]

---

[12] So translates O. S. Wintermute in *The Old Testament Pseudepigrapha* 2 (ed. James H. Charlesworth; Garden City, NY: Doubleday, 1983) 87 (hereafter cited as Charlesworth).

[13] The rabbis also taught that when a child is not circumcised, his future reward is not automatically imperiled. Such a lack is, in the opinion of the later rabbis at least, a sin of his father (*Shulhan Arukh,* 'Yoreh Dea' 260.1). Sabbath laws took precedence over circumcision laws for children born by caesarean section. So for later rabbinic tradition, it was not even necessary to be circumcised on the eighth day to be Jewish, part of Israel, or deserving of the world to come.

[14] Note that blood here appears to refer to the blood of pagan sacrifice.

They will look to the great glory of the
one God and commit no wicked murder, nor deal in
dishonest gain, which are most horrible things.
Neither have they disgraceful desire for another's spouse
or for hateful and repulsive abuse of a male.
Other men will never imitate their way
or piety or customs, because they desire shamelessness.
On the contrary, they deride them with mockery and laughter.
Infantile in their foolishness,
they will falsely attribute to
those what wicked and evil deeds they themselves commit.
Sib. Or. 4.24–39[15]

Here again murder, theft, and other specifics are mentioned as primary prohibitions for all humanity to observe. Pagan sacrifice is entirely forbidden. Note the three sins of the Gentiles: idolatry, which leads to the next two, promiscuity and violence.

Pseudo-Phocylides mentions the general principles of Jewish ethics without mentioning the ceremonial Torah. One of the testimonia reports that it ended with the exhortation that: 'purifications are for the purity of the soul, not of the body' (l. 228).[16] Of course, Pseudo-Phocylides and the *Sibyllines* are too uncertain for firm dating, though they are conventionally understood to be first-century documents. In any case, they do help us understand the intellectual atmosphere of the Jewish Hellenistic world. The earlier writer Aristeas likewise says, 'Honouring God is done not with gifts or sacrifices but with purity of soul'.[17] These sentiments come from the prophets, who rebuked the misuse of the cult. But they are used in Hellenistic Judaism to argue against the necessity of temple worship, both for Jews in the diaspora and Gentiles. It is also part of a proselyte literature designed to convince pagans of the inherent morality of Judaism and bring them to (but apparently no closer than) the status of God-fearers, in the first instance. If they later chose to convert to Judaism, that was even better, but it was their own, unforced and rational decision.

---

[15] Tr. by J. J. Collins in Charlesworth 1, 384.
[16] Tr. P. W. van der Horst in Charlesworth 2, 582.
[17] Räisänen, *Paul and the Law* (Philadelphia: Fortress, 1983) 36, 38.

The Apostolic Decree and Paul

Luke tells us something about the status of the discussion about the Noachian commandments in first-century Judaism. Acts 15.20, 15.29, and 21.25 describe an apostolic decree defining a minimum of practice for the new Gentile Christians:

> Therefore my judgment is that we should not trouble those of the Gentiles who turn to God, but should write to them to abstain from the pollutions of idols and from unchastity and from what is strangled and from blood. For from early generations Moses has had in every city those who preach him, for he is read every sabbath in the synagogues. (15.19–21)

> That you abstain from what has been sacrificed to idols and from blood and from what is strangled, and from unchastity. (15.29)

> Thus all will know that there is nothing in what they have been told about you but that you yourself live in observance of the law. But as for the Gentiles who have believed, we have sent a letter with our judgment that they should abstain from what has been sacrificed to idols and from blood and from what is strangled and from unchastity. (21.24–25)

In other words, the Christian discussion of Gentiles is evidence that the issue of the legal and ceremonial responsibilities of Gentiles was being debated in Judaism too, even if the argument had special characteristics within the Christian community. The apostolic decree, as Luke transcribes it, is neither exactly the laws of the resident sojourner nor the Noachian commandments; it is a peculiar, ambiguous mélange, perhaps even a combination of both. The new Christian 'God-fearers' (*sebomenoi* or *phoboumenoi*), as such Gentiles are sometimes called, had to abstain from idol sacrifices (εἰδωλοθύτων) and from blood (αἵματος) — perhaps from eating blood entirely, or perhaps from blood sacrifices, as the *Sibylline Oracles* says, or perhaps from bloodshed. They also had to stay away from πνικτῶν — evidently a ritual requirement of some sort, perhaps avoidance of animals which had been throttled and killed as prey, hence a translation of the Hebrew term *terefa*, or, as the later

13

church sometimes interpreted it, from animals killed and prepared by stewing or boiling. In my opinion πνικτός refers to *terefa* because πνικτός is a reasonable Greek translation of the Hebrew word denoting the carcass of an animal caught as prey and because abstinence from *tref* foods is one of the most basic requirements of Jewish food laws. Similarly, the resident sojourners were expected to observe the basic moral code of the Jews, staying away from forbidden marriages, incest, and unchastity (πορνείας).[18]

The question is, What kind of a code is the apostolic decree? Is it moral or cultic? What does it forbid? Which model does it evince? Even terms like 'moral' and 'cultic' must be used cautiously because they contain some ambiguities as well. The apostolic decree can hardly be a complete moral code, because such obvious sins as theft are entirely missing, although they are present in the rabbinic formulation of the Noachian commandments. Thus, the apostolic decree is not exactly what the Noachian commandments are supposed to be. Obviously, Christians are expected not to steal, although that is not covered in the decree. Probably the Ten Commandments and other virtue lists were in effect for all the community. Εἰδωλόθυτα is often taken to be cultic, while εἰδωλολατρία would be moral. But the rabbis might see the issue differently. No doubt they would see both as morally wrong, but the term εἰδωλολατρία is too general; thus it is less helpful than εἰδωλόθυτα, which has the advantage of specifying which types of behavior are forbidden. At issue here are only the rules specifically appropriate for those Gentiles who do not convert to Judaism. Thus, these laws are not exactly the Noachian commandments, because they assume a social situation where the Christians are subject to other moral standards as well. But neither are they exactly the received rules for resident sojourners because there are fewer rules and the situation is somewhat different. Obviously, the apostolic decree, as it stands, is another formula of the same type as both of them but adapted to a unique purpose — to guide Jewish Christians and Gentile Christians living together. In other words, in the apostolic decree, some issues

---

[18] For more detail on these issues see Wilson, *Luke and the Law* (Cambridge: Cambridge University Press, 1983) 87–100.

were taken for granted because they were obviously eschewed by all Christians.[19] The decree concerned only those rules that Jewish Christians might impose on Gentile Christians to allow them to live in their midst.

S. Wilson suggests that Luke understood the apostolic decree as a universal moral code, like the Noachian commandments, because he appears to interpret αἷμα as bloodshed and from the stories that he relates about Peter it is clear that he already knew the food laws and ceremonial laws of Judaism were now suspended. Thus, Luke sees the code simply as a universal moral code for Gentiles. Furthermore, there is a significant textual variant in the Western text, which adds a negative version of the golden rule at this point and eliminates the πνικτός clause. Thus, the textual tradition, which is most easily understood as a theologically sophisticated early gloss, underlines the argument that the church has followed Luke in taking a 'moral' rather than a 'ceremonial' interpretation of these early Christian laws.

In this regard, the interpretation of the Greek words αἷμα and πνικτός is crucial for understanding the original intent of the apostolic decree. Whatever πνικτός means it seems clearly ceremonial or ritual, ensuring that the approach of the first church council was at least partly 'ceremonial' as well as 'moral'. The ambiguity in the rules hides a change in church perspective over time and it possibly also conceals a deliberate attempt to express both sides of the conflict, perhaps even a strategy not to needlessly alienate one Christian community. Here we lay bare one of Luke's basic methods. He cannot drop out the original edicts of the conference, but he places them in a context which changes their import somewhat, in line with his more universal perspective. As it is, αἷμα and εἰδωλόθυτα can be interpreted ceremonially or ethically. In their original Jewish context there would not be much need to distinguish; but the import of the rules was probably to make the earlier Gentile Christians pure enough to interact with their Jewish coreligionists.

I agree with S. Wilson's suggestion that moral universalism was not necessarily the original intent of the decree. There is little point in

---

[19] See the helpful articles by Kirsopp Lake, 'The Apostolic Council of Jerusalem,' and 'Paul's controversies,' *The Beginnings of Christianity: The Acts of the Apostles, Additional Notes* (Grand Rapids: Baker, 1966) 5: 195–211 and 212–23.

detailing 'ritual' requirements after they are suspended. The ritual requirements must be more original, reflecting a time in the church when the Gentiles were viewed by the framers of the decree more like resident sojourners, who must conform their practice to the minimum practice within the community. It must have come from a time when Luke's summary historical theology had not yet penetrated, a time that Luke has no interest in detailing accurately and perhaps did not even understand. Thus, the history of the apostolic decree is incomplete as it now stands.

There are comparable problems in reading the Christian evidence as there are in reading the Jewish evidence. Just as there are problems reading the history of Noachian commandments, so too there are insoluble problems in tracing the history of the apostolic decree which is, indeed, known to us in greater detail outside rabbinic sources. But it turns out that these two documents should be seen as strategies to resolve the same problems — two chapters in the same history; and seen as such, the same tendency towards universalization will become evident in both communities.

All of these formulations are attempting to deal with a similar issue from a variety of social situations. Once the social significance of the different formulations is outlined, the reasons for the ambiguity will become clearer. The difference between the Noachian commandments and the rules for the sojourner is clear from a social point of view. The resident sojourner must, because of his close association with the Israelites, observe some of the laws of Judaism, while the Noachian commandments refer to the ultimate disposition of Gentiles and thus entirely to Gentiles who are not observant. The resident sojourners may be ethical or not; the issue is irrelevant. The law of the sojourner is formulated for the benefit of the Israelites who need not tolerate certain impieties within their own political or social territory.

The social issue in the Noachian commandments is quite different. With the Noachian commandments first a different theological question arises: Can God completely reject the Gentiles? Both Christians and rabbinic Jews answer, 'No!' but they formulate the process of inclusion in different ways. In the rabbinic consensus, the Gentiles need not observe any Jewish laws. The sole question is whether they can be righteous, hence worthy to inherit the world to come. The issue has to do with the place of Israel within the wider category of humanity.

The original historical context suggests the social function of the two models. They correspond to the two different but related social situations of Jews in the Hellenistic world. The first, the resident sojourner, refers to a situation where Jews are in the majority and have political power. In that situation they can maintain that Gentiles ought to perform certain Jewish rituals — including circumcision — if they want to eat the passover sacrifice. This formulation of a *ger*, a resident sojourner, later becomes the major legal basis for discussions of conversion in Judaism. Rabbinic discussion uses the same word to cover two concepts, stimulating the distinction between an ordinary *ger* and a *ger tsedek*, a full convert.

Thus, the issue of how to accommodate Gentiles depends on the social landscape. It is not directly linked to the existence or destruction of the temple or the land of Israel/diaspora split. But one can see that both history and geography have an effect on which model will be adopted in specific situations. In the land of Israel under Israelite law, the resident sojourner is the easiest model to apply. But wherever Jews are not the majority of the population or have very limited political power to affect or control their neighbors, the second model can become more relevant. In such a situation, there is even a danger of Gentile backlash in being too open to converting Gentiles. There is ample evidence of the concern of the pagan community that the Jews and Christians were stealing their children.[20] In these situations, the concept of a righteous Gentile, who eschews sin but does not explicitly embrace the special rules of Judaism, would have a positive value. So before the third century when the mature doctrine is voiced in rabbinic Judaism, certain ambiguities would naturally obtain. In areas around Palestine with a Jewish majority and certain rights of self-rule, one set of procedures would be more relevant. In other areas, the other might. During the hostilities with Rome when circumcision was forbidden, the only alternative for an interested Gentile would have been to be-

---

[20] See my *Paul the Convert: The Apostolate and Apostasy of Saul the Pharisee* (New Haven: Yale University Press, 1990) 84–96.

17

come a God-fearer. So too in mature Christianity and Judaism, both of which work with a Gentile majority as the given, the concept of righteous Gentile is much more important. In the first and early second century, the situation was more fluid, as the Christian evidence shows. The ambiguity of the Christian formulation of the apostolic decree merely underlines the imprecision of the earliest discussions of the issues.[21]

Of course, there would never have been any necessity or purpose for adopting this vocabulary within the Christian church had the moral and ethical universalism so evident to Luke been evident to the earliest Christians. The vocabulary was probably adopted because some Christian Jews viewed the first Gentile Christians through the rubric of the law of the sojourners. They might convert to Judaism if they wished. But if they did not seek such a right, evidently by circumcision, they should at least have made some cultic or ceremonial accommodations to Jewish observances so that the whole group could interact. Conversion to Judaism is thus not the only cultic approach to the inclusion of Gentiles within the community. It is merely the most conservative one. Possibly this is why James and Peter agreed that circumcision was not necessary; they may have understood that there was another option — the Gentiles did not have to become Jews but they may have had to make other ceremonial accommodations. This is logical because the earliest church was largely a Jewish majority with a small Gentile minority. While many Jewish Christians seemed positive to the idea of being one community with Gentiles, many thought that some kind of accommodation to the ritual purity of the Jewish community should and could be reached. Only a few took Paul's position that no ritual accommodations were necessary. Furthermore, Paul himself was forced

---

[21] Whether αἵματος refers to a moral action or a ritual one is not entirely clear in church tradition, which has taken it both ways. Traces of the decree appear in Revelation 2.14, 20, 24; *Didache* 6.3; Justin *Dial.* 34–35; Tertullian, *Apol.*; Eusebius *H.E.* 5.1.26 in a letter dated 177 C.E., from Lyons; Minucius Felix *Octavius* 30; *Sib. Or.* 2.93; *Pseudo-Clementine Homily* 7.8.1. The early Christians more closely approximate the ordin-ances of *Jubilees* than did the third-century rabbis. Thus the ambiguity in the Christian evidence as to whether the term αἷμα refers to a Jewish rule of slaughter or bloodshed shows that this ambiguity was rather early. For a basic bibliography see John Hurd, *Origin*, 250–53.

to compromise in place after place, by saying that although Christian freedom demanded no ceremonial observance, no ἔργα τοῦ νόμου, Christian unity demanded that the strong always accommodate to the feelings of the weak for the sake of peace in the community.

This ambiguity about the true referent of the apostolic enactments has a positive social function for the Christian community even after Paul, as the maximalist Gentile position grows inexorably stronger. Take the issue of αἷμα – whether *blood* be idolatrous, ethical, or ritual. Paul tells Gentiles that they are free from the law, but they should consider other Christians' feelings. For them, Luke's αἷμα is ethical — bloodshed. Other Christians insisted that Gentiles observe at least some of the laws. Or they may have assumed, as Paul did when he was a Pharisee, that converts must keep all the laws, but that resident sojourners need not. Obviously, Paul is fighting against there becoming two classes of Christians. After Paul, the ambiguity served to allow both opinions to be precedented in the text. So a variety of perspectives is protected by a certain ambiguity in Luke's rendering of the apostolic decree. One can see that there is no need to make accommodations unless the opposing group is the vast majority. But it is possible that Paul himself may have sought this compromise as a way to gain legitimacy for his Gentile congregations.[22]

---

[22] Of all the possible reconstructions of Paul's career, and especially his policy about the Jewish law, that proposed by John Hurd in *The Origin of 1 Corinthians* seems the most logical. With allowances for the fact that the course of events does not necessarily follow the most logical path, I shall outline Hurd's solution. According to his reconstruction of the events, the regulations contained in the apostolic decree were not part of Paul's original preaching at Corinth because they had not yet been formulated. Paul adopted them after the council, in which he participated, and sent a letter to the Corinthians later, informing them of his intentions to live by the compromise adopted at the Jerusalem council. None of this is possible if one assumes that Paul discredited the system of works-centered righteousness of Judaism. But it is possible if the position of Paul was against the aspects of Jewish law that separated his Gentile congregations from the Jewish Christian ones. This was a religious issue driven by a sociological fact. Because the events are still unresolved and the majority of New Testament scholars in fact favor the alternative ordering, I shall not assume either reconstruction but instead try to stick to the specific issues. Evidently, when the Corinthians received Paul's letter informing them of their responsibilities, they immediately responded by challenging his lack of consistency. Paul then replies again (1 Corinthians 7–14) in an attempt to preserve the principles of his earliest teaching, without transgressing his agreement with the other church fathers. The result is his policy of freedom tempered by a diplomatic policy of

The result of this policy of conciliation could easily have produced confusion for Paul's hearers and readers. He begins by assuming that the Gentiles need not observe any of the Jewish laws, in effect assuming the model of the Noachian commandments. The dominant model of some of the other church fathers is apparently close to that of the rules of the sojourner, not the Noachian commandments. This means, in effect, that they understood that there were a few Gentiles mixed into a larger Jewish sect. Paul, on the other hand, reflects the position of a majority of Gentiles in which a few Jewish Christians lived.

Nowhere does Paul openly discuss the apostolic decree. Either he did not know it (because it had not yet actually been formulated by the church in the way that Luke expresses it), or he chooses to ignore it. In that case, it is plausible to argue that to have acknowledged the modified sojourner model which underlies the apostolic decree would have jeopardized Paul's radical position on Christian freedom. Instead Paul begs moderation and continues to argue that the Gentiles are to be added to the community of the faithful through the model of the Noachian commandments, with no specific rules of Judaism in place, especially not circumcision. Either of the two alternatives is understandable within the Christian formulation of the discussion. But one must realize that even if the church had not formally ratified anything like the apostolic decree, it is quite likely that early Jewish Christian communities were automatically applying their Jewish understanding of what was necessary for Gentiles to join their midst. The issue was certainly alive, as Paul's letters so amply testify, even if the specific solution had not yet formally evolved.

One of the clearest evidences for a first-century discussion of universalism in Judaism actually comes from Rom 2.12–16. Most New Testament scholars think this pericope is an anomaly because it contradicts their understanding of Paul's critique of 'works righteousness'. I will try to show that Paul is affirming a version of the formulation of universalism found in the Judaism of his day, in order to make an

conciliation, which begs the Corinthians to observe the rules of the council, at least to the extent that they can understand them (Hurd, 259–70). This policy is only possible if one understands Paul to be operating as a rabbi would, on a case by case basis, without an overwhelming critique of works righteousness.

argument about the unity of the church. In Romans 2 Paul seems to assume that Gentiles, as well as Jews, can get the rewards of Torah, even though they do not observe the ceremonial laws:

> All who have sinned without the law will also perish without the law, and all who have sinned under the law will be judged by the law. For it is not the hearers of the law who are righteous before God, but the doers of the law who will be justified. When Gentiles who have not the law do by nature (φύσει) what the law requires, they are a law to themselves, even though they do not have the law. They show that what the law requires is written on their hearts, while their conscience also bears witness and their conflicting thoughts accuse or perhaps excuse them on that day when, according to my gospel, God judges the secrets of men by Christ Jesus. (Romans 2.12–16)

Paul may or may not be arguing in Rom 1.18 – 3.20 that everyone is under the sway of sin, and my purpose here is not to debate exactly what this is supposed to mean for the human condition. I take his statements as being less ontological than observational – that is, he observes that everyone sins. But, in any event, there are secondary effects to his argument which give us interesting insights into the place of law in Jewish life. Paul states that all sinners are judged by the law, while all righteous persons are upheld by it. This judgment is equivalent to natural law (φύσει). He also implies that this doctrine is what Jews teach (2.21), strongly suggesting that he knows the equivalent of a doctrine of the Noachian commandments. In other words, Romans 2 is not so much an anomaly in Paul's thinking as it is a statement that Jews recognize the universal value of righteousness (however he later applies this argument). I would say as well, though there is no space here to demonstrate in detail, that Paul also believes that all people, not just Jews, must repent and enter the way through faith. There is no separate covenant of law for the Jews. Furthermore, neither Gentiles nor Jews need to be concerned about any of the fleshly observances of Judaism — food laws, ceremonies and holidays, circumcision. But obviously that does not excuse the faithful from living moral lives. They must also observe the basic moral laws of life through the spirit rather than through the flesh. Paul does not distinguish between ceremonial

21

laws and moral laws per se. He distinguishes between flesh and spirit. But the effect of his distinction, as I will show, is to valorize moral life while denigrating ceremonial life. In other words, it is Paul's opinion that the Gentiles must be transformed by their faith in the risen, spiritual Christ so that they are to be treated as righteous Gentiles and not to be made to observe any part of the ceremonial law. They are not to be treated as resident sojourners but as equals. On the other hand, Paul believes that Jews too must be transformed by their faith in the risen, spiritual Christ so that they will treat the Gentiles as brothers and sisters and not demand that they observe the ritual requirements of resident sojourners, either righteous or unrighteous. In the event that the weak Jewish Christians are unable to do so, the stronger Jewish and Gentile Christians are to act charitably toward them and not give them cause for offense, for the unity of the church is more important than food laws.

What is difficult about my reading is that it avoids making the critique of works centered righteousness the basic assumption of Paul's preaching career. Two important counterarguments may be cited in opposition to my perspective: (1) There is no other evidence that any Jews in the first century separated the special laws of Judaism from the moral laws; (2) there is no place where Paul himself makes any distinction between Jewish law and the Noachian commandments. We have already seen that both these arguments are simply selective readings of the evidence.

My argument, however, is not that Paul separates special laws of Judaism from the moral laws — he only separates the fleshly observances from the spiritual ones. That is his unique or almost unique vocabulary. What I maintain instead is that the distinction of *ceremonial* from *moral* law is a better gloss on what he actually says than to maintain that he is criticizing works centered righteousness. That concern is characteristic of a later time.

Furthermore, it is not strictly true that no one distinguished between ceremonial and moral rules. Philo gives direct evidence of a group of Jews who studied and revered Torah but did not practice it in *Migr. Abr.* 87–88. He calls them the *radical allegorizers* and he criticizes their perspective severely. But he never calls them apostates. Theoretically, this group does not need to be organized or confined to cult. There

22

were doubtless many Jews deeply influenced by Hellenistic culture who simply gave up many of the peculiar laws of Judaism but still identified as Jews. Paul himself essentially is converted by his vision of Christ from the perspective of a Pharisee — a right-wing one at that — to a perspective that is more characteristic of left-wing Pharisees and more 'Hellenistic' Jews.[23] Of course, Paul's discussion of the centrality of faith, his insistence that all need transformation, and his specific language for flesh and spirit are unique and mark him off from other Hellenistic Jewish writers. But on the issue of the practice of the law and the salvation of the Gentiles, he appears quite close to several positions within Judaism. This is understandable particularly in the diaspora where the social situation demanded a different solution than merely to insist that Gentiles accommodate to Jewish practice. A more intellectual approach was needed, one that explained what the God of all history intended for the Gentiles, especially the righteous ones. Like more moderate Jews, Paul knew that God would not abandon them. Unlike most moderate Jews, he had been given a special revelation that outlined God's plan and he was called to be the great agent of that plan.

There are also a few places where Paul speaks quite plainly about the difference between Jewish and Gentile practices. I want to begin first with the phrase, 'the works of the law'. I take James D. G. Dunn's article on the topic as my basis.[24] And I am aware that Dunn does not exactly equate the phrase 'works of the law' with the ceremonial laws, only with their effects in community. But I want to generalize a bit further than he. One should distinguish between the denotative meaning of the phrase 'works of law' and its referent. (It is clear to all who study the connotations of words that the denotation and referent of a word are different. When we say 'The White House' we *denote* a building, not the president, but we can be *referring* to him.) Dunn is correct in saying that the phrase 'works of law' does not *denote* the ceremonial

[23] By Hellenistic, I would include all the sects of Judea as well, because they are all a product of Hellenism. I do not mean to set Palestinian or rabbinic Judaism in opposition to Hellenistic Judaism.

[24] James D. G. Dunn, 'Works of the Law and the Curse of the Law (Galatians 3.10–14),' *NTS* 31 (1985) 523–42.

23

laws. But I think that 'Jewish ceremonial laws' is the *referent* of the term in Paul's discussions, as does Dunn, if I understand him correctly. In other words, 'the works of the law' does not refer to the entire law in the places that Paul uses it.[25] It appears to *refer to* (as distinct from *denote*) merely the special laws of Judaism or everything except more or less what the Noachian commandments demand of Gentiles:

> We ourselves, who are Jews by birth and not Gentile sinners, yet who know that a man is not justified by *works of the law* but through faith in Jesus Christ, even we have believed in Christ Jesus, in order to be justified by faith in Christ, and not *works of the law*, because by *the works of the law* shall not all be justified. (Gal 2.15–16)

Paul is saying that the special laws of Judaism are not relevant for salvation. Strictly speaking, this is an understandable option within pharisaism and, as it seems, a diaspora Jewish position too. If it is true that the righteous of all nations have a place in the world to come, then the special laws of Judaism are not the agency for the salvation of all. That is the effect of the 'all' in Galatians 2.16. But it is clear from Paul's discussions of dietary laws in Corinthians and Romans that he is no longer a Pharisee, not because he admits that non-Jews do not have to practice Jewish law to be saved but because he says that Jews do not have to observe them either. They are voluntary for everyone. No one who says this can be a Pharisee in good standing. However, Paul is still a Jew. He is an ex-Pharisee who still uses his pharisaic position to inform his judgment and, in terms of practice, probably just an ordinary Hellenistic Jew. But that is the subject of another paper.

As is clear, I do not conclude with Gaston and Gager that Paul is offering two different views of salvation — one for Jews by means of the law, another for Gentiles by means of Christ.[26] Rather he feels that

---

[25] See Michael Winger, *The Law in Paul's Writings* (Ph.D. diss., Columbia University, 1989).

[26] Lloyd Gaston, *Paul and the Torah*; John Gager, *The Origins of Anti-Semitism: Attitudes Towards Judaism in Pagan and Christian Antiquity* (New York: Oxford University Press, 1983). These scholars base their work on Krister Stendahl, 'Paul and the Introspective Conscience of the West,' *HTR* 56 (1963) 199–215. Stendahl, however, does not share the radical separation of missions — a lawful mission for Jews, a lawless

the spirit of Christ has brought a change for everyone. That change does not nullify Torah, although it does make totally volitional one's adherence to the *special* laws of Judaism, which he expresses variously as *the fleshly laws of Judaism* in Romans 7 or *the works of the law*, as he says above.

Paul is maintaining here that one has to have faith in Jesus to be saved. And he is not necessarily denying that the Torah still remains intact. He can be stating that the special laws no longer need to be practiced because they are fleshly works, not spiritual ones. The special laws are part of Scripture, which must be known and understood, but they can be allegorized, as they were for the extreme allegorizers. In the Christian case, the issue is inherent to any discussion about how Jewish Christians and Gentile Christians can interact as a single community. For Paul, to be transformed into the spirit means that the fleshly laws — circumcision, the food laws, and the rest – are no longer necessary; they are in some sense voluntary, although he concedes that they can be practiced for the sake of church unity. The vocabulary of this distinction is uniquely Paul's and it was not used by any subsequent Jewish or Christian group.

We can see parts of this in his letter to the Galatians:

> Now I Paul say to you that if you receive circumcision, Christ will be of no advantage to you. I testify again to every man who receives circumcision that he is bound to keep the whole law. (Gal 5.2–3)

If one receives circumcision, one is bound to follow the entire law because one has converted to Judaism. Paul says that what is necessary is that all be transformed by the spirit, which is in modern parlance a different kind of conversion. It follows that when one is not circumcised, one does not have to keep the whole law. But it does not follow that one need not keep some parts of it. We have seen that many Jews and Christians assumed that part of the law was encumbent upon non-

mission for Gentiles — that both Gager and Gaston promote, preserving instead the ambiguity in Paul's writings about the relationship between Gentile and Jewish missions. Stendahl actually seems closer to my position than theirs.

Jews who wished to live with Jews. He even tells us that the Christians who are making this deal are not as pious as Pharisees. And as an ex-Pharisee he has nothing but contempt for that position (Gal 6.12–13):

> It is those who want to make a good showing in the flesh that would compel you to be circumcised, and only in order that they may not be persecuted for the cross of Christ. *For even those who receive circumcision do not themselves keep the law*, but they desire to have you circumcised that they may glory in your flesh.

So his argument seems to us to be very subtle, but it may have been exceedingly clear to those living in the social situation he addresses. He says that *if one wants to be Jewish* one has to go beyond what the circumcisers are doing and become a Pharisee, as Paul himself was a Pharisee. Evidently, he sees the circumcisers in Galatia as promoting a kind of watered-down Judaism. They keep some of the laws but not others. And they do not practice the pieties of the Pharisees. For pharisaic Judaism and for Paul, the ex-Pharisee, this solution appears hypocritical. Like the later rabbis Paul also says that circumcision and pseudo-Judaism is not necessary for righteousness.

 But Paul's message goes considerably beyond the issue of Gentiles. Instead, Paul is primarily concerned with the process of transformation by faith that brings justification — a process that he sees as universal, required for both Jewish and Gentile converts to Christianity. Still, he has agreed that the feelings of Jewish Christians are to be considered in practical community. So even though Gentile Christians have the freedom to eat anything and not to observe any of the festivals of Judaism, yet they should forbear where others may be offended by their behavior. Thus Paul's arguments do not burst through Jewish parochialism; they absolutely depend on knowing that he is relying on what the rabbis will call the 'Noachian commandments'. Rather, he is fighting against both the conversion to Judaism model and the model of the resident sojourner, which apparently had been active in the early Christian community, because they had already been active in Judaism. Instead he promulgates a new conception of conversion, which involves a spiritual metamorphosis.[27] But he is willing to accept some of the rules of the sojourner

---

[27] See *Paul the Convert*, 117–49 for more detail.

if that will achieve peace and unity within his community of Christians. Indeed, his usage merely gives us one more piece of evidence that Judaism contained such ideas, even before the redaction of the Mishnah.

One Community of Circumcised and Uncircumcised

From one perspective, Paul has retreated to the position of the extreme allegorizers in Judaism, different from the purity community of the Pharisees. That in itself is not unique, although certainly his idea of a single community of repentant sinners, made up of Jews and Gentiles describes the Hellenistic house church more than any other social institution of his day.

The effect of Paul's preaching and his vision of a new, unified Christian community was the destruction of the *ritual* distinction between Jew and Gentile within the Christian sect. In other words, Paul was breaking down a ritual boundary within Christianity, not a boundary between saved and unsaved. The same ritual boundary — between Jews and non-Jews — was assumed by almost all Jews, even if some did not treat it seriously. While many Jews admitted that righteous Gentiles were saved, they differed wildly in estimating the number of saved Gentiles. And most Jews who wrote about the issue insisted on some ritual distinctions between Jewish and Gentile communities, especially in cases where no conversion was anticipated and yet some contact between them was expected.

From one perspective, Paul's action was a provocative if not unique development within Judaism. The virtually unprecedented aspect of Paul's mission was that he recommended that Gentile converts ignore the ritual law to become one community with the Jewish Christians, *while yet claiming that the antinomian actions fulfilled the purpose of Torah*, which could easily seem to a Jew like the charge of 'leading astray'. Whether Paul was innocent or guilty of the charge of apostasy depends entirely on one's perspective about his actions, not on the actions themselves. Paul risked the charge of apostasy for his recommendations, and he knew he could be characterized as an apostate when he admits ironically that to return to practice of Torah would be the same as admitting that he was a transgressor (Gal 2.18) from the perspective of some Jews and 'faithless' Christians (from Paul's point of view).

27

Of course, Paul denies that he is a transgressor, since the application of Torah has been overturned by the crucifixion and resurrection of Christ: 'But, if in our endeavour to be justified in Christ, we ourselves were found sinners, is Christ then an agent of sin? Certainly not! But if I build up again those things which I tore down, then I prove myself a transgressor.'[28]

Thus, Paul is not only saying that the model of the sojourner is incomplete. He is also saying that the whole idea of ceremonial laws in Judaism needs revision. When one places Paul in his Jewish context a new Paul emerges. He is not a Paul who negates all law entirely. Rather he holds some law in abeyance, based on the precedent of the sojourner within the community, for the purposes of creating a single community of those transformed in Christ. He goes even further in suggesting that none of the rules of the flesh are now truly compulsory. Yet he seeks accommodation in the same way that Hellenistic Jews sought it, but for a whole new reason and with the proviso that he sees transformation by faith into the body of Christ as a real, ongoing event which has necessitated social innovation. And since Paul is the only Pharisee in the entire history of Judaism to give us his personal observations we should take him very seriously, not merely because he says he is a Pharisee, but because we can demonstrate that his social observations about the ceremonial choices available to Jews and Christians alike are accurate to the first century, even though he was himself a convert from Pharisaism to a new and rather strange apocalyptic form of Judaism and suspected of being an apostate.

But I would also say that Paul's social observations are not the end of his important remarks for Jewish historians. Christian and Jewish exegetes of Paul should take his transformation passages more seriously. In them he shows us glimpses of Jewish mysticism as it was practiced in the first century, even though he identified the Glory of the Lord, the human figure of God which Ezekiel saw, with the crucified Christ. Even so, he

---

[28] See Gaston's discussion of 'Paul and the Law in Galatians Two and Three,' in *Anti-Judaism in Early Christianity* (ed. G. Peter Richardson; Waterloo, Ontario: Wilfred Laurier University Press, 1986); John Gager, *Origins*, 233. Gaston's translation of παραβάτην as 'apostate' is somewhat tendentious, even though pretty much the same sense can be rendered from the passage by translating it simply as 'transgressor'.

is the only Jewish mystic to give us personal confessional accounts of his mystical experiences in the first 1500 years of Jewish mysticism.[29]

What is important for us here is that Paul's writings are more understandable when they are placed in the context of rabbinic literature as well as the writings of Luke his biographer, but only when we have discovered the methodological principles for interleafing them. When the story is reassembled, Paul gives us clear evidence about the status of Jewish discussion about universalism in the first century. Both Judaism and Christianity, under the influence of the events of the Hellenistic period and the dominant cultural forces of the day, argued not just for universalism but also for toleration of differences within monotheistic religion.

There are at least two meanings of the term universalism. One is that all will turn into a single truth (uni+versus) that holds throughout the cosmos. Even the apocalyptic Jews believed this much. What distinguishes both rabbinic Judaism and early Christianity is that their minority social positions forced them to express their universalism in a temperate way. They tried to accommodate others to a certain extent.[30] Rabbinic Judaism admitted that righteous Gentiles existed and that they were part of God's plan without conversion. Paul at least counseled tolerance of positions that differed from his own for the purposes of preserving Christian unity. For the historian, as well as the believer in a culturally plural world not unlike that of late antiquity, I am sure that both the Jewish and Christian communities have a great deal to learn from consulting the documents of the other tradition and treating them historically to discover more about their own. Reading Paul is not reading other people's mail. It is reading mail meant for all of us, however we may construe Paul's message.

---

[29] See my *Paul the Convert*, esp. 34–71.

[30] Wayne A. Meeks, 'The Polyphonic Ethics of the Apostle Paul', *The Annual of the Society of Christian Ethics* (1988) 17–29; *The Moral World of the First Christian* (Philadelphia: Westminster, 1986) 94–119; Troels Engberg-Pedersen, 'I Corinthians 11:16 and the Character of Pauline Exhortation,' *JBL* 110 (1991) 679–89.

2

'Yes,' 'No,' 'How Far?': The Participation of Jews and Christians in Pagan Cults

Peder Borgen

Introduction

Research on Judaism has gradually moved away from regarding the traditional distinction between Palestinian (normative) Judaism and Hellenistic Judaism as of basic importance. By extension, the distinction between the Palestinian Jewish church and the Hellenistic church does not provide us with a satisfactory basis for categorization.[1] Thus, although the differences between Palestine and the Diaspora are not to be ignored, one should pay more attention to the complexity of Judaism both within Palestine and in the Diaspora, as well as look at the variety of tendencies which existed within Christianity as it emerged within Judaism and spread out into other nations. Although the present study

---

[1] The champion of 'normative' Judaism is G. F. Moore (*Judaism* 3 vols., [Cambridge, Mass.: Harvard University Press, 1927–30]); correspondingly, E. R. Goodenough (*Jewish Symbols in the Greco-Roman Period*, [New York: Pantheon 1953] esp. 1.3–58) stresses the distinctiveness of Hellenistic Judaism. Among scholars who argue against this sharp distinction, see especially R. Meyer, *Hellenistisches in der rabbinischen Anthropologie* (Stuttgart: W. Kohlhammer, 1937); M. Hengel, *Judentum und Hellenismus* (Tübingen: Mohr-Siebeck, 1969); G. Delling, 'Perspektiven der Erforschung des hellenistischen Judentums,' *HUCA* 45 (1974) 133–76. See also P. Borgen, *Bread from Heaven* (Leiden: Brill, 1965); H. Marshall, 'Palestinian and Hellenistic Christianity: Some Critical Comments,' *NTS* 19 (1973) 217–75; P. Borgen, *Philo, John and Paul* (Atlanta: Scholars Press, 1987) 207–32; M. Hengel, *The 'Hellenization' of Judaea in the First Century after Christ* (London: SCM, 1989); A. Kasher, *Jews and Hellenistic Cities in Eretz Israel* (Tübingen: Mohr-Siebeck, 1990); A. Kasher, U. Rappaport, G. Fuks, eds., *Greece and Rome in Eretz Israel* (Jerusalem: Yad Izhak Ben-Zvi. The Israel Exploration Society, 1990).

concentrates on data from the Diaspora, the assumption is that to some degree corresponding differences existed in Palestine as well.

The complexity of Judaism and early Christianity may be studied from different angles. In this paper, the focus is on the attitudes to pagan cults which emerge in encounters with the non-Jewish and non-Christian world. Some of the ideas behind the various forms of behavior will be presented. The purpose is to exemplify these different attitudes rather than to study all aspects of the situation in one particular place. Thus the data utilized will come from Asia Minor, Greece, Alexandria, and Egypt and will cover a span of some centuries, with an emphasis on the first century C.E.

In studying Judaism, Josephus and Philo are important sources. In addition other literary documents will be used, as well as archaeological material. Some of the sources, especially the archaeological data, give information about specific cases, while other sources reflect attitudes in the form of polemic, apologetics, or advice. In the discussion of early Christianity, some emphasis will be given to Paul, especially the problems he deals with in 1 Corinthians 8 and 10. Both chapters will be examined on the basis of the understanding that they are parts of the same letter.[2] Other sections of the New Testament, such as some passages in Revelation, contain other important data. Only occasionally will Christian and gnostic sources from the second century C.E. and onwards be drawn into the discussion. As one would expect, the data does not only occur in a variety of forms, but different tendencies are expressed and different historical situations are reflected. Nevertheless, the picture of Judaism and Christianity that may be gained in this way seems more adequate than the picture that was drawn when the material was selected and categorized on the basis of the distinction between Palestinian (normative) Judaism and Hellenistic Judaism and, correspondingly, between the Palestinian church and the Hellenistic church. In the analysis some consideration will be given to the various types of sources.

---

[2] See various introductions such as H. Conzelmann, *Der erste Brief an die Korinther* (MeyerK 5; 11th ed.; Göttingen: Vandenhoeck & Ruprecht, 1969) 13–15.

The Problem

Within Judaism there exists a long tradition of polemic against pagan cults. This polemic was taken over by Christianity, at first as it existed within the context of Judaism, and then also when it spread into the Greco-Roman world with an identity of its own. Accordingly, for Gentiles to join Judaism and Christianity meant to leave the worship of the many gods and turn to the one God and worship Him. Thus, according to Philo, *Virt.* 102–4, the proselytes have abandoned the images of their gods, and the tributes and honors paid to them, and have turned away from idle fables to the clear vision of truth and the worship of the one truly existing God. Similarly, in Gal 4.8–9 Paul tells us that the Galatians formerly were in bondage to beings that by nature are no gods and now have come to know God. And according to 1 Thess 1.9 the Thessalonians have turned to God from idols.

In the pluralistic towns and cities of the Roman world it was difficult to separate the worship of the one God from the worship of the many gods. Thus the attitudes among both Jews and Christians varied along a wide scale, from different forms of participation to strict isolation. The question of how far one might go was a pressing one in the daily life of many.

Paul's letters reflect this problem and the boundary question is discussed in some detail in his first letter to the Corinthians.[3] C. K. Barrett's essay 'Things Sacrificed to Idols' offers a convenient point of departure for our discussion. His conclusion is, '… in the matter of εἰδωλόθυτα … Paul was not a practising Jew.' … 'Paul is nowhere more un-Jewish than in this μηδὲν ἀνακρίνοντες' (1 Cor 10.25).[4] An alternative understanding will be proposed in this essay: since on the

---

[3]   Besides 1 Corinthians, see Romans 14; Gal 5.19–21; cf. 1 Thess 4.1–8; 2 Cor 6.14–18, etc.

[4]   C. K. Barrett, 'Things Sacrificed to Idols,' *NTS* 11 (1965) 138–53, esp. 146–47. Barrett's view is shared by H. Conzelmann (*An die Korinther*, 208 n. 14). Barrett states that 'in permitting the eating of εἰδωλόθυτα, Paul allows what elsewhere in the New Testament was strictly forbidden. In particular, he contradicts the requirements of the Apostolic Decree' (p. 149). According to Barrett, Paul's attitude with regard to εἰδωλόθυτα brought him into uncomfortable controversy with the Cephas group (p. 150). Barrett has developed further Manson's suggestion that the question about sacrificial food was raised at Corinth by Peter (T. W. Manson, 'The Corinthian Correspondence (1) and (2),' *Studies in the*

level of daily life there was a variety of behavioral patterns among Jews relative to pagan cult, there were Jews and Christians who followed a practice similar to that of Paul, and some even went further than he did.[5] Paul's first letter to the Corinthians demonstrates that there was tension among persons who followed different applications of the rule that one should not take part in pagan worship.

'Yes'

The task then is to sketch some of the different practices of the Jews with regard to pagan cults and to discuss some of the data in the New Testament against this background.

Some years ago, W. C. van Unnik demonstrated that Josephus' version in *Ant.* 4.126–158 of the story in Num 25.1–16 about the seduction of the Hebrew youth by the Midianite women reflects the pressures Jews felt from society at large. Josephus reads into the biblical story arguments used by Jewish apostates in his own time.[6] This pas-

---

Gospels and Epistles [ed. M. Black; Manchester: Manchester University Press, 1962] 190–224.) Other scholars, such as H. Conzelmann (*An die Korinther*, 163 n. 9), rightly state that there is no basis for connecting the Cephas group with the apostolic decree. Conzelmann may also be right in his view that the apostolic decree was not known in Corinth (163–64). They were however familiar with lists of vices forbidding participation in idolatry (1 Cor 6.9). In my essay 'Catalogues of Vices, The Apostolic Decree and the Jerusalem Meeting,' *The Social World of Formative Christianity and Judaism: Essays in Tribute to Howard C. Kee* (ed. J. Neusner, P. Borgen, E. Frerichs, and R. Horsley; Philadelphia: Fortress, 1988) 126–41, another approach to the problem is suggested. In the New Testament the catalogues of vices, including the apostolic decree, list vices in a summary fashion. Thus, they had to be further specified and applied to specific situations and cases, as is illustrated by the problems in the Corinthian congregation.

[5] Cf. the way in which A. F. Segal assumes that there was a variety of attitudes and practices among ordinary Jews with regard to the food laws: 'Although Jewish commensality was frequently noted by Roman and Greek writers, we do not know how ordinary Jews, as opposed to strict Pharisees, observed the dietary laws in the first century. Since there was no explicit law forbidding Jews and gentile from eating together, we must assume that some, possibly many, ate with gentiles, despite qualms. There was obviously a range of practice that we cannot precisely reconstruct …', *Paul the Convert* (New Haven: Yale University Press, 1990) 231.

[6] W. C. van Unnik, 'Josephus' Account of the Story of Israel's Sin with Alien Women in the Country of Midian (Num 25.1ff.),' *Travels in the World of the Old Testament: Festschr. M. A. Beek* (ed. M. S. H. G. Heerma van Voss et al.; Assen: Van Gorcum, 1974) 241–61.

sage and other sources reflect aspects of polemical exchanges between Jews and non-Jews due to problems of separation and integration.

Although Num 25.1–16 does not say anything about a counsel of Balaam, Josephus follows a broad Jewish tradition when he interprets this passage on the basis of Num 31.16: 'Behold, these (the women of Midian) caused the people of Israel, by the counsel of Balaam, to act treacherously against the Lord.' Balaam's counsel to the pagan king Balak was that the Midianites should send their comeliest girls to the Israelite boys in order to seduce them and make them renounce the laws of their fathers and the true God and worship the gods of the Midianites and Moabites (*Ant.* 4.129–30).

Some of the Jewish men then accepted the belief in a plurality of gods and sacrificed to them in accordance with the established rites of the people of the country. They revolted against Moses and his decrees (*Ant.* 4.131, 139, 145–49). Josephus interprets the revolt in Greek terms, as a fight for freedom against tyranny. The leader of the revolt, Zambrias, wants self-determination and freedom from the tyrant Moses:

> But *me* thou [Moses] shalt not get to follow thy tyrannical orders; for thou hast done nought else until now save by wicked artifice, under the pretext of 'laws' and 'God', to contrive servitude for us and sovereignty for thyself, robbing us of life's sweets and of that life of self-determination, which belongs to free men who own no master (δεσπότης) ... not to live as under a tyranny, hanging all my hopes for my whole life upon one. And woe be to any man who declares himself to have more mastery over my actions than my own will.' (*Ant.* 4.146 and 149)

To be free, ἐλεύθερος, was a cherished Greek ideal and it is here defined as being αὐτεξούσιος, having 'self-determination' in the sense of the power to make an independent decision without being forced.[7]

Although Josephus disagrees with this charge made by Zambrias, he formulates it in such an appealing way that he probably draws on

---

[7] W. C. van Unnik, 'Josephus' Account', 255–57. See Epictetus, *Diss.* 4.1.62 and 68. On 'freedom', see H. Schlier, ἐλεύθερος, *TWNT* 2.484ff. See further R. MacMullen, *Enemies of the Roman Order* (Cambridge, Mass.: Harvard University Press, 1967) 9–13.

points of criticism of the Law of Moses that had been leveled by non-Jews and apostates against the nation. In *Ap.* 2.173–74 Josephus even characterizes Moses and his legislation in a way that makes Zambrias' polemic quite understandable, logical and to the point: Moses is praised because he ordered the life of his people from its earliest youth and left nothing to the self-determination (οὐδέν ... αὐτεξούσιον) of the individual. Moses made the Law the standard and rule, that the Jews might live under it as under a father and despot (δεσπότης).[8]

Views held by non-Jews in Josephus' own time also find their expression in the words of the girls:

> 'Seeing then ... that ye have customs and a mode of life wholly alien to all mankind ... it behoves you, if ye would live with us, also to revere our gods (ἡμῖν συνοικεῖν καὶ θεοὺς τοὺς ἡμετέρους σέβειν). ... Nor can any man reproach you for venerating the special gods of the country whereto ye are come, above all when our gods are common to all mankind, while yours have no other worshipper.' They must therefore either fall in with the beliefs of all men or look for another world, where they could live alone in accordance with their peculiar laws ... (*Ant.* 4.137–38.)

Similar opinions are also voiced by non-biblical persons mentioned in Josephus' writings. Thus, according to Josephus, when Agrippa, the son in law of Augustus, visited the East during the years 16-13 B.C.E. the Ionians made a petition to him claiming that 'if the Jews were to be their fellows, they should worship their [the Ionians'] gods.' (εἰ συγγενεῖς εἰσιν αὐτοῖς Ἰουδαῖοι, σέβεσθαι τοὺς αὐτῶν θεούς, *Ant.* 12.125–26; cf. 16.58–59). A corresponding idea is communicated in *Ap.* 2.66: 'Why then, if they are citizens, do they not worship the same gods as the Alexandrians?' (... *quomodo ergo ... si sunt ciues, eosdem deos quos Alexandrini non colunt?*). Also in *Mek.* Exod 15.2, in an exposition of Song of Songs 5.9 a similar point is made by pagan polytheists: 'Come and mingle with us.'[9] The general separation of the

---

[8] W. C. van Unnik, 'Josephus' Account', 256–57.

[9] See Y. Baer, 'Israel, the Christian Church, and the Roman Empire,' in *Scripta Hierosolymitana* 7, *Studies in History* (ed. A. Fuks and I. Halpern; Jerusalem: Magnes, 1961) 82.

Jews from others is further documented in non-Jewish sources, such as Diodorus Siculus, *Bibliotheca Historica*, Fragments of Book 34.1: '[the Jews] alone of all nations avoided dealings with any other people and looked upon all men as their enemies'.

The main points of Josephus' interpretation of Num 25.1–16 are in this way confirmed by parallel statements found in other sources. It is obvious that his exegesis reflects the problem of apostasy in his own time. Such Jews who apostatized, following the example of the biblical Zambrias, said 'Yes' to participation in pagan cults and left Judaism.

These ideological exchanges of a polemical nature presuppose the experience of separation and apostasy/integration, but they do not report in any direct way on specific cases in empirical life. Archaeology can at times give more direct empirical evidence, although it may be difficult to interpret with certainty. Some inscriptions suggest that individual Jews compromised with polytheism and with society at large. It is difficult to decide, however, whether they still remained members of the Jewish community or left it. The examples which follow illustrate how certain Jews integrated extensively and said 'yes' to pagan society, although probably without renouncing Judaism.

From Cyrene we know that in the year 60 C.E. the Jew Eleazar son of Jason had a prominent administrative position as a guardian of the laws (νομοφύλαξ) in the city, and his name is found together with those of two high priests of Apollon on an inscription in honor of a pagan deity. Eleazar probably did not renounce Judaism, because he did not follow the custom of exchanging his Jewish name for a Greek one.[10]

From an inscription dated about 150 B.C.E. and found in Iasos in Asia Minor we learn about a Jerusalemite, Nicetas, who as a resident alien (μέτοικος) made a donation of one hundred drachmas to the festival of Dionysus. Since he came from Jerusalem, he was probably a

---

[10] The inscription of the *nomophylakes* of Cyrene is published in *QAL* 4 (1961) 16, no 2. See S. Applebaum, *Jews and Greeks in Ancient Cyrene* (Leiden: Brill, 1979) 178 and 186; and G. Delling, *Die Bewältigung der Diasporasituation durch das hellenistische Judentum* (Göttingen: Vandenhoeck & Ruprecht, 1987) 60.

Jew.[11] In Acmonia in inland Asia Minor the family of the Tyrronii produced an 'Archisynagogos', Tyrronius Cladus, and a high priest of the imperial Cult, Tyrronius Rapon.[12] It is obvious that the synagogue leader was a member of the Jewish community. It is impossible, however, to decide whether Nicetas and Tyrronius Rapon were actually members of the Jewish community and identified themselves as Jews. It should not, however, be taken for granted that they had left the Jewish community.

As for early Christianity, we have only literary sources from the first century C.E. Some of these literary sources exemplify how some Christians integrated extensively and said 'yes' to pagan society, but nevertheless remained within the Christian congregation. Thus in spite of the polemic leveled by John in Revelation against Christians who participated in polytheistic cults, these passages give evidence that this kind of compromise with the pagan community existed in the Christian congregations in Pergamum and Thyatira. Thus the *ekklesia* in Pergamum was divided on the question of how to relate to the polytheistic community at large. Some adhered to the teaching that Christians were to be integrated with society and thus could take part in pagan cults. In Pergamum as in other cities it was difficult to function without being involved in polytheistic cults because such cults were woven together with most aspects of the life of the city.[13]

John labeled the teaching of these members of the congregation as the teaching of Balaam. J. Roloff considers it unlikely that this phrase 'the teaching of Balaam' was coined by John himself. Rather it was

[11] P. Jean-Baptiste Frey, ed., *Corpus Inscriptionum Iudaicarum* 2 (Rome: Pontificio Istituto di Archeologia Cristiana, 1952) 15, no 749; see G. Kittel, 'Das kleinasiatische Judentum in der hellenistisch-römischen Zeit,' *TLZ* 69 (1944) col 15; P. Trebilco, *Jewish Communities in Asia Minor* (Cambridge: Cambridge University Press, 1991) 182.

[12] W. M. Calder, ed., *Monumenta Asiae Minoris Antiqua* 6 (*Monuments and Documents from Phrygia and Caria* ed. W. H. Buckler and W. M. Calder; Manchester: Manchester University Press, 1939) no 264 and no 265; A. R. R. Sheppard, 'Jews, Christians and Heretics in Acmonia and Eumeneia,' *AnSt* 29 (1979) 170–80.

[13] See E. Ohlemutz, *Die Kulte und Heiligtümer der Götter in Pergamum* (Darmstadt: Wissenschaftliche Buchgesellschaft, 1968); E. V. Hansen, *The Attalids of Pergamum* (2nd ed.; Ithaca and London: Cornell University Press, 1971) 434–70; W. Radt, 'Vom Leben in der Antiken Stadt,' *AW* (1978) 3–20; *Pergamon. Geschichte und Bauten, Funde und Erforschung einer antiken Metropole* (Köln: DuMont, 1988) esp. 179–285.

used by the criticized persons themselves. If so, they regarded Balaam positively as a prototype of gnostic prophets.[14] A more satisfactory context is the one provided above where the Ionians claimed that if the Jews were to be their fellows, they should worship the Ionian gods. As seen already the same point is made by Josephus in his interpretation of the Balaam story. To John, therefore, to yield to such pressures from the gentile surroundings would mean to 'hold the teaching of Balaam who taught Balak to put a stumbling block before the sons of Israel ...' (Rev 2.14). To John they said 'Yes' and were apostates. In their own eyes, however, although they said 'yes' they functioned within the pagan community without leaving the Christian congregation.

The inducement to worship the gods of the many might come from within the Jewish and Christian communities themselves. Thus, in his paraphrase of Deut 13.1–11 Philo presupposes that there were Jews who, on the basis of inspired prophetic oracles, were encouraged to worship the gods recognized in the different cities. Philo also refers to family members or friends who might urge Jews to fraternize with the multitude, frequent their temples, and join them in their libations and sacrifices (*Spec.* 1.315–16).[15]

Similarly, in Thyatira Jezebel claimed to be a prophetess while also teaching the people in the *ekklesia* to participate in pagan cults: 'But I have this against you, that you tolerate the woman Jezebel, who calls herself a prophetess and is teaching and beguiling my servants to practice immorality and to eat food sacrificed to idols' (Rev 2.20).

---

[14] J. Roloff, *Revelation* (Minneapolis: Fortress, 1993) 51–52.

[15] LXXDeut 13.7b: '... worship foreign gods' ... (λατρεύσωμεν θεοῖς ἑτέροις), and Philo, *Spec.* 1.316: '... fraternize with the many (συνασμενίζειν τοῖς πολλοῖς) and resort to the same temples and join in their libations and sacrifices ...' LXXDeut 13.10 implies that the seducer is to be reported to the authorities, while Philo, *Spec.* 1.316, rephrases this to mean that the report on the seducers is to be sent to all lovers of piety. See T. Seland, *Jewish Vigilantism in the First Century C.E. A Study of Selected Texts in Philo and Luke on Jewish Vigilante Reactions against Nonconformers to the Torah* (Ph.D. diss., Trondheim, 1990) 63–80, 98–107, 123–37. It should be added that in another passage Philo tells of how Jews felt the attraction of pagan cults with their poetry and music, beautiful sculptures and paintings, *Spec.* 1.28–29. A broader discussion of Philonic material is given by K.-G. Sandelin, 'The Danger of Idolatry According to Philo of Alexandria,' *Tem* 27 (1991) 109–50.

Neither John in the edict to Thyatira nor Philo in his paraphrase of Deut 13.1–11 elaborates upon the exact content of the prophetic messages favoring participation in the polytheistic cults of the many. Philo mentions the (inspired) oracles and pronouncements (λόγια καὶ χρησμοί) of the false prophet (*Spec.* 1.315), and John refers to (false) prophetic teaching (διδαχή; Rev 2.24, cf. 2.20).

Having discussed apostasy and having identified a form of integration which is meant to stop short of leaving Judaism and Christianity respectively, I shall now comment on attitudes held and actions suggested by those who regarded both groups as renegades. First we shall look at the attitudes of Jews such as Philo and Josephus. In Numbers 25 the punishment for the Jewish apostates was death. Philo follows this view in his use of the Phinehas story in *Spec.* 1.54–56. If needed, their execution was to be carried out on the spot.[16] Josephus (*Ant.* 4.14–44) tells a somewhat different story: Moses did not order the trespassers to be killed, but tried to win them back by way of conversion (μετάνοια). When this failed, Phinehas and other zealous Jews killed many of the transgressors.[17] Correspondingly, in Rev 2.16 Jesus Christ gives the congregation in Pergamum the alternative of repentance or the sword, where the latter is understood by John as being the sword of his mouth.

By these examples from Jewish and Christian sources we have illustrated how some Jews said 'Yes' to participation in pagan cults to such an extent that they became apostates or were treated as apostates by some. Moreover, we have seen that there were also Jews (see Philo, *Spec.* 1.315–16) and Christians (Rev 2.14, 20) who attempted to remain Jews and Christians and at the same time compromised to a large extent with the pagan surroundings. They said 'yes', some in a limited way, but others went as far as to participate in pagan worship.

'No' and 'How Far'

With this background in mind, how is the controversy among the Christians in Corinth to be understood, and what is Paul's own view

---

[16] See the detailed discussion in T. Seland, *Jewish Vigilantism*, esp. 123–25.

[17] In another context Philo (*Praem.* 162–64) also offers apostates the possibility of conversion.

and attitude? To judge from Paul's first letter to the Corinthians, he himself and some others with him reasoned up to a certain point along a line similar to that followed by the false prophet in Deut 13.1–11 and *Spec.* 1.315–16 and by the prophetess Jezebel in Rev 2.20: Paul correspondingly refers to revealed insight, *gnosis*, and both he and some other Christians in Corinth practised limited integration with society at large, but were more restrictive in their practice than those in Thyatira and Pergamum who followed the false prophet, Jezebel and the teachings of Balaam. According to Paul, he himself and the others reasoned on the basis of accepted insights:

> 'We know that all of us possess knowledge.'
> οἴδαμεν ὅτι πάντες γνῶσιν ἔχομεν (1 Cor 8.1).
> 'We know that an idol is nothing in the world,
> and that there is no God but one.'
> οἴδαμεν ὅτι οὐδέν εἴδωλον ἐν κόσμῳ,
> καὶ ὅτι οὐδεὶς θεὸς εἰ μὴ εἷς (1 Cor 8.4).

These two statements taken together meant that the *gnosis* consisted of insights drawn from the view that no idols had any existence. From this view, which is also documented in Jewish sources,[18] Paul and the others (1 Cor 8.1, 4) drew the conclusion that they could eat sacrificial meat. Paul did not regard paganism as an *adiaphoron*, however, since he warns the Corinthians against participating in the sacrificial act in pagan worship (1 Cor 10.1–22). The warning in 10.7 refers back to the incident of the golden calf: 'Do not be idolaters as some of them were; as it is written, 'The people sat down to eat and to drink and rose up to dance' (Exod 32.6). In 1 Cor 10.8, moreover, he refers to Num 25.1–18, the seduction of the Hebrew youth by Midianite women, and reports that twenty-three thousand Israelites fell on a single day. In 1 Cor 10.14–22 Paul gives further warnings against actual participation in idolatrous worship.

Philo, Josephus, Paul, and John say 'no' to participation in pagan cults. In everyday life, the negative attitude of refusal led to the question of 'how far', meaning 'where is the boundary line to be drawn?'

---

[18] For the view that idols are nonbeings or demons, see Deut 32.17; Ps. 95.5; *Enoch* 19.1; 99.7; *Jub.* 1.11; *m. 'Abod. Zar.* 2.3. Cf. Justin *Apol.* 5.1, 2; 12.5; 19.1; 21.6.

For example, Philo's 'no' did not prevent him from praising the pagan gymnasium. He indicates that Jews sent their children to it for their education and he declares that the parents benefit the children's physical wellbeing by means of the gymnasium and the training given there, and they have given them mental training by means of letters, arithmetic, geometry, music, and philosophy (*Spec.* 2.230). Philo's writings even betray such an expert knowledge of Greek sports that he himself probably was active in athletics during his youth.[19] He also tells that he watched boxing, wrestling, and horse-racing (*Prob.* 26 and *Prov.* 58). In the gymnasia there were numerous statues of deities, and the games in which the students participated were religious festivals. An inscription was found in Cyrene dating from 3-4 C.E. dedicated to Hermes and Heracles with a list of ephebes in which five of the names are obviously Jewish.[20]

Although Philo refers to the triennial festivals of wrestling, boxing, etc., he does not approve. He states that a Jew should try to avoid taking part, but if compelled to do so, should not hesitate to be defeated (*Agr.* 110–21). Correspondingly, R. simeon ben Lakish is said to have once been a professional gladiator, which he justified on the ground of grim necessity (*b. Git.* 47a).[21]

Jews also frequented the theaters, in spite of the fact that the performances included pagan cultic activity. For example, in the theater in Priene in Asia Minor there was an altar in the middle of the front row — the horseshoe shaped row with the seats of honor. The altar was dedicated to the god Dionysus.[22] Philo frequented the theater in Alex-

---

[19] H. A. Harris, *Greek Athletics and the Jews* (Cardiff: University of Wales Press, 1976) 90–91; A. Mendelson, *Secular Education in Philo of Alexandria* (Cincinnati: Hebrew Union College Press, 1982) 26; L. Feldman, 'The Orthodoxy of the Jews in Hellenistic Egypt,' *JSS* 22 (1968) 224–26; R. R. Chambers, *Greek Athletics and the Jews: 165 B.C.-A.D. 70,* (Ph.D. diss., Miami University, 1980) 129–44; M. Hengel, *Judaism and Hellenism* (Philadelphia: Fortress, 1974) 1.70–74.

[20] The inscription is published in *QAL* 4 (1961) 20, no 7. See S. Applebaum, *Jews and Greeks,* 177, 219.

[21] P. Borgen, 'Philo of Alexandria,' in *CRINT* II.2, 253 and n. 103. There was disagreement among rabbis on the question of whether or not a Jew might watch gladiator fights, *t. 'Abod. Zar.* 2.7.

[22] Ekrem Akurgal, *Ancient Civilizations and Ruins of Turkey* (4th ed.; Istanbul: Haset Kitabevi, 1978) 196–98.

andria, and in Miletus in Asia Minor an inscription in the theater read 'Place of the Jews, who also are godfearing'. The inscription was written sometime between 100 B.C.E. and 200 C.E.[23] According to the rabbinic material attendance at theaters was generally prohibited because of the idolatrous activities that took place. A Jew might go to an amphitheater, however, if the state required him to do so.[24] There were both strict and more lenient views among the rabbis as to whether or not Jews could attend pagan wedding parties.[25] Among those Jews who said 'no' to participating in pagan cults, Philo and others drew the boundary line in such a way as to enable them to participate extensively in sports and cultural activities.

The question of food and meals was another difficult issue for both Jews and Christians in relationship to pagan cultic life. In most of the cases mentioned above where Jews participated in pagan sacrifice, they would also have shared in pagan sacrificial meals. A quotation from *t. Hul.* 2.13 implies that some Jews in Caesarea Maritima joined in pagan rituals and sprinkled blood from a slaughtered animal for idolatrous purposes in addition to offering its fat parts for idolatrous purposes:

> If one slaughters an animal in order to sprinkle its blood for idolatrous purposes or to offer its fat parts for idolatrous purposes, such meat is considered as sacrifices of the dead. If it had already been slaughtered, and one sprinkled its blood for idolatrous purposes and offered its fat parts for idolatrous purposes. ... This happened in Caesarea.'[26]

---

[23] J.-B. Frey, ed., *Corpus Inscriptionum Iudaicarum* 2.14–15, no 748. See H. Hommel, 'Juden und Christen im kaiserzeitlichen Milet. Überlegungen zur Theaterinschrift,' *IstM* 25 (1975) 167–95; L. Feldman, 'Orthodoxy', 226–27.

[24] L. Feldman, 'Orthodoxy', 226, with reference to *b. 'Abod. Zar.* 18b; G. G. Porton, *GOYIM. Gentiles and Israelites in Mishnah-Tosefta* (Atlanta: Scholars Press, 1988) 250, with reference to *t. 'Abod. Zar.* 2.5–7.

[25] See H. Blaufuss, *Roemische Feste und Feiertage nach den Traktaten ueber fremden Dienst (Abodah Zarah) in Mischnah, Tosefta, Jerusalemer und babylonischem Talmud* (Nürnberg: Stich, 1909) 37–38.

[26] Translation from L. I. Levine, *Caesarea under Roman Rule* (Leiden: Brill, 1975) 45.

Sacrificial food is only one part of the much larger spectrum of eating traditions which serve as a boundary line between the Jews and others. This general separation might also be touched upon here since it pertains to our topic. As already noted the historian Diodorus Siculus stated that the Jews 'alone of all nations avoided dealings with any other people and looked upon all men as their enemies'. He adds that the Jews had introduced their laws in order to 'share table (τραπέζης κοινωνεῖν) with no other nation'. The same attitude toward separation is also seen in several other places, such as *Jub.* 22.16 ('do not eat with them') and 3 Macc 3.4. However, this general impression needs to be specified further and in some cases to be modified. Although Joseph in *Joseph and Aseneth* 7.1 had a table of his own and did not eat with the Egyptians, he nevertheless had a meal in the house of Pentephres, the Egyptian priest of Heliopolis. Similarly, although the *Letter of Aristeas* records that the Jewish delegates dined with the pagan king Ptolemy II Philadelphus, here it is explicitly stated that the food was chosen and served in accordance with the habits of the Jews, and that no pagan acts of worship took place (*Ep. Arist.* 181–86).

Philo indicates another solution to the problem in *Jos.* 202: Joseph held a banquet for Egyptians and Jews together by entertaining each group in accordance with their different ancestral practices. Philo himself probably adopted this practice of a selective eating. He tells that he had taken part in ill-regulated meals at which he had to fight by means of *logos* (as learned from the Laws of Moses) in order to win the noble victory of self-mastery (*Leg. All.* 3.156). Since the purpose of the dietary laws of Moses, according to Philo, is to control the unruly (pagan-like) desires and to get rid of extravagance (*Spec.* 4.100–31),[27] such 'ill-regulated (ἀδιάγωγος) and extravagant meals' as mentioned in *Leg. All.* 3.156 probably meant that forbidden food was served, possibly also in a pagan cultic setting.

In rabbinic writings there are numerous warnings against Jews eating with Gentiles,[28] including the *Baraita 'Abod. Zar.* 8a: 'If a Gentile held

[27] Concerning ethical interpretation of the dietary laws, see S. Stein, 'The Dietary Laws in Rabbinic and Patristic Literature,' in K. Aland and F. L. Cross, eds., *Studia Patristica* 2 (Berlin: Akademie-Verlag, 1957) 146–48.

[28] See Str-B IV.1, 374–78.

a banquet for his son and invited all the Jews in his town, notwithstanding that they eat their own food and drink their own wine, the scripture charges them, as if they had eaten of the sacrifices of the dead.' Such a casuistic formulation seems to presuppose, however, that some Jews would accept such invitations and bring their own food with them. Moreover, there are passages, such as *m. 'Abod. Zar.* 5.5 and *m. Ber.* 7.1, which deal with questions arising from Gentile guests sharing tables in the home of Jews.

A specific historical case is reported by Paul in Gal 2.11–14. Although details are not given, Paul makes it clear that 'some who came from James' stressed separation during the meals so that Jews could follow their own customs. Since Paul at the meeting in Jerusalem had reached a general agreement on circumcision and a division in the allocation of work areas between himself and Peter (Gal 2.1–10), 'some who came from James' might have advocated that Jews and Gentiles were to have different meals but in the same room, in accordance with Philo's picture of the banquet arranged by Joseph (*Jos.* 202).[29]

Returning to the problem area of pagan cults, some further comments should be made on the participation in meals in pagan settings and the use of sacrificial food in general. Philo tells about some pagans who when sacrificing to the emperor Gaius poured the blood upon the altar and took the flesh home and feasted themselves on it (*Gaium* 356). Although Philo mentions pagan temples and worship in several places, his information about sacrifice and things connected with it are difficult to analyze because he largely interprets them in ethical thought-categories. Thus pagan sacrifice represents vice while the sacrifice as prescribed in the Laws of Moses symbolizes virtues (cf. *Spec.* 1.192–93).

---

[29] H. D. Betz (*Galatians* [Philadelphia: Fortress, 1979] 108) comes close to this understanding: 'If Cephas' shift of position resulted in "separation", this must have been the demand made by the "men from James". If they made this demand, it was made because of their understanding of the Jerusalem agreement (cf. 2.7–9). The separation of the mission to the Jews from that to the Gentiles would imply that Peter would retain his Jewish way of life, and this included first of all the dietary and purity laws. As a result, cultic separation would have to be observed also during table fellowship with Gentile Christians.'

In *Ebr.* 14–15, 20–29, 95 some specifics can be traced.[30] The Scriptural reference is Deut 21.18–21 concerning a disobedient son who does not listen to his father and mother (*Ebr.* 14). The accusations brought against the son are listed as 'disobedience, contentiousness, paying of contributions, and drunkenness' (*Ebr.* 15). The 'paying of contributions' (συμβολῶν εἰσφορά) means that the person joined a social association or club. Religious activities always played a role at such gatherings. On the whole Philo sharply criticizes people who joined such clubs as well as the practices of the clubs, implying that some Jews did join. He argues that the lifestyle in the club is characterized by gluttony and indulgence, so that by paying their contributions they are actually mulcting themselves in money, body, and soul (*Ebr.* 20–22). The disobedient son made a god of the body, worshiping Apis, the vanity most honored by the Egyptians, whose symbol is the golden bull of Exodus 32.

> Round it the frenzied worshipers make their dances and raise and join in the song, but that song was not the sweet wine-song of merry revelers as in a feast or banquet, but a veritable dirge, their own funeral chant, a chant as of men maddened by wine, who have loosened and destroyed the tone and vigor which nerved their souls. (*Ebr.* 95)

The disobedient one learns from others, joins 'the many' and also consents to initiate evil himself (*Ebr.* 23–26).

From this it is seen that Philo ties the excessive indulgence in food and the pagan god together as a worship of the body as god. He calls this a lifestyle of 'irregularity' (ἐκδιαίτησις). Philo uses this term and the corresponding verb to mean acting against the laws of Moses and subverting the Jewish customs and abandoning the old Jewish ways of communal life (*Somn.* 2.123; *Jos.* 254; *Mos.* 1.31, 241, 278, 298; 2.167, 270; *Spec.* 3.126; *Praem.* 98; *Flac.* 14, 50). To Philo participation in the religious meals in a club was both a breaking of the Jewish dietary laws and eating forbidden and idolatrous food.

---

[30] See P. Borgen, *Philo, John and Paul,* 227–28; concerning club life in Alexandria, see *Bread from Heaven,* 124–25, with reference to I. Heinemann, *Philons griechische und jüdische Bildung* (Darmstadt: Wissenschaftliche Buchgesellschaft, 1962) 431.

Philo seems here to exclude the possibility that Jews could enter the social clubs of the non-Jews. He does not exclude this possibility completely, however, since in *Ebr.* 20 he says, 'As for contributions and club subscriptions, when the object is to share the best of possessions, prudence, such payments are praiseworthy and profitable.' To Philo prudence, φρόνησις, means wisdom which guides and regulates human life in accordance with the divine laws of Moses (*Praem.* 79–81; see also *Mos.* 1.25; 2.189, 216; *Spec.* 1.191–93, 277; 2.18, 62, 257–59; *Virt.* 180). So Philo is of the opinion that Jews might join non-Jewish social clubs and be permitted to keep their own customs and standards of behavior. He does not specify how this could be done, however. As to the problem of the cultic aspects (sacrifices, etc.) in club activities, Philo does not specify how a Jew should behave in order to avoid taking part in idolatrous worship. Such specification is also lacking when he reports on experiences he has had when attending performances in the theater and the hippodrome (*Prob.* 26 and *Prov.* 58).

Before returning to New Testament material, I shall comment on the (later) rabbinic sources. It would lead us too far to survey all the relevant material, and it would be nearly impossible to date the various traditions. G. G. Porton, who has studied the interrelations between Jews and Gentiles in Mishna and Tosepta, concludes that the rabbis were not quite as strict as one might think. He writes:

> Mishnah-Tosefta display a rather practical attitude toward the gentiles as idolators. On the one hand, Israelites must avoid any direct or indirect contact with gentile religious rites ... the texts support the view that unless it is clear that the gentile is engaging in religious activity, the Jews need not be concerned with interacting with non-Jews. . . . Furthermore, the authors of Mishnah-Tosefta seem to have assumed that the individual Jews could determine when the gentile was an idolator, so that much of the concern with idolatry was internalized. . . . The goal was to avoid idolatry, while at the same time existing and flourishing in an environment which necessitated daily contact with idols and their worshippers. . . . [31]

[31] G. G. Porton, *GOYIM*, 258.

It is even possible that some rabbis limited the definition of idolatry to direct participation in idolatrous worship. *m. Sanh.* 7.6 may be understood in this way: 'The idolator (is culpable) no matter whether he worships or sacrifices or burns incense or pours out a libation or bows himself down to it or accepts it as his god or says to it, Thou art my god.'[32]

As for the attitude taken by Jews towards pagan deities, note that some individuals, in contrast to Paul and the majority of Jews in general, had a positive understanding of them and even thought that Moses had founded polytheistic worship. Thus Artapanus claimed that Moses established the Egyptian cults: '[Moses] divided the state into 36 nomes and appointed for each of the nomes the god to be worshiped, and for the priests the sacred letters, and that they should be cats and dogs' (Eusebius, *Praep. Evang.* 9.27.4).[33] Moreover, as mentioned above, Jews in Cyrene had their names written on an inscription dedicated to Hermes and Heracles.[34] An inscription from Upper Egypt demonstrates that a Jew worshiped a god in the temple of Pan.[35]

As already shown, Paul sided with the predominant Jewish traditions in saying an emphatic 'no' to idolatry (1 Cor 10.7, 14.22). Idolatry is a central term in catalogues of vices from which the (Christian) proselytes should abstain (1 Cor 6.9; Gal 5.20; 1 Pet 4.3; Col 3.5; Eph 5.5; Rev 9.20; 22.15.) The practical problem remained, however, how to decide exactly where the boundary line was to be drawn. Therefore in many cases there would be disagreements and differing solutions. 1 Corinthians 8 and 10 gives us an insight into the diversity of viewed and approaches present in such cases.

In Paul's report on the congregation in Corinth, it is evident that there were persons who were strict in their drawing of the boundary line, and others who on the basis of their spiritual *gnosis* were more lenient and drew the line at actually taking part in the sacrificial ce-

---

[32] Y. Baer, 'Israel', 82–89. *m. Sanh.* 7.6 is cited on p. 89; Borgen, *Philo, John and Paul,* 227.

[33] J. Charlesworth, *The Old Testament Pseudepigrapha* (Garden City, NY: Doubleday, 1985) 2.899.

[34] See n. 20, above.

[35] J.-B. Frey, ed., *Corpus Inscriptionum Iudaicarum* 2.1537–38; G. Delling, *Die Bewältigung,* 86 n. 584.

remony itself. The stricter ones had a comprehensive definition of the sacrificial act:

> Some, through their familiarity (τῇ συνηθείᾳ) up to the present with idols, eat the food as something sacrificed to an idol (ὡς εἰδωλόθυτον); and their conscience (ἡ συνείδησις), being weak, is defiled (1 Cor 8.7).

The adjective εἰδωλόθυτος means 'sacrificed to idols' and the corresponding noun in the neuter 'meat offered to idols'. The proselyte catalogue in Acts 15.20, 29 and 21.25 (with two main versions in the manuscripts and several variations) in referring to idolatry stresses the aspect of sacrificial food by using the terms τὰ εἰδωλόθυτα (15.29); τὸ εἰδωλόθυτον (21.25) and τὰ ἀλισγήματα τῶν εἰδώλων (15.20: 'the pollutions of idols').[36] Elements of such lists, namely eating things sacrificed to idols and adultery, are also found in Rev 2.14, 20. Although these Greek terms isolate a certain aspect of idolatry — namely food — they might, nevertheless, have had various applications for practice in daily life. Those who applied the terms broadly, then, understood a meal consisting of food from sacrifices, either in an idol's temple (1 Cor 8.7, 10) or at home (10.28), to be an integral part of idolatrous worship.

Thus we have seen that in everyday life, the attitude of 'no' led to the question of 'how far', meaning 'where is the boundary line to be drawn?' Various Jews and various Christians drew the boundary differently with regard to sports, cultural activities, meals and with regard to being present where idols were placed and polytheistic worship was performed. Paul refers to guidance on these matters from *gnosis*, and he also refers to the concept of conscience (συνείδησις). The role of this latter concept is then to be analyzed.

Syneidesis in 1 Corinthians 8 and 10

The concept of 'conscience', συνείδησις, is used by Paul in 1 Cor 8.7, 10, 12; 10.25, 27–29. The word was not a philosophical term in

---

[36] For the understanding of the so-called apostolic decree as being a proselyte catalogue of vices, see my 'Catalogues of Vices' (n. 4, above).

Stoicism, but rather has its roots in the common language of daily life.[37] The word means basically 'knowing together' with someone else or with oneself, and may have various shades of meaning. P. J. Tomson refers to the study by H.-J. Eckstein, who discerns the following potential meanings: 'Mitwissen, Bewusstsein, Gewissen, Inneres.' Tomson states that 'especially in view of the correlation with one's outward actions, the last word is more effectively rendered "intention".'[38] Tomson associates this meaning of *syneidesis* with the conscious intention which is a decisive halakhic factor, especially in the area of laws concerning idolatry. R. Eliezer, for example, followed a strict rule about a Jew who slaughters for a non-Jew: 'The unspecified intention … of a Gentile is towards idolatry' (*m. Hul.* 2.7).

How then is 1 Cor 8.7–12 to be understood?

> However, not all possess this *gnosis*. But some, through being hitherto accustomed to idols, eat food as really offered to an idol; and their *syneidesis*, being weak, is defiled. … Only take care lest this liberty of yours somehow become a stumbling block to the weak. For if anyone sees you, a man of *gnosis*, at table in an idol's temple, might he not be 'edified' if his conscience is weak, to eat food offered to idols? … Thus, sinning against your brethren and wounding their *syneidesis* when it is weak, you sin against Christ.

Tomson maintains that the concept of halakhic intention illuminates the meaning of the first, essential sentence.

> The minds of the neophytes are still dominated by their awe of pagan deities … Thus when eating pagan food which they know may well have been consecrated to the gods, the 'delicate', whose consciousness is still dominated by idolatry, eat it ὡς εἰδωλόθυτον, 'as idol food'. … To these delicate, and these alone, Paul is ready to apply R. Eliezer's principle: 'The unspecified intention of gentiles is towards idolatry.' The consciousness of the delicate is

---

[37] H.-J. Eckstein, *Der Begriff Syneidesis bei Paulus* (Tübingen: Mohr-Siebeck, 1983) 65–66.

[38] P. J. Tomson, *Paul and the Jewish Law: Halakha in the Letters of the Apostle to the Gentiles* (Assen: Van Gorcum/Minneapolis: Fortress, 1990) 211, esp. n. 110.

'defiled', i.e. it is not yet pure and directed towards the Creator. By inconsiderate behaviour, the 'knowing' can 'edify' the 'delicate consciousness' towards idolatry, and 'wound' its relation to Christ.[39]

Tomson's interpretation is generally convincing. There are some weak points, however. First, he translates ἀσθενής as 'delicate' instead of 'weak'. By doing this he fails to discuss the term adequately in its Hellenistic context as well as from its Jewish aspect. In his essay 'Determinism and Free Will in Paul' (see below pp. 231–55) A. J. Malherbe shows how, according to the Stoic theory of cognition, it is because of a person's weakness that he gives his assent to false judgments. Thus, 'weak' does not just mean that a person is sensitive. 'Paul associates weakness with cognition; and he recognizes the importance of habituation for their condition.'[40] The 'weak' did not possess *gnosis* (1 Cor 8.7).

Second, the translation of *syneidesis* as intention does not adequately express that the term as used by Paul in 1 Corinthians 8 and 10 implies a consciousness based on certain sets of criteria and standards. Thus, Paul's use can be more precisely understood on the basis of the general characterization of the word given by H.-J. Eckstein with reference to its Greek usage from the first century B.C.E. onwards: 'A consciousness that rationally or emotively condemns or endorses one's own acts based on moral or nonmoral criteria.'[41] In connection with food and sacrifice the meaning can then be formulated in this way: the conscious and existential classification of food on the basis of a person's experiences and of criteria held by him. 1 Cor 8.7 may then be paraphrased in this way: Due to their experiences from participation in pagan sacrifice and the criteria gained from this, the conscious and existential classification of the food made by the recent converts was that it was sacrificial food offered to idols. In this way the act of eating became a sacrificial act and the persons partook of the table of demons (1 Cor 10.21). The

[39] P. J. Tomson, *Paul and the Jewish Law*, 215–16.
[40] See p. 234. Malherbe refers to *SVF* 1.67; 3.177; Plutarch, *adv. Colot.* 1122C; Cicero, *Tusc. Disp.* 4.15.
[41] H.-J. Eckstein, *Der Begriff Syneidesis bei Paulus*, 56.

conscious and existential engagement of the converts was defiled, according to Paul, because it was drawn into pagan worship.

In 1 Cor 8.10–11 the specific case is recorded of a man of *gnosis* reclining in a temple of idols. The person who has *gnosis* does not classify this meal as an idolatrous meal, but the conscious and existential understanding of the meal on the part of the recent converts will, by seeing the person of *gnosis* in this situation, be 'built up' to classify it as a case of eating food sacrificed to idols. Paul here seems to assume that the recent convert will interpret this positively and see it as permission to participate in polytheistic sacrificial meals. This may lead him to attempt a syncretistic fusion of Christianity and polytheistic worship. According to Paul, the convert is in this way destroyed.

This Pauline passage might be compared with Philo, *Ebr.* 14–15, 20–29, 95. Philo addresses the problem of whether a Jew might join pagan associations and clubs, corresponding to the case described by Paul where a Christian participates in a meal in an idol's temple. Philo is even more negative with respect to this than Paul. He thinks that in general the Jew would in such a case join in with the others and worship pagan gods, while Paul restricts himself to the actual meal and thinks that the weak convert is the one who in this setting is drawn into idolatrous worship by eating food offered to idols. Philo does not completely exclude the possibility of Jews joining, however, if they want to share the virtue of prudence.

This passage in Philo supports Tomson's general thesis that Paul draws on Jewish ideas about the importance of the attitude, intention, and criteria held by a person when one is judging whether food is sacrificial or not. Tomson's analysis, however, needs to be supplemented by further examination of the Hellenistic ideas which have also influenced Paul.

Paul gives instruction for two more cases in 1 Cor 10.25–29. Verses 25–26 present a rule based on Scripture:

Πᾶν τὸ ἐν μακέλλῳ πωλούμενον ἐσθίετε
μηδὲν ἀνακρίνοντες διὰ τὴν συνείδησιν.
τοῦ κυρίου γὰρ ... (Ps 24.1 is cited).

In v. 27 the rule is then applied to the normal case in which the unbelievers invite to dinner:

51

εἴ τις καλεῖ ὑμᾶς τῶν ἀπίστων καὶ θέλετε πορεύεσθαι πᾶν τὸ
παρατιθέμενον ὑμῖν ἐσθίετε
μηδὲν ἀνακρίνοντες διὰ τὴν συνείδησιν.

There is an exception to this application of the rule, however, when a
person explicitly says that it is sacrificial meat (v. 28):

ἐὰν δέ τις ὑμῖν εἴπῃ, Τοῦτο ἱερόθυτόν ἐστιν, μὴ ἐσθίετε
δι' ἐκεῖνον τὸν μηνύσαντα καὶ τὴν συνείδησιν.

It is difficult to decide whether the person who says 'This is sacrificial
food' (Τοῦτο ἱερόθυτόν ἐστιν, v. 28) is himself a pagan polytheist, or
one of the Christian 'weak' persons. He is probably meant to be a
pagan, since the word ἱερόθυτον is the common form used by polytheists themselves, while Paul in 1 Cor 8.7 uses the Jewish pejorative form,
εἰδωλόθυτον.[42]

What then is the meaning of 'because of the one who has declared
and the consciousness' (τὴν συνείδησιν; 10.28)? In verse 29 Paul
makes it clear that he is referring to the consciousness of the other
person, probably the one who made the declaration. If so, the person
has made the meal an act of pagan worship, and for that reason the
Christians are to abstain from eating. There is here a conflict between
two sets of criteria and two classifications of the meal: (1) the Christian
in his freedom takes part in the meal with gratefulness and gives thanks.
The scriptural basis is Ps 24.1: 'the earth is the Lord's, and everything
in it' (1 Cor 10.25–27, 30). (2) The polytheist draws his criteria from
the polytheistic sacrificial practice and 'theology'. His conscious and
existential classification (συνείδησις) is that it is sacrificial food, which
he understands to be part of polytheistic sacrificial ritual.

The problem arises when Christians and polytheists take part in a
meal and both claims are made. One can then assume that to the
polytheist it will not be problematic to include the Christian person
and his God in a sacrificial act to one or more of his gods. If so, the

---

[42] A pagan: H. Lietzmann and W. G. Kümmel, *An die Korinther I/II* (HNT 9; 4th
ed.; Tübingen: Mohr-Siebeck, 1949) 51–52; C. K. Barrett, *A Commentary on the First
Epistle to the Corinthians* (2nd ed.; London: Black, 1971) 241–42; H. Conzelmann, *An
die Korinther*, 210; P. J. Tomson, *Paul and the Jewish Law*, 216. A 'weak' Christian: Chr.
Maurer, σύνοιδα κτλ, *TWNT* 7: 914.

pagan person's understanding and spoken claim that 'this is sacrificial meat' will draw the Christian into acts of syncretistic worship. When the meal and the food in this way function as part of a sacrifice, then the principle of freedom does not apply any more. Paul says that the Christian must in that case abstain from eating (1 Cor 10.28–29).

The interpretation of 1 Cor 10.30 is still somewhat problematic: 'If I partake with thankfulness, why am I denounced because of that for which I give thanks.' The partaking mentioned here seems to contradict the advice given in verse 29 that the Christian should not eat. One might then relate verse 30 to the whole section of vv. 25–29 which deals with the question of a Christian partaking of a meal with unbelieving Gentiles. Another possibility is that verse 30 presupposes selective eating by a Christian. When he is partaking of the meal, he is to abstain from eating that which is claimed to be pagan sacrificial meat, but he is not to be denounced for partaking and eating that over which he has said his prayer of thanksgiving. In support of this interpretation one might refer to the emphasis on πᾶν, 'all, everything, whatever' in verses 25 and 27. This seems to imply that the claim, 'this is sacrificial meat (food)' does not refer to all the various kinds of food which are thought to be served at the meal. Paul's description of the cases here is so brief that it is impossible to reach a certain conclusion as to which of these two alternatives is the correct one.

On the basis of this interpretation of 1 Cor 10.25–30, the interpretation of the formulaic phrase μηδὲν ἀνακρίνοντες διὰ τὴν συνείδησιν in vv. 25 and 27 (cf. v. 28 and Rom 13.5) may be paraphrased in this way: Other people's conscious and existential classifications of food on various sets of criteria do not as such call for any questioning by the Christians, for God is the Creator so that they can for that reason eat whatever is served. When someone explicitly states that the food is sacrificial, the situation is different and the rule does not apply.

Tomson has rightly related 1 Cor 10.25, 27 to rabbinic ideas and practice. In contrast to R. Eliezer some of the Sages held the same view as Paul, that there were Gentiles of whom it was known that they did not worship idols. 'According to the latter opinion, in questions of "implicit intention" it was unnecessary to "inquire further" and have the gentile make his intention explicit.'[43]

To summarize, the term *syneidesis* as used by Paul in 1 Corinthians 8 and 10 implies a consciousness based on certain sets of criteria and standards. In connection with food and sacrifice the meaning can then be formulated in this way: the conscious and existential classification of food on the basis of a person's experiences and of criteria held by him. 1 Cor 8.7 may then be paraphrased in this way: Due to their experiences from participation in pagan sacrifice and the criteria gained from this, the conscious and existential classification of the food made by the recent converts was that it was sacrificial food offered to idols. In this way the fact of eating became a sacrificial act and the persons partook of the table of demons (1 Cor 10.21). The conscious and existential engagement of the converts was defiled, according to Paul, because it was drawn into pagan worship.

As for the meaning of 'because of the one who has declared and the consciousness (τὴν συνείδησιν)' in 1 Cor 10.28, Paul makes it clear in verse 29 that he is referring to the consciousness of the other person, probably the one who made the declaration. If so, the person has drawn the meal into the sphere of pagan worship, and for that reason the Christians are to abstain from eating.

Other Guiding Concepts

As already shown above, on the basis of the Jewish belief that God was the only God, Paul stated that food from sacrifices was not really idolatrous since the gods had no existence (1 Cor 8.4, 8). And from the conviction that Israel's God was the Creator, as stated in Ps 24.1, 'the earth is the Lord's, and everything in it', he drew the conclusion that Christians might eat whatever is sold in the meat market (1 Cor 10.25). This meant that neither Jewish dietary laws nor the objections to eating pagan sacrificial meat were to be followed. The same reasoning is found in the *Letter of Aristeas* in a question asked of the Jewish high priest Eleazar: '... why, since there is one creation only, some things are

---

[43]   Tomson, *Paul and the Jewish Law*, 219.

considered unclean for eating' (*Ep. Arist.* 129)? In his answer, however, Eleazar did not draw the conclusion that the Jewish dietary laws were to be abandoned (*Ep. Arist.* 130–71), while Paul did, on the basis of a reasoning similar to that indicated in *Ep. Arist.* 129.

It is worth noticing that Paul cites phrases which are akin to those found in Zambrias' speech according to Josephus in *Ant.* 4.145–49. Zambrias championed freedom (ἐλευθερία) and self-determination (τὸ αὐτεξούσιον) against the Laws of Moses, and Paul expresses a similar idea when he quotes 'everything is permissible to me', πάντα μοι ἔξεστιν (1 Cor 6.12; with a minor variation in 1 Cor 10.23) and also refers to freedom, ἐλευθερία (1 Cor 10.29). Moreover, the issues are similar — illicit marriage with a pagan woman in *Ant.* 148 and intercourse with a prostitute in 1 Cor 6.12–20; participation in pagan sacrifice in *Ant.* 149 and the eating of sacrificial food in 1 Cor 10.28. In contrast to Zambrias, Paul modifies the idea of freedom on the basis of the Old Testament tenet that God is the Creator (1 Cor 6.16; 8.4–6, 10.26). He also draws on Christology and other motifs, and thus he interprets the principle of freedom in such a way as to exclude sexual immorality and participation in pagan sacrifice.

The Jewish ephebes in Cyrene who took part in the activities in the gymnasia and whose names were included on an inscription in honor of Hermes and Heracles, the Jew who in Upper Egypt worshipped a god in a temple of Pan,[44] and Christians who followed the teachings of Balaam in Pergamum (Rev 2.14) and of the prophetess Jezebel (Rev 2.20), did not abstain from what took place in an idol's temple. Did Paul allow Christians to dine in an idol's temple (εἰδωλεῖον)? According to 1 Cor 8.10 he was open to this possibility: 'For if any one sees you, a man who has *gnosis*, at table in an idol's temple …'. Some scholars take this statement at face value, while others regard it as a rhetorical example. Grammatically, the conditional formulation implies that such a situation may occur. It seems too easy to say that Paul's example was an impossible one. Accordingly, he must have considered it possible for a man who has *gnosis* to join in a meal in a dining room

---

[44] Cf. Philo's warnings against Jewish 'prophets' who would lead Jews to mingle with the many (*Spec.* 1.315–16).

in a pagan temple, without taking part in the cult ceremonies. Again it is a question of where to draw the line.[45] Although Paul did not prohibit the eating of sacrificial food as such, those who took part in the sacrificial ritual offered the sacrificial meat to demons and not to God (1 Cor 10.19–22). Thus he applied a functional interpretation of εἰδωλόθυτον — when persons offered the meat as sacrifice, it implied a demonic context, while outside of this direct context, it was ordinary food even when the setting for the meal was the dining room in a temple.[46]

In this way Paul in 1 Corinthians 8 and 10 drew the boundary line just at the pagan altar table when sacrifices were performed. Apart from this, the belief in the one God, the Creator, allowed the possibility of eating sacrificial food either in an idol's temple or at home. Paul may here be illustrating how Philo could accept that Jews joined pagan clubs and still followed Jewish principles (*Ebr.* 20).[47]

In conclusion, on the basis of different sources it has been demonstrated that on the level of daily life there was a variety of behavioral patterns among Jews relative to pagan cults. Thus, there were Jews and

[45] P. J. Tomson (*Paul and the Jewish Law*, 196–97) agrees with J. C. Hurd (*The Origin of I Corinthians* [London: S.P.C.K., 1965]) that Paul's question in 1 Cor 8.10 is clearly rhetorical. Tomson thinks that the fact that σέ is left out in P46 and some other manuscript witnesses, may be read as reflecting the impossibility of Paul's rhetorical example (196 n. 45). Against Tomson it must be said that P46 shows that the scribe wished to weaken the fact that the formulation in 1 Cor 8.10 allows for Paul's example to be possible. See H. Mosbech, *Sproglig Fortolkning til Foerste Korinterbrev* (2nd ed.; Copenhagen: Gyldendal, 1951) 107. C. K. Barrett ('Things sacrificed to Idols', 148–49; *First Epistle to the Corinthians*, 188 n. 1, and 195–96) and H. Conzelmann (*An die Korinther*, 176–77 and 205–6) are among those who take 1 Cor 8.10 to refer to a real possibility.

[46] As for entering a pagan temple as such, Josephus tells that Jewish envoys together with many Jews in Rome met before the council gathered by Caesar (Augustus) in the temple of the Palatine Apollo (*J.W.* 2.80ff.; *Ant.* 17.301ff.).

[47] It would be beyond the scope of this paper to discuss Christian and (anti-) gnostic material in the time after the New Testament. The survey given above makes clear, however, that there is no need to look at material on Gnosticism in order to explain the various attitudes towards pagan sacrifice and sacrificial food in Paul's letters and in the book of Revelation. The variety of attitudes reflected in Jewish sources give us sufficient background for understanding the struggle in early Christianity in the New Testament period. For a survey of the post-New Testament material, see J. C. Brunt, 'Rejected, Ignored, or Misunderstood? The Fate of Paul's Approach to the Problem of Food Offered to Idols in Early Christianity,' *NTS* 31 (1985) 113–24.

Christians who followed a practice similar to that of Paul, and some who went even further than he did. Tension between different views and practices existed, as is also seen in Paul's first letter to the Corinthians chapters 8 and 10.

Appendix: Religious Complexity in the Pagan World

It may be of interest to note that parallel variations in attitudes were also held by non-Jews. For example, only Greeks might be initiated into the Eleusian mysteries, and foreigners were barred access to the temple of Hera at Argos.[48] In some temples slaves were not admitted to take part in the worship.[49] In some temples men were excluded and in others women, etc.[50]

On the other hand some cults were inclusive and open, among them the worship of the Ephesian Artemis with its great festivals to which pilgrims came from near and far. In an inscription from Ephesus the following lines are found: 'Since the goddess Artemis, leader of our city, is honored ... among Greeks and also barbarians . . . .'[51] In a similar way several cults were civic in nature and their celebrations were events for all the inhabitants of a city or a province, sometimes also including pilgrims who came from afar to take part. For example, the imperial cult in Asia Minor was celebrated both in sanctuaries and elsewhere, such as in the central square, in the council house, in the theaters, sports arenas, etc. The involvement of the whole community meant that householders per-

---

[48] Theodor Wächter, *Reinheitsvorschriften im griechischen Kult*, RVV 9.1 (Giessen: Alfred Töpelmann [J. Ricker], 1910) 118–22; S. Eitrem, *Opferritus und Voropfer der Griechen und Römer*, VSII.HF. 1914. No. 1 (Kristiania: Jacob Dybwad, 1915) 217. Concerning intolerance among non-Jews, see Josephus, *Ag. Ap.* 2.259–70.

[49] Wächter, *Reinheitsvorschriften*, 123–25.

[50] Wächter, *Reinheitsvorschriften*, 125–34.

[51] The inscription is published in C. T. Newton, ed., *The Collection of Ancient Greek Inscriptions in the British Museum*, Part III, *Priene, Iasos and Ephesos*, edited by E. L. Hicks, 2 (Oxford: Clarendon, 1890) 142–45, no 482 (and addendum on p. 294). See R. Oster, 'Holy Days in Honour of Artemis,' *New Documents Illustrating Early Christianity* (1987) 4.75. The phrase 'both Greeks and barbarians' is also used by Apollonios of Tyana (*Ep.* 97) regarding the various peoples who were admitted to the temple of Artemis. The same wording is used by Paul in Rom 1.14, as well as by Philo (*Mos.* 2.12, 18, etc.).

formed sacrifices on altars outside their houses when the processions passed by. Noncitizens and foreigners were occasionally included in invitations to the feasts. Banqueting played an important role in the celebrations. It is worth pointing out that the veneration of the emperor went together with the worship of various gods.[52]

In some cults the rules for admission stressed ethical virtues. Of particular interest in this connection is a syncretistic cult group in Philadelphia (Alasehir) in Lydia. An inscription gives us a valuable insight into this cult of the late second or early first century B.C.E. The ordinances were given by divine revelation to a person by the name of Dionysios in his sleep. Dionysios allows entry into this cultic association to those who qualify on ethical grounds without debarring anyone based on sex or class:

> When coming into this *oikos* let men and women, free people and slaves, swear by all the gods neither to know nor make use wittingly of any deceit against a man or a woman, neither poison harmful to men nor harmful spells. . . . Apart from his own wife, a man is not to have any sexual relation with another married woman, whether free or slave, nor with a boy nor a virgin girl. . . . A free woman is to be chaste . . . .[53]

Thus religious pluralism was characterized by diversity and complexity. In addition the dining arrangements varied. At some temples the dining rooms were adjacent to the sanctuary itself. This was the case in the Asclepeion-Lerna complex north of the forum of Corinth.[54] The temple of Asclepius is located on the higher level to the east, and on the lower level to the west there was a peristyle court, with access to three dining rooms with eleven couches in each. These rooms were attached to the foundation area of the temple, and a ramp led from the temple

[52] S. R. F. Price, *Rituals and Power: The Roman Imperial Cult in Asia Minor* (Cambridge: Cambridge University Press, 1984) 109–14, 229–33.

[53] Stephen Barton, 'A Hellenistic Cult Group and the New Testament Churches,' *JAC* 24 (1981) 7–41, esp. 9; Otto Weinreich, 'Stiftung und Kultsatzungen eines Privatheiligtums in Philadelphia in Lyden,' SHAW.PH 16 (Heidelberg: Carl Winter, 1919) 1–68.

[54] See Carl Roebuck, *Corinth XIV: The Asclepieion and Lerna* (Princeton: Princeton University Press, 1951) 51–55.

on the upper level to the courtyard and the dining rooms on the lower level. The rooms were in use from the fourth century B.C.E. to the fourth century C.E. Inside the holy *temenos* of the Heraion at Argos there was a separate banquet hall.[55] Similarly, the banquet hall at Perachora north of Corinth was located in the vicinity of the sanctuary.[56] In such dining rooms it seems that parties might possibly have had their meals according to their own liking, if they so wished, since the rooms were not part of the sanctuary proper where the alter was located, and at least some of them did not have sufficient space for a permanent altar in addition to the couches and transportable tables.

In some places the banquet hall had the altar in the center, however, and the dining was by necessity an integral part of the sacrificial ceremony. The so-called 'Podium Hall' (24 x 10 m.) in Pergamum exemplifies such a hall for sacred meals. The hall received its name by the excavators because a podium, approximately 1 m. high and 2 m. deep, runs along the walls of the structure. The participants lay on the podium with their heads toward the center of the room. In the middle section of the room the entrance was through the door on the one side and on the opposite side there was a niche with an altar before it. There might be room for seventy cult participants in the hall. Reclining together they took their sacred meals. The food was placed on a marble slab which ran along the front edge of the podium. The hall was dedicated to the god Dionysus and probably belonged to a cultic association.[57] In such a cultic dining room it would have been impossible not to be drawn into the sacrificial act itself.[58]

---

[55] G. Gruben, *Die Tempel der Griechen* (2nd ed.; München: Hirmer, 1976) 106–7.

[56] R. A. Tomlinson, 'Perachora: the remains outside the two sanctuaries,' *ABSA* 64 (1969) 164–72; Michael Vicker, *Greek Symposia* (Oxford: The Joint Association of Classical Teachers, n.d.) 2–3.

[57] Wolfgang Radt, *Pergamon. Geschichte und Bauten, Funde und Erforschung einer antiken Metropole*, 224–28; cf. *Pergamon. Archaeological Guide* (2nd ed.; Istanbul: Türkiye Turing ve Otomobil Kurumu, 1978) 20–21, where Radt had preliminarily suggested that it was the hall of an oriental cult.

[58] The Deputy Director of the Department of Culture and Tourism, Ankara, Ms Nimet Berkok, and the Director of the Ephesus Museum, Selahattin Erdemgil, have given me very helpful professional assistance in the study of ancient archaeological sites in Turkey. The insights thus gained have contributed to the perspective followed and to some of the specifics mentioned in this essay.

3

Paul and the Hellenistic Schools: The Evidence of Galen

Loveday Alexander

If we have learned anything from the last twenty years of New Testament scholarship, it is that 'thought' does not operate in a kind of disembodied noetic sphere independent of personal and social structuring. Thought is an activity of thinkers, and thinkers are tied in to certain patterns of behavior, restricted to certain specific forms of communication, by the society they live in. It seems appropriate, therefore, in a volume devoted to situating Paul within his Hellenistic context, to take a step back from conceptual comparisons to consider the broader question of the social matrix in which both the Pauline churches and the Hellenistic philosophers were operating. Are there any fruitful comparisons to be made between the social structures of the Pauline churches and the Hellenistic schools? Were the two groups engaged in any way in the same sort of activity? Were they competing, in market terms, for the same group of consumers? How did they set about attracting adherents, and how did they keep them? What strategies did they develop to meet the ongoing needs of disciples (or students)? And how were their activities related to the wider political and social structures of the Greco-Roman world?

The cornerstone of study in this area must be Arthur Darby Nock's brilliant monograph *Conversion*.[1] In what follows I follow Nock's basic thesis that to the casual pagan observer the activities of the average synagogue or church would look more like the activities of a school than anything else. Teaching or preaching, moral exhortation, and the exegesis of canonical texts are activities associated in the ancient world

---

[1] A. D. Nock, *Conversion: The Old and the New in Religion from Alexander the Great to Augustine of Hippo* (London: Oxford University Press, 1933) chap. 11.

with philosophy, not religion. Moreover, as Nock argues, the whole idea of 'conversion' from one set of beliefs and way of life to another is at home among the philosophical schools of antiquity in a way that it is not in the pluralistic, polytheistic world of ancient religion. Only the mystery religions could provide anything analogous to this experience, and, as Ramsay MacMullen has recently and persuasively reminded us, we should not overestimate the influence and importance of the mysteries across the whole spectrum of Greco-Roman religion. For the average inhabitant of the cities of the Empire, east or west, 'religion' meant something public, something to do with sacrifices and processions and festivals, and something that carried the sanction of long practice in a particular locality. It was not a private affair, and it did not normally demand exclusive loyalty.[2]

If we attempt to explore the analogy between church and school in a more detailed way, however, we soon run up against a number of unresolved problems. These are set out most clearly by Wayne Meeks, whose *The First Urban Christians* provides the classic treatment of the topic.[3] Vague phrases like 'the school of Paul', as Meeks points out, do not help us much unless some attention is paid to questions of structure. Is the term properly used of a specialist, central Pauline 'academy', clustered around the master in his lifetime and dedicated to the preservation of the Pauline tradition after his death?[4] Or could the local Pauline congregation be regarded as a 'school'? What ancient models are there for the 'school' in either sense? Edwin Judge, in one of the most concerted attempts in recent years to construct an imaginatively cogent position for Paul in Greco-Roman society, argues that the activities of the Pauline 'retinue' can most easily be compared with those of a traveling sophist and his disciples. But, as Judge himself acknowledges, there are no parallels among the sophists to Paul's establishment of ongoing 'nurture groups' which continue to exist after the teacher

[2] R. MacMullen, *Paganism in the Roman Empire* (New Haven: Yale University Press, 1981) 112–30.
[3] W. A. Meeks, *The First Urban Christians* (New Haven: Yale University Press, 1983) 81–84.
[4] Meeks, *First Urban Christians,* 82 and nn. 43–45 (p. 223).

has left.[5] It may be easier to find parallels for this aspect of the Pauline mission among the philosophical schools, especially the Pythagoreans and Epicureans. Unfortunately we have little reliable information on the former, and there is still much to investigate about the latter.[6] Moreover it is a fair question to ask how far the Pythagoreans and Epicureans are typical of the ancient schools in general. The prevailing picture of 'a closed organization of initiated disciples' which scholars have gleaned from these groups is not obviously reflected, for example, among the Stoics (Meeks, *First Urban Christians*, 83). This last point raises an issue that has been perceptively developed by Stanley Stowers, and takes us back to the question of the social context of philosophical teaching: How far is Paul's activity as a preacher comparable to the teaching activity of the Greco-Roman philosophers?[7]

There is, however, a more fundamental unease about the comparison between church and school. Deeper than any awareness of apparent differences of structure is the gut feeling that, at bottom, 'going to school' and 'going to church' are two entirely different kinds of activity. Despite Nock's arguments, the comparison seems to be an attempt to assimilate two fundamentally different phenomena. Even its earliest critics had noted the cultic side of Christianity. Tacitus calls the movement a *superstitio* (*Ann.* 15.44), and Pliny records the practice of singing 'a hymn to Christ, as to a god' (*Epist.* 10.96). The evidence for cultic practice in the Pauline churches is thin, but they clearly had regular meetings, a commemorative meal, and a ritual of initiation which demarcated 'outsiders' from 'insiders'.[8] The maintenance of group

[5] E. A. Judge, 'The Early Christians as a Scholastic Community,' *JRH* 1 (1960–61) 4–15, 125–37, esp. 135.

[6] On the Pythagoreans, see now Gillian Clark, *Iamblichus on the Pythagorean Life* (Translated Texts for Historians 8; Liverpool: Liverpool University Press, 1989). On the Epicureans, the work most often cited is N. DeWitt, 'Organization and Procedure in Epicurean Groups,' *CP* 31 (1936) 205–11; but attention should now be paid to the flood of new work on the Epicureans resulting from intensive study of the Herculaneum discoveries; cf. the bibliography cited below, n. 9. Clarence E. Glad (*Adaptability in Epicurean and Early Christian Psychagogy: Philodemus and Paul*) [Ph.D. diss., Brown University, 1992]) treats some of this material.

[7] S. K. Stowers, 'Social Status, Public Speaking and Private Teaching: the Circumstances of Paul's Preaching Activity,' *NovT* 26/1 (1984) 59–79.

[8] Meeks, *First Urban Christians*, chap. 5. The New Testament passages are conveniently summarized in R. P. Martin, *Worship in the Early Church* (London: Marshall, Morgan and Scott, 1964).

identity continues to be important. Paul's letters to his churches pursue an active program of 'resocialization' in which group members are encouraged 'to conceive of only two classes of humanity — the sect and the outsiders' (Meeks, *First Urban Christians*, 86). Any 'scholarly' or 'academic' pursuits were 'ancillary' to the movement (Meeks, *First Urban Christians*, 84). Conversely, cultic activities are broadly seen as peripheral to the academic and intellectual world of the Hellenistic schools. Parallels to the behavior patterns of Christian groups are sought among the most 'religious' of the philosophical schools, which are, however, recognized as exceptional even in the Greco-Roman world.

Clearly the issues raised here are too wide-ranging to be addressed within the scope of a single article. The process of comparison, undertaken seriously, must involve a detailed examination of both sides of the analogy. We must ask not only, What features of the churches made them look like schools? but also, What features of the schools made them look like churches? In particular, we need to know much more about the social organization of the Hellenistic schools before we can hope to assess their usefulness as a social model for the Pauline churches. Until relatively recently, histories of the schools tended to confine their interests to ideas.[9] All I can hope to do here is to survey a small corner of the terrain in the hope that it will provide a useful triangulation point for the larger project. The Greek doctor Galen, writing in Rome at the end of the second century C.E., obviously cannot be used directly to throw light on first-century Christianity. But he provides an invaluable (and often neglected) perspective on the schools from the viewpoint of an acerbic contemporary observer, which enables us to see some of the ways the Hellenistic schools were comparable to the churches. Moreover, he also happens to be the first pagan writer to mention the Christians and

---

[9]   I have dealt at more length with some of these topics in my article, 'Schools, Hellenistic' in the *Anchor Bible Dictionary* (New York: Doubleday, 1992) V. 1005–11. On the schools in the Roman period, see the splendid bibliography in *Philosophia Togata: Essays on Philosophy and Roman Society* (ed. M. Griffin and J. Barnes; Oxford: Clarendon, 1989) 260–81.

the schools in the same breath. And for this alone he merits our consideration.[10]

Faith or Reason?

In 1949 Richard Walzer published a fascinating collection of passages in which Galen refers explicitly to both Jews and Christians.[11] Three of these texts (Walzer refs. 3–6) are of particular interest to us, for in them Galen treats both Judaism and Christianity as defective philosophies, characterized by faith as opposed to reason. Briefly, the point of passage (1) is that 'the followers of Moses and Christ' find it difficult to adapt to new ideas; that of passage (2) is that they place too much reliance on 'undemonstrated laws', that is, on axioms which have to be taken on trust rather than being demonstrated by proper logical means. Passage (3), which Walzer entitles 'Faith and Reason', takes the last point further; here the complaint is that 'the followers of Moses and Christ' teach their pupils 'to accept everything on faith':

Passage (1): (Walzer, *Galen* 14: *De puls. diff.* 3.3, Kühn 8.657):

θᾶττον γὰρ ἄν τις τοὺς ἀπὸ Μωσοῦ καὶ Χριστοῦ μεταδιδάξειεν ἢ τοὺς ταῖς αἱρέσεσι προστετηκότας ἰατρούς τε καὶ φιλοσόφους.

One might more easily teach novelties to the followers of Moses and Christ than to the physicians and philosophers who cling fast to their schools.

Passage (2) (Walzer, *Galen* 14: *De puls. diff.* 2.4, Kühn 8.579):

[10] Since Galen is writing in the second century C.E. it is clear that the term 'Hellenistic' cannot be used here in a strict chronological sense. Nevertheless when dealing with the schools, 'Hellenistic' seems preferable to 'Greco-Roman', which in this context creates an artificial distinction. I use the word, therefore, simply to indicate that I am discussing a phenomenon widespread in the postclassical Greek-derived culture of the Mediterranean world.

[11] R. A. Walzer, *Galen on Jews and Christians* (London: Oxford University Press, 1949). Walzer's material is summarized and discussed in R. L. Wilken, *The Christians as the Romans Saw Them* (New Haven: Yale University Press, 1984) chap. 4.

... ἵνα μή τις εὐθὺς κατ᾽ ἀρχάς, ὡς εἰς Μωσοῦ καὶ Χριστοῦ διατριβὴν ἀφιγμένος, νόμων ἀναποδείκτων ἀκούῃ, καὶ ταῦτα ἐν οἷς ἥκιστα χρή.

... in order that one should not, at the very beginning, as if one had come into the school of Moses and Christ, hear talk of undemonstrated laws, and that where it is least appropriate.

Passage (3): (Walzer, *Galen* 15: Frag. of Εἰς τὸ πρῶτον κινοῦν ἀκίνητον, surviving only in Arabic):

If I had in mind people who taught their pupils in the same way as the followers of Moses and Christ teach theirs — for they order them to accept everything on faith — I should not have given you a definition.

The detailed background to these criticisms is set out by Walzer. Essentially the issue is the same in all three passages, namely Galen's insistence on employing proper logical procedures to test and weigh all assertions, rather than relying on simple loyalty to a dogmatic creed. This is the point which, for Walzer, marks the fundamental difference between Jews and Christians on the one hand and Greek philosophers on the other (Walzer, *Galen*, 51). The conflict is defined, as Tertullian saw it, in terms of a deep ideological rift between 'Athens' and 'Jerusalem' (Walzer, *Galen*, 37). But this is not the obvious way to read Galen's rhetoric. There is no question that these passages point to a deep divide — Galen on one side and the Jews and Christians on the other. But to interpret this as a divide between 'Hebraism' and 'Hellenism' is to overlook the fact that, on the specific point at issue, Galen places most of his Greek and Roman contemporaries, including the adherents of the philosophical and medical schools, on the same side of the gulf as the Jews and Christians. The essential point of passages (1) and (2) is that the 'followers of Moses and Christ', whatever their deficiencies as philosophers, are *in this respect* no worse than — in fact may even be superior to – the adherents of the schools. Dogmatic adherence to a particular school or 'sect', whether philosophical or medical, is Galen's own personal bugbear; the Christians and Jews are

65

only introduced as incidental ammunition in the real debate.[12] So Jews and Christians are not lone examples of credulity and superstition. In fact, for Galen 'the followers of Moses and Christ' are treated here as two among many contemporary schools which show a devoted — and in Galen's eyes culpable — loyalty to their own particular dogmas.

Galen certainly is not interested in the Christians and Jews for their own sake. He is not making a statement about Jews and Christians ('Jews and Christians are behaving like philosophical schools') but one about the sects ('the philosophical schools are behaving like Jews and Christians'). This evidence is therefore quite distinct from any second-century apologetic attempts to claim a special status for Christianity as the primordial 'philosophy'. On the contrary, if Galen speaks of the 'school' of Christ it is not because Christianity in general — or a particular group of Christians — has taken steps to bring itself up to his own exacting standards of rational behavior, as Walzer implies (*Galen*, 75–86). Rather, the whole force of the rhetoric implies that the philosophical and medical schools are being compared (to their detriment) with the Christians in their normal irrational state. Origen makes a similar point in the *Contra Celsum*: if you feel that 'faith' plays too great a role in the life of the average Christian, Origen argues, you should look at the average Stoic, or Platonist, or Peripatetic, or Epicurean, who is just as reliant on 'faith' (I. 10). But it is not a specially 'academic' or 'rationalist' Christianity which merits the comparison: it is the ordinary experience of the Christian 'multitude', in Origen's words, which is mirrored in the philosophical schools.

The fact that Galen has no real interest in either Judaism or Christianity actually makes his evidence all the more valuable for our purposes. The rhetoric would not work unless the comparison was seen (by the readership as well as the writer) to have a certain plausibility. Thus we may fairly conclude that for Galen and his audience, both Jews and Christians can properly be described in the terminology of the schools as 'those who follow Moses and Christ' (τοὺς ἀπὸ Μωσοῦ καὶ

---

[12] Cf. Walzer, *Galen*, 37–43, 45–48: the object of attention is Archigenes. Galen's views on the sects are repeated in *De ordine librorum suorum* 1 and in *De libris propriis* 1 and 9, and in *Passions* 8 and *Errors* (see n. 14 below). *De Sectis* gives a more detailed account of the medical sects.

Χριστοῦ), in the 'school of Moses and Christ' (Μωσοῦ καὶ Χριστοῦ διατριβήν), engaged in 'teaching' their 'pupils' and not easily 'taught' to change their minds (μεταδιδάξειεν). Elsewhere Galen reveals that he knows something of the content of that teaching: 'Moses' is associated with the doctrine of Creation, and the Christians with 'parables'.[13] But here the parallel is conceived phenomenologically, in terms of social structures, rather than in terms of any similarity at the conceptual level. It is the teaching activities of Jews and Christians, and the traditions which by implication lie behind them, which qualify both groups to be regarded as 'schools': there are 'teachers' and 'pupils' in the present, and their teaching is traced back to a revered founder in the past through either written or oral tradition.

Galen does not limit the comparison to the philosophical schools. The phenomenological approach is valuable again here. Galen is not interested in the ideas propounded by the different schools but in the underlying attitudes and behavior patterns of their adherents, and these may be observed, in his view, not only across the whole range of philosophies but also among the followers of the various medical sects. It is a useful reminder that the study of the school as a social structure in the ancient world must be distinguished from the study of particular ideas or theoretical concerns. Certainly Galen provides no warrant for the common assumption that only the philosophical schools provide a proper analogy for the early Christian groups, much less for our tendency to look for parallels among the more 'religious' of the philosophical schools (incidentally, Galen does not discuss the Pythagoreans). Many of the structural features that we associate with the philosophical schools are in fact found across a wide range of subjects and disciplines. This factor should be borne in mind in any broader assessment of the schools as a social phenomenon, especially with regard to the question of social status.

Galen thus provides us with a rather ironical view of Christianity as a 'school' which encourages reliance on 'faith' rather than reason and

---

[13] Walzer, *Galen*, 11–13, 15–16. The discussion of Moses occurs in *De usu partium* 11.14 (Kühn 3.904); also in *Galenus De Usu Partium*, ed. G. Helmreich (Leipzig: Teubner, 1907; repr. Amsterdam: Hakkert, 1968). The discussion of the 'parables' of the Christians survives only in Arabic.

whose adherents are noted for their loyalty to the received wisdom inculcated by their teachers. This is not a flattering view, but it is hardly surprising. What is more striking is that, for Galen, the philosophical and medical schools of his day are characterized by the same sort of behavior. 'Going to school', in other words, is not as different from 'going to church' as we might expect. I shall now explore some further aspects of the behavior of the schools, as observed by Galen, which confirm this impression.

The Search for a Teacher

Galen's own experience of the schools started at the age of fifteen when, under the guidance of his father, he began a tour of the various teachers offering their services in his home town of Pergamon. The process is described in *On the Passions of the Soul* 8:

> After I had completed my fourteenth year, I attended lectures by philosophers from my own city — mostly under a Stoic who was a disciple of Philopator, but for a short time, also, under a Platonist, a disciple of Gaius. ... Meanwhile, I studied under another teacher from my home town, a disciple of Aspasius the Peripatetic, on his return from a long sojourn abroad. After him, I had another teacher from Athens, an Epicurean. For my sake, my father made a close investigation of the lives and doctrines of all these men and went along with me to hear them.[14]

This is a classic example of the 'search for a teacher', paralleling more famous searches like those of Josephus and Justin Martyr.[15] In Galen's case it ended not in a 'conversion' to a particular philosophy but in a radical scepticism which Galen inherited from his father and which

---

[14] Περὶ ψυχῆς παθημάτων and Περὶ ψυχῆς ἁμαρτημάτων (cited hereafter as *Passions* and *Errors*), Kühn 5.1–103. Greek text most readily available in *Galenus: Scripta Minora*, ed. J. Marquardt, I. Müller, G. Helmreich (Leipzig: Teubner, 1884; repr. Amsterdam: Hakkert, 1967), 1.1–81. English translation in P. W. Harkins & W. Riese, *Galen on the Passions and Errors of the Soul* (Columbus: Ohio State University Press, 1963).

[15] Nock, *Conversion*, 107–110; 255–57; and Niels Hyldahl, *Philosophie und Christentum* (AThD 9; Kopenhagen: Munksgaard, 1966).

became the lynchpin of his own attitude to the schools for the rest of his life:

> He went on to say that I must not be hasty in proclaiming myself a member of one sect, but that I must inquire, learn, and form my judgment about these sects over a considerable period of time. ... These ... were the injunctions I received from my father and I have observed them up to the present day. I did not proclaim myself a member of any of those sects of which, with all earnestness, I made a careful examination, but I continued undaunted in the face of day by day occurrences throughout my life ... (*Passions* 8: Harkins 58–59; Kühn 5.43; *SM* 1.33)

Despite the many parallels, there is no need to write off this 'search' as a literary convention. The sampling of a number of different teachers was a normal part of the educational process. Teaching was throughout most of antiquity a private enterprise affair. A 'university' city meant no more than a city where a large number of teachers operated, making it easier for their would-be students to move from one to another. Completion of the full *enkyklios paideia* meant not enrolling in an institution which covered the whole curriculum but finding enough individual teachers, concurrently or successively, to cover all the subjects a gentleman's education was deemed to include.[16] It was inevitable that students (and their parents) would try out a number of teachers before deciding on a significant financial and emotional commitment (prudent teachers might demand fees in advance). Origen, indeed, regards the successive sampling of a number of teachers as positively beneficial (*C. Cels.* 3.19).

Motives for choosing — or rejecting — a teacher range from the mundane to the exalted. A letter found at Oxyrhynchus gives us the disarmingly frank lament of a first-century student in Alexandria over the difficulty of finding a satisfactory teacher. Behind the unfamiliar

---

[16] S. F. Bonner, *Education in Ancient Rome from the elder Cato to the younger Pliny* (London: Methuen, 1977) 146–62; M. L. Clarke, *Higher Education in the Ancient World* (London: Routledge and Kegan Paul, 1971) 1–10 (esp. 7–8); H. -I. Marrou, *A History of Education in Antiquity* (from the 3rd ed. of the French original; New York: Sheed and Ward, 1956) 290–95.

educational procedure we glimpse a not-too-serious undergraduate, short of cash and slightly worried about his father's reaction to 'the business about the theatre' and the 'smashing-up' of a chariot, whose excuses sound endearingly like those of the students we know today. Neilus' 'search' and that of his friends is constantly frustrated. One teacher has left the city, and since the chariot accident cannot possibly be reached; another has died. A third is rejected as 'too careless', a fourth as too 'provincial'. Neilus himself feels that 'apart from paying useless and excessive fees there is no good to be had from a teacher', but he is sure that he will make up the work on his own by listening to a few epideictic orators.[17]

In Galen's view, by contrast, most students were only too ready to give a quasi-religious allegiance to their chosen teacher, on grounds which Galen considered far from rational. The process is rather like choosing racing colors, he complains on another occasion. The choice of a sect has little to do with studying their doctrines or distinguishing true arguments from false. People choose the school their father belonged to, or one which was admired in their home town (*De ord. libr. suorum* 1: Kühn 19.50, *SM* 1.80). Sometimes conviction comes 'all of a sudden' on listening to a particular teacher discoursing 'on the end of life, <on happiness>, and on misery': in these cases, the response of faith is in inverse proportion to the intellectual attainments of the would-be disciple (*Errors* 3: Harkins 84; Kühn 5.72; *SM* 1.55–56). As we have seen, Origen makes very much the same point in *C. Cels.* 1.10.

Galen's own reasons for refusing allegiance to any of the sects he tried were (on his own account) more serious. Their quarrelsomeness was one factor (*De libr. propr.* 11: Kühn 19.40; *SM* 2.116), but more fundamental was the philosophers' failure to follow the procedures of 'scientific demonstration' (*Errors* 3: Harkins 82; Kühn 5.70; *SM* 1.54).[18] Yet even Galen sees no contradiction in the admission that his own

---

[17] *P. Oxy.* 2190.9–11, 16, 25, 29, 30–36, tr. Hunt. Bruce Winter has made a detailed study of this text (*Paul and Philo among the Sophists: a Hellenistic-Jewish and a Christian Response* [Ph.D. diss., School of History, Philosophy and Politics, Macquarrie University, 1988]).

[18] Further, M. Frede, 'On Galen's Epistemology,' *Galen: Problems and Prospects* (ed. V. Nutton; London: Wellcome Institute, 1981) 65–86.

decision to study medicine rested ultimately on something much less rational — his father was guided in the choice of career for his son by 'a very clear dream' (*De ord. libr. suor.* 4: Kühn 19.59; *SM* 2.88.15ff.). It is a salutary reminder that the possibility of supernatural revelation was not ruled out by the most intellectual of Greek thinkers. Socrates, after all, professed to be guided to the end of his life by the words of the oracle and his own particular *daimon.*

Nurture and Loyalty

The suddenness (or the shallowness) of this kind of 'conversion' experience might well be expected to cause problems for the student, and it is not surprising to find that the schools adopted a number of different strategies for maintaining the allegiance of their adherents. The part played by epistolary literature in this process is now well documented,[19] but philosophers also insisted on the value of daily conversation with a philosopher and observation of his lifestyle (Seneca, *Epist.* 6.5–6). If he could afford it, there was nothing to stop the would-be philosopher from attending his teacher's classes — and paying his fees — for twenty years or more, like Lucian's gullible Hermotimus, whose relationship with his *didaskalos* (teacher) was clearly as expensive and addictive as long-term attachment to a psychoanalyst (Lucian, *Hermotimus* 741, 748–49). The seriously wealthy might keep a philosopher on the payroll as a member of the household, or maintain one in an independent establishment, like Philodemus, for the edification of a wide circle of adherents.[20] Cicero and Plutarch both provide evidence for the establishment of regular gatherings to celebrate the founder's birthday, not only among the Epicureans, but also among the Platonists.[21] The quasi-

---

[19] Most conveniently discussed in A. J. Malherbe, *Paul and the Thessalonians: The Philosophic Tradition of Pastoral Care* (Philadelphia: Fortress, 1987) chap. 3; for Malherbe's more detailed studies, see the full bibliography in *Greeks, Romans, and Christians: Essays in Honour of Abraham J. Malherbe* (ed. D. L. Balch, E. Ferguson, W. A. Meeks; Minneapolis: Fortress, 1990) 367–71.

[20] E. Rawson, *Intellectual Life in the Late Roman Republic* (London: Duckworth, 1985) 79–83. On Philodemus, see bibliography in *Philosophia Togata* (cited above, n. 9) 267–68.

[21] Epicurus: Cicero, *De fin.* 2.31; Plutarch, *Adv. Col.* 1117A. Plato: Cicero, *De nat. deor.* 2.32.

religious veneration felt by the Epicureans for their founder was notorious in antiquity,[22] but it would be erroneous to suppose that the Epicureans were alone in this. In an important article on 'Philosophical allegiance in the Greco-Roman World', David Sedley claims that 'in the Greco-Roman world, especially during the Hellenistic and Roman periods, what gives philosophical movements their identity is less a disinterested quest for the truth than a virtually religious commitment to the authority of a founder figure'.[23] Sedley's prime example of this phenomenon is taken from the Epicureans, but he insists that all the Greek philosophical schools follow the same pattern, with only occasional exceptions.

It is hardly surprising, therefore, to find that the uncritical attitudes which so disturbed Galen regarding the choice of a school were a continuing feature of the life of a disciple. In fact, Galen suggests that teachers deliberately set out to 'brainwash' their most impressionable students. Teachers prefer students who are either 'naturally dull' or 'untrained in the elements of learning ... since a disciple who is naturally intelligent and has had previous training in the elements will straightway look with scorn on these charlatans. ... For they are accustomed to win their own disciples over [to these vices] beforehand, so that they never submit to offer their ears to such arguments as I have employed up to this point. It is very easy for a teacher who speaks with a dignified mien to persuade uneducated lads. ...' (*Errors* 3: Harkins 82–83; Kühn 5.69–70; *SM* 1.54).

Techniques like these would naturally result in a strong sense of differentiation between the disciple group and 'outsiders', with students forewarned against external criticism. That there were opportunities for discussion with outsiders also seems clear, although according to Galen most teachers evaded such discussion wherever possible. Galen himself had no objection to the intervention of bystanders in his own classes: 'I took lads who had no previous training in learning and taught them to recognize true arguments. If any of those present wished

[22] Cicero, *Tusc.* 1.48; *De nat. deor.* 1.43; Lucretius, *De rerum natura* 5.8 (with Bailey's notes *ad loc.*); Plut. *Adv. Col.* 1117B.

[23] D. Sedley, 'Philosophical Allegiance in the Greco-Roman World,' in *Philosophia Togata*, 97–119.

to do so, I asked them to propose sophisms to these young men. ...'
(*Errors* 3: Harkins 85; Kühn 5.73–74; *SM* 1.57). Similarly, he obviously took it on himself as an adult observer to put propositions to
other philosophers:

> I have often had experience with those philosophers who quarrel
> with and pretend not to understand any position which is at
> variance with their own. At any rate, I have discussed with many
> philosophers on many occasions the question of what ways of life
> are in accordance with any given end. ... Those philosophers
> who have grown old and are wise in their own conceit were the
> only ones who contradicted my position; when those who were
> present laughed them to scorn, they turned on their taunters and
> heaped abuse on them. (*Errors* 3: Harkins 86–87: Kühn 5.76;
> *SM* 1.59).

Not all the philosophers even bothered to contradict the questioner:

> That they choose to flatter themselves and that they are not
> seeking the truth we can recognize from the very fact that they
> argue individually against an opinion only among their own fol-
> lowers, but accuse all others of being in error. If I should gather
> them all together into the same place, they refuse to stand their
> ground; they offer a man's modesty as their excuse and say that
> they cannot speak when a crowd is present. They maintain this
> even though they are not too modest to speak every day when
> they have twenty, thirty, or more listeners. (*Errors* 5: Harkins 99;
> Kühn 5.92–93; *SM* 1.72–73).

'It is very strange,' Galen comments ironically a little further on, 'that
no-one commends any of these wise men except the members of their
own flock' — that is, the loyal disciples who were expected to (and
clearly did) back their own teacher against all comers.

Public or Private?

Where was all this teaching going on? In the passages just quoted,
Galen appears to imply a public setting in which bystanders and chance

passersby could interrupt the teacher; Lucian, by contrast, talks of a 'notice on the door, saying in large letters: "NO PHILOSOPHY CLASS TODAY"' (Lucian, *Herm.* 750), which seems to imply that teaching takes place in an enclosed space, probably the master's house. In fact, as we know from many ancient sources, teaching was carried on in a wide variety of locations, both indoors and out: Stowers provides an excellent summary of a range of evidence on this point (see above, n. 7).

The divergence between public and private locations goes back at least as far as Socrates and the Sophists of fifth century Athens. Socrates teaches in the streets and public spaces of the city, Gorgias in the house of a patron — though the occasion is no less 'public'.[24] The patronage pattern was an enduring one, whether in the occasional form of a meal, used typically by the Cynics as a vehicle for teaching, or in the more stable form where a wealthy man could offer a teacher or philosopher a permanent — if dependent — position in his household.[25] Many teachers used their own homes for teaching, effectively assimilating their pupils to a position of proxy sonship. This position is reflected in the Hippocratic Oath, which at this point simply reflects the age-old apprenticeship system of the crafts.[26] Some of the most prestigious philosophical schools simply repeated this pattern on a larger scale. Plato's Academy with its famous grove was his own private property, as was the Garden of Epicurus. The Stoa, on the other hand, and the Peripatos, were public spaces belonging to the city where the sessions of the philosophers took place. Even schoolboys were taught in the open, in the street, or in the Agora or Forum; or a master might hire a room over a shop if he wanted a little more privacy.[27]

As Stowers correctly observes, implicit in this pattern is a question of status. The public spaces of the city were not places which no-one

[24] Plato, *Gorgias* 447a–c. On the Sophists, see further G. B. Kerferd, *The Sophistic Movement* (Cambridge: Cambridge University Press, 1981).

[25] Cynics: cf. A. J. Malherbe, ed., *The Cynic Epistles: a Study Edition* (SBLSBS 12; Missoula: Scholars Press, 1977) *passim.* Household: cf. n. 23 above and E. Rawson, 'Roman Rulers and the Philosophic Adviser,' in *Philosophia Togata,* 233–57.

[26] Hippocrates, *Oath* 5–15. On the persistence of the 'family' pattern for medical teaching, cf. P. M. Fraser, *Ptolemaic Alexandria* (Oxford: Clarendon, 1972) 1.357–58; on medical education in general, I. E. Drabkin, 'On Medical Education in Greece and Rome,' *BHM* 15 (1944) 333–51.

[27] Bonner, *Education* (cited above, n. 16), chap. 10.

happened to own; they were owned by 'the public', that is by the sovereign people of the city — which sometimes even had designated areas created precisely for the purposes of teaching.[28] A stranger from a different city could not automatically assume the right to teach there. Hence the preference of the Sophists, who were non-Athenians, for the patronage of a wealthy citizen, who could offer not only premises for the meeting (and material support for the speaker) but also — and perhaps equally important — a form of *proxenia* for the visitor. Arguably the fourth-century dispute over the status of philosophy was at least in part a dispute over the right to use the public teaching space of the city; Plato's political success, and the enduring popularity of the martyred Socrates, ensured that in later centuries the philosopher's cloak was sufficient at least to win the visiting teacher a *prima facie* right to use that space. But the right to use public space also entails public responsibilities. Socrates was executed for denying the gods of the city and 'corrupting' its young men, and the ultimate success of the Academy depended in large part on Plato's claim that philosophy was an indispensable training for public life — that is, for a life spent in the service of the city. Philosophers who opted out of that responsibility were always vulnerable, as may be seen from the problems experienced by the so-called 'Stoic opposition' in first-century Rome.[29] It is perhaps no coincidence that the Cynics, who placed themselves firmly in the Socratic tradition and were always liable to incur the same charges, also proclaimed the ideal of 'world citizenship' in place of narrow city loyalties.[30] Conversely the Epicureans, who avowedly eschewed public utility as a philosophical aim, were also the most private and withdrawn of the philosophical schools in terms of their teaching location.

But the evidence of Galen cited in the previous section (which can be confirmed from other sources) suggests that in other respects the

---

[28] Vitruvius, *De architectura* 5.11.2: constituantur autem in tribus porticibus exhedrae spatiosae, habentes sedes, in quibus philosophi, rhetores reliquique, qui studiis delectantur, sedentes disputare possint.

[29] R. MacMullen, *Enemies of the Roman Order* (Cambridge, Mass.: Harvard University Press, 1966) chap. 2; M. Griffin, *Seneca: a Philosopher in Politics* (Oxford: Clarendon, 1976) chap. 10, esp. 339–46, 360–66.

[30] Malherbe, *The Cynic Epistles*, 210.20–21.

distinction between public and private may be less important than it appears. The public sessions he describes are not in any direct sense 'evangelistic': these are not 'street corner preachers' addressing passersby directly. They are — following normal practice in the ancient world — simply teachers holding their classes in a public place. This creates a two-tier pattern of audience participation: the inner ring of disciples, who will not question the master in public (though they may do so privately afterwards), and the outer ring, 'those present', who are either uncommitted, like Galen himself, or perhaps committed to a rival group. These will cheerfully listen, observe, and try to argue with the teacher; they may heckle or mock, depending on temperament. This pattern does not quite fit the distinction we are inclined to make between 'teaching' (to insiders) and 'preaching' (to outsiders). 'Conversion' may result from such encounters — that is, a passerby may be attracted by the teacher and ask to be enrolled in the inner circle of disciples; but formally the mode of speech involved is not 'evangelism' or the winning of new converts but the instruction of an already committed band of adherents.

The Schools and the New Testament

It is often pointed out that the use of sociological models carries with it the risk of anachronism. One may be tempted to force the ancient evidence into a mould into which it will not readily fit. In theory it should be possible to avoid that problem by using models from the ancient world; but the danger here is that of concealed anachronism — using ancient concepts but unconsciously interpreting them in an anachronistic fashion. Robert Jewett has demonstrated the perils of thinking we understand the concept 'church' when we try to reconstruct the problems of a Pauline congregation.[31] By the same token, looking at the schools through the eyes of a contemporary provides some protection against assuming too confidently that we understand the concept 'school'.

[31] R. Jewett, *The Thessalonian Correspondence: Pauline Rhetoric and Millenarian Piety* (Philadelphia: Fortress, 1986) 136–42.

Galen's evidence permits us to refine our view of the schools in a number of useful ways. The schools themselves appear less 'academic' (in the modern sense), less 'rational', than we might have expected. Galen confirms the accusations of Origen and Justin (*Dial.* 2.2) that 'faith' played just as important a role in the schools as it did in the church, and that teachers encouraged an attitude of uncritical loyalty to the school and its founder. Group identity was strong, and teachers devoted themselves to the defence of entrenched positions against straw opponents. Disinterested intellectual debate, at least by Galen's standards, was a rarity, more likely to occur among outsiders than in the schools themselves: in the colloquium described at the end of *On the Errors of the Soul*, the philosophers are put to rout by the logical skills of a passing master builder (*Errors* 5–7: Harkins 99–107; Kühn 5.93–103; *SM* 1.73–81). In this perspective, the attempt of the second-century apologists to claim for Christianity the status of a 'philosophy' does not seem as pretentious as is often thought; and even Luke's account of the arranged debate on the Areopagus between Paul and 'certain of the Epicurean and Stoic philosophers' (Acts 17.18) should not be dismissed as totally implausible. Moreover Galen demonstrates that the philosophical schools should not be treated in isolation. The same behavior patterns can be seen among the medical sects (a parallel Origen also observes; *C. Cels.* 3.12). Widening our definition of a 'school' may be one way to rid the model of its implicit social limitations. Not all schools were restricted to the leisured elites.

What about the structural questions raised at the beginning of this paper? At the verbal level, Galen gives no sanction for speaking of a 'school of Paul': the Jews and Christians he knows are identified as belonging to 'the school of Moses' or 'the school of Christ' rather than to any contemporary teacher. Paul himself, of course, would have approved (1 Cor 1.13). The coupling with 'Moses' may also suggest a resolution to the problem of identifying at what level it is appropriate to pursue the analogy between church and school. There were specialist academies within rabbinic Judaism in Galen's time,[32] but would Galen

---

[32]   *b. Sanh.* 32b, cf. H. L. Strack and G. Stemberger, *Introduction to the Talmud and Midrash* (Minneapolis: Fortress, 1992) 11–12. On Rabbinic schools, see further D. Goodblatt, *Rabbinic Instruction in Sassanian Babylonia* (Leiden: Brill, 1975).

have been acquainted with them? It is hard to believe that diaspora Judaism (especially in Alexandria, with its vigorous Jewish intellectual life) did not have something analogous to the rabbinic academies. But the fact is that we have no evidence for them. We must therefore take seriously the alternative possibility suggested by Nock: for outsiders like Galen, the most visible location in Judaism where school-like activities took place was not the rabbinic academy but the local synagogue. This suggestion is borne out by the well-known passages where Philo describes the weekly synagogue meetings as 'schools' (διδασκαλεῖα) and the Sabbath as an opportunity for 'studying philosophy' (φιλοσοφεῖν) (*Spec. Leg.* 2.62; *Hypothetica* 7.13).

If we ask the same question about Christian teaching at ground level, we come up with a similar answer. Certainly by Galen's day there were specialist Christian 'academies' in existence, like the contemporary *diatribe* of Pantaenus in Alexandria (Eusebius, *Hist. eccl.* 5.10). Eusebius mentions in passing that the church in Alexandria had been running a *didaskaleion* for some time. Specialist 'academies' of a slightly different type have also been hypothesized for the first century, and their activities are readily explicable in terms of the Hellenistic schools.[33] But all of these raise the same problem from our perspective as the rabbinic academies: is Galen likely to have known of such institutions, even if they could be proved to have existed? It is simpler by far to conclude that, for Christians as for Jews, it was his knowledge of local congregations with their 'apostles, prophets, and teachers' (1 Cor 12.28–9; cf. Rom 12.8; *Did.* 11 and 13), which prompted Galen's description of the 'followers of Christ' and their students ('disciples').[34]

[33] Cf. n. 4 above. The concept of a 'school' appears sporadically in New Testament scholarship, often with little attempt at concrete visualisation of what the word might imply in terms of social organization; cf. R. A. Culpepper, *The Johannine School* (SBLDS 26; Missoula: Scholars Press, 1975) chap. 1. To cite two further examples, the 'College of the Apostles' proposed by B. Gerhardsson in *Memory and Manuscript* (ASNU 22; Lund: Gleerup, 1961) would be on the face of it pursuing activities rather different from the scholarly group whose hand Zuntz discerned behind the early stabilization of the text of the Pauline letters (G. Zuntz, 'The text of the Epistles,' *RB* 59 (1952) 5–22; repr. in *Opuscula Selecta*, Manchester: Manchester University Press, 1972, 252–68, esp. 268). Yet both might reasonably be called 'schools'.

[34] My guess is that although Christian terminology apparently distinguished 'teachers' from 'prophets' and 'apostles', any of the three would have been categorized as

The teaching missions of Paul and the other apostles can readily be assimilated to the patterns of operation of the Hellenistic teachers. Like them, Paul (the one of whom we know most) used a variety of locations for his teaching activities: the private houses of a patron, his own workshop, a rented public building. Like the Sophists and other Hellenistic travelling teachers, both Paul and Peter traveled with a 'disciple circle' or 'retinue' (to use Judge's term) from place to place. They set up new disciple circles on arrival, and left behind a number of supporters in the local community who would count themselves adherents to the sect. (Acts, though not Paul, uses the word 'disciples' — that is, 'students' — for all Christians, as does Matt 28.19.) The chief difficulty in pursuing the analogy arises, as we noted at the outset, when we try to identify the community setting in which this teaching took place. The normal way of resolving this difficulty is to look at the 'nurturing' strategies of the schools (especially the Epicureans), and as we have indicated above (pending further investigation), that may well provide the best parallel. Another possibility on this tack is to look beyond the philosophical schools to medicine and other crafts. Could the 'trade guilds' — if we only knew more about them — provide the missing analogue to the ongoing Christian community? This is another area that could well repay more detailed investigation.

There is, however, an alternative line of attack, and that is to define the 'community context' of the schools in a broader way. It is no coincidence that the Epicureans, the closest of the philosophical schools structurally to the Christians, were also the most withdrawn from the public life of the Greek *polis*. For most of the philosophical schools, as we have shown, the public arena was the *polis* itself. The city provided both a social matrix and a physical location for their teaching activity. If we look at the Pauline churches from this perspective, we note that Paul is at pains to constitute his converts as 'the people of God'.[35] This means, in effect, that their position was analogous to that of the Jewish groups which had a semiautonomous existence alongside the citizen

---

'teachers' by a pagan observer. Lucian picks on the term 'prophet' for Peregrinus (*Peregr.* 11), but bears witness to the same pattern of itinerant speakers, reliant on community support, well into the second century.

[35] Meeks, *First Urban Christians*, 85–86.

body of the host community.[36] For such a parasitic *politeuma*, using the public spaces of the host city was problematic. Like the Cynics, one might be questioned, as Paul was in Athens (Acts 17), or ejected, as he was in Philippi (Acts 16). One solution was to use a private house, relying on the *proxenia* of a patron like Titius Justus (Acts 18.7) or Gaius (Rom 16.23). But there was another possibility. The Pauline strategy of using the synagogue (if we can accept the account of Acts) meant in effect using the 'public space' of the Jewish community and attempting to win a right for Christian teachers to operate within its teaching space. When that failed, the logical step was to fashion local adherents of the new teaching into a new *politeia*, with its own code of political conduct (πολιτεύεσθε; Phil 1.27) and its own *metropolis* or mother-city (Gal 5.26; Phil 3.20; cf. also Eph 2.19; Heb 12.22–23). Continued propagation of the teaching of Christ could then take place within the 'public space' of this new community — in the *ekklesia* or 'assembly' of the people of God (the term is a political one for both Greeks and Jews).[37] On this reading, we do not need to look for an analogue to the *ekklesia* in the putative group activities of some types of philosophical school. It was the *polis* itself that functioned as the social matrix for the schools and that provided public space for their teaching, and in the same way the *ekklesia* of the Christian 'people' provided a location for the activities of Christian teachers.[38]

This political aspect of teaching location may explain another puzzling feature — the relatively private nature of early Christian activity,

---

[36] The precise status of Jewish groups in the Greco-Roman city is disputed. P. Trebilco (*Jewish Communities in Asia Minor* [SNTSMS 69; Cambridge: Cambridge University Press, 1991]) provides a convenient summary of the evidence, but see also T. Rajak, 'Jews and Christians as Groups in a Pagan World,' *To See Ourselves as Others See us: Christians, Jews, 'Others' in late Antiquity* (ed. J. Neusner and E. S. Frerichs; Chico: Scholars Press, 1985) 247–62.

[37] This point was made some years ago by Edwin Judge in 'Contemporary Political Models for the Interpretation of the New Testament Churches,' *RThR* 22 (1963) 65–75. I am indebted to Pandang Yamsat for drawing my attention to this point in his Sheffield Ph.D. thesis, *The Ecclesia as Partnership* (1992).

[38] As Wayne Meeks has argued in a recent paper, in ethical matters it was the whole Christian movement which functioned as 'point of reference' for Christians in the way that the *polis* did for the citizen of a Greek city (W. A. Meeks, 'The Circle of Reference in Pauline Morality,' *Greeks, Romans, and Christians* [cited above, n. 19], 305–17).

highlighted by Ramsay MacMullen.[39] Unlike the philosophers, the Christians could not claim a right to the public teaching space of the *polis*. Paul's unusual activity in Athens (Acts 17), if historical, perhaps represents a tentative attempt to 'test the waters', but it is not repeated. Justin's more consolidated presentation of Christianity as a 'philosophy' could be another, more plausible move in this direction. But it would be wrong to conclude that because there is (as MacMullen shows) little evidence for public evangelizing, the 'school of Christ' was uniquely inward looking and enclosed. MacMullen acknowledges that the Christians were assiduous in instructing their disciples *after* their conversation.[40] But this is exactly the pattern we find in the Hellenistic schools. If the two-tier pattern of instruction we observed in Galen is common, as I believe it is, then instruction addressed primarily to disciples — 'preaching to the converted' — is precisely what we would expect to find. Of course it will be rare in the first two centuries to find Christian instruction going on in the Forum or the Agora, but that is simply a matter of location, not a serious difference in patterns of communication. Any outsider who found his or her way to the meeting point, be it indoors or out-of-doors, could listen in on the proceedings, just as in the schools. It seems clear that this was an accepted pattern of behavior for the 'godfearers' in the synagogue. Equally, Paul seems to expect such outsiders to be present at Christian meetings (1 Cor 14.16, 23–25). The 'outsider' is described as an ἰδιώτης, the same word as Galen uses to describe non-philosophers ('laymen') in *Errors* 7 (Harkins 107: Kühn 5.103; *SM* 1.81.5); and as Stowers has acutely observed, Paul also uses the very Socratic verb ἐλέγχειν for the 'conviction' which may lead such an observer to cross the boundary between 'outsider' and 'disciple'.[41] Thus I believe MacMullen is correct in saying that formally speaking all Christian discourse in the first century, and much of it in the second century, is 'instruction' rather than 'evangelism' addressed directly to outsiders. But the same might well be said of much of the activity of the Hellenistic schools.

[39] R. MacMullen, *Christianizing the Roman Empire* (New Haven: Yale University Press, 1984).

[40] MacMullen, *Christianizing*, 33–34, with notes.

[41] Stowers, 'Social Status' (cited above n. 7), 69.

Conclusion: Comparison or Contrast?

In this essay I have tried to show two things: (1) that Christians could plausibly be seen as the adherents of a school by an outsider like Galen; and (2) that the Hellenistic schools were in many aspects of structure and behavior remarkably like the early church. That is not to argue that *everything* in early Christianity can be explained on the model of the school. Alongside Galen's description of the 'school of Christ' we must set Celsus' comparison of Christians with 'begging priests of Cybele and soothsayers, and worshippers of Mithras and Sabazius, and whatever else one might meet, apparitions of Hecate or of some other daemon or daemons' (Origen, *C. Cels.* 1.9). But Galen deserves to be taken just as seriously (that is, with just the same quantity of salt) as Celsus. A just description of early Christianity as a social phenomenon must take account of both viewpoints. Moreover, I believe that Galen's passing remarks will be vindicated by further research. We are slowly learning to appreciate the intellectual complexity of Pauline discourse, as a number of essays in this volume have shown; and Paul's vision of church life shows a clear tendency to elevate the rational and cognitive over against the ecstatic.[42] In terms of social structure, too, the model of the school has distinct advantages over the more familiar models of the household or the association, neither of which normally produces literature, or sees itself as part of a worldwide movement: there are a number of potentially valuable comparisons to be made in this area, as I hope to show at a later date. But there will always be areas on both sides where comparison gives way to contrast, and that is right and proper. All I have tried to do is to establish that the model of the school is an important tool for the imaginative understanding of Paul's world and the options open to him for penetrating it, as well as for understanding the reactions of that world to Paul. And if we accept the usefulness of this model we may be able to move our study of Paul's

---

[42] Cf. the highly cognitive definition of 'edification' in 1 Cor 14.6–12 (even music is only valuable if it has an intelligible message), and the insistence on using the 'mind' (*nous*) in vv. 13–19. Cf. further S. K. Stowers ('Paul on the Use and Abuse of Reason,' *Greeks, Romans, and Christians* [cited above n. 19], 253–86), who argues convincingly against the view that Paul elevates 'faith' at the expense of 'reason' in 1 Corinthians 1–4.

Hellenistic context forward from the amassing of parallels towards a more concerted 'compare and contrast' exercise with both Hellenistic and rabbinic schools, which will enable us to achieve a firmer understanding of Paul's historical achievement.

4

Transferring a Ritual: Paul's Interpretation of Baptism in Romans 6

Hans Dieter Betz

Recent studies have shown that Paul's interpretation of baptism, especially as regards Romans 6, still presents problems of extraordinary complexity for New Testament scholarship.[1] A whole range of questions is at stake, beginning with the simple meaning of words and extending into context, argumentation and composition. One of these questions concerns the theme of this conference and the volume originating from it: Paul's Hellenistic context. A prior question is: How should we approach this question of the Hellenistic context? What do we mean by 'context'?[2]

It is often taken for granted that with respect to contexts 'Hellenistic' is to be seen in opposition to 'Jewish', but this contrast is ambiguous. In the Hellenistic era, which begins with Alexander the Great and extends up to the Roman era, Judaism itself is a Hellenistic phenomenon, whereas 'Jewish context' refers to the specific conditions within Judaism at this time which had their roots in pre-Hellenistic Palestine. In the following, however, we shall take 'Hellenistic context' in a different way. Assuming the terms of modern scholarship, there is a Hellenistic cultural perspective which has its roots in Greece and is manifested in historical texts and phenomena. This Hellenistic perspective can to

---

[1] Besides the recent commentaries see the erudite work by Alexander J. M. Wedderburn, *Baptism and Resurrection: Studies in Pauline Theology against Its Graeco-Roman Background* (WUNT 44; Tübingen: Mohr-Siebeck, 1987).

[2] See also my article 'Hellenismus,' *TRE* 15 (1986) 19–36, and the 'Einführung' to my collected essays *Hellenismus und Urchristentum: Gesammelte Aufsätze I* (Tübingen: Mohr-Siebeck, 1990) 1–9.

an extent explain in its own terms what Paul was doing as an apostle of Jesus Christ. A specific instance of this is provided by Paul's interpretation of baptism. If the apostle's letters constitute the foreground, his Hellenistic context would point out the cultural and religious presuppositions for explaining what Paul was doing in his interpretations of the ritual. There are of course different ways of approaching the question of Paul's Hellenistic context. One can begin with the secondary literature on the subject, which has its own history,[3] or one can speculate about Paul's education. The way we shall approach the question, however, is by comparing the apostle with similar figures operating in the world of Hellenistic religions.

Before turning to this subject matter, the major problems concerning baptism ought to be briefly stated:

1.   Paul's doctrine of baptism as set forth in Romans 6 is characteristically different from what he says about baptism in his other letters.

2.   Before Romans, Paul cites what appears to be a baptismal formula in Gal 3.26–28. This formula summarizes a theology of baptism with which the Galatian churches must have become familiar when Paul founded them.

3.   The treatment of baptism is more explicit in the Corinthian correspondence, where the theological understanding of the ritual is, however, different from Galatians. Also, in 1 Corinthians Paul expresses strong reservations with regard to some aspects of baptism. While admitting that he baptized some members of the church at the time of its beginning (1 Cor 1.13–17), at least when he wrote the letter he distanced himself from baptizing people, saying that he did not regard it as the central part of his apostolic office. He also sees a connection between the problems the Corinthian church is experiencing internally and the understanding — or misunderstanding — of the ritual by some church members. There appears to have been a difference between Paul's and the Corinthians' concept of baptism.

---

[3]   This is Wedderburn's approach. He was preceded by Günter Wagner, *Das religionsgeschichtliche Problem von Römer 6,1–11* (AThANT 39; Zürich: Zwingli, 1962); ET: *Pauline Baptism and the Pagan Mysteries: The Problem of the Pauline Doctrine of Baptism in Romans VI.1–11 in the Light of Its Religio-Historical 'Parallels'* (Edinburgh: Clark, 1967).

4. While in the other letters Paul's own concept of baptism remains largely in the background, he spells it out more clearly in Romans 6–8. In Rom 6.3–10 he sets forth a new kind of baptismal theology. The relationship between this new elaboration of baptismal doctrine and the formula in Gal 3.26–28 needs to be explored. Moreover, why and how can it be explained that the apostle presents baptism in Rom 6 as the Christian *initiation* ritual? How are we to understand the various shifts that have taken place in regard to the interpretation of baptism in the early church?

Paul as Founder Figure

Viewed from a Hellenistic perspective, Paul's activities as an apostle of Jesus Christ, when compared with those of other figures operating in the area of religion, do not look unique. Associating Paul with other founder figures should not be taken to mean, however, that he 'founded Christianity'.[4] Rather, what we wish to examine is his activity of founding churches as part of his mission. How did such foundations actually

---

[4]   No special investigation seems to exist. Earlier works by Heinrich Weinel (*Paulus als kirchlicher Organisator* [Freiburg: Mohr-Siebeck, 1899]); and Friedrich Wilhelm Maier (*Paulus als Kirchengründer und kirchlicher Organisator*. Aus dem Nachlass herausgegeben von Günter Stachel [Würzburg: Echter, 1961]) provide merely a discussion of pertinent New Testament passages. For a reflection about the 'disappearance' of the founder figure in religion, see Richard M. Meyer, 'Mythologische Fragen, III. Ein religionsgeschichtliches Dogma,' *ARW* 10 (1907) 101–3. Meyer suggests that the founder figure has disappeared because of a romantic reaction against the *tres impostores* of eighteenth-century Rationalism. This reaction took religion to be the product of a slow and popular development. As a contrast Meyer refers to Jacob Burckhardt's essay, 'Die Religion', in his *Weltgeschichtliche Betrachtungen*, vol. 7 of his *Gesamtausgabe* (Basel: Schwabe, 1929) 28–42, esp. 31: 'Wie weit sind die Religionen *gestiftet*? Jedenfalls sind sie wesentlich als die Schöpfung einzelner Menschen oder einzelner Momente, d.h. eben der Fixierungsmomente ruckweise, strahlungsweise entstanden. Ein Teil der Menschen hält mit, weil der Stifter oder das Ereignis gerade *den* Punkt des metaphysischen Bedürfnisses getroffen hat, der in den lebendigsten Menschen empfunden wird, die große Masse hält mit, weil sie nicht widerstehen kann, und weil alles Bestimmte ein Königsrecht hat gegenüber dem Dumpfen, Unsicheren und Anarchischen . . . Allmählich können die Religionen *nicht wohl entstanden* sein, sonst besässen sie den siegreichen Glanz ihrer Blütezeit nicht, welcher der Reflex eines grossen einmaligen Moments ist.' Indeed, a conflict of two powerful dogmas! For this century at least, the romantic reaction buttressed by sociology and psychology has dominated, but this does not make it an eternal truth, especially not if the alternatives are being forgotten.

happen? What were the ritual, legal, and organizational procedures that no doubt took place at the occasion of these foundations? Unfortunately, Paul's letters speak of these occasions only in general terms, leaving specific descriptions aside because the addressees knew them anyway.[5] Even the book of Acts describes the founding of churches only in general terms, and there are no early inscriptions concerning foundations of Christian churches such as we possess for Jewish synagogues[6] and Greek cults.[7]

Yet, there can be no doubt that Paul's founding activities had parallels in the Hellenistic world. Although we have evidence of other such founder figures, not very much is known about them. There is also no modern scholarly investigation of the phenomenon.[8] There must have been, however, a considerable number of those founder figures at work precisely at the time of Paul's mission. These people were specialists in founding cults. They knew the traditions, the myths, the rituals, and the procedures to be followed. They were experienced travelers and served as advisers, often collaborating with governmental authorities.

Paul's mission can best be compared with the activities of those who introduced foreign gods and cults into a city. There must have been

---

[5]   Paul uses foundation language in describing his work. He functions as 'master builder', laying the foundation, which is none other than Jesus Christ. In the final analysis God is the primary founder (1 Cor 3.6–7, 10–12; cf. Rom 15.20). Reminding the addressees of the events at the time of their foundation is an important part of the arguments in 1 Thess 1.5–10; 3.4; 4.6 (cf. 2 Thess 2.15; 3.6); Gal 1.8–9; 5.21; 1 Cor 2.1–5; 11.2, 23; 15.3. Different images are used in Eph 2.20: The foundation consists of the apostles and the prophets, while Christ is the 'cornerstone'.

[6]   See Baruch Lifshitz, *Donateurs et fondateurs dans les synagogues juives: Repertoire des dédicaces grecques relatives à la construction et à la réflection des synagogues* (Cahiers de la Revue Biblique 7; Paris: Gabalda, 1967). For additional material see Emil Schürer, *The History of the Jewish People in the Age of Jesus Christ* (revised and edited by Geza Vermes, Fergus Millar and Matthew Black; vols. I–III/2 [Edinburgh: Clark, 1973–1987]); Martin Hengel, 'Der alte und der neue Schürer,' *JSS* 35 (1990) 19–72 (with the appendix on inscriptions by Hanswulf Bloedhorn, pp. 64–72); *The 'Hellenization' of Judaea in the First Century after Christ* (London: SCM, 1989).

[7]   See the collection of inscriptions by Franciszek Sokolowski, *Lois sacrées de l'Asie Mineure* (Ecole française d' Athènes: Travaux et mémoires, fasc. 9; Paris: Boccard, 1955); *Lois sacrées des cités grecques* (Ecole française d' Athènes: Travaux et mémoires, fasc. 18; (2nd ed.; Paris: Boccard, 1969).

[8]   See Timothy Cornell and Wolfgang Speyer, 'Gründer,' *RAC* 12 (1982) 1107–71. On Paul, see 1148–49.

innumerable cases of such introductions, some of which became famous because they were described vividly by Hellenistic writers or because their cult inscriptions have been discovered by modern scholarship.

One of the most common ways of introducing new cults into a city was by founding a cult association.[9] These associations established the institutional groundwork for the development of a cult. They took responsibility for building a sanctuary and for running its affairs on a continuing basis henceforth. In effect, Paul's churches are such religious associations. This statement can be sustained, although the term Paul chose to designate the church association (ἐκκλησία) is a secular concept, meaning 'assembly'.[10] He does not use the term συναγωγή, also meaning 'assembly', even though church foundations often began in synagogues.[11] In other words, Paul's foundations were not to be new synagogues.[12] In a similar way, the apostle does not typically use terms describing Greek and Roman religious associations.[13] He is certainly right in avoiding these terms because the church is fundamentally different from the ordinary foundation of a Greek or Roman cult: The early Christian churches have no special buildings, no temples, no altars, no cult statues, no sacred annual festivals or calenders, no priests or other sacred officials officiating at sacrifices. In spite of these structural differences, however, Paul's foundations can be profitably compared with other cultic associations. Different from other associations such as schools or professional guilds, the early churches established divine worship by setting up local administrators and facilities appropriate for the worship of the Christian

[9]   See Arthur Darby Nock, 'The Historical Importance of Cult-Associations,' *CLR* 38 (1924) 105–9; '*Magistri* and *Collegia*,' in his *Essays on Religion and the Ancient World* (Cambridge, Mass.: Harvard University Press, 1972) 1.409–13; 'The Gild of Zeus Hypsistos,' in *Essays*, 1.414–43; Martin P. Nilsson, *Geschichte der griechischen Religion* (3rd ed.; München: Beck, 1974) 2.113–31; Peter Herrmann et al., 'Genossenschaft,' *RAC* 10 (1978) 83–155; Walter Burkert, *Ancient Mystery Cults* (Cambridge, Mass.: Harvard University Press, 1987) 30–53: 'Organizations and Identities'.

[10]   The basic term used is ἐκκλησία, which is then modified by genitive attributes. It is difficult to say when this term was first introduced; perhaps, it was pre-Pauline (cf. Gal 1.22; 1 Thess 2.14; Matt 16.18; 18.17).

[11]   At least this is the picture conveyed by Acts (6.9; 9.2, 20; 13.5; etc.)

[12]   The remarkable exception is Jas 2.2, where a Christian synagogue is envisioned.

[13]   See also Burkert's comments, *Ancient Mystery Cults*, 51–53.

God. There were also rules and regulations for ritual performances and for forming moral ethos. Among the peculiar features of these early churches is the fact that the appropriate structures were not put in place all at once, but we can observe the founder Paul still developing these structures in his letters.[14] What took place, therefore, when a church began was some kind of foundational act, but we have no information about what precisely happened.[15] At any rate, Paul's letters show that some foundational activities continued even after the foundation itself in the sense that the shaping of rituals and the setting of moral standards for Christian behavior constitutes most of the content of the letters.[16]

Perhaps similar developments took place in other cults as well, but we do not have information to substantiate it. At any rate, in Paul's view the foundation of the church marked the beginning of a longer building process. Laying the foundation was one thing, building the house of the church community was another. The latter took more time and was considerably more complicated. This required the apostle to direct his constant attention to the upbuilding of the church community, an effort that seems at first to have been all-consuming. This effort goes along with the nearly total disinterest in erecting specially marked physical structures and monuments during the first generations, which is so characteristic of later Christian church life. No foundation inscriptions or identifiable remnants of house churches have been found from the early years of Christian church life. This lack of evidence does not seem to be accidental but is a result of the peculiar nature of Christian church foundations. When Paul speaks of the 'temple of the Holy Spirit' (1 Cor 6.19) or the 'temple of God' (1 Cor

---

[14] See Wolfgang Speyer, 'Gründer', 1149: 'Die Bekehrung und Bildung einer Gemeinde traten meist nicht als ein einmaliger, Aufsehen erregender Akt, sondern als ein sich allmählich entfaltender Prozeß in Erscheinung.'

[15] See Adolf von Harnack, *Die Mission und Ausbreitung des Christentums in den ersten drei Jahrhunderten* (4th ed.; Leipzig: Hinrichs, 1924) 1.79–107.

[16] It is at this point that Paul can be compared with philosophers. Some founders of Hellenistic cults apparently had connections with philosophy. Reforming cults was one of the concerns of philosophers; see Betz, *Hellenismus und Urchristentum*, 186–88. For Paul, see Abraham J. Malherbe, 'Paul: Hellenistic Philosopher or Christian Pastor?' in his *Paul and the Popular Philosophers* (Minneapolis: Fortress, 1989) 67–77.

3.16–17; cf. 2 Cor 6.16; Eph 2.21), he is not referring to physical buildings, which in his view are incidental.[17]

In Hellenistic religions, one of the methods for founding new cults was by the transferral of rituals, myths, statues, and cult personnel from one place to another (*Kultübertragung*). Many newly established cults were in fact due to *Kultübertragung*.[18] These transferrals also involved redesigning myths and rituals to accommodate them to local conditions. Temples were built in imitation of other temples. Statues could be transported from another location or newly created by imitating famous prototypes; hymns were composed, patterned on other hymns; official titles were derived from elsewhere, and so forth. That is to say, cult transferrals nearly always involved modifications and adaptations to the new environment. This could also entail imposing upon an earlier cult, or reforming it completely. Such changes, just as the new foundations, had to be legitimated by divine authority. Legends then told of these authorizations, often in the form of visions. As a consequence, new myth had to be woven into old myth. Local or regional traditions were used to create an identity for the new foundation. All of these developments required the cooperation of cult experts on various levels. *Mutatis mutandis* all this can also be said of the work of the apostle Paul.

A few examples must suffice to show what kind of persons were involved in Hellenistic cult foundations. Thanks to Tacitus and Plutarch we are informed about the role a certain Timotheos of Athens played in

---

[17] Not incidentally, the language of 'building' (οἰκοδομέω κτλ) and 'house' (οἰκία κτλ) that Paul uses so frequently is almost entirely figurative and refers to the corporate life of the Christian community. See Ernst Dassmann and Georg Schöllgen, 'Haus II (Hausgemeinschaft),' *RAC* 13 (1986) 801–905; Friedrich Ohly, 'Haus III (Metapher),' *RAC* 13 (1986), 905–1063; Margaret M. Mitchell, *Paul and the Rhetoric of Reconciliation: An Exegetical Investigation of the Language and Composition of 1 Corinthians* (HUTh 28; Tübingen: Mohr-Siebeck, 1991) 99–111.

[18] See on this concept the important Heidelberg dissertation, begun under Albrecht Dieterich, by Ernst Schmidt, *Kultübertragungen* (RVV 8/2; Giessen: Töpelmann, 1909). Schmidt deals with the transferral of the Magna Mater from Pessinus to Rome (204 B.C.E.), Asklepios from Epidauros to Rome (293–291 B.C.E.), the creation of the Sarapis cult in Alexandria (ca. 300 B.C.E.). He also collects a number of Christian hagiographical examples from a later period and provides a list of features typical of legends concerned with cult transferrals.

the foundation of the cult of Sarapis under Ptolemy I. Soter (305–283 B.C.E.). A high-ranking Athenian from the Eumolpids, he was serving as an ἐξηγητής with the mysteries of Demeter and Persephone at Eleusis when he was called upon by the Egyptian king to be a consultant, as we would say today, assisting in the organization of the new cult of Sarapis.[19] Tacitus relates what he had received as information concerning this foundation — that is, the foundation legend:

> The Egyptian priests tell the following story, that when king Ptolemy, the first of the Macedonians to put the power of Egypt on a firm foundation, was giving the new city of Alexandria walls, temples, and religious rites, there appeared to him in his sleep a vision of a young man of extraordinary beauty and of more than human stature, who warned him to send his most faithful friends to Pontus and bring his statue hither; the vision said that this act would be a happy thing for the kingdom and that the city that received the god would be great and famous; after these words the youth seemed to be carried to heaven in a blaze of fire. Ptolemy, moved by this miraculous omen, disclosed this nocturnal vision to the Egyptian priests, whose business it is to interpret such things. When they proved to know little of Pontus and foreign countries, he questioned Timotheus, an Athenian of the clan of the Eumolpidae, whom he had called from Eleusis to preside over the sacred rites, and asked him what this religion was and what the divinity meant. Timotheus learned by questioning men who had traveled to Pontus that there was a city called Sinope, and that not far from it there was a temple of Jupiter Dis, long famous among the natives: for there sits beside the god a female figure which most call Proserpina. . . . (*Hist.* 4.83)[20]

---

[19] See Schmidt, *Kultübertragungen*, 47–81, 116–20; P. M. Fraser, *Ptolemaic Alexandria* (Oxford: Clarendon, 1972) 1.246–58 and notes; 'Current Problems concerning the Early History of the Cult of Sarapis,' *Opuscula Atheniensia VII* (Lund: Gleerup, 1967) 23–45; John E. Stambaugh, *Sarapis under the Early Ptolemies* (EPRO 25; Leiden: Brill, 1972); Wilhelm Hornbostel, *Sarapis: Studien zur Überlieferungsgeschichte, den Erscheinungsformen und Wandlungen der Gestalt eines Gottes* (EPRO 32; Leiden: Brill, 1973).

[20] The translation is that of the LCL edition. See also Ronald Syme, *Tacitus* (Oxford: Clarendon, 1958) 2.674–76.

Another version of the story is related by Plutarch *De Iside et Osiride* 28, 361F–362A. The source from which Plutarch obtained his information may be Manethon, who appears in the passage as a collaborator of Timotheos:[21]

> Ptolemy Soter saw in a dream the colossus of Pluto in Sinope though he had previously neither known nor seen what its form was like; and it ordered him to transport it as quickly as possible. Since he had not known, and was quite at a loss to find out, where it had been set up, when he explained the vision to his friends, a much-traveled man by the name of Sosibius was found, who said that he had seen in Sinope a colossus of the type the king thought he had seen. The king therefore dispatched Soteles and Dionysius, who after a long time and with difficulty, but not without the aid of divine providence, stole it from there and took it away. When the colossus had been transported and examined, Timotheus the interpreter and Manetho the Sebennyte concluded that it was an image of Pluto, inferring this from the Cerberus-dog and the serpent; and they convinced Ptolemy that it represented no other god than Sarapis; for it did not come from there bearing his name, but only after being transported to Alexandria did it acquire the name of Sarapis, which is the Egyptian appellation of Pluto.

The difficult historical questions regarding this story can be left aside at this point.[22] As it is, the story shows the features typical of a foundation legend, culminating in the dream vision and suggestion to establish the cult. This foundation involved the transfer of a cult statue from Pontus in Asia Minor to Egypt, a transaction that could only be accomplished by theft, strangely to be legitimated by divine providence. Interpretation of visions and identification of the god were the responsibility of experts like Timotheos and Manethon. While Timotheos was an expert in Greek religion, Manethon, a high-ranking Egyptian priest

---

[21] The translation is that of J. Gwyn Griffiths, *Plutarch's De Iside et Osiride* (Cambridge: University of Wales Press, 1970) 161.

[22] See the commentary by Griffiths, 393–400.

or high priest who wrote on Egyptian religion in Greek, made sure the new cult was assimilated to local traditions.[23]

The result of what must have been a major effort was the god Sarapis, a newly created deity of the Macedonian kingdom in Egypt who exhibited both Greek and Egyptian characteristics. For the Egyptians the god reflected Osiris,[24] for the Greeks Zeus or Helios.[25] According to Plutarch, there was also an affinity between Sarapis and Dionysos.[26]

What did king Ptolemy have in mind when he established the cult of Sarapis? Having no older myth of his own, Sarapis was obviously intended to provide religious legitimacy for this first Macedonian ruler on the Egyptian throne. New legends circulated to undergird this new foundation. Arrianus (*Anab.* 7.26.2), claiming to depend on the royal diaries (the *Ephemerides*), relates that shortly before the death of Alexander the Great in Babylon the god Sarapis was consulted by the friends of the king. The question was 'whether it would be better for Alexander to be brought into the temple of the god and after prayer to be healed by the God'. The reply was, 'that he should not be brought into the temple but that it would be better for him if he abode where he was'.[27] For Ptolemy, who had transferred Alexander's mortal remains from Babylon to Alexandria, there was no better way to legitimate his own place as Alexander's successor than to establish the cult of this god Sarapis in Alexandria. And so he did.[28]

Why then did Ptolemy not simply transfer the cult of Sarapis from Babylon? The fact is that as of this day there is no evidence that there was a Babylonian Sarapis cult. The whole story about the oracle of

[23] On Manethon, see Wolfgang Helck, 'Manethon,' *Der Kleine Pauly* 3 (1979) 952–53. The fragments of the author are assembled in the LCL edition and translation of *Manetho* by W. G. Waddell (London: Heinemann, 1940).

[24] See Griffiths, *Plutarch's De Iside*, 399–400.

[25] Griffiths, 401.

[26] Griffiths, 400.

[27] Cited according to the LCL edition and translation of *Arrian* by E. Iliff Robson (London: Heinemann, 1958) 2.292–95. Plutarch (*Alexander* 76) also mentions the consultation of the oracle. For the question of the royal diaries, see Schmidt, *Kultübertragungen*, 72–74; Fraser, 'Current Problems', 32–35.

[28] See on this point Schmidt, *Kultübertragungen*, 71–81: 'Die Schaffung des Gottes'; Nilsson, *Geschichte*, 2.154–58.

Sarapis before Alexander's death is fiction, inserted into the royal diaries at a later time, perhaps even by Ptolemy himself who was in possession of the document.[29]

Another possible explanation is that the god consulted in Babylon was not at that time known as Sarapis, but was a similar Babylonian deity who was later identified with Sarapis.[30] At any rate, Ptolemy needed a new god who was connected with Alexander's death, who was Greek as well as Egyptian in character, and who provided a special foundation for the Ptolemaic regime. These roles were filled by Sarapis.

Even the name of the god was artificially contrived, coined after the theriomorphic Osiris-Apis.[31] Yet, the statue made by the famous sculptor Bryaxis[32] was of human form. It shows the familiar curly-headed and bearded Zeus-type head bearing the *kalathos*. This anthropomorphic figure was Greek in conception, but slightly Egyptianized.[33] The intended result was accomplished — the god was worshipped throughout Egypt and the Graeco-Roman world. Sarapis was held to be a universal deity (*pantheos*).[34]

When Timotheos was consulted by the king, he had already been in Egypt, assisting in the establishment of the cult of the Eleusinian goddesses Demeter and Kore in a place called Eleusis near Alexandria.[35] Again, this establishment involved some kind of cultic transfer. To be sure, one should not expect that the Eleusinian mysteries were simply transferred to Egypt.[36] The widespread conviction that the mysteries could be celebrated in their

---

[29] See Fraser, 'Current Problems', 33–34.

[30] On attempts to connect Sarapis with Babylon, see Schmidt, *Kultübertragungen*, 75–76; Fraser, 'Current Problems', 29, 45.

[31] See Griffiths, *Plutarch's De Iside*, 395–96, 399.

[32] Athenodoros, according to Clemens Alexandrinus (*Protr.* 4.48.5); see Griffiths, *Plutarch's De Iside*, 399–400; Hornbostel, *Sarapis*, passim.

[33] See Griffiths, *Plutarch's De Iside*, 399–401.

[34] Griffiths, 401. See also Ladislav Vidman, 'Isis und Sarapis,' *Die orientalischen Religionen im Römerreich* (ed. Maarten J. Vermaseren; EPRO 93; Leiden: Brill, 1981) 121–56; Hans Dieter Betz, *The Greek Magical Papyri in Translation*, vol. 1: *Texts* (Chicago: The University of Chicago Press, 1986) 388 *s.v.* 'Sarapis (Serapis)'.

[35] On Timotheos, see Otto Weinreich, 'Timotheos, 19,' *PRE*, 2. Reihe, 12. Halbband (1937) 1341–42.

[36] See on this point Ulrich von Wilamowitz-Moellendorff, *Der Glaube der Hellenen* (3rd ed.; Darmstadt: Wissenschaftliche Buchgesellschaft, 1959) 2.336–37; Nilsson, *Geschichte*, 2.94.

proper form only at Eleusis would have advised against it.[37] There were, however, other mysteries similar to the Eleusinian mysteries or influenced by them. Nilsson is on the right track when he says: 'Although the Eleusinian mysteries were not transplanted to Alexandria, the cult of Demeter was set up there and reshaped under Eleusinian influence. In the same way, the mysteries of Demeter and Kore in Pergamon were reorganized under Eleusinian influence and opened to men.'[38]

The archaeological remains of the cult, which are significant, point to Graeco-Egyptian mysteries as well. This raises the question of how the cult was related to the Eleusinian mysteries in Attica. Perhaps it was part of the Eleusinian cult propaganda, for which Timotheos was an eminent representative, established in order to plant mysteries outside of Attica. This strategy could have had the purpose of enhancing the fame of Eleusis in Attica rather than detracting from it. By assimilating local traditions, the Alexandrian mysteries seem to have developed in somewhat different directions. Conceivably, something like a hierarchical ranking among the mysteries existed in various places, similar to what we know from Apuleius about the mysteries of Isis and Osiris in Egypt and Rome. By contrast, denying the existence of Alexandrian mysteries altogether[39] seems as implausible as assuming that all celebrations must have been alike. The famous *synthema* regarding the birth of Aion by Kore certainly points to mysteries, but it may have been characteristic of the Alexandrian cult and not of all others.[40] On the whole, Nilsson's cautious assessment looks convincing:

---

[37] Nilsson, *Geschichte*, 2.94.

[38] Nilsson, 2.94

[39] See Fraser, *Ptolemaic Alexandria*, 1.200–01; 2.340–42. Walter Burkert (*Ancient Mystery Cults*, 37–38) surveys the evidence and concludes: '. . . it seems that the Alexandrian festival took place in a temple, without previous initiation; it was not a mystery celebration but rather belonged to an Egyptian setting. Eleusis wished to remain unique, and largely succeeded in doing so.'

[40] See Albrecht Dieterich, *Eine Mithrasliturgie* (3rd ed.; Darmstadt: Wissenschaftliche Buchgesellschaft, 1966) 213; 256; Otto Weinreich, 'Aion in Eleusis,' *ARW* 19 (1916–1919) 174–90; reprinted in his *Ausgewählte Schriften I* (Amsterdam: Grüner, 1969) 442–61; Eduard Norden, *Die Geburt des Kindes* (Leipzig: Teubner, 1924; reprinted Darmstadt: Wissenschaftliche Buchgesellschaft, 1958); Wilhelm Bousset, 'Der Gott Aion,' in his *Religionsgeschichtliche Studien: Aufsätze zur Religionsgeschichte des Hellenistischen Zeitalters* (NovTSup 50; Leiden: Brill, 1979) 192–230, esp. 228–30; Burkert, *Ancient Mystery Cults*, 37–38, with notes.

Mysteries also were part of the cult of Demeter in Alexandria. They were doubtless not a copy of the Eleusinian ones, but probably influenced by them. Everything else that is known about Timotheos shows that he may be credited with such an arrangement, not least his role in the creation of the new cult of Serapis. It is probably also the same Timotheos who wrote about the Phrygian Great Mother. He is a most interesting figure, since he combined practical religious activity with a theoretical interest, which may be called theological in the modern sense. In both respects he is typical of his time.[41]

Indeed, according to Pausanias[42] and Arnobius,[43] Timotheos was also working on the cults of the Phrygian Attis and Cybele.[44] His role in the composition of the Pessinuntian myth of Attis seems to have been more than simply writing up what tradition had handed down; he seems to have created what in his view the myth should relate as well.[45]

Founder figures like Timotheos and Manethon were not exceptional. The mysteries of Andania in Messene, about which we are informed by Pausanias[46] and a famous inscription from 92/91 B.C.E.,[47] were founded by Mnasistratos[48] who, according to the inscription, provided the sacred books in which the tradition was written up; he also marched at the head of the procession and was entitled to some of the income of the cult. There can be little doubt that Mnasistratos had organized the cult,

---

[41] Nilsson, *Geschichte*, 2.95 (my trans.); see also 2.156–58, 641, 649.

[42] Pausanias 7.17.10–12. See Nilsson, *Geschichte*, 2.96–98, 101–2.

[43] Arnobius *Adv. nat.* 5.5–7.

[44] This Timotheos is the same Eumolpid; see Hugo Hepding, *Attis, seine Mythen und sein Kult* (RVV 1; Giessen: Töpelmann, 1903) 103–4.

[45] See Hepding, *Attis*, 37–41, for a synopsis of the texts; for commentary see 103–10.

[46] Pausanias 4.1.5–7, 8–9; 2.6; 3.10; 26.6–8; 27.1–3; 33.4–6.

[47] For the text see Sokolowski, *Lois sacrées des cités grecques*, no 65 (pp. 120–34). A translation is provided in Marvin W. Meyer, *The Ancient Mysteries: A Source Book* (San Francisco: Harper & Row, 1987) 47–59. For bibliography see Nilsson, *Geschichte*, 1.478 n. 5; 2.96 n. 8; Sokolowski, 120–21.

[48] He is mentioned also in another inscription from Argos, dated 94 B.C.E., as having the office of hierophant. See Otto Kern, 'Mnasistratos, 1,' *PRE*, 30. Halbband (1932) 2255–56; Nilsson, *Geschichte*, 2.96–97.

and he may also have been the author of the rules laid down in the inscription. Similar things could be said about other such inscriptions, for example, the Iobacchoi inscription from Athens, dated 178 C.E.[49] This inscription contains not only the rules of the cult society but also the minutes of the procedure in which these rules were adopted. One of the priests named must have been the author of the rules.

Another founder figure of repute was Methapos of Athens, whom Pausanias names as τελεστὴς δὲ καὶ ὀργίων [καὶ] παντοίων συνθέτης (4.1.17). He is said to have established the mysteries of the Kabeiroi at Thebes, but he also had a hand in the organization of the mysteries at Andania and Phlya (4.1.7–8).[50] That many of these founder figures were active in the establishment of mystery cults was not uncommon. The popularity of mystery celebrations in the Hellenistic period can hardly be overestimated. Also Alexander of Abonuteichos belongs to this category of founder figures. When he set up the new cult of the god Glykon, he connected it with Athens and instituted an annual three-day mystery celebration patterned on Eleusis.[51] Although Lucian's description is highly satirical, the basic facts leave no doubt that Alexander's foundation was a serious religious institution. The same can be said about Peregrinos Proteus, another target of Lucian's satire.[52] As Philostratos shows, reforming cults even required the assistance of philosophers like Apollonios of Tyana[53] who went against the local priests

---

[49] For the text and bibliography, see Sokolowski, *Lois sacrées des cités grecques*, no 51 (pp. 95–101); a translation is provided by Meyer, *The Ancient Mysteries*, 95–98. See also Nilsson, *Geschichte*, 2.359; 361; Walter Ameling, 'Der Archon Epaphrodeitos,' *ZPE* 61 (1985) 133–47; Luigi Moretti, 'Il regolamento degli Iobacchi ateniesi,' *L'Association dionysiaque dans les sociétés anciennes* (Collection de l'Ecole française de Rome 89; Paris: Boccard, 1986) 247–59.

[50] See Otto Kern, 'Methapos,' *PRE*, 30. Halbband (1932) 1379; Nilsson, *Geschichte*, 1.669; 2.97–98.

[51] Lucian, *Alex.* 38–40. For bibliography see Nilsson, *Geschichte*, 2.472–75, 528.

[52] Lucian, *De morte Peregrini*, whose cult was begun by his disciples. See Hans Dieter Betz, *Lukian von Samosata und das Neue Testament: Religionsgeschichtliche und paränetische Parallelen* (TU 76; Berlin: Akademie-Verlag, 1961) 124–31.

[53] See Gerd Petzke, *Die Traditionen über Apollonius von Tyana und das Neue Testament* (SCHNT 1; Leiden: Brill, 1970) 207–16; Wolfgang Speyer, 'Das Bild des Apollonios von Tyana bei Heiden und Christen,' in his *Frühes Christentum im antiken Strahlungsfeld: Ausgewählte Aufsätze* (WUNT 50; Tübingen: Mohr-Siebeck, 1989) 176–92.

when necessary.[54] Also the philosopher Plutarch, who served as a chief priest of Apollo at Delphi, helped shape religion through his writings on the Delphic oracle and other religious topics.[55] Another fascinating case is presented by the cult of Mithras. As Reinhold Merkelbach has shown, the history of this cult in the Hellenistic and Roman periods consists of a sequence of reforms, in which Mithraism was changed from a Persian religion into a Hellenistic and Roman mystery cult.[56] These reforms must have been undertaken by imaginative cult reformers: 'M. P. Nilsson hat die Vermutung ausgesprochen, "daß die Mithrasmysterien eine einmalige Schöpfung eines unbekannten religiösen Genies" waren; wir können diese Ansicht nur bestätigen.'[57]

Also very interesting is the inscription documenting the establishment of a private mystery cult in Philadelphia in Lydia (first century B.C.E.).[58] The inscription contains the foundation legend as well as the ordinances of the new cult. This cult is said to have been founded by a certain Dionysios in his house (οἰκία), after he had a dream vision in which Zeus revealed the laws of the cult now inscribed in stone. The inscription all but admits that the cult has been imposed on an older cult of Agdistis, the Phrygian manifestation of the Great Mother, who continues in the new situation as an overseer.[59] A different feature of the new cult is that the members celebrate mysteries and that high moral standards are set and enforced by an oath. The high emphasis on ethics shows the influence of philosophy.[60]

---

[54] See Hans Dieter Betz, 'The Problem of Apocalyptic Genre in Greek and Hellenistic Literature: The Case of the Oracle of Trophonius,' reprinted in *Hellenismus und Urchristentum*, 184–208, esp. 186–88.

[55] See Hans Dieter Betz, ed., *Plutarch's Theological Writings and Early Christian Literature* (SCHNT 3; Leiden: Brill, 1975).

[56] Reinhold Merkelbach, *Mithras* (Königstein i.T.: Hain, 1984) 64–70, 75–77. See my reflections on this important book in *HR* 26 (1986) 87–89.

[57] Merkelbach, *Mithras*, 77. The quotation is from Nilsson, *Geschichte*, 2.675.

[58] For the text and bibliography see Sokolowski, *Lois sacrées de l' Asie Mineure*, no 20 (pp. 53–58); for the interpretation see the commentary by Otto Weinreich, *Stiftung und Kultsatzungen eines Privatheiligtums in Philadelpheia in Lydien* (SHAW.PH 1919.8; Heidelberg: Winter, 1919); S. C. Barton and G. H. R. Horsley, 'A Hellenistic Cult Group and the New Testament Churches,' *JAC* 24 (1981) 7–41.

[59] See Weinreich, *Stiftung*, 31.

[60] See Hans Dieter Betz, *Galatians* (Philadelphia: Fortress, 1979) 184–85 n. 26.

More evidence regarding founder figures could be adduced, but the examples given will have to suffice. They clearly show the leading role of founder figures at a time that saw a large expansion of cults, whether by new establishments or reformation of older cults, in the course of which transferral from one place to another was a common feature. Many of the new foundations originated in the East.[61] In the course of their reception in the West they were adapted and changed so as to meet new religious and cultural expectations. Many of the Eastern cults developed into mystery cults which seem to have enjoyed a rising popularity.[62] The development of the mysteries of Isis and Osiris, or Mithras, provides impressive examples for such transformation. Even the new Imperial Cult had to have mystery-religion rituals.[63]

The use of mystery-cult terminology and conceptuality was not limited to the mysteries themselves. Even philosophers like Plato or Jewish thinkers like Philo of Alexandria employed mystery-cult language.[64] Later, the mystery cults themselves became means for communicating philosophical wisdom.[65]

I am suggesting that the apostle Paul should be viewed as analogous to these Hellenistic founder figures, a suggestion that is not altogether new but that needs to be reaffirmed because of recent criticism.[66] The

---

[61] For a survey of the material, see Wedderburn, *Baptism and Resurrection*, 90–163.

[62] See my article 'Magic and Mystery in the Greek Magical Papyri,' *Hellenismus und Urchristentum*, 209–29.

[63] See Henri W. Pleket, 'An Aspect of the Emperor-Cult: Imperial Mysteries,' *HTR* 58 (1965) 331–47; Simon R. F. Price, *Rituals and Power: The Roman Imperial Cult in Asia Minor* (Cambridge: Cambridge University Press, 1984), 190–91; Duncan Fishwick, *The Imperial Cult in the Latin West: Studies in the Ruler Cult of the Western Provinces* (vols. I/1–2; EPRO 108; Leiden: Brill, 1987).

[64] See the excellent study by Christoph Riedweg, *Mysterienterminologie bei Platon, Philon und Klemens von Alexandrien* (UaLG 26; Berlin: de Gruyter, 1987).

[65] See Burkert, *Ancient Mystery Cults*, 66–68.

[66] This is not the place to respond in detail to the work of Wedderburn (*Baptism and Resurrection*) whose criticism of previous attempts to relate Paul and the mystery religions must be taken seriously. The problem with his hypothesis is that it remains entirely negative. 'It is the role of the study of the background of the New Testament to be ancillary to the interpretation of the New Testament — but an indispensable ancillary. I am conscious that in some ways this study has made the hermeneutical task of interpreting both the ancient mysteries and Paul more difficult. For we can no longer interpret either in the light of the other: the mysteries were not saying the same thing as Paul, nor was Paul borrowing his ideas from the mysteries. Each must now be considered in its

apostle Paul was indeed involved in the transferral of a religion that began in Palestinian Judaism and had Jesus of Nazareth as its primary founder. Paul's mission was to expand early Christianity into the Gentile world. In the course of this transferral, the traditions, rituals, and organization of Palestinian Christianity underwent substantial changes. As Paul's letters testify, he was one of the leading figures responsible for Jewish Christianity's transformation and for finding a place for the church in the larger world of Graeco-Roman antiquity. The transferral and concomitant reinterpretation of baptism provide us with a classic example of this process.

The Jewish Origins of Baptism

The historical origins of baptism have yet to be clarified; all we have at present are various theories concerning these origins.[67] At least there is certainty about the one point of concern to us: The Christian ritual of baptism has in some way developed out of Judaism. One should not assume, however, that only one Jewish form of baptism was practised at the time of early Christianity. Therefore the questions have to be formulated in this way: From which one of the Jewish forms of baptism did Christian baptism develop? Since at the beginning there were different forms of Christian baptism as well, did they all come from the same Jewish ritual, or did the transition occur at several points in different ways? Did the ritual itself change, or only its interpretation? Or did both the procedure and the interpretation change?

own light. The interpretation of Paul is my task, and it is only just beginning. Yet it is, I hope, not an inconsiderable beginning, to have set a large warning sign at the entry to what I believe to be a 'dead-end' in Pauline studies, the interpretation of Paul's doctrine of union with Christ as derivative from the mystery-cults of his day' (396). This last paragraph of the massive volume leaves in the air entirely, perhaps not accidentally, what is to be made of the material and the analysis in Wedderburn's book. Indeed, the interpretation of Paul's doctrines of baptism and resurrection has barely begun.

[67] These theories do not need to be discussed here. For the present state of the question see recent commentaries on Mark 1.1–11 and its parallels; Adela Yarbro Collins, 'The Origin of Christian Baptism,' *StL* 19 (1989) 28–46; also Kurt Niederwimmer, *Die Didache* (KAV 1; Göttingen: Vandenhoeck & Ruprecht, 1989) 158–64.

It appears that both the procedure and the interpretation of baptism changed in the new Christian contexts. These changes did not take place once and for all but only successively and in various ways in different places. This situation can easily explain why at the beginning of Christianity we find a variety of forms of baptism — not just one. At the same time, other rituals not continued in the Christian context seem to have had influence in other ways — for example, the language of purification continues in spite of the discontinuation of repeated ritual ablutions in early Christianity.[68] Proselyte baptism,[69] even after Jewish proselytism ceased to be an issue, may have influenced the conversion ritual practised in the Christian mission.

On the whole it can be said with confidence that Christian baptism somehow developed out of the baptism of John the Baptist. This form of baptism was summed up by the phrase βάπτισμα μετανοίας εἰς ἄφεσιν ἁμαρτιῶν (Mark 1.4).[70] Although our information is regrettably limited, this form of baptism was unique at the time.[71] It can be described as an eschatological sacrament of penitence.[72] As Mark 1.4–5 reports it, Jews from all over Judea went out to the river Jordan in response to John's message, confessed their sins, and were baptized in the Jordan. This baptism was a one-time 'seal' publicly indicating a promise of *teshubah* on the part of the baptized as well as of forgiveness of sins at the Last Judgment.

---

[68] For the language of 'washing' and 'cleansing' as applied to baptism, see 1 Cor 6.11; Eph 5.26; Tit 3.5. Generally speaking it is interesting that this language is taken up mostly in later texts (see also Acts 22.16; Heb 10.22; Jas 4.8; 1 Pet 3.20–21; 2 Pet 1.9, etc.)

[69] The origin and meaning of Jewish proselyte baptism is a problem all its own. See Schürer, *History*, 3.173–74, 642; Louis H. Feldman, 'Proselytes and "Sympathizers" in the Light of the New Inscription from Aphrodisias,' *REJ* 148 (1989) 265–305.

[70] This description is confirmed by Luke 3.3; cf. βάπτισμα μετανοίας, Acts 13.24; 19.4; *Gospel of the Ebionites* (Epiphanius *Pan.* 30.13.6; 30.14.3); Justin Martyr *Dial.* 88.7. The texts are assembled in Kurt Aland, *Synopsis Quattuor Evangeliorum* (13th ed.; Stuttgart: Deutsche Bibelgesellschaft, 1985) 22.

[71] For the present state of the question and bibliography, see Hartwig Thyen, 'Johannes der Täufer,' *EKL* 2 (1989) 834–35; Otto Böcher, 'Johannes der Täufer,' *TRE* 17 (1988) 172–81.

[72] Cf. especially Josephus' description (*Ant.* 18.116–19), using the phrase ἐφ' ἁγνείᾳ τοῦ σώματος, ἅτε δὴ καὶ τῆς ψυχῆς δικαιοσύνῃ προεκκεκαθαρμένης (117). The interpretation is disputed; cf. Böcher, *TRE* 17.174, lines 45–53.

101

This baptism of John had nothing to do with repeated ablutions, conversion of Gentile converts, or initiation into the Jewish religion. Those who were baptized were already Jews, but they were previously negligent Jews who turned from pro forma adherence to serious performance of the requirements of the Jewish religion. As a one-time definitive act this baptism came at least close to what later was called a sacrament. It had a 'magical' quality to it, although its validity was certainly conditional on the subsequent faithful observance of the Torah. The ritual was performed on the authority of John as the prophet of the end time; its efficacy must therefore be seen by analogy to other prophetic promises,[73] but the expectation of the imminent end of the world that John held gave his baptism its definitive character.

There are many questions with regard to this baptism for which we have no answer: How did John develop this form of baptism? Did he invent it *de novo*, or were there antecedents? Did he consciously modify existing rituals? What happened to this baptism after the death of John, when his personal authority could no longer be counted on? Since in fact there was a continuation of the ritual among his followers, what was its basis of authority then and how did the changes affect its interpretation?[74]

Whatever the answers to these questions may be, the evidence in the New Testament is most likely historically accurate in suggesting that Christian baptism somehow developed from the baptism of John.[75] The transferral of the ritual, however, did not occur easily.[76] There had to be some drastic changes affecting the practice of the ritual itself as well as its theological interpretations. Most importantly, the authority of John the Baptist had to be transferred to Jesus, which involves the difficult question whether Jesus himself practised baptism, and if so, which form of baptism it would have been (cf. John 3.22; 4.1–2). The river Jordan lost its special significance;[77] Christian baptism could be

[73] See Böcher, *TRE* 17.173, section I.3.

[74] Böcher, section I.4.

[75] Böcher, 177, section II.3.

[76] For the church of Corinth this applies especially to Apollos, who was baptized by John's baptism (Acts 18.24–25), and to his group (1 Cor 1.12; 3.4–6 [see below]).

[77] For the allegorical meaning of the Jordan, see Richard Reitzenstein, *Die Vorgeschichte der christlichen Taufe* (Leipzig & Berlin: Teubner, 1929) 254: 'der Jordan bedeutet bei den Mandäern nur das Taufwasser'.

performed in any kind of 'living water' (*Did.* 7.1–2).[78] Even those elements that continued to play a role, such as eschatology, forgiveness of sins, and the ethical implications had to be reinterpreted so as to fit into the new Christian context.

The Appropriation of Baptism in Primitive Christianity

When carefully examined, the New Testament sources indicate that the appropriation of baptism by primitive Christianity did not occur in a harmonious and unified way. What we encounter, rather, are the problems one should expect in this case of complex ritual transferral.

One of the earliest sources concerning this question is the correspondence of Paul. Strangely, however, he never states openly where, by whom, or by what method he himself was baptized. His baptism can only be inferred from his references to the baptism of Christians, among whom he includes himself by implication. If Paul was baptized, what kind of baptism was it? Acts 9.18 assures us that Paul was baptized, but the notice is singular and exceedingly short: καὶ ἀναστὰς ἐβαπτίσθη.[79] By whom was Paul baptized? Was it Ananias? Was it done by 'the church' of Damascus? What kind of baptism would the Damascus Christians have practised? No answers can be given to these questions. If Paul was baptized by the Christians of Damascus, they were still a part of Judaism. Otherwise, Saul/Paul would have had no reason to persecute that Christian group. If prior to his 'conversion' Paul was a Torah-observing Jew, the type of baptism performed by John the Baptist would hardly apply to him. Neither would proselyte baptism be appropriate. His baptism could only have been some kind of association ritual performed for those who joined the 'disciples' (μαθηταί) who were still members of the synagogues of Damascus.[80] The story in Acts 9 speaks of 'synagogues' (συναγωγαί) in Damascus. Does this

---

[78] Niederwimmer, *Die Didache*, 161–63.

[79] See Erich Fascher, 'Zur Taufe des Paulus,' *TLZ* 80 (1955) 643–48.

[80] Acts, our only source concerning 'Christianity' in Damascus, leaves unclear in which way the 'Christians' were organized. When Paul persecutes them, he goes to the synagogues (Acts 9.2, 20), where he finds 'disciples' (9.10, 19, 25, 26); the term 'church' is not used.

indicate that one of these synagogues was that of the 'disciples' of Jesus (9.2)? Was it only this synagogue that practiced baptism? The notion of Acts that Paul received his 'Christian' baptism in the house of Judas in Damascus (9.11) appears to be an anachronism, projecting back later Christian performances; the reference to Paul's baptism, which the author of Acts repeats only once in the later accounts of chapters 22 and 26 (in 22.16), may have come down to him as part of the Ananias legend. Thus, the facts about Paul's baptism remain elusive.

Difficulties with baptism are apparent in 1 Corinthians. Surprisingly, Paul shows uneasiness with regard to the ritual when he expresses gratitude for not having baptized any Christians at Corinth, except for Crispus, Gaius, and the household of Stephanas (1 Cor 1.14–16), among them perhaps Fortunatus and Achaicus who may have been his sons or slaves (1 Cor 16.15–18).[81] Paul sharply denies that baptizing converts is part of his missionary work: 'Christ did not send me to baptize but to preach the gospel' (1.17).

Indeed, his account of his call and commission by Christ (Gal 1.16) does not mention baptism. Also, the book of Acts never shows Paul baptizing (cf. Acts 16.15, 33); for Acts εὐαγγελίζεσθαι (see Acts 13.32; 14.7, 15; 16.10; 17.18; 20.24) and βαπτίζειν are two different matters. Baptism is the task of apostles like Peter (Matt 28.19; Acts 2.38, 41; 8.16; 10.48) and Philip (8.36, 38), but Paul and Barnabas are not called apostles (except 14.4, 14). Thus, it may not be surprising that Paul never mentions baptism in 1 Thessalonians. When he says in 1 Thess 2.7 that he *could* claim the privileges which the apostles of Christ are entitled to, he nonetheless abstains from doing so; in fact, the title of apostle does not appear in the prescript to 1 Thess 1.1.[82] In the light of this evidence, one would ask: Why did Paul then baptize in Corinth? Did he baptize because he felt he had to, or did he simply not suspect any detrimental consequences at that time?

The fact that in 1 Corinthians Paul lays claim to the title of apostle

---

[81]   See Wolfgang Schenk, 'Korintherbriefe,' *TRE* 19 (1990) 620–40, esp. 625, lines 3–5.

[82]   See Traugott Holtz, *Der erste Brief an die Thessalonicher* (EKK 13; Zürich, Einsiedeln, Köln: Benziger; Neukirchen-Vluyn: Neukirchener, 1986) 77–81.

of Christ Jesus (1 Cor 1.1; 4.9; 9.1, 2, 5; 15.7–9) may have been connected with his baptisms. Taking this step seems inevitable, if he wanted to be counted equal with other apostles, especially Cephas, and Apollos, both of whom, if we trust the tradition, baptized.[83] Apparently, Paul did not foresee at the time that σχίσματα and ἔριδες would result from such baptisms and that the allegiances between baptized and baptizers would prove stronger than the unity in the church (1 Cor 1.10–17; 3.4–15). When Paul points to this connection between dissension and baptism, he simultaneously evaluates the brief history of the Corinthian church. From his words we can infer that Christianity at Corinth began with groups formed around the missionaries who had baptized them. Three such groups are named: the parties of Paul, Cephas, and Apollos (leaving the questionable Christ party aside). What kind of baptism did these groups hold dear?

Paul ironically describes his own view of baptism as εἰς τὸ ὄνομα τοῦ κυρίου ἡμῶν Ἰησοῦ Χριστοῦ (1 Cor 1.13, 15; 6.11; cf. 1.2; 5.4; 10.2). This baptism was certainly a conversion ritual. Upon hearing and accepting the message of the gospel, individuals or households became members of the church, ἡγιασμένοι ἐν Χριστῷ Ἰησοῦ, κλητοὶ ἅγιοι, σὺν πᾶσιν τοῖς ἐπικαλουμένοις τὸ ὄνομα τοῦ κυρίου ἡμῶν Ἰησοῦ Χριστοῦ ἐν παντὶ τόπῳ. They became what Paul calls ἡ ἐκκλησία τοῦ Χριστοῦ ἡ οὖσα ἐν Κορίνθῳ (1.2; cf. 1.9).

This concept looks similar to, if not the same as, that used by other Christian missionaries, in particular Peter (Acts 2.38; 10.48; cf. 8.16; Matt 28.19). The baptism of Apollos, however, seems to have been different. At least, this would be the case if Acts 18.25 is right in saying that Apollos 'knew only the baptism of John'. The 'disciples' of John in Ephesus were associated with Apollos. They were baptized εἰς τὸ Ἰωάννου βάπτισμα (Acts 19.3), a ritual declared insufficient by Paul who then had them baptized εἰς τὸ ὄνομα τοῦ κυρίου Ἰησοῦ, to which he added the gift of the Holy Spirit by the laying on of hands

---

[83] For Cephas see Matt 28.19; Acts 2.38; cf. 2.41; 8.16; 10.48; for Apollos see 18.24–25; 19.1–7.

(Acts 19.5–6). Thus, when Paul began at Corinth and baptized some of the new converts he seems to have adjusted to the common ritual 'in the name of our Lord Jesus Christ'. Yet, as we learn from Gal 3.27, and also from a glimpse at 1 Cor 12.13 and its context, Paul's own concept of baptism was different.[84] Therefore, when the quarrels broke out at Corinth, the parties in that quarrel were separated by, among other things, different concepts of baptism. The Cephas people held on to baptism 'in the name of our Lord Jesus Christ'; the Apollos group may have continued John's baptism (unless they were 'corrected' by Paul), while at the time of writing 1 Corinthians Paul refrained from baptism altogether. Paul did not object in principle to all baptism, of course. Neither was the quarrel merely a matter of a misunderstanding of the apostle's baptismal theology. Rather, the confusion arose when the different groups Paul attempted to unite in the church maintained different baptismal interpretations. In addition, these concepts were open to mutual criticism. From Paul's later perspective the formula 'in the name of our Lord Jesus Christ' expressed Christian salvation only insufficiently. While Apollos' baptism was not even fully Christianized but stood halfway between Judaism and Christianity, Cephas' concept created a link between the baptized and their Lord Jesus Christ only through the ὄνομα, that is, by 'magical' application of the name of Christ. Such a link merely *modo magico* failed to spell out the ethical and communal obligations entered into by the baptized. Thus, one could be baptized in the name of Jesus Christ and still commit the violations of Christian ethos the apostle tries to rectify in 1 Corinthians 5–15.

The other obstacle to church unity that Paul underscores is the client relationship characterizing the groups. Just as the (Christian?) disciples of John the Baptist at Ephesus were held together by their allegiance to their master — that is, by εἰς τὸ Ἰωάννου βάπτισμα (Acts 19.3), so Paul sees the Corinthian factions divided by the allegiances to the initiators of their respective baptisms. This involves the grave error of confusing the name of the leader with the name of the redeemer.

---

[84] We should keep in mind that baptism 'in the name of our Lord Jesus Christ' is mentioned in Paul's authentic letters only in 1 Corinthians, while the initiation formula is cited and interpreted in Gal 3.26–28; 1 Cor 12.13; and Romans 6.

In 1 Corinthians, therefore, Paul does not develop his own doctrine of baptism as initiation, except for mentioning it once in 12.13. By stressing his limited baptismal activity in the past, the apostle tries to stay above the fray. He is no longer interested in being at the same level with the other apostles (cf. 9.1–2; 15.3–10), but emphasizes his special role as founder of the Corinthian church. As far as the Corinthians' own practices of baptism are concerned, he can be remarkably tolerant, condoning even baptism for the dead (15.29).[85] For him the more important issue is reconciling the factions with each other and preserving the community of the church.[86] It should be clear, however, that merely abstaining from baptism could not solve the problem. Sooner rather than later Paul had to come to terms with baptism.

Paul's Interpretation of Baptism as Initiation

If we look at the rather complicated picture regarding baptism in 1 Corinthians, Paul's own baptismal theology is not easy to discern. My thesis is that he did not fully develop it before Romans. What he develops in Romans, however, is based on the older formula of Gal 3.26–28.[87] When Paul cites this formula in Gal 3.26–28, there can be no question that he does so with approval. If he had not fully approved of it, he would not have given baptism the high status in the argument that it has in that letter. The formula must have been known to the Galatians from the beginning, so that its citation amounts to a reminder. Since Paul founded the churches of Galatia, we can also assume that it expresses his theology. It should be noted, however, that some of the features of that formula are not repeated elsewhere (cf. 1 Cor 12.13; cf. 10.2). In fact, what Paul presents in Romans 6 is a complete reinterpretation of the older formula of Gal 3.26–28.

The basic concept of the older formula is indicated by the phrase εἰς Χριστὸν ἐβαπτίσθητε (Gal 3.27; Rom 6.3), a phrase which is at once interpreted by the metaphor of putting on Christ like a garment: Χριστὸν ἐνεδύσασθε (3.27). Clearly, therefore, εἰς Χριστόν does not mean

---

[85] See Wedderburn, *Baptism and Resurrection*, 7, 288–89, with further literature.

[86] See Mitchell, *Paul and the Rhetoric of Reconciliation* (above n. 17), *passim*.

[87] See my *Galatians*, 181–201.

here 'in the name of Christ'.[88] Rather, the formula sums up the soteriological implications of the salvation event 'in Christ'. Conferring the status of 'sons of God' upon the baptized results in a change of status not only before God but also in respect of social rank. All new members in the church are one in the body of Christ (ἐν Χριστῷ Ἰησοῦ), and this includes their equality of social status: 'There is neither Jew nor Greek; there is neither slave nor freeman; there is no male and female' (3.28).

Baptism 'into Christ' means, therefore, being incorporated into the body of Christ and having some form of union with Christ. These notions, to be sure, must be compared with initiation rituals as we find them especially in Hellenistic mystery religions.[89] Of course, careful distinctions have to be made between these mystery cults, since each of them is characterized by its own features. Different deities require different initiations. And yet, there are common features, too. To what extent these initiations use similar patterns or are dependent on one another is a question we cannot pursue here.

When Paul interprets baptism in Romans 6 as an initiation ritual, he does so because he intends to overcome the difficulties he has experienced especially in Corinth. Initiating new members into the church means that they must become full participants in Christian salvation, that is, in the crucifixion and resurrection of the redeemer. Initiation is more than a mere conversion ritual. Membership in a corporate body

---

[88] Cf. also Hubert Frankemölle, *Das Taufverständnis des Paulus: Taufe, Tod und Auferstehung nach Römer 6* (SBS 47; Stuttgart: Katholisches Bibelwerk, 1970) 41–53; Lars Hartman, 'Baptism "Into the Name of Jesus" and Early Christology,' *StTh* 28 (1974) 21–48; 'Into the Name of Jesus,' *NTS* 20 (1974) 432–40; 'La formule baptismale dans les Actes des Apôtres: Quelques Observations relatives au style de Luc,' *A Cause de l'Evangile: Mélanges offerts à Dom Jacques Dupont* (LD 123; Paris: Cerf, 1985) 727–38; Ulrich Wilckens, *Der Brief an die Römer* (Röm 6–11) (EKK VI/2; Zürich, Einsiedeln, Köln: Benziger; Neukirchen-Vluyn: Neukirchener, 1980) 11, 48–51. Wilckens, with many others, assumes that baptism εἰς Χριστόν is a short way of saying εἰς τὸ ὄνομα Χριστοῦ Ἰησοῦ, but in fact the two expressions refer to fundamentally different doctrines. See Wedderburn, *Baptism and Resurrection*, 57 n. 20.

[89] See the helpful surveys provided in the articles by Peter Gerlitz, 'Initiation/ Initiationsriten,' *TRE* 16 (1987) 156–62; Mircea Eliade et al., 'Initiation,' *The Encyclopedia of Religion* 7 (1987) 224–38; Christoph Elsas and Balthasar Fischer, 'Initiationsriten,' *EKL* 2 (1989) 664–71. Wedderburn (*Baptism and Resurrection*, 360–92) discounts their applicability.

such as a local church is different from a social club in that this membership is in the 'body of Christ'. Baptism merely 'in the name of' cannot suffice, as the abuses in Corinth have demonstrated. Rather, baptism understood as an initiation presupposes that conversion has taken place, and that a process is to begin in which the new member is incorporated into the church as the body of Christ. This process is a lifelong process, so that baptism is only its beginning act. This process also involves several required steps. Perhaps the three-part schema described by van Gennep can be applied here as well: There is the *séparation* from the previous way of life and environment, the *marge* or precarious transition from the old to the new status, and *agrégation* or the integration into the new cultic community.[90]

In the case of Romans, the three stages are of course stated in terms of Paul's theology of the death and resurrection of Christ, and the Christian's participation in it — change from sinfulness to new Christian ethos; transition from the old to the new life; membership in the church; and finally the eschatological union with Christ.

Why then did Paul wait until Romans to fully explain his views on baptism? Or did he hold these views before but did not make it a special topic? Did he develop the doctrine in Romans especially for the benefit of the addressees in Rome? How much did the situation of the Roman church have to do with Paul's exposition in Romans?[91] Admittedly, these questions can be raised but not definitively answered; only a few considerations can be offered.

It appears unlikely that Paul held this baptismal theology prior to Romans but simply kept it hidden. There would have been reasons enough to make it public, although this judgment can be reached only retrospectively. Gal 3.26–28 shows a theology that is in some ways similar to that of Romans. Yet, the combination of theologoumena in

[90] Arnold van Gennep, *Rites of Passage,* trans. Monica Vizedom and Gabrielle L. Caffee (Chicago: University of Chicago Press, 1960); for the present discussion see Barbara G. Meyerhoff et al., 'Rites of Passage,' *The Encyclopedia of Religion* 12 (1987) 380–402.

[91] We do not know which views on baptism were held in Rome. The Roman Christians certainly practised baptism and had a theology going with it, but it must have been somewhat different from Paul's. For other theories about baptismal theology in Rome, see Wedderburn, *Baptism and Resurrection,* 37–69.

Romans is not found prior to that letter, even though some of the basic ideas are present earlier in Galatians. The formula of Gal 3.26–28 as a whole is not repeated in Romans. Instead, one may say, the formula has been replaced by the far more extensive section in Rom 5.1–8.39. The concept of dying and rising together with Christ *in baptism* is not found prior to Romans.[92] Rather, Paul connects death and resurrection together with Christ with his own apostolic existence, which serves as the paradigm for the church to imitate (see Gal 2.19–20; 6.14, 17; 2 Cor 4.10–11; Phil 3.10–11).[93] By contrast, in Romans Paul avoids setting himself up as a paradigm, and the language of imitation is not used at all.[94] Indeed, it would have been odd if he had asked the Romans to imitate an apostle whom they do not yet know in person.[95]

Thus, it is not too much to assume that, while baptism became more and more the accepted entrance ritual in the churches, Paul's shifting attitudes regarding it looked ambiguous to outsiders. The Corinthian crisis may at last have forced him to reconsider his position on baptism. Perhaps reports about it had reached the Roman church as well.[96] At any rate, Romans demonstrates that the apostle had finally seen the need to present a fully-developed doctrine of baptism.

How then did he develop this doctrine? As he does in other instances, we can see him reaching back into the arsenal of theological formulae, in this instance the formula in Gal 3.26–28, which is then interpreted on a large scale in Romans 5–8. This interpretation is that of baptism as the Christian initiation ritual. We have seen that in transferral of cults their new contextualization of rituals often took the

---

[92] Wedderburn (*Baptism and Resurrection*, 70–84) has persuasively argued that the doctrines held in Col 2.12–13 and Eph 2.5–6 were hardly those held by the Roman Christians, and that Paul did not write Romans 6 to 'correct' their ideas.

[93] See my book *Nachfolge und Nachahmung Jesu Christi im Neuen Testament* (BHTh 37; Tübingen: Mohr-Siebeck, 1967) 137–89.

[94] *Nachfolge*, 174–76.

[95] Paul's concept of himself as the 'imitator of Christ' seems to be connected with his personal acquaintance with the readers (see 1 Cor 11.1; Phil 3.17; 4.8–9). Since the Romans do not know him face to face, imitating him was not a possibility (cf. Rom 1.10–13; 15.22–29, 32). The deutero-Pauline Ephesians (5.1) changes the concept to 'imitation of God'. See Betz, *Nachfolge*, 137 n. 1.

[96] As far as our texts go, there is no reason to suspect that Paul's doctrine of baptism was a concern in Rome (cf. Rom 3.5–8; 6.1–2). Perhaps the Romans had no clear ideas about what Paul's position was, so that his exposition in Romans 6–8 served to clarify it.

form of initiations. Paul's case is in principle just another example of this phenomenon. If this thesis is granted, it may also help us to understand how the new doctrine as developed in Romans is fully integrated into the overall argument of the letter. Although this question of the overall argument cannot be answered here, it may suffice to say that the doctrine of baptism is part of the discussion of the Christian experience of salvation in chapters 5–8. Baptism marks the point at which the individual Christian is 'implanted' (6.5) into the salvation process, a process which extends from Adam to the Parousia. After dealing with the meaning of the ritual itself in Rom 6.3–11, Paul takes up, point by point, what he regards as the *beneficia Christi* in 6.12–8.39.

When he refers to the ritual as ἐβαπτίσθημεν εἰς Χριστὸν Ἰησοῦν (6.3), this concept is the same as Gal 3.27, εἰς Χριστὸν ἐβαπτίσθητε and 1 Cor 12.13, εἰς ἓν σῶμα ἐβαπτίσθημεν (cf. 10.2: εἰς τὸν Μωϋσῆν ἐβαπτίσθησαν), but it is different from the other concept of baptism 'in the name of our Lord Jesus Christ' (1 Cor 1.13, 15). Perhaps the Roman Christians were familiar with the phrase ἐβαπτίσθημεν εἰς Χριστὸν Ἰησοῦν (6.3), a phrase that is open to several interpretations, but baptism 'into his death' seems to be something unusual: ἢ ἀγνοεῖτε ὅτι, ὅσοι ἐβαπτίσθημεν εἰς Χριστὸν Ἰησοῦν, εἰς τὸν θάνατον αὐτοῦ ἐβαπτίσθημεν; (6.3).

The argument drawn is introduced by the rhetorical question: ἢ ἀγνοεῖτε . . .; Rhetorically, this question can simply remind the readers of what they already know, or it can make them aware of consequences they ought to recognize.[97] Since the consequence is peculiarly Pauline, the apostle may propose his interpretation as new but compatible and even agreeable with what they have been familiar with thus far. Given Paul's theological presuppositions, his conclusion is logical indeed. If he describes the Christian experience as Χριστῷ συνεσταύρωμαι (Gal 2.20)[98] and συμμορφιζόμενος τῷ θανάτῳ αὐτοῦ (Phil 3.10),[99] baptism is the logical point of inception of this experience. For Paul,

---

[97] See also Wedderburn, *Baptism and Resurrection*, 46–48.
[98] See Betz, *Galatians*, 186–89, referring to Gal 2.19; 5.24; 6.14.
[99] See Betz, *Nachfolge*, 143–53, 179–85.

being crucified with Christ is first of all an experience of faith that precedes the ritual of baptism.[100] The experience also transcends baptism in that it characterizes the life of the believer throughout, so that Paul can speak of sharing Christ's death and resurrection without referring to baptism.

At the moment, however, when Paul decides to interpret baptism as initiation into the experience of salvation in Christ, then the ritual could easily be taken as the point of inception of that experience. Baptism into Christ, to be sure, involves the ritual performance of what in its meaning is circumscribed by the wider mythico-historical framework of the Adam-Christ typology (Rom 5.12–21).

Parallel to the tradition of 1 Cor 15.3–4, therefore, the βάπτισμα εἰς τὸν θάνατον also means συνταφῆναι αὐτῷ διὰ τοῦ βαπτίσματος (Rom 6.4a). Partaking in the death and burial of Christ, then, is the necessary precondition for sharing in the hope of the resurrection together with him (6.4b).

Most difficult and thus most controversial is the meaning of Rom 6.5: εἰ γὰρ σύμφυτοι γεγόναμεν τῷ ὁμοιώματι τοῦ θανάτου αὐτοῦ, ἀλλὰ καὶ τῆς ἀναστάσεως ἐσόμεθα. Does this sentence describe the *performance* of the baptismal ritual, or does it explain what the ritual *means?* If it is the former, then those exegetes are right who see in the sentence the description of a *Mysteriendrama*, in which submersion under the water represents death and burial, and emergence from the water resurrection from the dead. This interpretation became famous in the ancient church especially through the *Mystagogical Catecheses* of Cyril of Jerusalem (died 387).[101] In the twentieth century this interpretation was revived, supported by insights of the *Religionsgeschichtliche Schule*, by the Abbott of Maria Laach, Dom

---

[100] See Wedderburn, *Baptism and Resurrection*, 49.

[101] See the edition by Auguste Piédagnel, *Cyrille de Jérusalem. Catéchèses Mystagogiques* (2nd ed.; Sources Chrétiennes 126; Paris: Cerf, 1988). On the whole tradition see Hugh M. Riley, *Christian Initiation: A Comparative Study of the Interpretation of the Baptismal Liturgy in the Mystagogical Writings of Cyril of Jerusalem, John Chrysostom, Theodore of Mopsuestia and Ambrose of Milan* (The Catholic University of America: Studies in Christian Antiquity 70; Washington, D.C.: The Catholic University of America Press, 1974).

Odo Casel (1886–1948)[102] and his followers.[103] Interesting and stimulating as this interpretation was and still is,[104] New Testament scholars are now in agreement that it does not apply to Paul himself.[105] Paul, however, should be seen as the first theologian who showed the way to this interpretation which was subsequently developed further by the authors of Colossians, Ephesians, and a host of other authors.[106] The difficulties of Rom 6.5 can be best approached with two contexts in mind. There is first the context of vv. 2–5, within which v. 5 attempts to explain what has been stated in vv. 3–4.[107] Then, Paul's larger argumentation should be taken into consideration. The sentence of v. 5, being an explanatory statement, provides the terms needed to connect the ritual of baptism with the christological and soteriological meaning that Paul

---

[102] See especially his basic article, 'Zur Kultsprache des Heiligen Paulus,' *ALW* 1 (1950) 1–64, 140–42. This article caused an entire generation of learned discussion among and with the Benedictines of Maria Laach. Odo Casel had already summed up his views in a review in *JLW* 14 (1938) 197–224. See the bibliographies by Osvaldo D. Santagada, 'Dom Odo Casel: Contributo monografico per una Bibliografia generale delle sue opere, degli studi sulla una dottrina e della sua influenza nella teologia contemporanea,' *ALW* 28 (1967) 7–77; Angelus A. Häussling, 'Bibliograhie Odo Casel 1967–1985,' *ALW* 28 (1986) 24–42; 'Bibliographie Odo Casel 1986,' *ALW* 29 (1987)189–98.

[103] See especially Viktor Warnach, 'Taufe und Christusgeschehen nach Römer 6,' *ALW* 3 (1954) 284–366; 'Die Tauflehre des Römerbriefes in der neueren theologischen Diskussion,' *ALW* 5 (1958) 274–332.

[104] See Lothar Lies, 'Kultmysterium heute – Modell sakramentaler Begegnung: Rückschau und Vorschau auf Odo Casel,' *ALW* 28 (1986) 2–21; Angelus A. Häussling, 'Eine bleibende Herausforderung, Odo Casel neu zu lesen: Zu zwei neuen Auswahlbänden,' *ALW* 29 (1987) 371–94.

[105] Against Casel and his followers see Rudolf Schnackenburg, *Das Heilsgeschehen bei der Taufe nach dem Apostel Paulus: Eine Studie zur paulinischen Theologie* (MThS 1/1; München: Zink, 1950); *Baptism in the Thought of St. Paul: A Study in Pauline Theology,* trans. G. R. Beasley-Murray (New York: Herder & Herder, 1964); 'Todes- und Lebensgemeinschaft mit Christus: Neue Studien zu Röm 6, 1–11,' *MThZ* 6 (1955) 32–53; Karl Hermann Schelkle, 'Taufe und Tod: Zur Auslegung von Römer 6, 1–11,' *Vom christlichen Mysterium: Gesammelte Arbeiten zum Gedächtnis von Odo Casel* (ed. A. Mayer; Düsseldorf: Patmos 1951) 9–21; Frankemölle, *Das Taufverständnis,* 16–17, 70–71; Dieter Zeller, 'Die Mysterienkulte und die paulinische Soteriologie (Römer 6, 1–11),' *Suchbewegungen: Synkretismus-Kulturelle Identität und kirchliches Bekenntnis* (ed. H. P. Siller; Darmstadt: Wissenschaftliche Buchgesellschaft, 1991) 42–61.

[106] See the excellent study of the history of exegesis by Robert Schlarb, *Wir sind mit Christus begraben: Die Auslegung von Römer 6, 1–11 im Frühchristentum bis Origenes* (BHTh 31; Tübingen: Mohr-Siebeck, 1990).

[107] So correctly Frankemölle, *Das Taufverständnis,* 61.

intends to give it. It is to be understood, of course, that, seen from the outside, the ritual has little resemblance to the meaning.

The two key terms σύμφυτος and ὁμοίωμα, brought in to explain matters, should be expected to come from contexts in which they explain comparable phenomena. The first, σύμφυτος, is a New Testament hapaxlegomenon,[108] while the second, ὁμοίωμα, is found elsewhere in Paul (Rom 1.23; 5.14; 8.3; Phil 2.7) and Revelation (9.7);[109] these other usages are, however, only of limited help.[110] Paul's choice of these terms was certainly deliberate; he intended them to illuminate two essential problems raised by rituals in general. The first term, σύμφυτος, states the effect the ritual has, while the second, ὁμοίωμα, determines the relationship between the image of something and that something itself.

The adjective σύμφυτος alludes to agricultural processes and conveys the idea of separate entities growing together.[111] As a metaphor the term was applied also to the interpenetration of the human and the divine.[112] Most difficult is the term ὁμοίωμα, for which no adequate investigation — or even translation — exists that examines the whole evidence from antiquity.[113] The problems have often been pointed out

[108] See especially Ceslaus Spicq, *Notes de lexicographie néotestamentaire* (OBO 22/2; Fribourg: Editions universitaires; Göttingen: Vandenhoeck & Ruprecht, 1978) 2.844–46.

[109] For discussion we can here refer to the standard Greek lexica; none of them, however, achieves clarity of the issues because they do not go beyond lexicography.

[110] The creedal formula in Ignatius (*Trall.* 9.1–2) makes a similar point and may indeed by based on Rom 6.4–5, but baptism is not mentioned and ὁμοίωμα is applied to the resurrection, not the death of Christ. See Schlarb, *Wir sind mit Christus begraben*, 58–59, 214.

[111] See especially Origen in several places; see Schlarb (*Wir sind mit Christus begraben*, 214) for the passages. Rufinus translates σύμφυτος as *complantatus*, i.e. *complantari similitudini mortis Christi*.

[112] There is no space here to discuss the interesting digression on the origin of human civilization in Dio Chrysostom, *Or.* 12.27–37. Primitive humanity is said to have been close to the deity: ἅτε γὰρ οὐ μακρὰν οὐδ' ἔξω τοῦ θείου διῳκισμένοι καθ' αὑτούς, ἀλλὰ ἐν αὐτῷ μέσῳ πεφυκότες, μᾶλλον δὲ συμπεφυκότες ἐκείνῳ . . . (28). The passage is often cited as a parallel to Rom 6.5. It is influenced by Epicurean and Stoic notions, which makes it comparable to Rom 1.19–23 and Acts 17.27–28. The passage also makes a comparison (σχεδὸν οὖν ὅμοιον) of the cosmic religion of the primitive people with initiation into the mysteries (*Or.* 12.33–34).

[113] See Warnach, 'Taufe und Christusgeschehen,' 302–10, and against him Eduard Stommel, 'Das "Abbild seines Todes" (Römer 6, 5) und der Taufritus,' *RQ* 50 (1955) 1–

and can therefore be summarized here.[114] Is τῷ ὁμοιώματι the dative object for σύμφυτοι γεγόναμεν? Or is it an instrumental dative meaning that 'we have become united (with Christ) through the likeness of his death,' whereby 'likeness' refers to baptism, and σύμφυτοι requires an additional object αὐτῷ?[115] There is now a virtual consensus that τῷ ὁμοιώματι is the object of σύμφυτοι, so that the translation should read: 'we have been united with the likeness of his death'. Why, however, 'with the likeness', if 'with his death' is meant? It seems obvious that ὁμοίωμα is an *abstractum* referring to baptism.[116] Yet, does ὁμοίωμα point to the ritual of baptism descriptively, or to the notion of baptism theologically?

The larger context of Paul's argument requires an explanation of how he relates a ritual performed in the present with Christ's death, which is a matter of the past. Apparently, in Paul's mind, using the term ὁμοίωμα in reference to baptism should have clarified the matter.

Given the lexicological background of the term ὁμοίωμα[117] and its main synonyms (εἰκών, μίμημα), the usage in v. 5 intends, it seems, the ritual as ritual: This ritual is a ὁμοίωμα. Indeed other terms would not be appropriate because no cult image (εἰκών) is used and no dramatic episodes (μιμήματα) are performed.[118] Thus, baptism is *only* a ὁμοίωμα, a *similitudo*.[119] As a technical term, ὁμοίωμα would indeed, as Viktor Warnach has rightly seen, come close to the *Kultsymbol*,[120] the ritual as it makes mythic realities present in symbolic fashion. For such

21; Schnackenburg, *Baptism*, 49–53; 'Todes- und Lebensgemeinschaft', 32–53; Otto Kuβ, *Der Römerbrief* (Regensburg: Pustet, 1957) 299–303; Frankemölle, *Das Taufverständnis*, 60–73.

[114] See Ernst Käsemann, *Commentary on Romans* (Grand Rapids: Eerdmans, 1980) 167–69.

[115] Cf. Walter Bauer, *A Greek-English Lexicon of the New Testament and Other Early Christian Literature* (Frederick Danker et al., eds.; Chicago: The University of Chicago Press, 1979), *s.v.* ὁμοίωμα, 1: 'if we have been united (i.e. αὐτῷ with him; cf. vs 4: συνετάφημεν αὐτῷ) in the likeness of his death (= in the same death that he died).'

[116] Differently Wilckens, *Der Brief an die Römer*, 2.14–15.

[117] Cf. Johannes Schneider, 'ὁμοίωμα,' *TDNT* 5.191–98.

[118] See Betz, *Nachfolge*, 174.

[119] This is the equivalent in the Vulgate; cf. Tertullian *De resurr.* 47.11–12 (CCSL 2.986): *simulacrum mortis Christi* (so according to Schlarb, *Wir sind mit Christus begraben*, 214).

[120] Warnach, 'Taufe und Christusgeschehen', 306–7.

115

rituals we possess a number of examples, so that Paul's explanation could be expected to be understandable for his readers. Cult symbols are understandable to those initiated, but they look obscure to outsiders.[121]

If this explanation of ὁμοίωμα is accepted, it constitutes further evidence that Paul is consciously shaping baptism as an initiation ritual. Symbolic rituals were characteristic of initiations. What would initiation in terms of Paul's theology mean if not the entering into union with Christ's death as salvation event? By making Christ's death and burial a present experience for the believer, he was made a participant physically as well as spiritually in that salvation event. The term ὁμοίωμα, by designating the ritual as ritual, distinguishes between the crucifixion of Christ as a historical act of the past and its present representation. Also, baptism covers only death and burial, while participation in the resurrection is a consequence of the future (6.5b).[122]

Baptism, understood in this way, conveys not only experience but also conviction and knowledge. Terms signifying knowledge pervade the passage, in particular vv. 6–11. In this regard as well Paul is in conformity with ancient initiation ceremonies. They also communicate both experience and knowledge to the initiates, a knowledge that encompasses life and death. Most importantly, initiations mark the beginning of a person's 'transformation' (μεταμορφοῦσθαι), a soteriological concept fundamental for Christian ethics.[123]

Conclusion

Viewing Paul from the Hellenistic perspective can be illuminating in-

[121] For collections of examples, see J. Gwyn Griffiths, *Apuleius of Madauros, The Isis-Book (Metamorphoses, Book XI)* (EPRO 39; Leiden; Brill, 1975) 294–308; Betz, *Hellenismus und Urchristentum*, 151–53. Cf. also the *symbola Pythagorea*, and on them Nilsson, *Geschichte*, 1.703–8.

[122] The question is whether ὁμοίωμα should also be applied to the resurrection (v. 5b). Most scholars see here a difference between Paul and the deutero-Paulines (Col 2.12; 3.1; Eph 2.5–6). See Frankemölle, *Das Taufverständnis*, 63–64; 72–73.

[123] See on this issue my article, 'The Foundations of Christian Ethics According to Romans 12.1–2,' *Witness and Existence: Essays in Honor of Schubert M. Ogden* (ed. Philip E. Devenish and George L. Goodwin; Chicago: The University of Chicago Press, 1989) 55–72 (German: 'Das Problem der Grundlagen der paulinischen Ethik [Röm 12, 1–2],' *ZTK* 85 [1988] 199–219).

deed.[124] His apostolic activities of founding churches can be placed alongside those of other founder figures establishing religious institutions in the Hellenistic period. Although we do not possess detailed reports about what happened during the initial visits of the apostle that led to church foundations,[125] his letters reveal that the founding act was only the beginning of a longer process. That process can be observed in the letters, and they are in fact part of the process.[126] The history of the ritual and interpretation of baptism provides insight into one of the aspects of new religious foundations: the institution of rituals. Such institution involves the performance as well as the interpretation of any given ritual.

As far as baptism is concerned, the ritual itself was a transferral from Judaism. This transferral took place in stages and involved multiple recontextualizations. The process was anything but well planned and harmonious; it reflected the different movements, tensions and controversies within nascent Christianity as it slowly found its way out of the Jewish into the Gentile world. We were able to trace the history of baptism from John the Baptist, for whom it was a sacrament of penitence, to an early Christian conversion ritual, and finally to Paul, who in his last letter, following the Corinthian crisis, interprets baptism as the Christian initiation ritual. During the early course of this history, the actual performance of the ritual appears to be *extra controversiam*; in fact, it is of so little interest that we do not possess precise information about how it was to be performed.[127] Was it done by ablution or submersion, in a river, in a basin, or just anywhere? By contrast, the

---

[124] There are certainly other such insights not covered by this paper. Morton Smith ('Pauline Worship As Seen by Pagans,' *HTR* 73 [1980] 241–49) pointed out that pagans, when reading Paul's letters or witnessing his activities in person, could have concluded that Paul was a magician. Cf. also 'Transformation by Burial (I Cor 15.35–49; Rom 6.3–5 and 8.9–11),' *Eranos-Jahrbuch* 52 (1983) 87–112. See on this point my discussion in *Hellenismus und Urchristentum*, 236–38, 253–61.

[125] Cf. Harnack, *Mission*, 1.448 n. 1: 'Einen detaillierten Bericht über die Entstehung einer Christengemeinde besitzen wir nicht'. Cited by Wolfgang Speyer, 'Gründer,' *RAC* 12 (1982) 1149.

[126] See furthermore my article, 'Christianity as Religion: Paul's Attempt at Definition in Romans,' *JR* 71 (1991) 315–44.

[127] The concerns about performance first appear in *Did* 7.1–4; see Niederwimmer, *Die Didache*, 158–64.

entire emphasis is on the meaning of baptism, and indeed this meaning changed considerably, given the respective theological and social contexts in which it was interpreted. Therefore, while the performance was apparently transferred without much change, the interpretation had to be recontextualized. Paul's letters reveal that he accepted the transferral of the ritual but considered its interpretation to be inadequate. At least this seems to be the conclusion he had drawn from the Corinthian crisis. For this reason, in his letter to the Romans he undertook the full recontextualization of baptism in terms of his theology. Interpreting baptism as the Christian initiation ritual then also explains why there are so many analogies to other Hellenistic initiations, especially those from the mystery religions, while the baptismal theology in Romans 6 is so originally and unmistakably that of the apostle Paul.

5

Enthymemic Argumentation in Paul: The Case of Romans 6[1]

David Hellholm

For Nils A. Dahl

1. Introduction

Most of the letters written by the apostle Paul, alone or together with
co-workers[2], are argumentative texts[3] in which Paul argues with his
addressees and with his antagonistic propagandists. They thus constitute a theological sub-class of 'public-institutional argumentation'.[4] As
a consequence of this it is necessary — with Wilhelm Wuellner[5] and
others[6] — to investigate more closely the argumentative character of
the letters.[7] This has to be done here on a limited scale, since we must

---

[1]   For a more exhaustive treatment, see the longer version of this essay to be pub-
lished in my *New Testament and Textlinguistics: Collected Essays I* (Tübingen: Mohr-
Siebeck, in preparation). For computer assistance I am obliged to my son, Christer D.
Hellholm. Texts and translations of classical texts are in most cases (sometimes with
minor alterations) according to LCL. For Arist., *Ars rhet.*, see now the English transl. by
G. A. Kennedy (*Aristotle on Rhetoric. A Theory of Civic Discourse.* Newly translated with
Introduction, Notes, and Appendixes, New York/Oxford: Oxford University Press, 1991).

[2]   Cf. W. H. Ollrog, *Paulus und seine Mitarbeiter* (WMANT 50; Neukirchen-Vluyn:
Neukirchener Verlag, 1979) 183–89; W. Klein, 'Argumentation und Argument,' *LiLi* 10
(1980) 13.

[3]   The *argumentative* text-type stands in opposition to the *narrative*, the *descriptive*,
the *expository*, and the *instructive* text-types; see E. Werlich, *Typologie der Texte* (UTB
450; Heidelberg: Quelle & Meyer, 1975) 30–39.

[4]   W. Klein, 'Argumentation', 11ff., especially 19; F. Siegert, *Argumentation bei Paulus*
(WUNT 34; Tübingen: Mohr-Siebeck, 1985) 18.

[5]   Cf. W. Wuellner, 'Paul's Rhetoric of Argumentation in Romans: An Alternative to
the Donfried-Karris Debate over Romans,' *The Romans Debate* (ed. K. P. Donfried; 2nd
ed.; Peabody: Hendrickson, 1991) 145f.

[6]   E.g. F. Siegert, *Argumentation bei Paulus.* Cf. H. D. Betz's analysis of the argumentative structure of Galatians (*Galatians* [Hermeneia], Philadelphia: Fortress, 1979).

[7]   The argumentative character can be very different due to various types of argumentation. Two main groups can rather easily be discerned, however (cf. P.-L. Völzing,
Begründen, Erklären. Argumentieren [UTB 886; Heidelberg: Quelle & Meyer, 1979]

confine ourselves to analyzing the argumentative strategy of Romans 6 only.

2. The Text-Form 'Argumentative Text'

The specific text-form 'argumentative text',[8] which — depending on the depth of abstraction[9] — can be located on either of the levels 'Mode of writing' or 'Type of text', is characterized by explicitly formulated 'contrastive form sequences'.[10] The 'consequence-relations'[11] which occur within the framework of an argumentative discussion are — from a semiotic point of view[12] — of three kinds: (a) *syntactically* the consequence-relations are characterized by the fact that one link in the text-relation constitutes the *conclusion* while the others constitute *premises*;[13] (b) *semantically*, in the consequence-relation the truth of the

---

130ff.): First, texts with predominantly logical-theoretical argumentation with the aim of convincing (τὸ ἐνδεχόμενον πιθανόν [Arist., *Ars rhet.* 1355b]; see J. Sprute, *Die Enthymemtheorie der aristotelischen Rhetorik* [AAWG.PH 124; Göttingen: Vandenhoeck & Ruprecht, 1982] 69–109) or seeming to convince (τὸ φαινόμενον πιθανόν [Arist., *Ars rhet.* 1355b]; see Sprute, *Enthymemtheorie*, 109–15) the interlocutors intellectually (πίστις; see H. Lausberg, *Elemente der literarischen Rhetorik* [5th ed.; Munich: Hueber, 1976] 25f.; 34f; J. Martin, *Antike Rhetorik* [HAW II.3; Munich: Beck, 1974] 95ff.; W. Klein, 'Argumentation', 17ff.). The second group consists of texts with predominantly practical-pragmatic argumentation with the aim of persuading the interlocutors emotionally (ἦθος and πάθος; see especially M. H. Wörner, *Das Ethische in der Rhetorik des Aristoteles* [AlbR.PPh 33; Freiburg/Munich: Alber, 1990]).

[8] For this text-type see especially J. Kopperschmidt, 'An Analysis of Argumentation,' *Handbook of Discourse Analysis* (ed. T. A. van Dijk; London: Academic Press, 1985) 159–68.

[9] Cf. D. Hellholm, 'The Problem of Apocalyptic Genre,' *Early Christian Apocalypticism: Genre and Social Setting* (*Semeia* 36; ed. A. Y. Collins; Atlanta: Scholars Press, 1986) 30.

[10] Cf. Werlich, *Typologie*, 36.

[11] See H. Schnelle, 'Zur Explikation des Begriffs "Argumentativer Text",' *Linguistische Probleme der Textanalyse* (JIdS 35; ed. H. Moser; Düsseldorf: Schwamm, 1975) 67.

[12] The adequate exploitation of the threefold semiotic schema is as important with regard to argumentative as with regard to narrative textanalyses; for the latter cf. Hellholm, *Das Visionenbuch des Hermas als Apokalypse* (ConBNT 13:1, Lund: Gleerup, 1980) 27–52; see also 'Problem'.

[13] The valid *syntactic form* does not, however, presuppose that the premises are true; see K. Marc-Wogau, *Logik, Vetenskapsteori, Argumentationsanalys* (Tema; Stockholm: Liber, 1968) 64; J. Allwood, L. G. Andersson, and Ö. Dahl, *Logic in Linguistics* (CTL; Cambridge: Cambridge University Press, 1977) 16; A. Menne, *Einführung in die Logik* (UTB 34; 2nd ed.; Munich: Franke, 1973) 93. One such syntactic form that establishes the logical validity of the inference is the familiar first figure *Barbara*:

conclusion is dependent on the *truth of the premises*;[14] (c) *semantic-pragmatically* — as is already indicated by the Aristotelian differentiation between the scientifically acceptable συλλογισμὸς ἀποδεικτικός on the one hand, and the συλλογισμὸς διαλεκτικός and συλλογισμὸς ῥητορικός [= ἐνθύμημα] respectively on the other — the truth of the conclusion is dependent on the truth of the premises *as acknowledged by the interlocutors*; thus, the truth-value is limited exclusively to what is accepted by both partners, and the scientific or ontological truth-value is not a consideration. Within the communication process, however, this kind of consequence-relation possesses sufficient validity to achieve the intended effect.[15]

2.1. Theoretical vs. Practical Argumentation

Every attempt to solve a controversy by means of argumentative strategies is dependent on whether the underlying problem is based (a) on the reliability of the information offered, (b) on the acceptance of an obligation or evaluation, or (c) possibly on a combination of both. Thus, in an argumentation we have to deal with theoretical as well as with practical problems or a combination of the two.[16]

Another difficulty especially in connection with practical argumentation lies, as Wolfgang Klein has emphasized, in the fact that 'Äußerungen

---

Premise 1: All a's are b's;
Premise 2: All b's are c's;
Conclusion: Therefore: all a's are c's.
   'And it is in virtue of having this form that the inferences are valid. Such inferences are said to be *formally* valid' (J. Lear, *Aristotle: the Desire to Unterstand* [Cambridge: Cambridge University Press, 1988] 214). See Arist., *Topica* 101a1–17; *Soph. El.* 176b31–33; 166b21ff.
[14]   It is a characteristic of the deductive syllogism that if the inference is valid and the premises are true, then the inference can be called 'binding' (cf. Marc-Wogau, *Logik*, 63; Allwood, Andersson, and Dahl, *Logic*, 15; Menne, *Logik*, 93).
[15]   See T. Ballmer, 'Einführung und Kontrolle von Diskurswelten,' *Linguistische Pragmatik* (SLKW 12; ed. D. Wunderlich; Wiesbaden: Athenaion, 1975) 184: 'Wie in der *Syntax* die Wohlgeformtheit und in der *Semantik* die Wahrheit als Grundbegriffe dienen, so muß auch die *Pragmatik* ihren Grundbegriff haben, auf dem die pragmatische Theorie aufgebaut werden kann' (italics mine). As the basic concept for pragmatics Ballmer introduces the term 'Erfolg'.
[16]   Cf. Kopperschmidt, 'Analysis', 161; D. Wunderlich, *Studien zur Sprechakttheorie* (stw 172; Frankfurt/Main: Suhrkamp, 1976) 257.

in der natürlichen Sprache grundsätzlich vage, kontextabhängig, mehr-
deutig und illokutiv gesehen polyfunktional sind'.[17]

2.2. Macrostructural vs. Microstructural Argumentation Analysis

With regard to argumentative texts there is a need to distinguish first of
all between partial micro-structural and global macro-structural analyses.
If, as Werner Kummer assumes, argumentation can be defined 'as a goal-
directed chaining of arguments',[18] one must, according to the levels of
complexity in an argumentation, differentiate further between at least (a)
the micro-structural level of individual propositions and speech-acts —
that is, the individual proofs as such; (b) the intermediate level of group-
ings of propositions and speech-acts — that is, the functional integration
of themes and illocutions created by the cluster of proofs with regard to a
specific thesis; and (c) the macro-structural level of a hierarchical conjunction of arguments — that is, the functional integration of the intermediate themes and speech-acts into the global argumentation with regard to the overarching thesis of the given text.[19]

2.3. The Argumentative Analytical Tools

The tools for analyzing argumentative texts can be derived from three
different, yet related, and to a certain degree overlapping fields: analytical philosophy, text-linguistics, and ancient rhetoric.

2.3.1. Tools from Analytical Philosophy

When pursuing argumentative analyses the interpreter's first task is to
detect the thesis advocated by the author.[20] An argumentation contains
a thesis and one or more statements whose function it is to support the
thesis. In the terminology of ancient rhetoric, the syllogism is made up

---

[17]   W. Klein, 'Argumentation', 25.
[18]   W. Kummer, 'Aspects of a Theory of Argumentation,' *Textsorten* (ed. E. Gülich
and W. Raible; AthSL 5; 2nd ed.; Wiesbaden: Athenaion, 1975) 29.
[19]   Cf. J. Kopperschmidt, 'Analysis', 161; see also M. Schecker, 'Argumentationen als
allokutionäre Sprechakte,' *Theorie der Argumentation* (ed. M. Schecker; TBL 76; Tübingen:
Narr, 1977) 75–138, who in connection with argumentative dialogue structures speaks
of a 'sequential approach' in contrast to a 'sentential approach' (p. 95 *et passim*); cf. also
D. Hellholm, *Visionenbuch*, 60.
[20]   See, e.g., Kopperschmidt, 'Analysis', 161–62.

of the *propositio*, which is followed by the *rationes* or as they are also called *praemissae*.[21] These statements together constitute the argument. The next step is the establishment of *pro-* and *counter-arguments* of various degrees promoted by proponent(s) and opponent(s) respectively.[22] In many cases, however, as Dieter Wunderlich correctly observes, 'it is not facts that are argued but attitudes: the pros and cons are attempts to settle disputed attitudes with the aim to win over the opponents to one's own attitude'.[23]

In order to obtain an overview of the arguments as far as the hierarchical arrangement in their micro-, intermediate-, and macro-structure is concerned, it is advisable first to pick out those arguments that speak directly in favor of the thesis — the *pro-arguments of the first rank* (PA^{1-n}). Then one has to identify those arguments which support the arguments of the first rank — the *pro-arguments of the second rank* ($PA^{1.1-n}$), etc. Likewise, after the pro-arguments have been ranked one must pick out those arguments that speak directly against the thesis — the *counter-arguments of the first rank* (CA^{1-n}), and then identify those arguments which support the counter-arguments of the first rank — the *counter-arguments of the second rank* ($CA^{1.1-n}$), etc.[24] The proponents' pro-arguments for the thesis can also function as counter-arguments against the opponents' counter-arguments on every level in the argumentation; likewise the opponents' counter-arguments against the thesis can function as pro-arguments for their own — mostly unarticulated — thesis, sub-theses, or pro-arguments respectively.

As far as the speech-act theoretical function of the arguments is concerned, the thesis constitutes an 'active illocution' while the pro- and counter-arguments constitute 'reactive illocutions'.[25] Our first task

---

[21] See Lausberg, *Handbuch der literarischen Rhetorik* (2nd. ed.; Munich: Hueber, 1973) 199f. [§ 371]; see also *Elemente*, 118f. [§ 370].

[22] Cf. further, e.g. Ch. Perelman/L. Olbrechts-Tyteca, *The New Rhetoric* (Notre Dame: Notre Dame University Press, 1969); S. Toulmin, *The Uses of Argument* (4th ed.; Cambridge: Cambridge University Press, 1974); A. Naess, *Kommunikation und Argumentation* (Scriptor 59; Kronberg/Ts.: Scriptor, 1975); D. Wunderlich, 'Pro und Kontra,' *LiLi* 10 (1980) 109–28; Ch. Perelman, *The Realm of Rhetoric* (Notre Dame: Notre Dame University Press, 1982); M. Kienpointner, 'Argument,' *Historisches Wörterbuch der Rhetorik 1* (ed. G. Ueding; Darmstadt: Wissenschaftliche Buchgesellschaft, 1992) 889–904.

[23] Wunderlich, 'Pro und Kontra,' 127.

[24] Cf. Naess, *Kommunikation*, 128–59; Kopperschmidt, 'Analysis', 162–65.

[25] See Raible, 'Argumentation als allokutionäre Sprechakte? Bemerkungen zur These von Michael Schecker,' *Theorie der Argumentation*, 143.

will be to work out the thesis and the arguments against and in favor of the thesis. This first step is of a semantic as well as a pragmatic nature.

2.3.2. Tools from Text-Linguistics[26]

One of the most important factors in connection with argumentative analyses is the observation that argumentation primarily occurs in dialogue form.[27] Thus our next step will be to analyze the dialogue structure in order to be able to recognize the development of the pro- and counter-argumentation.

In order to delimit the text into functional text-sequences or subtexts of different degrees, the following markers or signals on the surface level must be utilized in the hierarchical ranking given below:

(A) *Meta-communicative clauses (MCC)*: Such clauses function as signals for the beginning or end of an act of communication, that is, they make the linguistic communication situation the subject of a theme. These markers can be divided into two main groups, one with an encoding and the other with a decoding function. Each of these can thematize either oral or written acts of communication, for example, in Rom 6.1: τί οὖν ἐροῦμεν ... and 6.15: τί οὖν... . The importance of these meta-communicative clauses lies mainly in the fact that they serve as signals for changes between various levels of communication, that is for distinguishing between textinternal and textexternal communication levels and between various textinternal communication levels. Consequently they also signalize different dialogue phases and dialogue structures in a text.

(B) *Meta-argumentative clauses (MArC)*: Unlike the *MCC*, the *MArCs* do not function as indicators of the beginning and end of an act or acts of communication. Standing in a meta-relationship to the sentences they introduce, these *MArCs* serve as 'reminders' to the addressees. Examples from Romans 6 are: ἢ ἀγνοεῖτε ὅτι (v. 3) and οὐκ οἴδατε ὅτι (v. 16). The explicit *MArC*, however, can be replaced by other

---

[26] Concerning modern text-linguistics and ancient rhetoric, see especially H. Kalverkämper, 'Antike Rhetorik und Textlinguistik,' *Allgemeine Sprachwissenschaft. Sprachtypologie und Textlinguistik. FS P. Hartmann* (ed. M. Faust; Tübingen: Narr, 1983) 349–72.

[27] See Schecker, 'Argumentationen', 75–138, especially 96f., 104f.; in reaction to Schecker, see Raible, 'Argumentation', 139f., who refers to Aristotle's *Topica*, 101a (πρὸς δὲ τὰς ἐντεύξεις).

similar but indirect signals — so called substitutes (*MArCSub*), for example, by conditional clauses in the grammatical *modus realis* as is the case in 6.5 and 6.8.[28]

(C) *Meta-active clauses (MAC)*: *MACs* are, according to Paul-Ludwig Völzing, constituted by those sentences within an argumentation that question the validity of an action. Insofar as they dispute an action, they can be said to stand in a meta-relationship to that action.[29]

(D) *Meta-oppositional indicators (MOI)*: Johannes Schwitalla has observed how in opposing a thesis or a pro- or counter-argument an opponent frequently begins his or her argument with an expression indicating his or her opposition, 'die in einer Metarelation zu den Textteilen stehen, denen widersprochen wird, und zu denen, die die Korrektur enthalten'. Schwitalla calls such an expression a 'Widerspruchsindikator'. I prefer the designation 'meta-oppositional indicator' in order to bring out its meta-relationship over against what precedes and especially what follows. In Romans 6 we encounter two such *MOIs* of the same kind: μὴ γένοιτο (v. 2 and v. 15). Schwitalla has further pointed to the fact that *MOIs* often introduce a subsequent counter-argument: 'nach einem Widerspruchsindikator folgt die Korrektur dessen, was für falsch gehalten wird ...'.[30]

For the purpose of this essay the markers described above must suffice. These signals, which are recognizable on the surface level of the text, serve the purpose of allowing the recipients to recognize the textual macro-structure of the pro- and counter-argumentation within the dialogue between the proponent and his addressees or presupposed opponents.

2.3.3. Tools from Ancient Rhetoric[30a]

Argumentation is usually made up of a series of arguments and proofs.

---

[28] See F. Blaß, A. Debrunner, and F. Rehkopf, *Grammatik des neutestamentlichen Griechisch* (14th ed.; Göttingen: Vandenhoeck & Ruprecht, 1976) 302 [§ 372]; cf. also B. Frid, 'Römer 6, 4–5,' *BZ* 30 (1986) 194.

[29] See P.-L. Völzing, *Begründen*, 127.

[30] J. Schwitalla, 'Über Formen des argumentativen Widerspruchs,' *Theorie der Argumentation*, 40, 43.

[30a] See now W. F. Veit, 'Argumentation,' *Historisches Wörterbuch 1*, 904–14; E. Eggs, 'Argumentation,' *Historisches Wörterbuch 1*, 914–86; J. Klein, 'Beweis,' *Historisches Wörterbuch 1*, 1528–48.

These must be analyzed not only in view of their status as pro- or counter-arguments but above all in regard to the underlying communication situation and the types of proofs used by the author in his argumentation.

2.3.3.1. The Significance of the Communication Situation

In this connection it is imperative to realize that the most important characteristic of rhetorical argumentation is in fact the way in which the *communication situation* is put into focus.[31] The orator's most intense training was concerned with discovering how he could best convince and persuade the audience by optimally utilizing all the possible means that the rhetorical tradition put at his disposal.[32] It is the listener who is in focus. The conviction and persuasion is always a πιθανόν *for someone*.[33] However, if the listener is in focus in Aristotle's definition of rhetoric, it must also be emphasized — as Antje Hellwig correctly observes — that 'nicht irgendein Allgemeinwesen Mensch überzeugt werden (soll), sondern der in einer bestimmten Situation gegebene Hörer'.[34]

This thematization of the communication situation is reflected in many different ways in ancient rhetoric, not least in the distinction between various types of arguments and proofs, in the utilization of these types in the concrete act of argumentation, and in the choice of genre.

---

[31] Most urgent in rhetorical as well as in linguistic interpretations of texts is 'die explizite Rückbindung einer Argumentation an Sprechsituationen/ Dialogsituationen' as has been emphasized by Schecker, 'Argumentationen', 81 *et passim*; cf. also the apt remarks by C. J. Classen, 'Paulus und die antike Rhetorik,' *ZNW* 82 (1991) 7f.

[32] Arist., *Ars rhet.* 1.1. 1355b10–15; *Topica* 1.3.101b5–10. Cf. Lausberg, *Elemente*, 33 [§ 65]: 'Die Parteilichkeit (*utilitas causae*) der Rede sucht den Situationsmächtigen im Sinne der eigenen Parteimeinung und gegen die gegnerische Parteimeinung zu beeinflussen, damit der Situationsmächtige die Situation zum Vorteil der Partei des Redners ändere'.

[33] *Ars rhet.* 1.1. 1356b26: Ἐπεὶ γὰρ τὸ πιθανὸν τινὶ πιθανόν ἐστι κτλ; cf. also *Ars rhet.* 1358b1f.; 1.2. 1356a19; 1367b30; 1377b25; 1394a10. This aspect has lately been emphasized, and rightly so, by Wörner, '"Pistis" und der argumentierende Umgang mit reputablen Meinungen in der Rhetorik des Aristoteles,' *Argumente – Argumentation* (ed. J. Kopperschmidt and H. Schanze; Munich: Fink, 1985) 12; M. J. Lossau, Πρὸς Κρίσιν Τινὰ Πολιτικήν. *Untersuchungen zur aristotelischen Rhetorik* (Wiesbaden: Harrassowitz, 1981) 47ff.; Sprute, *Enthymemtheorie*, 77ff., 110ff., 133ff.

[34] A. Hellwig, *Untersuchungen zur Theorie der Rhetorik bei Platon und Aristoteles* (Hyp. 38; Göttingen: Vandenhoeck & Ruprecht, 1973) 47ff., especially 56f.; Aristotle, however, is ambiguous on this point.

2.3.3.1.1. The Distinction between Various Types of Rhetorical Arguments
The impact of the communication situation was first of all expressed in
an adherence to the dichotomic distinction between *theoretical* and *practical* argumentation noted above. In discussing the proofs in a rhetorical
argumentation, Aristotle differentiates between three types of arguments
or proofs of which the first two are of a pragmatic-practical, while the
third is of a theoretical nature: 'Now the proofs furnished by the speech
are of three kinds. The first depends upon the moral character of the
speaker (ἦθος), the second upon putting the hearer into a certain frame
of mind (πάθος), the third upon the speech itself (λόγος), in so far as it
proves (δεικνύναι) or seems to prove (φαίνεσθαι δεικνύναι).'[35] For the
sake of clarification it is important to emphasize already here (see below,
section 2.3.3.2.) that the *theoretical* (logical) argumentation can be either
epistemic or based on *reputable opinions*, while the *pragmatic-practical*
(non-logical) argumentation is *ethical* and/or *pathetic*. This means that
deductive and inductive arguments from ἔνδοξα are theoretical in nature; the pragmatic part here has mainly to do with the status of the
premises and the utilization and arrangements of the proofs.

Thus, arguments were of two main kinds divided into four sub-
types: (1) *theoretical* arguments consisting of (a) 'non-technical proofs
(πίστεις ἄτεχνοι; *probationes inartificiales*)', and (b) 'technical proofs
(πίστεις ἔντεχνοι; *probationes artificiales*)', the difference being that
the orator had only to make use of (χρήσασθαι) the former, while he
had to invent (εὑρεῖν) the latter;[36] (2) *practical* arguments consisting of
(c) 'ethical' proofs which presented the prepossessing character of the
rhetor, and finally (d) 'pathetic' proofs which created passions among
the judges, listeners or readers. (These can theoretically neither be true
nor false regardless of the status of the premises but as practical arguments pragmatically very effective!)

2.3.3.1.2. The Distinction between Epistemic and Rhetorical Proofs
The importance of the communication situation was brought out already in the distinction between *scientific or epistemic syllogisms* on the

---

[35] *Ars rhet.* 1.2.3. 1356a. See Wörner, 'Selbstrepräsentation im "Ethos des Redners",'
ZfS 3 (1984) 45; also '"Pistis"', 13f.; Lossau, Πρὸς Κρίσιν, 47–161.
[36] Arist., *Ars rhet.* 1.2.2. 1355b; Quint., *Inst. orat.* 5.1.1.

one hand and *dialectical* and *rhetorical syllogisms* on the other. The scientifically valid συλλογισμὸς ἀποδεικτικός[37] was based on true and primary (axiomatic) premises, while the συλλογισμὸς διαλεκτικός and the συλλογισμὸς ῥητορικός [= ἐνθύμημα] respectively[38] were based on generally accepted opinions,[39] which means that the truth of the conclusion is dependent upon the truth of the premises *as acknowledged by the interlocutors*; thus, the truth-value is limited exclusively to what is accepted by both partners, and does not bring the scientific or ontological truth-value into consideration. In fact, all rhetorical proofs depend upon ἔνδοξα.[40]

In the opening line of his *Ars rhetorica* Aristotle gives the much debated statement about the relationship between rhetoric and dialectic when he writes: ἡ ῥητορική ἐστιν ἀντίστροφος τῇ διαλεκτικῇ.[41] This definition in fact first indicates the analogy between the two methods: both accept reputable opinions (ἔνδοξα) as true premises in an inference. As *reputable opinions* Aristotle understands those opinions 'that commend themselves to all or to the majority or to the wise — this is, to all of the wise or the majority or to the most famous and distinguished of them'.[42] In this connection (and with regard to Paul's argumentation in Romans 6) it is essential to notice Aristotle's warning concerning contentious reasoning, when in his *Topica* 1.1. 100b he goes on to say that 'Reasoning is contentious if it is based on opinions

[37] *Topica* 1.1. 100a25-100b18; *Anal. post.* 1.2. 72a5. On the topic of *demonstrative syllogisms* cf. the commentary by Wörner, '*"Pistis"*', 10 who concludes that true and primary premises are axiomatic premises; cf. also K.-H. Göttert, *Einführung in die Rhetorik* (UTB 1599; Munich: Fink, 1991) 81–83.

[38] *Topica* 1.1.100a30; F. G. Sieveke, *Aristoteles Rhetorik* (UTB 159; Munich: Fink, 1980) 231f. n. 6.

[39] See Arist., *Topica* 1.1. 101b and *Ars rhet.* 1355a; further with regard to Aristotle, see Wörner, 'Enthymeme – ein Rückgriff auf Aristoteles in systematischer Absicht,' *Rhetorische Rechtstheorie* (ed. O. Ballweg and Th.-M. Seibert; Freiburg/Munich: Alber, 1982) 75–77; Wörner, '"Pistis"', 10ff.; M. Kraus, 'Enthymem,' *Historisches Wörterbuch der Rhetorik 2* (ed. G. Ueding: Darmstadt: Wissenschaftliche Buchgesellschaft, 1994) 1197–1222. More generally with regard to theory of argumentation, see D. Wunderlich, *Foundations of Linguistics* (CStL 22; Cambridge: Cambridge University Press, 1979) 43.

[40] See the ample discussion in Sprute, *Enthymemtheorie*, 74–114, especially 77ff. and 100ff.; P. Ptassek, 'Endoxa,' *Historisches Wörterbuch 2*, 1134–38.

[41] *Ars rhet.* 1.1. 1354a; see Hellwig, *Untersuchungen*, 43ff.; Lossau, Πρὸς Κρίσιν 15–20. Lossau, 'Dialektik,' *Historisches Wörterbuch 2*, 560–67.

[42] *Topica* 1.1. 100b; Raible, 'Argumentation', 141.

128

which appear to be generally accepted but are not really so, or if it merely appears to be based on opinions which are, or appear to be, generally accepted. For not every opinion which appears to be generally accepted is actually so accepted.'[43] It is clear from Aristotle's discussion in *Ars rhet.* 1.1. 1356a and in *Topica* 1.12. 105a10–19 that the affinity between dialectic and rhetoric is real also with regard to the parallelism between *syllogism* (συλλογισμός) and *induction* (ἐπαγωγή) in dialectic and *enthymeme* (ἐνθύμημα) and *example* (παράδειγμα) in rhetoric.[44]

One of the most important differences between dialectic and rhetoric, indicated by the term ἀντίστροφος, is the two additional pragmatic-practical proofs referred to above, namely, ἦθος and πάθος. Aristotle argues explicitly for the importance of the ἦθος-proof when he states that 'it is not the case, as some writers of rhetorical treatises lay down in their "Art", that the worth of the orator in no way contributes to his powers of persuasion; on the contrary moral character, so to say, constitutes the most effective means of proof'.[45] Thus, in conclusion Aristotle can state that 'since proofs are effected by these means, it is evident that, to be able to grasp them, a man must be capable of logical reasoning, of studying characters and the virtues, and thirdly the emotions. ... Thus it appears that Rhetoric is as it were an offshoot of Dialectic and of the science of Ethics, which may be reasonably called Politics'.[46]

Another decisive difference, also due to the relatedness to the audience, is the incorporation of *elocutio* (λέξις) and *dispositio* (τάξις) into the *partes artis* of rhetoric.[47]

2.3.3.1.3. The Distinction between the Three Genera Causarum

The significance of the communication situation is finally reflected in the interrelationship between the different types of audiences and the choice of rhetorical genre on the part of the orator. This is explicitly

---

[43] Cf. Sprute, *Enthymemtheorie*, 109ff.

[44] See the helpful discussion of the difference between παράδειγμα and ἐπαγωγή in Sprute, *Enthymemtheorie*, 80–88; cf. also Sieveke, *Aristotles*, 255; and Klaus, 'Induktion,' *Philosophisches Wörterbuch* (ed. G. Klaus, M. Buhr; 11th ed.; Leipzig: VEB Bibliographisches Institut, 1975) 565–67.

[45] *Ars rhet.* 1.2. 1356a; see the interpretation by Wörner, *Das Ethische*, 310.

[46] *Ars rhet.* 1.2.7. 1356a. The political character of Aristotle's rhetoric is emphasized most strongly by Lossau (Πρὸς Κρίσιν, *passim*, e.g. 12 and 18).

[47] Cf. Sieveke, *Aristoteles*, 227.

made clear in the thematization of the relationship between the communication situation and the three *genera causarum* in Aristotle's *Ars rhet.* 1.3.1–3. 1358b, where we read: 'The kinds of Rhetoric are three in number, *corresponding to the three kinds of hearers*. ... Therefore there are necessarily three kinds of rhetorical speeches, deliberative, forensic and epideictic. ...'[48]

These rhetorical text-genres[49] rarely appear in pure form — as is also the case with literary genres — but mostly mixed. It is most important, however, to discern the genre of the text as a whole,[50] which may have absorbed characteristics of other genres without changing the text-genre itself.[51]

It is significant that the forensic or judicial and the deliberative genres were argumentative (dominated by enthymemes and examples respectively), while the epideictic or demonstrative genre was much more esthetic in nature (dominated by amplification).[52]

With regard to the importance of the communication situation, it is imperative to realize — as we did above, when discussing the text-linguistic tools — that rhetorical argumentation occurs in *dialogue form* primarily in connection with the judicial and to some extent also the deliberative genres, while dialogue form is least pronounced in connection with the demonstrative genre.[53]

---

[48] See the semiotic deliberations in Arist., *Ars rhet.* 1.3.1. 1358a–b; cf. Lossau, Πρὸς Κρίσιν, 47, and the commentary on that passage by Lausberg, *Handbuch*, 51f. [§§ 53–61]. Kalverkämper, 'Antike Rhetorik,' 365.

[49] Cf. Arist., *Ars rhet.* 1.3.3–6. 1358b-1359a; Anaxim., *Ars rhet.* 1. 1421b. See further H. F. Plett, *Einführung in die rhetorische Textanalyse* (3rd ed., Hamburg: Buske, 1975) 15; H. Hommel, 'Griechische Rhetorik und Beredsamkeit,' *Neues Handbuch der Literatur-wissenschaft. Band 2: Griechische Literatur* (ed. E. Vogt; Wiesbaden: Athenaion, 1981) 367f.; R. Barthes, 'Die alte Rhetorik. Ein Abriβ,' *Rhetorik. Band 1: Rhetorik als Texttheorie* (ed. J. Kopperschmidt; Darmstadt: Wissenschaftliche Buchgesellschaft, 1990) 68.

[50] See Mitchell, *Paul and the Rhetoric of Reconciliation* (HUT 28; Tübingen: Mohr-Siebeck, 1991) 16.

[51] Cf., e.g. Lausberg, *Handbuch*, 132 [§ 243].

[52] Cf. Plett, *Einführung*, 16.

[53] Cf. Lausberg, *Handbuch*, 56 [§ 63]; with regard to dialectic, see Sprute, *Enthymemtheorie*, 53f.

2.3.3.2. The Distinction between Theoretical and Practical Types of Rhetorical Proofs

2.3.3.2.1. Theoretical – Logical Arguments[54]

When analyzing the argumentative structure of ancient texts the *inventio* of ancient rhetoric is, of course, an invaluable — although not always perfect — resource. This is due to the fact that ancient rhetoric was primarily directed towards the discovery of arguments with adherent proofs.[55] This was true of all genres, but especially of the *genus iudiciale*.

According to Aristotle, the basic types of argument in a rhetorical argumentation are *enthymemes* (ἐνθυμήματα) and *paradigms* (παραδείγματα), which means that theoretical arguments 'in fact uncover the most important field of possible rhetorical forms of argumentation'.[56] In spite of the importance Aristotle attached to the pragmatic arguments, the Aristotelian tradition still claimed the enthymemes to be 'the strongest of rhetorical proofs', since it is a kind of syllogism.[57]

As already stated, the theoretical argumentation can be carried out by means of *syllogistic-enthymemic* proofs or by means of *epagogic-inductive* proofs, mostly in the form of examples. In Aristotle's words: 'Now all orators produce belief by employing as proofs either examples or enthymemes and nothing else'.[58] According to the generally accepted opinion, the *enthymemes* are *incomplete* syllogisms in so far as either of the premises or the conclusion can be missing.[59] This definition of enthymeme is known to Aristotle[60] but, as Markus Wörner has shown, not really emphasized by him, since, according to Aristotle, that which is the *differentia specifica* distinguishing the enthymeme from the syllogism is its foundation on *probabilities* (εἰκότα) — that is, *the reputable*

---

[54] Arist., *Ars rhet.* 1.2.3. See Lossau, Πρὸς Κρίσιν, 51–114; Göttert, *Einführung*, 87–91; W. Klein, 'Argumentation', 17ff.

[55] Lausberg, *Handbuch*, 190–236 [§§ 348–430]; see also *Elemente*, 118–21 [§§ 370–76]; J. Martin, *Rhetorik*, 95–137; Plett, *Einführung*, 12f.; Classen, 'Paulus', 2f.

[56] *Ars rhet.* 1.2. 1356a–1356b and cf. Wörner, '"Pistis"', 15.

[57] *Ars rhet.* 1.1. 1355a; see Wörner, *Das Ethische*, 310; Kraus, 'Enthymem', 1202f.

[58] *Ars rhet.* 1.2. 1356b.

[59] Cf. Lausberg, *Elemente*, 119f. [§ 371]; L. Huth, 'Zur Rolle der Argumentation im Texttyp "Korrespondentenbericht",' *Theorie der Argumentation*, 378: 'Die sprachliche Form des *Argumentes* ist... nur in den seltensten Fällen das *Syllogismus*, sondern in der Regel das *Enthymem*'. Kraus, 'Enthymem', 1198f.

[60] Arist., *Ars rhet.* 1.2. 1357a; Sprute, *Enthymemtheorie*, 145.

opinions (ἔνδοξα).[61] The *paradeigmata* are constructed on the ground of a likeness in two steps: (a) as 'the result of induction (δι᾽ ἐπαγωγῆς) from one or more similar cases, and (b) when one assumes the general and then concludes (συλλογίσηται) the particular by an example'.[62]

As we have already seen, in contrast to epistemic syllogisms rhetorical syllogisms or enthymemes do not render scientifically established or absolutely true inferences but only inferences built on probabilities, due to the status of the premises as being true on the grounds of reputable opinions. If, however, the contending parties agree upon the premises, the conclusion follows by necessity as demonstrated above. The *paradeigmata* are inductive inferences that also emanate from premises and proceed to a conclusion, but here the inference is only valid with some degree of probability, since inferences by analogy miss the necessity of deductive inferences.[63]

With regard to the application of enthymemes and paradigms in the *syntagmatic structure* of actual argumentation, Wörner has correctly pointed to Aristotle's recommendation that it is appropriate, 'den Syllogismus ... *voranzustellen* und die zur Begründung verwendeten Beispiele gleichsam als Zeugen *nachzustellen*. In diesem Falle reicht oft ein Beispiel, wenn es zutreffend ist'.[64] This is confirmed by the structure of argumentative proofs in Romans 6 as will be demonstrated below.

2.3.3.2.1.1. Probationes Inartificiales

The 'non-technical proofs' (πίστεις ἄτεχνοι) existed and functioned without the help of the orator and his 'technique'. They consisted of precedents, laws and their inviolability, records, testimonies (especially by eyewitnesses; see Arist., *Ars rhet.* 1.2.2; Quint., *Inst. orat.* 5.1.2; Cicero, *de orat.* 2.116). Even though these proofs were not created by means of the rhetorician's technique but were found by him, it was his

---

61 Wörner, 'Enthymeme', *passim*, especially 76f.

62 *Ars rhet.* 2.25. 1402b; on this passage see especially Sprute, *Enthymemtheorie*, 86.

63 See Menne, *Einführung in die Methodologie* (Darmstadt: Wissenschaftliche Buchgesellschaft, 1980) 112–14; Wörner, 'Enthymeme', 88f.; Sprute, *Enthymemtheorie*, 80–88.

64 Wörner, 'Enthymeme', 88 (italics mine). See Arist., *Ars rhet.* 2.20.9 1394a.

duty to utilize them to the best of his ability.[65] Thus, the orator only had to make use of (χρήσασθαι) 'the non-technical proofs', whereas he had to invent (εὑρεῖν) the 'technical proofs'.[66]

This kind of proofs possessed the highest degree of credibility[67] and the method used was that of the *interrogatio*:[68] laws, documents, and witnesses were questioned!

2.3.3.2.1.2. Probationes Artificiales[69]

The 'artificial proofs' (πίστεις ἔντεχνοι) on the other hand had to be found — that is, they had to be worked out by the orator by different methods.[70] Three classes of artificial proofs were acknowledged: (a) *signa* (σημεῖα/τεκμήρια), (b) *argumenta* (συλλογισμοί/ἐνθυμήματα), and (c) *exempla* (παραδείγματα).[71]

(a) A *signum* is an external sign that can be perceived by our senses and that usually accompanies other facts (*causae*) and does so in such a way that an inference from the sign can be drawn with regard to these other facts.[72] As Lausberg has also pointed out, *signa* are most closely related to the *probationes inartificiales*, since they are not worked out by the rhetor but are given by the circumstances themselves. On the other hand *signa* differ from the inartificial proofs in so far as these 'sich sprachlich-explizit auf den im Prozeß zu behandelnden Sachverhalt beziehen, während die *signa* von sich aus nicht auf den im Prozeß zu behandelnden Sachverhalt zielen, sondern erst durch einen Erkenntnisvorgang mit dem Sachverhalt in Beziehung gesetzt werden'.[73]

---

[65] Cf. Lausberg, *Handbuch*, 191–93 [§§ 351–54]; Martin, *Rhetorik*, 96, 97–101; Sieveke, *Aristoteles*, 231f. n. 8.

[66] See Lausberg, *Handbuch*, 191 [§ 352].

[67] Cf. Lausberg, *Handbuch*, 192 [§ 354]; Martin, *Rhetorik*, 96.

[68] See especially Quint., *Inst. orat.* 5.7.8–37.

[69] Cf. Lausberg, *Handbuch*, 193–235 [§§ 355–426]; Martin, *Rhetorik*, 96, 101–19; Sieveke, *Aristoteles*, 231 n. 8.

[70] Lausberg, *Handbuch*, 193 [§ 355].

[71] Quint., *Inst. orat.* 5.9.1: *omnis igitur probatio artificialis constat aut signis aut argumentis aut exemplis.* However, see Lausberg, *Handbuch*, 194 [§ 357]: 'Manche Theoretiker rechnen die *signa* zu den *argumenta* (Quint., V.9.1: *nec ignoro plerisque videri signa partem argumentorum* ...), so daß nur zwei Klassen unterschieden werden: *argumenta* und *exempla*.'

[72] Lausberg, *Handbuch*, 195 [§ 358]; Anaxim., *Ars rhet.* 7.4. 1428a; 9.1. 1430a. Cf. especially Sprute, *Enthymemtheorie*, 88–109.

[73] Lausberg, *Handbuch*, 195 [§ 359].

Quintilian — as the Greeks before him — differentiated between *signa necessaria*, which the Greeks named τεκμήρια or ἄλυτα σημεῖα and which were conclusive, and *signa non necessaria*, which the Greeks called σημεῖα εἰκότα and which were inconclusive signs.[74] The method by which the rhetor puts the sign in relationship to the facts is — as in the case of *argumenta* — the inference by means of a rhetorical syllogism or enthymeme.[75]

(b) An *argumentum* is a proof that is developed from the case itself by means of logical inference on the part of the rhetor. The basis for the arguments, as we have seen, lies in statements that for the partners involved are indubitably true. In specifying Aristotle's *reputable opinions* Quintilian insists that there are seven different statements of such a degree of certainty that they can serve as a basis for an argument. Of these, two are of special interest to us in view of the arguments used by Paul in Romans 6: 'we may regard as certainties ... the things which are admitted by either party ... finally all that which is not disputed by our adversary' (*pro certis autem habemus ... si quid inter utramque partem convenit ... denique cuicumque adversarius non contradicit* [*Inst. orat.* 5.10.12f.; cf. 5.18.8]). The enthymeme is the method used to adduce proof for the argument from the case itself.

(c) The example (*paradeigma*) has its origin outside of the case. In the words of Heinrich Lausberg: 'Der Redner findet das *exemplum* ja vor wie einen unkünstlichen Beweis. Während aber die unkünstlichen Beweise von sich aus mit der Tat in Beziehung stehen und auf sie hinweisen, ist das *exemplum* von sich aus von der in der *causa* behandelten Tat völlig unabhängig. Die Inbezugsetzung des *exemplum* zur *causa* ist freie Schöpfung des Redners, der sich hierfür einer bestimmten Methode bedienen muß.'[76]

The *inductio* is the method used in connection with *paradeigmata*, as was demonstrated above. With regard to the *inductio* it is essential to draw attention to the fact that the basis for inductive reasoning lies in 'ein außerhalb der *causa* stehender *unbezweifelter* Sachverhalt. Von dieser

---

[74] Quint. *Inst. orat.* 5.9.3–16; cf. Arist., *Ars rhet.* 1.2.16–18 1357b.
[75] See Martin, *Rhetorik*, 106.
[76] Lausberg, *Handbuch*, 228 [§ 411].

Basis aus wird zur *causa* (die ein *dubium* ist) hin eine Beziehung herge-
stellt, die in der *Ähnlichkeit* besteht'.[77]
  In ancient as well as in modern argumentative texts argumentation
by means of formally complete syllogisms are rare. In most cases the
adversaries content themselves with different kinds of reduction (enthymemes) because they can presuppose premises left out to be known
or a conclusion not explicitly drawn to be self-evident.[78] The enthymemic
forms of the arguments must therefore be transformed into their underlying syllogistic structures.[79]

2.3.3.2.2. Practical — Nonlogical arguments[80]

In rhetorical handbooks from antiquity the *adhortatio* or παραίνεσις played
a subordinate role. However its presence cannot be denied since (Pseudo-)
Isocrates uses admonitions in his 'To Demonicus'[81] and Quintilian mentions rhetoricians who utilize exhortations in their systems.[82] In addition to
statements and questions, imperative formulations in rhetorical argumentation are also found in Aristotle's *Ars rhetorica*.[83] Furthermore, the *adhortatio*
is to be found above all in the figure called ἀποστροφή.[84]

---

[77] Lausberg, *Handbuch*, 230 [§ 419].

[78] See, e.g. Sprute, *Enthymemtheorie*, 131f; Kraus, 'Enthymem', 1199f.

[79] See E. U. Große, 'Von der Satzgrammatik zum Erzähltextmodell. Linguistische
Grundlagen und Defizienzen bei Greimas und Bremond,' *Text vs Sentence. Second Part*
(ed. J. S. Petöfi; PT 20.2; Hamburg: Buske, 1979) 613 n. 19: '… die Argumentation
(geschieht) fast immer in enthymematischen Formen. Die zugrundeliegenden Syllogismen
müssen daher rekonstruiert werden'.

[80] See especially Lossau, Πρὸς Κρίσιν, 115–61; Göttert, *Einführung*, 85–87; further
Wörner, '"Pathos" als Überzeugungsmittel in der Rhetorik des Aristoteles,' *Pathos, Affekt,
Gefühl* (ed. I. Craemer-Ruegenberg; Freiburg/Munich: Alber, 1981) 53–78; 'Selbst-
repräsentation', 43–64; 'Enthymeme', 73–98; *Das Ethische*, especially 310–34. Sprute,
Enthymemtheoric, see index, s.v. 'Charakterdarstellung'; F. H. Robling, 'Ethos. A. Der
Begriff', *Historisches Wörterbuch 2*, 1516-17; W. Fortenbaugh, 'Ethos. B.I. Antike',
Historisches Wörterbuch 2, 1517-25.

[81] Isocr., *Demon*. 9–11; cf. A.J. Malherbe, *Moral Exhortation. A Greco-Roman Sourcebook*
(LEC; Philadelphia: Westminster, 1986) 125f.; also *Paul and the Thessalonians* (Philadelphia:
Fortress, 1987) 70ff.; also, 'Hellenistic Moralists and the New Testament,' ANRW II.26.1
(ed. W. Haase and H. Temporini; Berlin: de Gruyter, 1992) 267–333, especially 281ff.

[82] Quint. *Inst. orat.* 3.6.47: '*Quattuor fecit Athenaeus* προτρεπτικὴν *στάσιν vel*
παρορμητικὴν *id est exhortativum* …' and cf. 9.2.11ff.

[83] *Ars rhet.* 2.23.11 1398b — 2.23.12ff. 1399a. Cf. Wörner, 'Enthymeme', 79.

[84] Plett, *Einführung*, 66; M. Vallozza, 'Adhortatio,' *Historisches Wörterbuch 1*, 100–04.

Most important of all in this connection, however, is the so called *ethos*-argument. In his treatment of various types of arguments Aristotle declares that 'proofs are established not only by demonstrative, but also by *ethical* argument — since we have confidence in an orator who exhibits certain qualities, such as goodness, goodwill or both.'[85] He concluded earlier that 'the orator persuades by moral character (ἦθος τοῦ λέγοντος) when his speech is delivered in such a manner as *to render him worthy of confidence*.[86] In fact the moral character (as we have seen) 'constitutes the most effective means of proof'.

It is important, however, to avoid the misunderstanding that the moral character primarily or exclusively referred to certain preconceived notions about the orator. This kind of misunderstanding is explicitly rejected by Aristotle himself when he claims that 'this confidence must be due to the speech itself (διὰ τὸν λόγον), not to any preconceived idea (διὰ τὸ προδε-δοξάσθαι) concerning the speaker's character'.[87] This, however, means that this kind of pragmatic-practical argument is on the one hand due to *virtuousness* (ἐπιείκεια) on the part of the orator and thus constitutes a non-technical proof, on the other 'aus einer *rednerischen* Aktivität hervorgebracht wird' and thus constitutes a piece of τέχνη — that is, an artificial or technical proof (but even as such it does not function as a theoretical proof!).[88]

Thus, as far as the ethical part of the practical means of persuasion is concerned there are, according to Aristotle, two aspects to be taken into consideration: (1) the moral character of the orator, which in turn is substantiated by (2) the speech itself.[89]

---

[85] *Ars rhet.* 1.8.6. 1366a. Quint. *Inst. orat.* 1. Prooemium 9; 2.15.1; 2.15.34; 12.1.1; 12.11.9; see also Kalverkämper, 'Antike Rhetorik', 366.

[86] *Ars rhet.* 1.2.4. 1356a; 3.17.11–12 1418a-b. See also Wörner, 'Selbstrepräsentation', 47 n. 8: 'Anaximenes bezeichnet die δόξα τοῦ λέγοντος als πίστις ἐπίθετος im Gegensatz zu den in den Kapiteln 7–14 behandelten πίστεις ἔντεχνοι. Mit der δόξα τοῦ λέγοντος meint er in etwa dasselbe wie Aristoteles mit ἦθος τοῦ λέγοντος (vgl. 1430a28; 1438b35; 1441b21; 1445b34; 1446a14)'.

[87] *Ars rhet.* 1.2.4. 1356a; see Wörner, *Das Ethische*, 327ff. especially 330.

[88] Wörner, 'Selbstrepräsentation', 47, and the previous note.

[89] Cf. Sieveke, *Aristoteles*, 232 n. 9: 'Die Einbindung von ἦθος wie auch von πάθος in den Komplex der πίστεις (Überzeugungsmittel), also in den Komplex der rhetorischen Argumentation, besagt, daß der Redner habituell durch seine Sprechweise so erscheinen muß, seine Worte so wählen muß, daß er Glauben erlangt (*ut probemus vera esse, quae defendimus*, Cicero, *de orat.* II 27.115). Um der Glaubwürdigkeit willen müssen Worte und Wesen des Redners in Einklang stehen (vgl. auch *Rhet.* II 1.3 hierzu)'.

From the point of view of philosophy of language texts can be analyzed with regard to their theoretical or practical status. The theoretical status of argumentative texts is expressed by their descriptive, informative, or logical function; the practical status is expressed by ancient rhetoricians in the labeling of the bias as *utilitas causae*.[90] This usage of language as a means of acting applies as far as the rhetoricians are concerned also with regard to descriptive narrative material: 'Die *narratio* ist selbst eine *probatio* in Erzählform, die *probatio* selbst eine nachträgliche Bekräftigung der *narratio* mit besonderer Betonung der Partei-*utilitas*'.[91]

In this connection it is important to realize that a text-sequence, a literary form, and even a single sentence within a text does not have a function of its own but only within the framework of a given structure of action or argumentation. This phenomenon has been emphasized lately among others by Margaret Mitchell, when she points to the necessity of a holistic interpretation of literary forms and argumentative proofs and their function within the framework of a rhetorical genre: 'The rhetorical genre and function of each part is determined by the compositional whole and cannot be correctly determined apart from it.'[92]

This means that the interpretation of the status and function of a paraenetical sequence is dependent on the overall structure and function of the entire text or sub-text of which the paraenetical sequence is a part.

Even if paraenesis did not play a major role in ancient rhetoric, it played a considerable role in popular philosophy. This has been shown with regard to Seneca by Hildegard Cancik in her investigation of Seneca's *Epistulae morales*. Of primary importance for our purpose is Cancik's observation of how paraenesis can function as an argument, when she distinguishes between two forms of argumentation: the theoretical-doxographical and the practical-paraenetical. Linguistically important is Dr Cancik's comparison of these forms of argumentation with the analytical-philosophical distinction between descriptive and prescriptive lan-

---

[90] Quint., *Inst. orat.* 4.3.14 and 5.11.16. For further discussion of theoretical and practical functions of language in modern linguistics and philosophy of language, see Hellholm, *Visionenbuch*, 52–58.

[91] Lausberg, *Handbuch*, 190 [§ 348].

[92] Mitchell, *Paul*, 16 *et passim*; cf. in linguistics already E. U. Große, *Text und Kommunikation* (Stuttgart: Kohlhammer, 1976) 26 and Raible, 'Zum Textbegriff und zur Textlinguistik,' *Text vs Sentence, First Part* (ed. J. S. Petöfi; PT 2.1; Hamburg: Buske, 1979) 67 and 69.

guage: 'Unter diesem Aspekt kann die Theorie (Doxographie) als deskriptive, die Paränese als präskriptive Sprache charakterisiert werden'.[93] Seneca's argumentation is according to Cancik 'eine mit rationalen und emotiven Mitteln arbeitende Methode zur Einübung sittlichen Verhaltens'.[94] Thus, the rational as well as the emotive arguments stand in the service of paraenesis! In view of our deliberations above the following statement of Dr Cancik is of importance: 'die Funktion des Exemplum als eines Elementes des präskriptiven Argumentierens läßt sich durch Aufbauanalysen paränetischer Partien bestimmen'.[95]

In addition Abraham Malherbe has drawn attention to the fact that 'Seneca's letters also contain many references to his own circumstances and conduct' and has furthermore pointed out that 'their ability to convince proceeds from the authoritative person of Seneca the teacher, who is conscious of the truth of what he writes'.[95a]

3. Paul's Argumentation in Romans 6

3.1. Analysis of Paul's Argumentation in Romans 6

3.1.1. Overview of the Dialogue-Structure and the Structure of Argumentation

1ST DIALOGUE PHASE (6.1–14)	2ND DIALOGUE PHASE (6.15–23)
CA¹ Meta-active argument (6.1)	CA² Meta-active argument (6.15)
PA¹ *Testimonium* (6.2)	PA⁵ *Exemplum/similitudo* (6.16)
PA² *Signum/testimonium* (6.3)	PA⁵ⁱⁿᶠ Inductive inference (6.17–18)
PA²ⁱⁿᶠ Deductive inference (6.4)	
PA³ᵃ *Argumentum* (6.5)	
PA³ᵃ:ⁱⁿᶠ Deductive inference (6.6–7)	
PA³ᵇ *Argumentum* (6.8)	
PA³ᵇ:ⁱⁿᶠ Deductive inference (6.9–11)	
PA⁴ *Paraenetic argument* (6.12–13)	PA⁶ *Paraenetic argument* (6.19b–22)
Affirmatio (6.14)	*Affirmatio* (6.23)

---

[93] H. Cancik, *Untersuchungen zu Senecas epistulae morales* (Spud. 18; Hildesheim: Olms, 1967) 16.

[94] Cancik, *Untersuchungen*, 15.

[95] Cancik, *Untersuchungen*, 25.

[95a] Malherbe, 'Hellenistic Moralists', 285 and further 285ff. with references to, e.g., Seneca, *ep.* 11.9; 13.15; 52.8 and Pliny, *ep.* 8.24.1.

3.1.2. Textanalysis

I shall now analyze the dialogue-structure and the structure of the arguments in detail in order to substantiate my understanding of how Paul argues in this text.

3.1.2.1. The Thesis as Stated in the Preceding Section

As mentioned earlier, in argumentation analyses one must first establish the thesis of the proponent. Only then is it meaningful to relate the pro- and counter-arguments of the disputing parties to each other.

The essential thesis that Paul is advocating in Romans is Justification by faith. This thesis is formulated both negatively and positively throughout the letter. Positively it is first and foremost encountered in the *propositio* (1.16–17).[95b] This positive formulation is repeated in 3.21f. and at the beginning of chap. 5.[96] The negative formulation of the thesis is found in 4.15b and in 5.12ff. Formulated negatively as well as positively we encounter the thesis in 10.4: 'For Christ is the end of the law, that every one who has faith may be justified.' This is true also of Romans 9–11 in general.[96a]

The section 5.20–21 forms the immediate thematic presupposition for Paul's argumentation in Romans 6, and it does so in a double way: Negatively it is stated in the formulation, 'The Law came in to increase the trespass'. Positively it is stated in the formulation, 'but where (οὖ δὲ ...)[97] sin increased, grace abounded all the more' (v. 20). As a presupposition for the

---

[95b] For a rhetorical outline of Romans, see Hellholm, 'Amplificatio in the Macro-Structure of Romans,' *Rhetoric and the New Testament.* Essays from the 1992 Heidelberg Conference (ed. S. E. Porter and T. H. Olbricht; JSNTS 90; Sheffield: JSOT Press, 1993) 123–51.

[96] See Conzelmann, 'Die Rechtfertigungslehre des Paulus: Theologie oder Anthropologie,' *Theologie als Schriftauslegung* (BEvT 65; Munich: Kaiser, 1974) 199: 'Der ganze Abschnitt Röm 5–8 erweist sich als ein Kommentar zum Credo unter dem Gesichtspunkt der Rechtfertigung durch Glauben ... Obwohl zwischen dem Anfang von Röm 5 und dem Schluß von Röm 8 die Begriffe der Rechtfertigung zurücktreten, trägt Paulus hier keine andere Erlösungslehre vor als vorher und nachher. Denn dieser Abschnitt ist nicht von der umgebenden Klammer zu lösen'; also *Grundriß der Theologie des Neuen Testaments* (EEvT 2; Munich: Kaiser, 1967) 263; N. Gäumann, *Taufe und Ethik. Studien zu Römer 6* (BEvT 47; Munich: Kaiser, 1967) 158ff.

[96a] See E. Brandenburger, 'Paulinische Schriftauslegung in der Kontroverse um das Verheißungswort Gottes,' *ZTK* 82 (1985) 34; W. Schmithals, *Der Römerbrief* (Gütersloh: Gerd Mohn 1988) 324f.

[97] Not ὅτι δὲ ... as Paul's opponents evidently misinterpreted his statement, see H. Schlier, *Der Römerbrief* (HTKNT 6; Freiburg: Herder, 1975) 191.

argumentation in chap. 6 this thesis is the last part of the sub-text 5.12–21 which constitutes the second proof in chap. 5 of the presence of the ζωή.[98]

As in the first sub-section of this part of chap. 5 (vv. 12–14) the thesis in v. 18 is followed by a sub-thesis (vv. 20–21) in which Paul brings in the law and its function in the dialectic between Adam and Christ on the one hand, and sin and grace on the other. Once again Paul brings in the problem that has played such an essential part in the letter up to this point — the law and its role. In view of the communication situation (to be discussed below in section 3.1.2.3.1.1) this is not accidental; on the contrary, it is altogether necessary.[99]

Finally, in the latter part of chap. 5 Paul deals with the situation of mankind as such. This is true with respect to the negative consequences of Adam's fall as well as with respect to the positive consequences of God's grace in Christ. In the first and third sub-texts (vv. 12–14 and vv. 18–21) Paul sets these consequences in relation to the Jewish law, which obtains an increasingly stronger negative profile. Here in v. 20 the law, contrary to v. 13, has not merely a recording function but also a provocative one.[100] It is essential to notice that within its own context this sub-section (i.e. vv. 18–21) functions as a *sub-thesis*; in its relation to chap. 6 it functions as the *thesis* for Paul's further argumentation.

How important the correct determination of the thesis is for a proper understanding of the course of argumentation in Romans 6, can be seen from Erich Dinkler's erroneous characterization of v. 2 as Paul's 'main thesis' in this chapter.[101] Here a pro-argument is mistaken for the thesis of the Apostle. The reason for this misinterpretation is obvious

---

[98] R. Bultmann, 'Adam und Christus nach Römer 5,' *Exegetica* (Tübingen: Mohr-Siebeck, 1967) 431. H. Hübner, *Biblische Theologie des Neuen Testaments, Band 2: Die Theologie des Paulus* (Göttingen: Vandenhoeck & Ruprecht, 1993) 244ff.

[99] Cf. Bultmann, 'Römer 5', 439: 'Wenn Paulus in V. 20f wieder auf den νόμος zu sprechen kommt, der schon V. 13f als eine zwischen Adam und Christus stehende Größe genannt worden war, so mag das Motiv zunächst ein apologetisches bzw. polemisches sein gegenüber der jüdischen Behauptung, daß das Leben durch das Gesetz vermittelt wird.'

[100] Cf., e.g., Schlier, *Römerbrief,* 176f.; O. Michel, *Der Brief an die Römer* (MeyerK 4; 5th ed.; Göttingen: Vandenhoeck & Ruprecht, 1978) 192. W. Bindemann, *Theologie im Dialog.* Ein traditionsgeschichtlicher Kommentar zu Römer 1–11 (Leipzig: Evangelische Verlagsanstalt, 1992) 188.

[101] E. Dinkler, 'Die Taufaussagen des Neuen Testaments,' *Zu Karl Barths Lehre von der Taufe* (ed. F. Viering; Gütersloh: Gerd Mohn, 1971) 71.

— the text of Romans 6 is interpreted in isolation from the rest of the letter as the dogmatic teaching of Paul concerning baptism.[102] No attention is paid to the argumentative character of this text-sequence within the framework of Paul's argumentation in Romans as a whole.[103]

3.1.2.2. The Dialogue-Structure of the Line of Reasoning

As I have indicated above, argumentation is in most cases carried out in dialogue form. The most striking feature in the composition of Romans 6 is its dialogue structure, which is indicated by means of meta-communicative, meta-active and meta-argumentative clauses as well as by meta-oppositional indicators. A survey of these meta-linguistic indicators shows the following picture of the dialogical structure of this chapter:

V.1: τί οὖν ἐροῦμεν;   MCC   V.15: τί οὖν;
    ἐπιμένωμεν τῇ ἁμαρτίᾳ   MAC/ ἁμαρτήσωμεν, ὅτι οὐκ ἐσμὲν
    ἵνα ἡ χάρις πλεονάσῃ;   (CA)   ὑπὸ νόμον ἀλλὰ ὑπὸ χάριν;
V.2: μὴ γένοιτο·   MOI   μὴ γένοιτο·
    οἵτινες ἀπεθάνομεν τῇ   (PA¹)
    ἁμαρτίᾳ πῶς ἔτι ζή-
    σωμεν ἐν αὐτῇ;
V.3: ἢ ἀγνοεῖτε ὅτι ...   MArC V.16: οὐκ οἴδατε ὅτι ...

The last rhetorical question in both dialogue phases introduce pro-arguments referring to common, well-known and accepted realities for all parties involved — in v. 3 to baptism, in v. 16 to slavery!

[102] The important question asked by R. Schnackenburg in his article 'Die Adam-Christus-Typologie (Röm 5, 12–21) als Voraussetzung für das Taufverständnis in Röm 6, 1–14,' *Battesimo e giustizia in Rom 6 e 8* (ed. L. De Lorenzi; SMB. Sb-e2; Rome: Abbazia S. Paolo, 1974) 37: 'Tritt sie (sc. baptism) für sein theologisches Denken hier in den Vordergrund, oder ist sie nur ein Motiv seiner Argumentation, die im übrigen ganz den Konsequenzen seiner Rechtfertigungs-und Erlösungslehre gewidmet ist?' is unfortunately answered only from the perspective of semantics while the pragmatic-argumentative setting is ignored. This leads Schnackenburg to give a positive answer only to the first alternative. Regarding the importance of the pragmatic aspect in connection with production of texts, see D. Breuer, 'Vorüberlegungen zu einer pragmatischen Textanalyse,' *Rhetoric. Band 1: Rhetorik als Texttheorie*, 95f.

[103] Correctly, however, N. A. Dahl, 'The Missionary Theology in the Epistle to the Romans,' *Studies in Paul* (Minneapolis: Augsburg, 1977) 83f.; further Gäumann, *Taufe*, 49 and 107; so already E. Lohse, 'Taufe und Rechtfertigung bei Paulus,' *KD* 11 (1965) 320; R. Tannehill, *Dying and Rising with Christ* (BZNW 32; Berlin: Töpelmann, 1967) 7f. and lately W. Schmithals, *Römerbrief*, 182.

As the rhetorical question in v. 1 connects with 5.20f. (ἁμαρτία vs. χάρις), so the corresponding question in v. 15 connects to v. 14 (ὑπὸ νόμον vs. ὑπὸ χάριν).

Both dialogue phases begin with *counter-arguments* in the formulation of the proponent followed by several *pro-arguments* of a rhetorical-theological as well as a practical-ethical nature. This dialogue-structure shows without doubt that the drawing line goes between v. 14 and v. 15 and not between v. 11 and v. 12 as is often argued.[104] The erroneous delimitation of chap. 6 is due to the misunderstanding that Paul here is introducing the doctrine of baptism or a new understanding of baptism instead of realizing that he is arguing his case, in which the practice and the doctrine of baptism function as part of the argumentation, that is, as proofs in the line of pro-arguments developed by Paul in the two dialogue phases of this chapter.

3.1.2.3. The Argumentative Structure of the Two Dialogue Phases

3.1.2.3.1. The Line of Argumentation in the First Dialogue Phase

3.1.2.3.1.1. The Counter-argumentation of the Adversaries
The counter-argumentation in the *first dialogue phase* is carried out by means of a *MCC* (τί οὖν ἐροῦμεν;) introducing, in the form of a citation formula, the CA[1], which in turn is constituted by a meta-active clause (*MAC*: ἐπιμένωμεν τῇ ἁμαρτίᾳ, ἵνα ἡ χάρις πλεονάσῃ;).

The CA is given in the formulation of the proponent regardless of how one wants to interpret the diatribe style of the counter-argument: (1) Questions formulated in diatribe style can be understood as plain rhetorical questions[105] within a *subiectio*, that is, as 'ein in die Rede hineingenommener *fingierter (also monologischer) Dialog* mit Frage und Antwort (meist mit mehreren Fragen und Antworten)':[106] (a) in a rhet-

---

[104] E.g. E. Käsemann, *An die Römer* (HNT 8a; 3rd ed.; Tübingen: Mohr-Siebeck, 1974) *ad loc.*, and J. D. G. Dunn, *Romans 1–8* (WBC 38A; Dallas: Word Books, 1988) *ad loc.* J. A. Fitzmyer, *Romans* (Anc B 33; New York: Doubleday 1993) 431f., 444.

[105] Cf. Schwitalla, 'Textliche und kommunikative Funktionen rhetorischer Fragen,' *ZGL* 12 (1984) 133 n. 2: 'Natürlich können auch Antworten auf rhetorische Fragen gegeben werden, die die in der rhetorischen Frage emphatisch negativ ausgedrückte Proposition explizieren.'

[106] Lausberg, *Handbuch*, 381 [§ 771] (italics mine); Plett, *Einführung*, 64; S. K. Stowers, 'Diatribe,' *Historisches Wörterbuch 2*, 627–33.

orical *subiectio* the (fictitious?) interlocutor in most cases is the opponent; (b) in other instances the orator may fictitiously pose the question to himself or have the questions posed to him; (c) in still other cases the question can be replaced by a quotation ascribed to the opponent.[107] (2) There is, however, nothing in a *subiectio* interpretation of a dialogue that in itself compels the interpreter or the reader to conceive of the *opponent(s)* or the *substance of the question(s)* as being fictitious; what is by necessity fictitious is only the dialogue, since the proponent has to formulate the question of the opponent(s) within the *fictitious dialogue*. Thus, neither the opponent(s) as interlocutors nor the questions posed need be fictitious, but are, at least in the *genus iudiciale*, in most cases very real.[107a]

The CA is further given in the formulation of the proponent regardless of whether one interprets the subjunctive ἐπιμένωμεν in the metaactive clause as *hortative* ('let us remain in sin …!') or as *deliberative* ('should we remain in sin… ?').

The main problem in securing the position behind the CA is further complicated by the fact that the modern interpreter of the counterarguments and of Paul's pro-argumentation for his thesis has to take his/her departure from one and the same *semantic* standpoint, namely, libertinism, which may *pragmatically* be ascribed either to Paul's adversaries or to their view of him and his theology:

[1]   the opponents *assert* a libertine view[108] — a position Paul rejects;

[2]   the opponents *accuse Paul* of libertinism[109] — an accusation Paul rejects.

---

[107]   See Lausberg, *Handbuch*, 381f. [§§ 771–74].

[107a]   Cf. Bultmann, *Der Stil der paulinischen Predigt und die kynisch-stoische Diatribe* (FRLANT 13; Göttingen: Vandenhoeck & Ruprecht, 1910; new printing ed. H. Hübner 1984) 12: 'Manchmal ist der Gegner nicht ein Vertreter der communis opinio, sondern er vertritt die bestimmte Anschauung einer *gegnerischen Philosophenschule*, etwa der Epikuräer oder des Skeptiker'; further Brandenburger, 'Schriftauslegung', 3f.

[108]   So W. Lütgert, *Der Römerbrief als historisches Problem* (BFCT 17.2; Gütersloh: Bertelsmann, 1913) 72ff., 111; Cranfield, *The Epistle to the Romans* (ICC; Edinburgh: Clark, 1977) 297 n. 1; similarly Gäumann, *Taufe*, 69 n. 7; P. Tachau, *'Einst' und 'Jetzt' im Neuen Testament* (FRLANT 105; Göttingen: Vandenhoeck & Ruprecht, 1971) 122; W. S. Campbell, 'Romans III as a Key to the Structure and Thought of the Letter,' *Romans Debate* (ed. Donfried) 261f.

[109]   So Käsemann, *Römer* 157: 'Doch ist Pls nach 3, 5ff. tatsächlich der Verführung zum Libertinismus beschuldigt worden, so daß man eher mit Verteidigung gegenüber einer Missdeutung der Rechtfertigungslehre zu rechnen hat'; Schlier, *Römerbrief*, 190; U. Wilckens, *Der Brief an die Römer* (EKK 6.2; Zürich/Neukirchen-Vluyn: Benziger/Neukirchener Verlag,

Here the interpreter is faced with the problem of reconstructing pragmatic presuppositions.[110] In the original communication situation this was less of a problem, since sender, addressees and adversaries in most cases knew (or at least thought they knew) each other's positions. When establishing the presuppositions the modern interpreter has methodically to take *textinternal* indications as well as *textexternal* information into account.[111]

From *textinternal* evidence it is obvious that the second option is the only possible one; this is clear from Paul's quotation in 3.8 of the adversaries' blasphemic accusation (καθὼς βλασφημούμεθα) of his alleged libertine statement: 'let us do evil that good may come (ποιήσωμεν τὰ κακά, ἵνα ἔλθῃ τὰ ἀγαθά)'.[112] This accusation is denied by Paul even with an oath (3.8b).

The *textexternal* considerations[113] point in the same direction, namely of

1980) 8f.; Conzelmann, *Grundriß*, 313; Schmithals, *Römerbrief,* 110; P. Lampe, *Die stadtrömischen Christen in den ersten beiden Jahrhunderten* (WUNT 18; 2nd ed.; Tübingen: Mohr-Siebeck, 1989) 55; Bindemann, *Theologie*, 188; Hübner, *Biblische Theologie 2*, 240 especially the list of Paul's quotations in Romans with the conclusion: 'Diese Fragen zeigen, wogegen sich Paulus verteidigen mußte: Wenn du das Gesetz beseitigst, öffnest du der Gesetzlosigkeit, also der Unmoral und Gottlosigkeit Tür und Tor'.

[110] Cf. H. Koester, *Introduction to the New Testament, II: History and Literature of Early Christianity* (dGL; Berlin/Philadelphia: de Gruyter/Fortress, 1982) 116f.: 'Therefore, the question of the identification of Paul's opponents is one of the most difficult questions of New Testament scholarship. At the same time it is also one of the most interesting problems, and without a reconstruction of the thoughts of the opponents, many sections of the Pauline letters would remain completely incomprehensible'; see also Classen, 'Paulus', 7f.

[111] For this differentiation, see Hellholm, *Visionenbuch*, 43, 80ff.; further Raible, 'Was sind Gattungen? Eine Antwort aus semiotischer und textlinguistischer Sicht,' *Poetica* 12 (1980) 335.

[112] Cf. U. Luz, 'Zum Aufbau von Röm. 1–8,' *TZ* 25 (1969) 175: 'Die in Röm. 3, 8 auftauchende und dort abgewiesene Frage wird in Röm 6, 1 wieder aufgenommen und in 6, 16 nochmals gestellt'; further cf. U. Schnelle, *Gerechtigkeit und Christusgegenwart: Vorpaulinische und paulinische Tauftheologie* (GTA 24; Göttingen: Vandenhoeck & Ruprecht, 1983) 74; B. Frid, 'Römer 6, 4–5', 188; Schmithals, *Römerbrief,* 110; Dahl, 'Missionary Theology', 83: 'If left unrefuted, it would be fatal to Paul's credibility in Rome'.

[113] K. Brinker, 'Textfunktionen. Ansätze zu ihrer Beschreibung,' *ZGL* 11 (1983) 135f.: 'Texte sind immer eingebettet in eine Kommunikationssituation; sie stehen immer in einem konkreten Kommunikationsprozeß, in dem Emittent und Rezipient mit ihren sozialen und situativen Voraussetzungen und Beziehungen die wichtigsten Faktoren darstellen.' W. Heinemann & D. Viehweger, *Textlinguistik. Eine Einführung* (RGL 115; Tübingen: Niemeyer 1991) 67: 'Das Bewußtsein des Sprechers (or writer's) ist ja vor dem Beginn des praktisch-gegenständlichen oder kommunikativen Handelns keine tabula rasa: Der Handelnde hat Erfahrungen gesammelt für das Ausführen einer bestimmten (und anderer) Tätigkeit(en), er hat Kenntnisse verschiedenster Art gespeichert, die er nun aktivieren muß, wenn sein Handeln oder Sprachhandeln "glücken" soll'.

Judaizing and/or Jewish synagogual propaganda against Paul and his law-free gospel, that was supposed to lead to lax conduct. Reasons for seeing such propaganda behind Paul's argumentation in Romans are in condensed form: (a) during his stay in Ephesus Paul had to experience how his churches in Galatia and Corinth were threatened by Judaizing adversaries;[114] (b) when writing Romans in Corinth Paul is just about to depart for Jerusalem in order to deliver the collection. How severe his situation in fact is can be discerned from Rom 15.30–32, where he first of all fears for his liquidation through the 'unbelievers in Judaea' — that is, the Judaizers/Jews, and secondly for the rejection of his collection on the part of the Jewish-Christian community in Jerusalem. This aspect has rightly been emphasized, although somewhat one-sidedly, by Jacob Jervell in particular;[115] (c) apparently Paul at the time of writing Romans fears that the Judaizing adversaries, who have challenged him in the East, either have already infiltrated or will soon infiltrate the church in Rom.[116] (d) Paul's intent in writing Romans was in my opinion to win the Roman church for his cause, in order to serve as the basis for his mission in Spain.[117]

The thesis of Romans as well as the line of argumentation in chap. 6 must be understood on the basis of these textinternal as well as textexternal considerations.[118] Conversely the line of argumentation in chap. 6 will have to confirm the supposition of Judaizing (and possibly also Jewish)

---

[114] Cf., e.g., Betz, *Galatians, passim*; P. Vielhauer, *Geschichte der urchristlichen Literatur* (dGL; Berlin: de Gruyter, 1975) 113–24.

[115] See J. Jervell, 'The Letter to Jerusalem,' *Romans Debate* (ed. Donfried) 53–64.

[116] See Vielhauer, *Geschichte*, 183; Wilckens, *Der Brief an die Römer 1* (EKKNT 6.1, Zürich/Neukirchen-Vluyn: Benziger/Neukirchener Verlag, 1978) 33–48; also *Römer 2* 10; further G. Bornkamm, 'Der Römerbrief als Testament des Paulus,' *Geschichte und Glaube, Zweiter Teil* (BEvT 52, Munich: Kaiser, 1971) 138; Brandenburger, 'Schriftauslegung', 14 and 27; J. Becker, *Paulus, Der Apostel der Völker* (Tübingen: Mohr-Siebeck, 1989) 367. P. Lampe, 'The Roman Christians of Romans 16,' *Romans Debate* (ed. Donfried) 221: 'The sharp polemic is directed against third persons: against possible heretics not belonging to the Roman church but maybe planning to infiltrate it. Paul may think of his opponents in the east …'.

[117] Cf. Brandenburger, 'Paulinische Schriftauslegung,' 7f.; see also Vielhauer in the previous footnote.

[118] Cf. H. Conzelmann ('χάρις κτλ', [*TWNT* 9; Stuttgart: Kohlhammer, 1973] 386) who correctly states: 'In R[ömer] 6, 1 wird der tatsächliche oder als möglich angenommene Vorwurf aufgegriffen, die Verabsolutierung des Gnadengedankens führe ins Libertinismus'; Conzelmann further thinks, incorrectly, that Paul rejects the reproach 'nur formal-pauschal, *nicht aber argumentierend*' (italics mine); so also Dinkler, 'Römer 6, 1–14 und das Verhältnis von Taufe und Rechtfertigung bei Paulus,' *Battesimo e giustizia in Rom 6 e 8* (ed. L. De

interlocutors in this letter to Romans. Decisive in this connection will be the issue whether the paraenetic-ethical parts (in PA⁴ and PA⁶) can also be interpreted on the background of this argumentative situation.

3.1.2.3.1.2. The Pro-argumentation of Paul

The pro-argumentation in both dialogue phases begins with a meta-oppositional indicator (*MOI*) rejecting apodictically CA¹ and CA²: μὴ γένοιτο![119] The *MOIs* are followed by 'the correction of that which is regarded to be false':[120] in the first dialogue phase the correction is comprised of four pro-arguments of which three are theoretical in nature, that is, inartificial and/or artificial (enthymemic), while the fourth is of a practical nature (paraenetic-ethical); in the second dialogue phase the correction is comprised of two pro-arguments of which the first is of a theoretical (*exemplum*), that is, of an artificial, and the second of a practical (paraenetic-ethical) type. Each of the dialogue phases are brought to a close by means of a confirming *affirmatio* restating in different words the thesis of 5.20f.

3.1.2.3.1.2.1. Pro-argument¹

Paul's first step is to reject the CA¹ by the apodictic meta-oppositional indicator (*MOI*): μὴ γένοιτο, which in itself shows how absurd he finds the consequence drawn by his opponents to be.[120a]

Following directly upon the *MOI* the PA¹ brings the necessary correction of what, as Paul sees it, is wrong. In his first proof Paul argues from what is common ground or a reputable opinion among all Christians: their death to sin! His use of οἵτινες[121] in the meaning of *quippe qui* + first person plural shows that he takes this theologoumenon to be a generally accepted fact. When witnessing himself of his own death to

---

Lorenzi) 86: 'Paulus antwortet nicht mit einem rational einsichtigen und linguistisch "transparenten" Gegen*beweis*, sondern mit der Gegen*frage*, die eigentlich eine Gegen*behauptung* aufstellt …'.

[119] Cf. A. J. Malherbe, 'MH ΓΕΝΟΙΤΟ in the Diatribe and Paul,' *HTR* 73 (1980) 231–40.

[120] See above ad n. 30. See also Malherbe, 'MH ΓΕΝΟΙΤΟ', 236: 'In all the places in Paul the rejection is supported by what immediately follows μὴ γένοιτο'.

[120a] Cf. Bultmann, 'Zur Auslegung von Galater 2, 15–18,' *Exegetica*, 395: 'das μὴ γένοιτο weist den (im Sinne des Paulus) absurden Satz zurück'.

[121] Cf. Blaß-Debrunner-Rehkopf, *Grammatik*, § 451, 1; W. Bauer, W. Gingrich, and F. W. Danker, *A Greek-English Lexicon* (2nd ed.; Chicago: University of Chicago Press, 1979) 587 s.v. ὅστις 2.b.

sin, he at the same time forces his readers as well as his adversaries to be eye-witnesses of their death to sin. Here he uses his own, his readers' as well as his adversaries' *testimonium* as a non-technical proof to refute the accusation of the counter-argument and does so by means of *interrogatio*, thus complying with the method belonging to the *testimonia*. It is important to emphasize that Paul in this chapter begins his argumentation by applying a proof of the highest degree of evidence.

Since neither the addressees nor the adversaries can respond to his first pro-argument, Paul in fact makes use of a true rhetorical question. The diatribe or the *subiectio* style, which Paul makes use of frequently in Romans and elsewhere, has to be interpreted on the one hand from the communication situation, on the other from the function it has within the framework of the type of argument Paul is utilizing. This means that we cannot from the outset take the diatribe or *subiectio* style as indicating that Paul is arguing with fictitious interlocutors or with himself only.[122]

When Günther Bornkamm was of the opinion that the question in CA[1] has 'das Recht einer formalen Logik' and further that the CA[1] 'nur die einzig mögliche Folgerung aus der Paulus eigener, soeben 5, 20 formulierter These für Leben und Verhalten der Glaubenden zu sein (scheint)',[123] then this statement would only be true if Paul had formulated his thesis in 5.20 as a *necessary condition*: ὅτι δὲ ἐπλεόνασεν ἡ ἁμαρτία, ὑπερεπερίσσευσεν ἡ χάρις. The adversaries in fact delineate Paul's theology as advocating a libertine conduct of life as a necessary condition for grace, that is, as a formal *replication* [p ← q], which can be formulated either in the affirmative:[124]

Premise 1: only when sin increases, grace abounds all the more;
Premise 2: now sin increases;
Conclusion: thus, grace abounds all the more;

---

[122] Thus, e.g. G. Bornkamm, 'Taufe und neues Leben (Röm 6),' *Das Ende des Gesetzes* (BEvT 16; 3rd ed.; Munich: Kaiser, 1961) 36f. Correct, however, U. Schnelle, *Gerechtigkeit*, 75: 'Paulus nimmt in Röm 6 einen gegnerischen Einwand auf, der nach Röm 3, 5–8 wirklich erhoben wurde und den Paulus in Röm 5, 20 geradezu provoziert'; so already H. Lietzmann, *An die Römer* (HNT 8; 5th ed.; Tübingen: Mohr-Siebeck, 1971) 65; and lately Schmithals, *Römerbrief*, 182, who reckons with Jews from the synagogue, not Judaizers, as adversaries; so also Bindemann, *Theologie*, 20–45 *et passim*.
[123] Bornkamm, 'Taufe', 36.
[124] Cf. Menne, *Logik*, 37; Menne, *Einführung in die formale Logik* (Darmstadt: Wissenschaftliche Buchgesellschaft, 1985) 31; G. Klaus, 'Replikation,' *Philosophisches Wörterbuch*, 1053.

147

or in the negative:

Premise 1: *only when* sin increases, grace abounds all the more;
Premise 2: now sin does not increase;
Conclusion: thus, grace does not abound.

In both instances sin is alleged as being the necessary condition for the abundance of grace: with sin, grace; without sin, no grace!

However, Paul does not formulate his thesis as a necessary but rather as a *sufficient* or as an *actual condition*, since he writes οὐ δέ and not ὅτι δέ.[125] Paul argues from the conviction that sin is an actual condition, which makes grace abound — that is, his thesis can be formulated as a formal *implication* [p → q] in *modus ponens* [((p → q) ∧ p) → q]:[126]

Premise 1: *always when* sin increases, grace abounds all the more;
Premise 2: now sin increases;
Conclusion: thus, grace abounds all the more.

Given the actual condition of sin, the sufficient condition for the abundance of grace is at hand.

Cranfeld has rightly underlined that 'the relative clause is placed at the beginning of the sentence in order to give more emphasis to "the consideration which contains within itself the answer to the false inference"'.[127]

With Hartwig Thyen we have to admit that it is an anachronism (ἔτι!),[128] in fact a logical *contravalence* (p >−< q)[129] to recognize that all Christians are dead to sin and at the same time accuse Paul of advocating a doctrine of justification that leads to the consequence: *pecca fortiter!*

---

[125] As has been pointed out by Schlier, *Römerbrief,* 190f.

[126] Cf. Menne, *Logik,* 36; also *Formale Logik,* 30; G. Klaus and W. Segeth, 'Implikation,' *Philosophisches Wörterbuch,* 550f. That Paul is also capable of developing valid proofs in *modus tollens* [Menne, *Formale Logik,* 30 [3.245]: ((p → q) ∧ −p) → −q] is convincingly shown by H.-H. Schade, *Apokalyptische Christologie bei Paulus* (GTA 18; 2nd ed.; Göttingen: Vandenhoeck & Ruprecht, 1984) 194f.

[127] Cranfield, *Romans,* 298.

[128] H. Thyen, *Studien zur Sündenvergebung* (FRLANT 96; Göttingen: Vandenhoeck & Ruprecht, 1970) 197; so also W. Schrage, 'Ist die Kirche das "Abbild seines Todes"?,' *Kirche, FS G. Bornkamm* (ed. D. Lührmann and G. Strecker; Tübingen: Mohr-Siebeck, 1980) 205.

[129] See, e.g., Menne, *Logik,* 39f.

148

Paul's own argument on the contrary is in fact either a logical *equivalence* (p ↔ q):[130] 'be dead to sin' is in fact equivalent to 'no longer live in sin': one cannot be dead and alive at the same time, or possibly an *implication* (p → q):[131] 'when the premise is true that we are dead to sin, then we no longer live in sin'. This first pro-argument is in itself conclusive.[132] On what occasion the Christian died to sin is not formulated here.[133] By means of this first pro-argument the aim of the opponents as formulated in the final clause of CA[1]: ἵνα ἡ χάρις πλεονάσῃ (corresponding to the final clause: ἵνα ἔλθῃ τὰ ἀγαθά in 3.8) is made null and void because its premises are invalid.

3.1.2.3.1.2.2. Pro-argument² and Pro-argument²ⁱⁿᶠ

Paul begins his second argument with a question in diatribe or *subiectio* style that functions as a 'reminder' in the form of a meta-argumentative clause.[134] He thereby reminds the addressees directly (and the opponents indirectly) of the decisive experience which they all share with all other Christians (including Paul), their baptism.[135] Paul is here utilizing a piece of circumstantial evidence containing a true *signum* — that is, a τεκμήριον, a sign of 'sensory perception' (τὸ αἰσθητόν)[136] which is at the same time a *testimonium*.[137]

PA[1], which — as we have seen — was a *pure testimonium* and consequently, through the phrase 'dead to sin', explicitly referred to the

---

[130] See, e.g., Menne, *Logik*, 38f.

[131] See, e.g., Menne, *Logik*, 36f.

[132] Thyen (*Studien*, 198f.) points out 'daß im Anschluß an Kapitel 5 schon 6, 2 in sich schlüssig ist' (198); Schmithals, *Römerbrief*, 185: 'Die Logik von V.2b ist zwingend; wer von der Macht der Sünde befreit ist, kann ihr in der Tat nicht mehr dienen.'

[133] See the discussion in Thyen, *Studien*, 198.

[134] Cf. E. Dinkler, 'Verhältnis', 86; Thyen, *Studien*, 201.

[135] Cf. Betz, 'The Mithras Inscriptions of Santa Prisca and the New Testament,' *Hellenismus und Urchristentum. Gesammelte Aufsätze* I (Tübingen: Mohr-Siebeck, 1990) 83 n. 78: 'The controversies between Paul and his opponents presuppose that ritualism played an important part in their theological views. Cf. Rom. vi 1ff.; 1 Cor. i 13ff.; Gal. passim'; so also W. A. Meeks, *The First Urban Christians* (New Haven: Yale University Press, 1983) 154: 'Allusions to baptism occur principally in passages in which Paul tries to correct misunderstandings or to argue on the basis of a common starting point ...'.

[136] The term τὰ αἰσθητά is used of *int. al.* baptism by Origen (Origenes, *Orat.* 5.1) in his description of how gnostic heretics reject cultic events; cf. K. Koschorke, *Die Polemik der Gnostiker gegen das kirchliche Christentum* (NHS 12; Leiden: Brill, 1978) 145.

[137] Dahl, 'Missionary Theology', 84: 'To further this purpose he appeals to their own experiences: they have been baptized into the death of Christ ...'. Cf. Paul's use of the proof 'testimonium' in connection with baptism in Gal 3.26–28; see Betz, *Galatians*, 185.

state of affairs (*causa*) that was to be dealt with in the argumentative process itself,[138] was in no need of further interpretation.

By contrast, PA[2], which was a *necessary signum* — even though it at the same time functioned as a *testimonium* — had to be correlated to the case itself by means of an epistemological process.[139] The artificial proof thus had to be 'found' or 'worked out' by the proponent by means of an adequate method in order for the *signum* to serve as a valid proof.

The method used when interpreting *signa* and *argumenta* is — as we have seen above — that of *ratiocinatio*/συλλογισμὸς ῥητορικός or ἐνθύμημα, which means that the proof of validity is to be sought in the *causa per se* by means of logical inference.

As ascertained above (in the synopsis) Paul first brings the argument (PA[2]) in 6.3 and only then does he bring the full and binding inference (PA[2inf]) in 6.4.

Even if Paul does not formulate the argument itself as a syllogism, it is nevertheless necessary that we reformulate Paul's *enthymeme* in such a way that we are able to understand how he argues intelligibly for his thesis and against CA[1] with the help of PA[2] and PA[2inf]. The first step in such an analysis is to establish the underlying *presuppositions* based on common knowledge from the situational context and then to work out the *implications* the addressees can infer from the textual context.[140]

That Paul here argues on the basis of a traditional understanding of baptism is clear from a series of indications:

(1) *Formal indications:*

(a) the meta-argumentative clause: ἢ ἀγνοεῖτε ὅτι ..., cf. Rom 7.1 from which text it is clear that this kind of phrase serves as a reminding signal:[141] ἢ ἀγνοεῖτε, ἀδελφοί, γινώσκουσιν γὰρ νόμον λαλῶ, ὅτι ὁ νόμος κυριεύει τοῦ ἀνθρώπου ἐφ' ὅσον χρόνον ζῇ;

---

[138] Lausberg, *Handbuch*, 195 [§ 359].

[139] Lausberg, *Handbuch*, 195 [§ 359].

[140] See J. Lyons, *Semantics* 2 (Cambridge: Cambridge University Press, 1977) 605f. Cf. further the remarks on Lyons' thesis by K. W. Hempfer, 'Präsuppositionen, Implikaturen und die Struktur wissenschaftlicher Argumentation,' *Wissenschaftssprache* (ed. T. Bungarten; Munich: Fink, 1981) 317, 322, 325f., and further Schwitalla, 'Formen', 33–35.

[141] Thus Lietzmann, *Römer*, 67; Tannehill, *Dying*, 12f.; Dahl, 'Missionary Theology,' 83; Käsemann, *Römer*, 157; Cranfield, *Romans*, 300; Wilckens, *Römer* 2, 11; Michel, *Römer*, 205; Bornkamm, 'Taufe', 37 n. 5; Bultmann, *Theologie des Neuen Testaments* (GNT; 9th ed.; Tübingen: Mohr-Siebeck 1984) 319; Gäumann, *Taufe*, 72f.; hesitantly Schlier,

(b) the corresponding formulation in 6.16: οὐκ οἴδατε ὅτι ... introducing a well-known and obvious example or similitude;[142]

(c) further it is substantiated by the relative pronoun ὅσοι being used with the meaning of πάντες οἵ[143] in combination with the 1st person plural of the verb: ἐβαπτίσθημεν.

(2) *Indications of substance:*

From the point of view of content it is plausible that this concept of baptism is traditional and thus a common ground for Paul as the author and the Roman Christians (and also the presumed adversaries) as the recipients. The formulation ἐβαπτίσθημεν εἰς Χριστὸν Ἰησοῦν in 6.3a reflects in my opinion a pre-pauline baptismal formula and that regardless of (a) whether the prepositional phrase εἰς Χριστὸν Ἰησοῦν is to be understood as an abbreviation of βαπτισθῆναι εἰς τὸ ὄνομα τοῦ κυρίου Ἰησοῦ (thus Acts 8.16; 19.5; *Did.* 9.5; *Herm.* 15.3)[144] or (b) as an abbreviation of βαπτισθῆναι εἰς τὸ σῶμα Χριστοῦ Ἰησοῦ (see below).[145] This alternative is to a certain degree substantiated by the parallelism between the following texts:

Gal 3.27: ὅσοι γάρ εἰς Χριστὸν ἐβαπτίσθητε, Χριστὸν ἐνεδύσασθε.

Römerbrief, 192; differently G. Wagner, *Das religionsgeschichtliche Problem von Römer 6, 1–11* (ATANT 39; Zürich: Zwingli, 1962) 291f. and H. D. Betz in this volume.

[142] In 7.1 Paul explicitly states that by means of the meta-argumentative clause ἤ ἀγνοεῖτε he refers to something known: γινώσκουσιν γὰρ νόμον λαλῶ. The phrase ἤ ἀγνοεῖτε ὅτι must not be confused with the similar but semantically opposed phrase οὐ θέλω δὲ ὑμᾶς ἀγνοεῖν or similar expressions which 'im Corpus Paulinum durchweg etwas Neues einführt' (G. Lüdemann, *Paulus und das Judentum* [TEH 215; Munich: Kaiser, 1983] 34f.). This was observed quite correctly already by Lietzmann (*Römer*, 67). Even S. K. Stowers (*The Diatribe and Paul's Letter to the Romans* [SBLDS 57; Chico: Scholars Press, 1981] 137), who throughout speaks of an 'imaginary interlocutor' in Romans, has to concede to the fact that 'the way that he (sc. Paul) addresses the Romans with ἤ ἀγνοεῖτε ὅτι is different from the practice in the diatribe where such expressions are directed toward imaginary interlocutors but usually not directly to the audience'. T. Schmeller's argumentation for an imaginary interlocutor of some kind is poor (*Paulus und die 'Diatribe'* [NTAbh 19; Münster: Aschendorff, 1987] 327f.). See also n. 107a.

[143] See Blaß-Debrunner-Rehkopf, *Grammatik*, 304, 1 and Bauer, Gingrich, and Danker, *Lexicon*, 586 s.v. ὅσος 2. with other references.

[144] Most commentators; on this formula see especially L. Hartman, 'Into the Name of Jesus,' *NTS* 20 (1974) 432–40; 'Baptism "Into the Name of Jesus" and Early Christology,' *ST* 28 (1974) 21–48; 'Auf den Namen des Herrn Jesus', *Die Taufe in den neutestamentlichen Schriften* (SBS 148; Stuttgart: Katholisches Bibelwerk, 1992), concerning Romans 6, see especially 69–78.

[145] Cf., e.g., Tannehill, *Dying*, 19f.; Thyen, *Studien*, 200f.; Käsemann, *Römer*, 157; Dinkler, 'Verhältnis', 109; Schrage, 'Kirche', 213; W. Schmithals, *Römerbrief*, 189. So also Betz in this volume.

Rom 6.3a: ὅσοι ἐβαπτίσθημεν εἰς Χριστὸν Ἰησοῦν ...
1 Cor 12.13: πάντες εἰς ἓν σῶμα ἐβαπτίσθημεν ... v. 12: ἕν
ἐστιν σῶμα, οὕτως καὶ ὁ Χριστός.

The structural similarity between these three texts as well as with Col
3.11 could support the supposition that in 6.3 we are facing a traditional formulation with regard to baptism. Then it would be safe to
suppose that the expression βαπτισθῆναι εἰς has the same meaning in
all three instances. In 1 Cor 12.13 the formulation εἰς ἓν σῶμα
βαπτισθῆναι refers to an initiation into the body of Christ: ἕν ἐστιν
σῶμα, οὕτως καὶ ὁ Χριστός. Thus Bultmann would be correct when
he draws the conclusion that 'instead of the complete formula it can
simply be phrased εἰς Χριστόν (Gal 3.27; 2 Cor 1.21), so that now
the Christian existence can be designated as an εἶναι ἐν Χριστῷ; see
Gal 3.28: πάντες γὰρ ὑμεῖς εἷς ἐστε ἐν Χρ. Ἰησοῦ.'[146] The parallelism between Rom 6.3a and the *traditional formulations* in Gal 3.27,[147]
especially the interpretation of βαπτισθῆναι εἰς Χριστόν as the incorporation of Christians 'into the "body of Christ" as an act of "cloth-
ing", whereby Christ is understood as the garment' in Galatians and
the explicit interpretation of baptism as a βαπτισθῆναι εἰς ἓν σῶμα
in 1 Cor 12.12f. speak in favor of Rom 6.3a as being traditional. If this
interpretation should be correct, the reference missed by many scholars
to the body of Christ in Romans 6 would in fact not be missing but
implicitly present by means of the implication that lies in the abbreviated formulation βαπτισθῆναι εἰς Χριστόν.[148]

(c) Another possible, and perhaps the most likely, interpretation of the
short-form εἰς Χριστόν is that the short-form as such is *traditional*,
which indeed is substantiated by the baptismal tradition quoted by Paul
in Gal 3.27 and cited above under (b). This short-form is polysemic in
the sense that it can be interpreted either as εἰς τὸ ὄνομα or as εἰς τὸ
σῶμα or simply taken as a general reference to the dead and risen Christ
Jesus. It is likely that Paul in this connection deliberately chose a *traditional expression*[149] *that was polysemic* and thus could be interpreted by the

---

[146] Bultmann, *Theologie*, 311f.
[147] See especially Betz, *Galatians*, 181–89 and literature referred to there.
[148] See Schrage, 'Kirche', 213 *et passim*.
[149] See below and n. 188.

Roman addressees depending on the baptismal tradition known to them. This polysemic short-form is in fact also the most adequate when serving as a premise in an enthymeme, whose conclusion is: 'we have died and are dead'. In either case the formulation is traditional.

In this way Paul firstly refers back to PA[1] and confirms the *testimonium*-proof given there; secondly, he makes explicit how through baptism the Christians have committed themselves to their death to sin (and possibly, although unlikely, in what way death from sin took place), and thirdly, he is able to show how the soteriological declaration is dependent on the common Christian creed.

The proposition-logical form of Paul's argument can be formulated as follows:

Premise 1: If our baptism to Christ implies participation in his death, [given] and
Premise 2: if we have been baptized to him [given];
Conclusion: ⟦then we have died (and are dead)⟧ [missing].

This is the fully developed syllogistic proof in *modus ponens*: $[((p \rightarrow q) \wedge p) \rightarrow q]$. But this is not the way Paul phrases his enthymemic proof, which is not surprising. As is easily discerned from the text itself premise 1 and premise 2 are given while the conclusion is missing, since it is self-evident.

As Ulrich Wilckens has emphasized, there is no parallel formulation in early Christian literature to Paul's formulation in Romans 6.3b: εἰς τὸν θάνατον αὐτοῦ ἐβαπτίσθημεν.[150] This causes Wilckens to draw the conclusion that the understanding of baptism as the place where Christians have died with Christ is Paul's own creative innovation. With regard to Paul's argumentative strategy, the determination of whether v. 3b is traditional, and thus generally known, is of decisive importance, as we must keep in mind Aristotle's and Quintilian's basis for a strategic argument, namely that this basis must be a *reputable opinion* (ἔνδοξον).[150a]

---

[150] Wilckens, *Römer 2*, 11.

[150a] Cf. the analogous observation in regard to the usage of traditional material in Paul's argumentative strategy by F. Siegert, *Argumentation*, 151 ad Romans 10.9f.: 'Für die Argumentationsanalyse ist daran (sc. Traditionsformeln mit "Sitz im Leben" beim Taufbekenntnis) wichtig, daß es ... Zentralpunkte des *Einverständnisses* innerhalb der Gruppe der Christen ... wären' (italics mine).

On the basis of our observations above regarding the formal indications, it is clear that not only v. 3a[151] or v. 3b[152] but the entire v. 3 is
traditional as far as its content,[153] and possibly also as far as its structure is
concerned.[154] This has been shown above to be true in regard to 3a.
Regarding 3b the following arguments — in spite of the lack of parallels
in Paul — speak in favor of taking this clause to be traditional as well:

(a) Paul could not have used the formal meta-argumentative introduction to PA²: ἢ ἀγνοεῖτε ὅτι ... expecting an affirmative answer,
had he only expected his readers' familiarity with the content of v. 3a.
The reason is quite obvious: (α) being self-evident v. 3a in itself is not
in need of this kind of meta-argumentative introduction, and (β) the
proper proof of the argumentation does not lie in the subordinate
clause (v. 3a) but in the main clause (v. 3b) of the sentence.

(b) Robert Tannehill has rightly pointed to the interrelationship
between the protasis and the apodosis of v. 3 and requested that every
interpretation of baptism as a βαπτισθῆναι εἰς Χριστόν must be able
to explain 'how Paul can move from this idea to the related idea of
baptism εἰς τὸν θάνατον αὐτοῦ and then interpret this participation
in Christ's death as he does in Rom 6.3ff.'[155] The only reasonable
explanation is that v. 3b is a common presupposition for Paul and the
anticipated readers (and possible adversaries) in Rome.[156] Only then
can v. 3 function as a *signum* answering the accusation of libertinism in
CA¹.

(c) As Niklaus Gäumann has argued, Paul would have had to explic-
ate his understanding of baptism as a baptism to death on a much
broader scale, had it been his own creative interpretation servicing the

---

[151] Thus Thyen, *Studien*, 202.

[152] Thus Käsemann, *Römer*, 157.

[153] Thus, e.g., Cranfield, *Romans*, 300; so already Bultmann, *Theologie*, 143f., and
also E. Larsson, *Christus als Vorbild* (ASNU 23; Lund: Gleerup, 1962) 52f.; P. Siber, *Mit
Christus leben* (ATANT 61; Zürich: Theologischer Verlag, 1971) 217f.; U. Schnelle,
Gerechtigkeit, 76.

[154] Thus Schmithals, *Römerbrief*, 191.

[155] Tannehill, *Dying*, 22.

[156] Cf. U. Schnelle, *Gerechtigkeit*, 76: 'Paulus will durch diese Tradition eine gemein-
same Basis mit der römischen Gemeinde herstellen'; Bindemann, *Theologie*, 188: 'Ent-
scheidend ist, daß der Apostel dieses Taufverständnis bei seinen römischen Gesprächs-
partnern offenbar als bekannt und anerkannt voraussetzen kann'.

rejection of CA[1].[157] Again, we must not forget that the *signum* 'baptism' here functions within an overarching line of argumentation and not as a doctrinal proposition concerning baptism: in the formulation εἰς τὸν θάνατον αὐτοῦ βαπτισθῆναι, θάνατος takes on the meaning of 'death to sin' (*dat. incomm.*) as is the case in PA[1]. Any other meaning of θάνατος here would cause a fallacy in Paul's pro-argument for his thesis, a pro-argument which is at the same time a counter-argument against CA[1].

So far we have only discussed the propositional-logical inference of Paul's PA[2]. This kind of inference, however, is not enough really to refute CA[1], since even if the addressees (and the adversaries) accepted the logic of Paul's argument — which they would probably have done — it is necessary for Paul to utilize the possibility of combining two kinds of arguments: the *signum* and the *testimonium*, which — as we have seen above — is directly indicated by his use of the relative pronoun ὅσοι with the meaning of πάντες οἵ in combination with the 1st person plural of the verb: ἐβαπτίσθημεν in the protasis as well as in the apodosis, although the meta-argumentative clause is phrased in the 2nd person plural. Thus the argument itself is formulated in inclusive terms.[158]

If we transform the proposition-logical inference of PA[2] into a syllogism proper, we encounter a syllogism of the 1st figure, namely an inference in *modus Barbara*:[159]

Premise 1:   *All* who have been baptized to Christ (M), have been baptized to his death (P) [partly given];

Premise 2:   *We all* (S) have been baptized to Christ (M) [given: ὅσοι ἐβαπτίσθημεν];[160]

---

[157] Gäumann, *Taufe*, 73 n. 46. This argument gains force in view of the fact that Paul was writing to a congregation to which he was for the most part unknown; so also Cranfield, *Romans*, 300.

[158] See Michel, *Römer*, 199: '*Wir-Stil des Bekenntnisses*'.

[159] Menne, *Logik*, 92f.: '4.711 MaP ∧ SaM → SaP Barbara ...: Wenn alle Tiere die Fähigkeit sinnlicher Wahrnehmung besitzen und alle Regenwürmer Tiere sind, so besitzen auch alle Regenwürmer die Fähigkeit sinnlicher Wahrnehmung'. Cf. also W. & M. Kneale, *The Development of Logic* (Oxford: Clarendon, 1978) 72f.

[160] Sprute, *Enthymemtheorie*, 91: 'Der Untersatz darf natürlich nicht fehlen, da ohne Feststellung, daß ein bestimmtes Indiz vorliegt, ein Indizienenthymem überhaupt nicht möglich ist'; Arist. *Anal. Pr.* 2.27. 70a24–27.

Conclusion: ⟦Thus, *we are all* dead (S and P)⟧ [missing].[161]

With regard to the inference in modus Barbara itself and also to the communicative force of the argument, it is important to observe that 'er beruht auf der *Transitivität* des Funktors *alle sind,* die so evident ist, daß Schlüsse der Form *Barbara* auch ohne Kenntnis der Logik meist leicht als richtig durchschaubar sind'.[162]

As far as the *signum* is concerned the only modus possible according to a piece of circumstantial evidence is Barbara.[163] It is constitutive of a *signum necessarium* that whenever the indication is present, so is that which is indicated. Since in many cases the middle term does not constitute a cause (αἴτιον), while in others it does, Jürgen Sprute is correct when he points out that 'ein Indiz daher nichts weiter als ein Anhaltspunkt, ein Symptom (ist), bei dessen Vorliegen man auf das Vorhandensein oder Eintreten von etwas anderem schließen kann, weil man weiß, daß immer dann, wenn das Indiz vorliegt, auch das betreffende andere vorhanden ist oder eintritt'.[164] Since the cause-effect-relationship is not of importance for the necessity of a sign, the necessity must be sought elsewhere, namely, in the fact that it functions without exceptions; the 'modal logical factor' must be interpreted as a 'universal qualifier'.[165]

Thus, PA² as a necessary sign does not in itself tell us anything about the cause-effect-relationship — as a σημεῖον ἀναγκαῖον within a line of argumentation for the thesis it does not say that death to Christ took place in baptism,[166] but it does say that in every case where someone has been baptized, death from sin can be deduced, since death *is con-*

---

[161] D. Wunderlich, *Foundations,* 50: 'The grammatical subject of the conclusion ... is called the major term S, the grammatical predicate of the conclusion is called the minor term P, and the term which is missing from the conclusion is called the middle term M.'

[162] Menne, *Logik,* 93.

[163] Arist., *Anal. Pr.* 2.27, 70a28–38. Cf. Sprute, *Enthymemtheorie,* 92f.

[164] Sprute, *Enthymemtheorie,* 93.

[165] Sprute, *Enthymemtheorie,* 94. In Aristotle's example that 'all who have a fever are ill' fever is a σημεῖον ἀναγκαῖον or τεκμήριον.

[166] Cf. Thyen, *Studien,* 203: 'Die Teilhabe am Christus geschieht allein ἐκ πίστεως, nicht διὰ τοῦ βαπτίσματος (Rom 5, 1)'; Schmithals, *Römerbrief,* 190: 'Folgt man anderen paulinischen Taufaussagen (1 Kor 12, 12f.; 6, 11; 2 Kor 1, 21f.; Gal 3, 27), so vermittelt die Taufe die Heilsgabe nicht, sondern *versiegelt* sie ...' (italics mine).

firmed in baptism. This understanding of baptism as an argument in the form of a τεκμήριον in PA² is in line with the fact that already PA¹ as a *testimonium* has given proof of the Christian's death to sin. Paul's argumentation in PA² runs as follows: 'Auf das "der Sünde-Gestorbensein" (V. 2) habt ihr euch durch eure Taufe ja ausdrücklich festgelegt'.[167] Whether Paul or the tradition he relies on in addition also understood baptism to be an αἴτιον must be left open. The συνταφῆναι of PA²ⁱⁿᶠ, however, seems to me in view of the credo (1 Cor 15.3–5: Χριστὸς ... ἐτάφη) to speak against baptism as being an αἴτιον (see below).

The way Paul relates baptism to the disputed *causa* is explicitly stated in v. 4 by means of an inferential οὖν! PA¹ was a pure *testimonium* and was therefore linguistically related explicitly to the state of affairs (ἀπεθάνομεν τῇ ἁμαρτίᾳ!) dealt with in the argumentative process. By contrast, since PA² is a τεκμήριον (though it also functions as a *testimonium*), it must be correlated to the *causa* itself by means of an epistemological process. This is what Paul explicitly does in the PA²ⁱⁿᶠ of v. 4, but contrary to PA¹ and PA² he does so with respect to the *positive* side of the argument.

In the first part (v. 4a) Paul only repeats, although with one important variation, his argument from v. 3. Here too he builds upon the credo (1 Cor 15.3–5), only this time he uses burial instead of death, thus underlining the reality of Christ's death.[168] The christological foundation of the soteriological reality is given implicitly by means of a semantic implication entailed in the explicitly stated soteriological consequence (συνετάφημεν ... αὐτῷ // Χριστὸς ... ἐτάφη) (p—𝟛q).[168a] I refrain on this occasion from elaborating upon the *negatively* formulated implication in v. 4a, since it mainly repeats the inference from v. 3. Nevertheless, as we will see below, it was necessary for Paul to repeat it in this inferential part of his argument.

In the second part (v. 4b) Paul carries out his *positive* proof by means of an inference in *modus ponens* formulated as a comparison: ὥσπερ

---

[167] Thyen, *Studien*, 203; Schmithals, *Römerbrief,* 190.

[168] See Larsson, *Vorbild,* 56; further especially Conzelmann, *Grundriß,* 85; also *1 Corinthians* (Hermeneia; Philadelphia: Fortress, 1975) 252; Thyen, *Studien,* 202f.

[168a] A *strict implication*: it is not possible that p is and q is not; cf. Menne, *Formale Logik,* 63: 'Bei einer strikten Implikation beruht diese ... auf einen notwendigen Zusammenhang beider Aussagen'.

... οὕτως. The emphasis in PA²ⁱⁿᶠ is on the *positive* proof. This is brought out in the way Paul here — contrary to his formulation of the negative proof in v. 4a — *explicitly* states the christological foundation: ἠγέρθη Χριστός. Thus here also the second part of the credo comes into play. Paul's proof in the second part runs as follows $[((r \rightarrow s) \wedge r) \rightarrow s]$:

> *Premise 1:* If Christ's resurrection implies a new life for the Christian [given; ὥσπερ ... οὕτως ...], and
> *Premise 2:* if Christ rose [given; ὥσπερ ἠγέρθη Χριστός],
> *Conclusion:* then we live in a newness of life [given (!); οὕτως ...].

As can be seen from this inferential survey, in his very formulation Paul has contributed not only the premises but also the conclusion, even though the argument is not given a syllogistic form.

In order to fully understand Paul's reasoning in PA²ⁱⁿᶠ we must further pay attention to the way Paul combines the *negative* and the *positive* inferences. This is necessary first of all in regard to the circumstantial proof in which he utilizes baptism as a τεκμήριον but secondly also in regard to how the emphasis in the proof has shifted from the negative consequences to the positive by means of the epistemological process employed. Paul relates the negative and the positive inferences to each other in such a way that they together constitute a logical inference of *combined propositions*. Formalized the result is as follows: $[(((p \rightarrow q) \rightarrow (r \rightarrow s)) \wedge (p \rightarrow q)) \rightarrow (r \rightarrow s)]$:[169]

---

[169] The relationship and similarity between simple hypothetical propositions and compound hypothetical propositions was explicitly recognized already by the philosopher Boethius (470–525 CE) although he could rely on Stoic models. I quote Boethius here in the translation of I. M. Bocheński, *A History of Formal Logic* (Notre Dame: Notre Dame University Press, 1961) 139, since his statement can serve as a direct commentary on Paul's way of arguing in PA²ⁱⁿᶠ: 'For when the hypothetical (propositions) which consist of simple ones are compared with those which are compound of two hypotheticals, (one sees that) the sequence (in both cases) is the same and the relations (of the parts to one another) remains, only the terms are doubled ... For in the proposition which says: "if A is, B is", and in that which says: 'if, if A is, B is, (then) if C is, D is' the place occupied in that consisting of two simple propositions by that which is first: "if A is", in the proposition consisting of two hypotheticals is occupied by that which (there) is first: "if, if A is, B is".'

Premise 1: If, if Christ's death is real, the death of the baptized is real [given in the repetition of the proof of PA² in v. 4a],

Premise 2: then if Christ's resurrection is real [given in the simple propositional proof of v. 4ba: ὥσπερ ...],

Conclusion: the new life of the baptized is also a reality [given in the simple propositional proof in v. 4bβ: οὕτως ...].

Now we are able to see why Paul had to repeat the negative part from PA² itself in v. 4a. It constitutes the first premise in the inference of combined propositions.[170] The inferential lead is stated *expressis verbis* in the text by means of the conjunction ἵνα combining the two propositions.

If the emphasis in PA² itself was on the negative aspect of death from sin, the emphasis in the inferential part is on the positive aspect of the new life. This is particularly apparent in the soteriological formulation of the second half of the inferential part, due to its turn towards the present-ethical aspect through the formulation: οὕτως καὶ ἡμεῖς ἐν καινότητι ζωῆς περιπατήσωμεν. This turn of the argument, however, is a necessity if Paul wants to say something that goes beyond what he argued for already in PA¹ and PA² and it is unavoidable if he would not be content with bringing only a *necessary* but also a *sufficient* answer to CA¹.[171]

We here see what Aristotle had already stressed so emphatically, that in an argumentation one has to bring proofs of such a kind that 'the demonstration should bear upon the particular point disputed',[172] in Paul's case, that justification by faith does not lead to libertinism. This claim on the part of his adversaries is denied — as we have seen — in two ways that complement each other: negatively — we are dead from sin, and positively — we live in a new life.

---

[170] This has been correctly observed already by R. Schnackenburg ('Todes- und Lebensgemeinschaft mit Christus. Neue Studien zu Röm 6, 1–11,' *MTZ* 6 [1955] 35).

[171] Cf. Thyen, *Studien*, 207; similarly Schmithals, *Römerbrief*, 191; Hartman, *Auf den Namen*, 73.

[172] *Ars rhet.*, 3.17.1. 1417b.

3.1.2.3.1.2.3. Pro-argument³ and Pro-argument³ⁱⁿᶠ

The third pro-argument is given in two partly parallel formulations: PA³ᵃ in vv. 5–7 and PA³ᵇ in vv. 8–11. This parallelism was first elaborated by Günther Bornkamm and has since been taken over by most commentators.[173] In spite of Bornkamm's (in many respects) convincing analysis it is necessary to draw attention to the fact that the parallelism is not as complete as he thought; a shift in emphasis takes place from PA³ᵃ to PA³ᵇ or rather, from PA³ᵃ:ⁱⁿᶠ to PA3ᵇ:ⁱⁿᶠ as will be shown below. This shift is partly in correspondence with the similar development in PA²ⁱⁿᶠ (from negative to positive proofs) and partly, and primarily, connected with the circumstance that in PA³ᵇ and PA³ᵇ:ⁱⁿᶠ Paul brings the theoretical argumentation of the first dialogue phase to completion, after which he proceeds in vv. 12–13 to the practical-ethical argumentation (PA⁴) of this dialogue phase. The soteriological consequences are kept together before the paraenetical consequences are elaborated upon.

First Paul brings PA³ᵃ in v. 5 followed by the inferential part PA³ᵃ:ⁱⁿᶠ. in vv. 6–7. Thereafter he repeats the pro-argument (PA³ᵇ) in v. 8 followed by a new inferential part (PA³ᵇ:ⁱⁿᶠ) in vv. 9–11. The two pro-arguments of the third rank (PA³ᵃ and PA³ᵇ) are both formulated as conditional clauses in the grammatical *modus realis*. This state of affairs together with the strengthening conjunction ἀλλά at the beginning of the apodosis in PA³ᵃ as well as the meta-argumentative clause πιστεύομεν ὅτι[174] at the beginning of the apodosis in PA³ᵇ give, as far as the communicative sense is concerned, a character of reality to the pro-arguments (*MArCSub*). In this way these conditional clauses correspond to the meta-argumentative clauses (*MArC*), ἢ ἀγνοεῖτε ὅτι and οὐκ οἴδατε ὅτι, at the beginning of PA² and PA⁵, both of which are placed at the beginning of each dialogue phase.[175]

---

[173] Bornkamm, 'Taufe', 38f.; so also, e.g. Michel, *Römer*, 201. It is a misunderstanding (a) of the relationship between vv. 4 and 5, and (b) of the structure of vv. 5–11, when Frid ('Römer 6, 4–5', 199 n. 52 – contra Bornkamm) maintains that there is 'keine Parallelität weder sachlich/inhaltlich noch argumentierend zwischen den Versen 5–7 und 8–10'.

[174] Cf. Gäumann, *Taufe*, 84; Schlier, *Römerbrief*, 199; Michel, *Römer*, 208; Schmithals, *Römerbrief*, 193.

[175] Cf. Tannehill, *Dying*, 13.

In this section of his argumentation Paul makes use of a proper *argumentum*, since he no longer refers to an αἰσθητόν, at least not directly. There is no direct indication in this section of proof that Paul is arguing from the τεκμήριον of baptism.[176] Rather, he is arguing directly from the credo in the form of the pistis formula (1 Cor 15.3–5) as the basis for the soteriological and ethical implications:[177] ὅτι Χριστὸς ἀπέθανεν ... καὶ ὅτι ἐτάφη ... // ... καὶ ὅτι ἐγήγερται ... καὶ ὅτι ὤφθη... .

However, as far as the *Sitz im Leben* of this credo formula is concerned Philipp Vielhauer is probably correct, when he writes: 'Die Pistis-formeln sind katechetische Formeln, die zweifellos beim Taufunterricht eine Rolle gespielt haben, vielleicht auch bei der Tauffeier abgefragt und aufgesagt wurden: aber sie sind nicht speziell auf die Taufe bezogen, sondern haben eine umfassende Bedeutung, wie ihre Verwendung in lehrhaften und ethischen Unterweisungen zeigt.'[178] The accent in PA³ as a proof is not on baptism but on the christological creed as a prerequisite for the soteriological and ethical consequences for the Christians. To be more precise, Paul here brings an argument which is a combination of an *argumentum a simili* and an *argumentum a modo*.[179] The argument from similarity expresses the parallelism as follows: 'Christ has died — we have died; Christ was raised — we shall rise.' The argument from manner expresses the relation as follows: 'Christ has died — we have died *with him* (σύμφυτοι; συν-); Christ was raised — we shall live *with him* (συζήσομεν).' That these two types of argument are being utilized by Paul here and elsewhere (e.g. 1 Thess 4.14ff.) is due to the fact that each of them contributes in its

[176] So also Thyen, *Studien*, 206 n. 5; Siber, *Mit Christus*, 217ff.; Schmithals, *Römerbrief*, 190; G. Lüdemann, *Paul, Apostle to the Gentiles* (Philadelphia: Fortress, 1984) 254 n. 101; cf. already H. Braun, 'Das "Stirb und werde' in der Antike und im Neuen Testament,' *Gesammelte Studien zum Neuen Testament und seiner Umwelt* (2nd ed.; Tübingen: Mohr-Siebeck, 1967) 156; Tannehill, *Dying*, 41.

[177] Other texts are: 1 Thess 4.14; 2 Cor 5.15; Rom 4.25; 14.9. See, e.g. W. Kramer, *Christos, Kyrios, Gottessohn* (ATANT 44; Zürich: Zwingli, 1963), 24–27; Gäumann, *Taufe*, 61–65 *et passim*; Conzelmann, *Grundriß*, 84; *1 Corinthians*, 251–57; K. Wengst, *Christologische Formeln und Lieder des Urchristentums* (SNT 7; Gütersloh: Gerd Mohn, 1972) 92–104; Vielhauer, *Geschichte*, 14–22, especially 18–20.

[178] Vielhauer, *Geschichte*, 22; similarly Schmithals, *Römerbrief*, 191.

[179] For these two types of arguments, see Lausberg, *Handbuch*, 217 [§ 394: *a simili*] and 214 [§ 390: *a modo*].

own way to bringing out the specific relationship between Christ and the Christians: the single argument *a simili* reveals the parallelism but not the inner relationship; the single argument *a modo* on the other hand brings out the relationship but not the difference between the redeemer and the redeemed Christians.[180] Not only the similarity but also the difference is explicitly brought out by means of the term ὁμοίωμα.[181]

The proposition-logical form in *modus ponens* of Paul's PA³ᵃ can be formulated as follows [((q → s) ∧ q) → s]:

Premise 1:   If we have grown together with the ὁμοίωμα[182] of his death, we *shall* surely be with [the ὁμοίωμα of?] his resurrection [given];

Premise 2:   {now we have grown together with the ὁμοίωμα of his death}[182a] [indirectly given: εἰ + ind. = *modus realis*];

Conclusion: then we *shall* grow together with [the ὁμοίωμα of?] his resurrection [given].

PA³ᵃ, however, only partly answers the objection to Paul's thesis given in CA¹; it serves instead as a prerequisite for the following inference in PA³ᵃ⁺ⁱⁿᶠ. The difficulty with PA³ᵃ lies in the apodosis clause with its

---

[180] Cf. Meeks, *Urban Christians*, 154: 'Foremost among the motifs that Paul takes for granted, known not only to members of groups he founded but also to the Christians in Rome, is the image of dying and rising with Christ. This is expressed not only in the *language of analogy* ("As Christ was raised from the dead ... so also we ...") but also in the *language of participation* ("We have been baptized into his death ...", Rom. 6:3f.), as well as by verbs compounded in *syn-* "with" (Rom. 6:4; 8 ...)' (italics mine).

[181] See Wilckens, *Römer 2*, 13; cf. also Larsson (*Vorbild*, 59) who, however, thinks that ὁμοίωμα refers to baptism; U. Schnelle, *Gerechtigkeit*, 82.

[182] Due to lack of space I must refrain here from an exegetical interpretation of the concept ὁμοίωμα and from the difficult question of its supplementary insertion into the apodosis. For the logical inference, which is my concern here, there is no need for an exact interpretation. At least one interpretation should be rejected though, namely, that it refers to baptism; see G. Beasley-Murray, *Baptism in the New Testament* (London: MacMillan, 1962) 135 n. 1; so already Schnackenburg, 'Todes- und Lebensgemeinschaft' 33–37; Bornkamm, 'Taufe', 42f.; further Gäumann, *Taufe*, 79; Thyen, *Studien*, 205f.; Siber, *Mit Christus*, 218–21; Schrage, 'Kirche', 208f.; Wilckens, *Römer 2*, 13ff.; Schmithals *Römerbrief*, 192; Dunn, *Romans*, 317. Differently H. D. Betz with references in this volume.

[182a] See n. 186.

162

future tense: ἐσόμεθα.[183] This is obviously the reason why Paul here (as in 6.4) after the pro-argument itself brings an inferential part connecting the argument with the accusation. The argument must, as we have seen before, be correlated to the *causa* itself by means of an epistemological process, and this is in fact what Paul does in v. 6, which he characterizes as such an inference by means of the inferential phrase τοῦτο γινώσκοντες ὅτι (or in v. 9: εἰδότες ὅτι), as he did by means of the inferential οὖν in PA[2:inf] in v. 4.[184]

In PA[3a:inf] the epistemological process is not formulated in *modus ponens* as one might have expected but rather for the sake of clarification according to the rule of '*transitivity of implications*' [((p → q) ∧ (q → r)) → (p → r)], which corresponds to the classical syllogism in the proposition-logical calculus.[185] Paul's argument here thus runs as follows:

> *Premise 1:* If our old man has been crucified with (Christ),
> then the sinful body has been abolished and
> *Premise 2:* {if the sinful body has been abolished}[186]
> then we are no longer enslaved to sin;
> *Conclusion:* ⟦thus: if our old man has been crucified with (Christ),
> then we are no longer enslaved to sin⟧.

Paul's formulation of PA[3a:inf] according to the rule of 'transitivity of implication' is quite obvious from the text itself: (a) ἵνα and (b) τοῦ +

---

[183] That is, as long as one understands the future tense as a real and not a logical future; cf. Conzelmann, 'Die Schule des Paulus,' *Theologia Crucis-Signum Crucis, FS E. Dinkler* (ed. C. Andresen and G. Klein; Tübingen: Mohr-Siebeck, 1979) 91 n. 37: 'Es ist eine vergebliche Ausflucht, die Futura von Röm 6 als "logische" eliminieren zu wollen'; also *Grundriß*, 299; 'Paulus und die Weisheit,' *Schriftauslegung*, 178; and 'Rechtfertigungslehre', 199 n. 51; so also Gäumann, *Taufe*, 48 n. 114; Käsemann, *Römer*, 161; Dunn, *Romans*, 318 and 322. Contra, e.g. Larsson, *Vorbild*, 71 and Thyen, *Studien*, 206ff.

[184] Thus, the inferential phrases τοῦτο γινώσκοντες ὅτι and εἰδότες ὅτι do not — contra Tannehill — have 'the same function as ἢ ἀγνοεῖτε in vs. 3' (*Dying*, 13). The participles γινώσκοντες and εἰδότες do not replace an imperative but rather an inferential indicative, contra Schlier, *Römerbrief*, 196 and with Käsemann, *Römer*, 161 and Dunn, *Romans*, 318.

[185] See Menne, *Logik*, 54f. with example; further I. M. Bocheński and A. Menne, *Grundriß der formalen Logik* (UTB 59; Paderborn: Schöningh, 1983) 46 [= 6.35].

[186] The line in this syllogism within {...} is not stated explicitly by Paul but is inferred from the previous line for the sake of clarity.

infinitive. The reason for Paul's formulation is equally obvious: by means of premise 2 he can explain the connection between the crucifixion of ὁ παλαιὸς ἡμῶν ἄνθρωπος with Christ and the freedom from our enslavement under the power of sin.[187] In fact he is in this way able to interpret PA[1] and the anachronism stated there (ἔτι); we should notice that here too Paul brings in the anachronism, this time by means of μηκέτι.

In contrast to what was the case in PA[3a], Paul directly defends his thesis in PA[3a:inf] and above all explicitly responds to the unreasonable and illogical conclusion drawn from his thesis by his opponents in CA[1]. However, he does so only as far as the *negative* side of his defense is concerned as the explication in v. 7 (PA[3a:inf/expl]) makes clear: ὁ γὰρ ἀποθανὼν δεδικαίωται ἀπὸ τῆς ἁμαρτίας.[187a]

The second part of PA[3] is partly a parallel to the first part. The proposition-logical form in *modus ponens* of Paul's PA[3b] (v. 8) can be formulated as follows $[((q \rightarrow s) \wedge q) \rightarrow s]$:

Premise 1: If we have died with Christ, we believe that we *shall* live with him [given];
Premise 2: {now we have died with him}[187b] [indirectly given: εἰ + ind. = *modus realis*];
Conclusion: then – we believe that – we *shall* live with him [given].

PA[3b], like PA[3a], only partly answers the objection to Paul's thesis given in CA[1]; like PA[3a] it serves as a prerequisite for the following inference, in this case in PA[3b:inf]. Again the difficulty lies in the apodosis clause with its future tense — συζήσομεν. The fact that here in PA[3b], as in PA[3a], Paul formulates the apodosis in the future tense, which actually does not correspond to his need in the line of argumentation against CA[1], is an indication that he is in all likelihood quoting a preformulated piece of tradition. This has recently been suggested by Walter Schmithals, who gives the following reconstruction of what he considers to be a

---

[187] Cf. Braun, 'Stirb und werde', 154.
[187a] Cf. Hartman, *Auf den Namen*, 74.
[187b] See n. 186.

"'Taufspruch' ... aus dem Taufgottesdienst, das etwa nach vollzogener Taufe von den Täuflingen gesprochen worden sein könnte".[188]

(1) ὅσοι ἐβαπτίσθημεν εἰς Χριστὸν Ἰησοῦν,
(2) εἰς τὸν θάνατον αὐτοῦ ἐβαπτίσθημεν (6.3);
(3) εἰ δὲ ἀπεθάνομεν σὺν Χριστῷ,
(4) πιστεύομεν ὅτι καὶ συζήσομεν αὐτῷ (6.8).

The future tense in the baptismal saying is obviously the reason why Paul here (as in 6.4 and 6.6), after the pro-argument itself, brings an inferential part connecting the argument with the accusation, since — as I have pointed out before — the argument must be correlated to the *causa* itself by means of an epistemological process. This is in fact what Paul does in vv. 9–11.[189] Paul here too indicates the inference by means of the inferential phrase εἰδότες ὅτι as he did by means of the inferential οὖν in PA^{2inf} in v. 4 and as he did by means of τοῦτο γινώσκοντες ὅτι in v. 6. PA$^{3b:inf}$ is, however, more developed and differently structured than PA$^{3a:inf}$.[190]

As in PA^{2inf}, so here too Paul carries out a *positive* proof, which is, however, first stated implicitly in v. 9 and then explicitly in conjunction with the negative proof in vv. 10–11.[190a] In PA$^{3b:inf}$ (v. 9) Paul — contrary to his formulation of the negative proofs in PA^{3b} (vv. 5–7) but

---

[188] Schmithals, *Römerbrief*, 191. For 6.8 as part of a pre-pauline Tradition, see F. Hahn, 'Taufe und Rechtfertigung,' *Rechtfertigung, FS E. Käsemann* (ed. J. Friedrich, W. Pöhlmann, and P..Stuhlmacher; Tübingen: Mohr-Siebeck, 1976) 109, who refers to 2 Tim 2.11(-13): εἰ γὰρ συναπεθάνομεν, καὶ συζήσομεν as a traditional parallel; so also Dunn, *Romans*, 322. Cf. Lohse, 'Wort und Sakrament in der paulinischen Theologie,' *Zu Karl Barths Lehre von der Taufe* (ed. Viering) 50: 'In den hellenistischen Gemeinden ist offensichtlich aus diesem Bezug auf das Kerygma eine genaue Entsprechung im Hinblick auf die Taufe abgeleitet worden...'; Bindemann, *Theologie*, 188. Did this baptismal tradition also originate in Antioch as other baptismal traditions in Paul (cf. Becker, *Paulus*, 107–19, especially 110ff. and 301)?

[189] The formulation of the apodoses in the future tense is not as Conzelmann, 'Schule', 91 suggests due to an 'eschatologischer Vorbehalt' (cf. 'Zum Überlieferungsproblem im Neuen Testament,' *Schriftauslegung*, 150; *1 Corinthians*, 268 n. 44) that has its ground in 'das enthusiastische Selbstverständnis eines Teils der Gemeinde in Korinth', from where Paul wrote Romans, but rather in the pre-pauline tradition as suggested by Schmithals and quoted above. Conzelmann reads the Corinthian situation into Romans, which is methodologically questionable.

[190] This is the reason why Bornkamm's parallelism is too rigid.

[190a] Cf. Hartman, *Auf den Namen*, 74f.

in congruence with the *positive* proof of PA^{2inf} (v. 4b: ἠγέρθη Χριστὸς ἐκ νεκρῶν) — explicitly states the christological foundation: Χριστὸς ἐγερθεὶς ἐκ νεκρῶν. Again, in that way Paul brings to expression that the emphasis in this second part of PA^3 is indeed on the *positive* proof after the first part had been confined to the negative proof. The christological foundation is certainly in focus, but when it is stated that the resurrected Christ will not be brought back under the power of sin and death, then it is clear to the addressees that this is also true of all baptized believers: 'Paulus formuliert deshalb den V.10 so, daβ der Satz von Christus spricht, der Leser aber zugleich an sich selbst denkt'.[191] This implication is explicitly formulated in the following explication encompassing both the negative and the positive argument in favor of the thesis and in opposition to CA^1.

In order to bring out the relevance of the correspondence between the christological creed and its implication for the baptized Christians with regard to its *negative* as well as its *positive* consequences for the rebuttal of CA^1, Paul brings in, for the first time in this chapter, an *explication of Christ's death and resurrection* in v. 10, in which his death is interpreted as 'death from sin once and for all' (τῇ ἁμαρτίᾳ ἀπέθανεν ἐφάπαξ) and his resurrection as 'life for God' (ζῇ τῷ θεῷ). This interpretation then constitutes the premise for the following conclusion about the Christians' soteriological status as being νεκροὶ μὲν τῇ ἁμαρτίᾳ ζῶντες δὲ τῷ θεῷ. That this conclusion is based on the Christians' participation in Christ's destiny is made clear by Paul when he adds that 'our death from sin' and 'our life for God' become a reality only ἐν Χριστῷ Ἰησοῦ. In this explicatory section of PA$^{3b:inf}$ Paul connects to the first and second parts of the pro-arguments — death with Christ *and* life with him. If we relate the implicit premise of PA^{3b} (v. 8): Christ's death implies our death (p → q) and Christ's resurrection implies our resurrection (r → s) with the premise of PA$^{3b:inf/expl}$ (vv. 10–11): Christ's death and life/(resurrection) (p ∧ r; v. 10) implies our death and life/(resurrection) (q ∧ s; v. 11), and if we further take into account the above mentioned interpretation of death and life/(resurrection) as 'death from sin' and 'life for God' in regard to Christ as well as in regard to the Christians, then we obtain a *'conjunctive coupling'* of

191 Schmithals, *Römerbrief,* 193.

the two sides, which has the following structure: $[((p \to q) \wedge (r \to s)) \to ((p \wedge r) \to (q \wedge s))].$[192]

That Paul here takes one step further is apparent from the fact that the 'conjunctive coupling' does not constitute an equivalence and consequently no tautology either. As a result of the reformulation of the implication Paul achieves two things: (a) the twofold *christological* creed: Christ's death and resurrection/life $(p \wedge r)$ is being kept together; (b) the *soteriological* status of the Christians in its *negative* and *positive* aspects: the Christians' death from sin and their life for God $(r \wedge s)$ can thus also be kept together, thereby constituting the direct background to the paraenetic-ethical argument in PA[4], which follows immediately.

It is most important to notice, as we did above, that while in PA[3a] and PA[3b] themselves the apodoses were formulated in the future tense (ἐσόμεθα and συζήσομεν respectively), in PA[3b:inf/expl] these formulations have been changed in a present-ethical direction. The result is that after the interpretation of Christ's death and resurrection as 'his death to sin' and 'his life to God' it is now stated in regard to the believers: οὕτως καὶ ὑμεῖς λογίζεσθε ἑαυτοὺς (εἶναι) νεκροὺς μὲν τῇ ἁμαρτίᾳ ζῶντας δὲ τῷ θεῷ ἐν Χριστῷ Ἰησοῦ.[193] In this way Paul here replies also in *positive* terms (as in PA[2inf] [v. 4]) to the accusation of CA[1]. In PA[3b:inf] we thus encounter a double consequence, which corresponds to the two parts of the christological creed as well as to the thesis advocated by Paul in 5.20f., namely, the death of Christians from sin once and for all (ἐφάπαξ) *and* their life for God in the present.[194]

3.1.2.3.1.2.4. Pro-argument[4]

I can only deal briefly here with the paraenetical argument (PA[4] in vv. 12–13). This practical proof is composed of three imperatives corresponding to the consequences of the thesis in 5.21aα (negative) and 5.21aβ (positive) as well as to the soteriological reality stated in 6.11bα (negative) and 6.11bβ (positive). The function of this paraenetic proof is first of all to reject the opponents' CA[1], but secondly also to admon-

---

[192] Bocheński and Menne, *Grundriß*, 47 [6.63].

[193] Cf. 2 Cor 5.14–15, and see Bultmann, *Der zweite Brief an die Korinther* (Meyer K. Sonderband; Göttingen: Vandenhoeck & Ruprecht, 1976) 153f.

[194] Cf. Schmithals, *Römerbrief*, 194.

ish the addressees to realize that justification in itself encompasses the obedient service to God, and to draw the right conclusion of their christological and soteriological status.[195]

PA[4] is structured in direct accordance with PA[3b:inf/exp]. First we encounter two negatively formulated imperatives (cf. v. 11bα), of which the first is an admonition to the Christians not to let sin reign in their deadly bodies (μὴ οὖν βασιλευέτω ἡ ἁμαρτία κτλ), and the second exhortation expresses the same concern only using figurative military language (ὅπλα ἀδικίας) (vv. 12–13a). Then we encounter one positively formulated imperative clause (cf. v. 11bβ) of which the first part is an admonition to yield oneself to God (τῷ θεῷ) followed by a second part again using military figurative language (ὅπλα δικαιοσύνης) (v. 13b); thereby the positively formulated imperative clause (as in PA[2inf]) takes up the negative presupposition (ὡσεὶ ἐκ νεκρῶν ζῶντας) for the positive admonition.

As mentioned above Seneca uses rational as well as emotive arguments in order to admonish people to live a moral life. Does this apply also to the way Paul argues in Romans 6? This would be the case if one could prove that Paul's adversaries or his addressees were libertines. As we have seen, however, a lot speaks against and — as it seems — only the paraenetical proofs (PA[4] and PA[6]) speak in favor of such a view. Rather, it seems as if the adversaries (and possibly even the addressees?) had been accusing (or suspecting) Paul of advocating a libertine conduct of life as a consequence of his 'doctrine of justification by faith'. But in that case, why does Paul here bring two paraenetical sections into his line of argumentation?

Paul's reason can only be discerned from a correct understanding of the paraenetical section as a partial proof in the overall argumentation in his struggle against the Judaizing and/or Jewish propaganda, which suggested that Paul gave the recommendation: 'let us do evil that good may come' (3.8). In chapter 6 Paul uses rational as well as emotive proofs but, contrary to Seneca, he does so not primarily in order 'to teach ethical conduct'[196] but in order to defend his doctrine of justification by faith and the consequences thereof.

---

[195] For the content of PA[4], which I cannot discuss here, see especially Gäumann, *Taufe*, 88–91, 129–33; Schmithals, *Römerbrief,* 194f.; Bindemann, *Theologie*, 191–95.
[196] See above, n. 94.

When Paul here — as in other letters — calls upon his addressees to live a life in conformity with their christological creed and their soteriological status, this is without doubt a genuine concern of his. This, however, does not mean that his addressees or his adversaries all were libertines. In regard to the Roman church this is out of the question, since he can end PA[5inf] with an expression of thanks: 'thanks be to God, that you who were once slaves of sin have become obedient from the heart ... and, having been set free from sin, have become slaves of righteousness' (vv. 17f.). This is a clear indication of how the paraenetical section functions as a *reminder* of what the addressees already know, as is the case also in Seneca and Pliny. In the words of A. Malherbe: 'There is ... a special, paraenetic function of remembrance'.[196a]

In addition to and at the end of the theoretical proofs in the first dialogue phase Paul, in accordance with Aristotle's claim that the moral character of the orator 'constitutes the most effective means of proof', brings in such a practical ἦθος-proof, which underscores precisely the moral character of the author by means of the admonition given in the text itself.[197] Thus, when Paul here admonishes (as he always does) the Christians to live according to their soteriological status, the propaganda of the adversaries is seen to be unwarranted. To show this is the very function of the paraenetical section.[197a]

3.1.2.3.1.2.5. Affirmatio[1]

Before turning to the second dialogue phase Paul gives a concluding indicative *affirmatio* (Affirm.[1]) to the pro-arguments developed so far

---

[196a] Malherbe, 'Hellenistic Moralists', 286.

[197] Cf. Fortenbaugh, 'Ethos. B. I. Antike', 1517: 'Wenn der Redner aber eher unbekannt ist oder einen schlechten Ruf hat, wird die Darstellung des Charakters wichtig'. Cf. the analogical procedure of Paul's in Rom 9–11; see Brandenburger, 'Schrift-auslegung', 7, and the similar function of 'the unique and long list of personal greetings' in Romans 16, which 'as a whole is a text of recommendation for Paul himself' (P. Lampe, 'Roman Christians', 218). Lampe explicates the hidden message of the list when he interprets it to say, 'Look at the many and honorable personal friends of mine in the midst of your church — and you will find that I, too, am trustworthy', and he concludes by emphasizing that 'Paul certainly needed all the recommendations he could get after he and his Law-free gospel had become so controversial in the east'.

[197a] See especially Dahl, 'Missionary Theology', 84: 'Refuting the alleged consequence, that his doctrine favored sinning, he turns the point around and exhorts his readers that they should put themselves and their capacities for action at the disposition of God, in the service of righteousness'.

and he does so by means of a *recapitulatio* of the thesis in 5.20f.: οὐ γάρ ἐστε ὑπὸ νόμον ἀλλὰ ὑπὸ χάριν.

3.1.2.3.2. The Line of Argumentation in the Second Dialogue Phase

The second dialogue phase encompasses vv. 15–23 as shown above and consists of a second counter-argument (CA²) as well as two pro-arguments made up of one theoretical proof, namely an inductive example (PA⁵ with PA⁵ⁱⁿᶠ), followed by a pragmatic-ethical exhortation (PA⁶) and concluded by yet another *affirmatio* (Affirm.²). In this essay I can only give a few hints at a proper interpretation of this second dialogue phase.

3.1.2.3.2.1. The Counter-argumentation of the Adversaries

After the reiteration of his thesis in Affirm.¹ Paul again brings in a counter-argument, this time formulated in direct correspondence with the rephrased thesis (v. 14). The counter-argumentation in the *second dialogue phase* is carried out by means of a *MCC* (τί οὖν;) introducing, in the form of a citation formula, the CA², which in turn is constituted by a meta-active clause (*MAC*: ἁμαρτήσωμεν, ὅτι οὐκ ἐσμὲν ὑπὸ νόμον ἀλλὰ ὑπὸ χάριν;). The formulation here seems to be Paul's own, since he takes up the affirmation from v. 14.

Again the CA shows the Judaizing and/or Jewish synagogual accusation made against Paul and the Hellenistic Christians because of alleged libertinism.[198]

3.1.2.3.2.2. The Pro-argumentation of Paul

The pro-argumentation in the second dialogue phase — as in the first — begins with a meta-oppositional indicator (*MOI*) rejecting apodictically CA²: μὴ γένοιτο![199] Also here the *MOI* is followed by 'the correction of that which is regarded to be false' but only after PA⁵ has been preceded by the meta-argumentative clause: οὐκ οἴδατε ὅτι ... introducing a well-known example or similitude. In this second dialogue phase the correction is comprised of two pro-arguments of which the

---

[198] See especially Wilckens, *Römer 2*, 34. The differentiation between CA¹ (v. 1) and CA² (v. 15) by P. Tachau, *'Einst' und 'Jetzt' im Neuen Testament* (FRLANT 105; Göttingen: Vandenhoeck & Ruprecht, 1972) 117 does not do justice to the line of arguments in the two dialogue phases.

[199] See above nn. 119f.

first is of an inductive-theoretical, that is, an artificial kind (*exemplum*), and the second of a practical (paraenetic-ethical) kind. The second dialogue phase is — like the first one — brought to an end by means of a confirming *affirmatio* restating in different words the theses of 5.20f. and 6.14 respectively.

3.1.2.3.2.2.1. Pro-argument⁵ and Pro-argument^{Sinf}

Paul's first step is to reject the CA² by the apodictic meta-oppositional indicator (*MOI*): μὴ γένοιτο, which again shows, how absurd he finds the consequence drawn by his opponents.

Following directly upon the *MOI* the PA⁵ brings the necessary correction of what in Paul's opinion is wrong. In his fifth proof Paul argues anew from what is common ground or reputable opinion among people in general in the ancient world, namely, that the slave has to obey his master.[200] That Paul here argues from common ground is clear from indications of a formal as well as a substantial kind:

(1) *Formal indication*: the meta-argumentative clause: οὐκ οἴδατε ὅτι ... repeating the corresponding formulation in 6.3: ἢ ἀγνοεῖτε ὅτι ...;[201]

(2) *Indication of substance:* from the point of view of content too, it is clear — as I have indicated already — that Paul refers to a reputable opinion about slavery in the ancient world; in an inductive proof the reputable opinion is indeed as urgent as in a deductive proof.[202]

Practically all inductive arguments are, as Aristotle claims, accomplished in two steps: (a) as 'the result of induction from one or more similar cases, and (b) when one assumes the general and then concludes the particular by an example'.[203] Thus it is necessary to analyze the

---

[200] See the texts in T. Wiedemann, *Greek and Roman Slavery* (Baltimore: John Hopkins University Press, 1981); cf. further S. Bartchy, *ΜΑΛΛΟΝ ΧΡΗΣΑΙ : First Century Slavery and the Interpretation of 1 Corinthians 7.21* (SBLDS 11; Missoula: Scholars Press, 1973) 11; Meeks, *Urban Christians,* 20–23; P. Lampe (*Stadtrömische Christen,* 68f.) refers to Dio Chrys., *Orat.* 15.22f.; A. Lindemann, *Die Clemensbriefe* (HNT 17; Tübingen: Mohr-Siebeck, 1992) 155 ad *1 Clem* 55.2.

[201] See above, n. 141 and n. 142.

[202] See above n. 77 and cf. further Lausberg, *Handbuch,* 233 [§ 422]: 'Die *similitudo* beschränkt sich also auf die Bereiche, die der allgemeinen, natürlichen Erfahrung jedes Publikums entsprechen: daher ihre Beweiskraft'.

[203] See above, n. 62.

formal structure of PA⁵. As often observed, Paul does not give a pure similitude but constructs it with the addressees already in mind.[204] Consequently the major premise is not spelled out but simply presupposed. If we fill in the missing premise by assuming the general and then concluding the particular we arrive at the following syllogistic proof in *modus Barbara*:[205]

> *Premise 1:* ⟦*All* slaves are required to obey their masters⟧ [missing!]
> *Premise 2:* *You* are slaves [given!]
> *Conclusion:* Thus, *you* are required to obey your master [whoever he may be!] [given as the similitude/example!]

The pro-argument itself consists of a *similitudo ex iure*, which is a form of *exemplum*.[206] The similitude is — like the example — a proof which is brought in from the outside. It is accomplished on the ground of likeness and requires a *tertium comparationis*.[207] The literary form is for the most part a brief allusion but can also consist of a more developed form of *narratio* or *descriptio*. The specific proof-function of the *similitudo ex iure* is created, 'wenn die *similitudo* statt aus allgemeinen Lebensbereichen aus dem Recht selbst genommen wird'.[208] In fact the *causa* of the similitude is mentioned indirectly by Paul in the preliminary reference to the *tertium* which follows directly upon the simile (v. 16b) in the form of an alternative subjugation: ἤτοι ἁμαρτίας εἰς θάνατον ἢ ὑπακοῆς εἰς δικαιοσύνην (v. 16c). Of significance with respect to the argumentative force of PA⁵ against CA² is the fact that in the *tertium* Paul does not focus on the ἔσχατον but on the present human existence.[209]

---

[204] See, for one, Schlier, *Römerbrief*, 206.

[205] See especially Sprute, *Enthymemtheorie*, 80ff.

[206] See Schlier, *Römerbrief*, 206; cf. also Gäumann, *Taufe*, 93; Cranfield, *Romans*, 322; Schmithals, *Römerbrief*, 198; Dunn, *Romans*, 341; Bartchy, *ΜΑΛΛΟΝ ΧΡΗΣΑΙ*, 58–59; Lampe, *Stadtrömische Christen*, 140–55.

[207] Cf. Plett, *Einführung*, 55; Lausberg, *Handbuch*, 231f. [§ 421].

[208] Lausberg, *Handbuch*, 234 [§ 425], who refers to Quint. *Inst. orat.* 5.11.32ff. Sprute, *Enthymemtheorie*, 87: 'Auf Grund des angeführten Beispiels [see *Ars rhet.* 1393b 4–8] müßte dies wohl für die Parabel dahin präzisiert werden, daß als Beispielfälle auch übliche Verhaltensweisen oder regelmäßige Geschenisabläufe gewählt werden können'.

[209] See Schmithals, *Römerbrief*, 198.

Paul also brings in an inference (PA^{5inf}, vv. 17–18) in order to cor-
relate the similitude used in PA^5 more fully to his case than in the
already noted preliminary reference to the *tertium* in v. 16c. In PA^{5inf}
Paul does not content himself with indicating the alternative subjugation alone; he goes on to give an interpretation of the similitude in
regard to the former and present status of the addressees which enables
him to respond directly to (CA^1 and) CA^2; as in the rest of this chapter,
he does so both *negatively* (ἦτε δοῦλοι τῆς ἁμαρτίας) and *positively*
(ἐλευθερωθέντες δὲ ἀπὸ τῆς ἁμαρτίας ἐδουλώθητε τῇ διαιοσύνῃ).
Thereby the emphasis lies decisively on the change, that is, the liberation and its consequence, as is clearly indicated by the thanksgiving
formula (*MArC*) with which Paul introduces PA^{5inf}.[210] The paradoxical
equation of ἐλευθερωθῆναι = δουλωθῆναι is not only substantiated in
God's absolute justice, as Ernst Fuchs argues,[211] but is already and
primarily due to the similitude itself with its alternative subjugation in
the following *tertium* (v. 16c). In order for the inductive interpretation
(PA^{5inf}) to function in regard to the παριστάνειν of the simile, this
equation was a necessity. The same argument could be used to justify
the difficult inserted sentence in v. 17b (ὑπηκούσατε δὲ ἐκ καρδίας
εἰς ὃν παρεδόθητε τύπον διδαχῆς) as has been argued by Wilckens,
who claims that 'das Gehorsamsmotiv in V17b durch V16 vorbereitet
und V16b ohne V17b nicht voll verständlich ist'.[212] The relation between v. 16b and 18 is established, however, by means of the already
discussed equation, which releases v. 17b from being an argumentative
necessity. On the contrary, the interpolation interferes with the distinct
antithesis of vv. 17–18 as was shown already by Bultmann in 1947,[213]
and it is, of course, not addressed to the Roman church but to the later
readers of the collection of Pauline letters.[214]

[210] Cf. Michel, *Römer*, 212.
[211] E. Fuchs, *Die Freiheit des Glaubens. Römer 5–8 ausgelegt* (BEvT 14; Munich:
Kaiser, 1949) *ad loc.*
[212] Wilckens, *Römer 2*, 35.
[213] Bultmann, 'Glossen im Römerbrief,' *Exegetica*, 283; for further arguments that cannot be given here, see, Michel, *Römer*, 212f.; Gäumann, *Taufe*, 94f.; Tachau, *'Einst' und
'Jetzt',* 117; Schmithals, *Römerbrief,* 199f.; Lindemann, *Paulus im ältesten Christentum* (BHT
58; Tübingen: Mohr-Siebeck, 1979) 26ff. Otherwise, e.g., Schlier, *Römerbrief,* 208–10;
Wilckens, *Römer 2*, 35–37; Fitzmyer, *Romans,* 449f.; Bindemann, *Theologie,* 192f.
[214] Rightly so Schmithals, *Römerbrief,* 200.

By means of PA[5inf] Paul not only brings the theoretical argumentation of the second dialogue phase to completion (as he did at the end of PA[3b:inf]), after which he proceeds to the practical-ethical argumentation (PA[6], vv. 19b–22) of this dialogue phase; he also underscores the fact that the choice of the addressees between the *negative* and the *positive* alternative subjugations has already been accomplished (indicative!) by them. This constitutes the direct background to the paraenetic-ethical argument (imperative!) that follows immediately in PA[6]. Again, the soteriological consequences are established before the paraenetical consequences are elaborated upon.[214a]

Before turning to the final argument, however, Paul inserts a statement about the type of argumentation he is using in this second dialogue phase. He does so by means of an *anaphorical* as well as *cataphorical meta-narrative clause (MNC)*[215] indicating his motivation for using an example/similitude of common human practice and its inductive analogical interpretation: ἀνθρώπινον λέγω διὰ τὴν ἀσθένειαν τῆς σαρκὸς ὑμῶν.[216] Here Paul explicitly states that at this stage in his argumentation he is bringing in an inductive similitude that has to be interpreted by means of an epistemological process of a different kind than the one used in dialogue phase one, where he was able to utilize the theological creed and the baptismal experience in his argumentation. He has to use an inductive proof because of the 'Erkenntnisschwäche der Leser'.[217] Thus, the rhetorical analysis of this chapter as a whole with its usage of

---

[214a] Cf. Bindemann, *Theologie*, 193.

[215] Correct Schlier, *Römerbrief*, 210; so also Wilckens, *Römer 2*, 37; Schmithals, *Römerbrief*, 200f. Only anaphorical: Lietzmann, *Römer*, 71; Michel, *Römer*, 213; Cranfield, *Romans*, 325f.; Dunn, *Romans*, 354f.; Fitzmyer, *Romans*, 450f.; only cataphorical: Fuchs, *Freiheit*, 45f.; Gäumann, *Taufe*, 97f.; neither-nor: Tachau, *'Einst' und 'Jetzt'*, 118: 'Die Redeweise ist also nicht wegen des Bildes vom Sklaven "menschlich", bezieht sich auch nicht auf das Nachfolgende, sondern ist einseitig aufgrund der ausschließlichen Hervorhebung des Indikativs'.

[216] Cf. Bauer, Gingrich, and Danker, *Lexicon*, 67 *s.v.* ἀνθρώπινον: '*speak in human terms* i.e. as people do in daily life Ro 6:19 (cf. Plut., Mor. 13C; Philo, Somn. 2, 288)'. It is a misinterpretation, when Gäumann, *Taufe*, 97 believes that in using this *MNC* Paul excuses himself for the inadequacy of his argumentation; so also Cranfield, *Romans*, 325; Michel, *Römer*, 213; Dunn, *Romans*, 345 and 354f.; Fitzmyer, *Romans*, 450. Correct Käsemann, *Römer*, 174.

[217] Thus Lietzmann (*Römer*, 71) who quotes Lipsius, and especially Schlier, *Römerbrief*, 210, and Schmithals, *Römerbrief*, 200f.

174

different types of proofs (deductive and inductive) enables us to arrive at a better understanding of this much discussed and misunderstood meta-narrative clause too.

3.1.2.3.2.2.2. Pro-argument⁶

I can only deal briefly here with the second paraenetical argument (PA⁶ in vv. 19b–22). This practical proof is given in the form of a traditional scheme of contrasts: τότε vs. νυνί as a practical-ethical rejection of CA².²¹⁸ It is composed of two sections: (1) firstly, a paraenetical exhortation to let the actual change of dominion (ὥσπερ – οὕτως) take on presentic-ethical consequences by means of putting 'once' and 'now' in contrast to each other (vv. 19b-c). This section brings (a) both an indicative reference to the addressees' former slavery under uncleanness and lawlessness *prior to* the change in dominion and its preteric-presentic consequences (εἰς τὴν ἀνομίαν) (b) and also a direct exhortation to serve righteousness now, that is, *after* the change in dominion and its presentic-ethical consequences (εἰς ἁγιασμόν); (2) secondly, a direct motivation for and indirect continuation of the paraenesis with reference to *this life* and *that which is to come* based on the paradoxical contrast between slavery 'once' and 'now'. This motivation contains (a) a reference to the time *prior to* the change of dominion (ὅτε) and its preteric-presentic (ἐφ' οἷς νῦν ἐπαισχύνεσθε) as well as its eschatological consequence (τὸ γὰρ τέλος ἐκείνων θάνατος), and (b) also a reference to the present, *after* the change of dominion (νυνὶ δέ) and its presentic (εἰς ἁγιασμόν) as well as its eschatological consequence (τὸ γὰρ τέλος ζωὴν αἰώνιον).

The function of this second paraenetic proof is — as with PA⁴ — first of all to reject the opponents' CA², but secondly also to admonish the addressees to realize that justification in itself encompasses the obedient service to God, and thus to draw the right conclusion of their christological and soteriological status. When Paul admonishes his ad-

---

²¹⁸ For the traditional provenance of this scheme, see already Bultmann, 'Literaturgeschichte, Biblische', *RGG*² III (Tübingen: Mohr-Siebeck, 1929) 1675–77, 1680–82, especially 1682; *Theologie*, 76 and 107; further Dahl, 'Form-Critical Observations on Early Christian Preaching,' *Jesus in the Memory of the Early Church* (Minneapolis: Augsburg, 1976) 33f.: 'The Soteriological Contrast Pattern'; Tachau, *'Einst' und 'Jetzt'*, especially 79–96, 116–23.

dressees to present their 'members as slaves to righteousness in order to live a consecrated life' (v. 19c), and when he further certifies that the fruit of their former life under the dominion of sin was of a shameful kind but that the fruit of their new life under the dominion of God is 'a consecrated life leading to eternal life' (vv. 20–22), then it is obvious first of all that Paul's own reputation cannot be called in question and secondly that his and the Jewish-Hellenistic gospel which produced the ἐλευθερία ἀπὸ τῆς ἀμαρτίας and the δουλεία τῷ θεῷ cannot be reproached for leading to libertinism. In addition to and after his theoretical proof in the second dialogue phase Paul brings in (as he did in the first dialogue phase) a practical ἦθος-proof (thereby once more aligning himself with Aristotle's claims that showing the moral character of the orator 'constitutes the most effective means of proof'). Here this proof underscores once more the moral character of the author and his message by means of the admonition given in the text itself. Consequently the propaganda of the adversaries misses the target; and this is indeed the real purpose of the paraenetical sections in Paul's strategy of argumentation in Romans 6.

3.1.2.3.2.2.3. Affirmatio²

Before ending the second dialogue phase Paul gives a concluding indicative *affirmatio* (Affirm.²) to the pro-arguments developed in this chapter, especially with regard to its eschatological consequences developed in the latter part of PA⁶, and he does so by means of a modified *recapitulatio* of the doxology of 5.21: τὰ γὰρ ὀψώνια τῆς ἀμαρτίας θάνατος, τὸ δὲ χάρισμα τοῦ θεοῦ ζωὴ αἰώνιος ἐν Χριστῷ Ἰησοῦ τῷ κυρίῳ ἡμῶν (v.23).

3.2. Synthesis of Paul's Argumentation in Romans 6

We may conclude that in his argumentative strategy in this chapter Paul makes direct use of the *probatio* of ancient rhetoric including inartificial, artificial (deductive and inductive) as well as practical proofs. The pro-argumentation consists in the *first dialogue phase* of

(PA¹) a *testimonium*;
(PA²) a *signum necessarium*/τεκμήριον;
(PA³) two partly paralleled *argumenta*;

(PA⁴) an *exhortatio* that functions as an argument;
and in the *second dialogue phase* of
(PA⁵) an *exemplum* in the form of a *similitudo ex iure*;
(PA⁶) an *exhortatio* that again functions as an argument.

Thus, in his pro-argumentation Paul makes use the *probationes* of ancient rhetoric and he does so according to their strength of evidence:

(1) The *inartificial* proofs like *testimonia* were — as we have seen — regarded as the strongest and most powerful ones,[219] and it is certainly not by chance that Paul begins his argumentation with precisely a *testimonium*.

(2) Among *artificial* proofs Aristotle identified (a) syllogistic-deductive *signa* and *argumenta* (in his terms ἐνθυμήματα) as well as (b) inductive *exempla* or *similitudines* (in his terms παραδείγματα) as by far the most important.[220] We have seen that Paul employed both in his argumentation in Romans 6. The interrelationship between these two theoretical types is formulated by Aristotle in his *Topica* in the following words: 'Induction (ἐπαγωγή) is more convincing and clear and more easily grasped by sense-perception and is shared by the majority of people, but reasoning (συλλογισμός) is more cogent and more efficacious against argumentative opponents.'[221] With regard to the order in which the arguments should be presented, Aristotle points out that examples should be used 'as a kind of epilogue/supplement to the enthymemes. For if they stand first, they resemble induction, and induction is not suitable to rhetorical speeches except in very few cases; if they stand last they resemble evidence, and a witness is in every case likely to induce belief'.[222] He goes on to say that it is therefore 'necessary to quote a number of examples if they are put first, but one alone is sufficient if they are put last'. As the above analysis has shown, Paul adheres fully to these rules in his argumentation in Romans 6, where he brings enthymemic-deductive as well as inductive proofs, and where

---

[219] See n. 67.
[220] Cf. *Ars rhet.* 1.2.10. 1356b. Of these two the enthymemes were regarded as the strongest, see *Ars rhet.* 1.1.11. 1355a.
[221] *Topica* 1.12. 105a; see also *Ars rhet.* 1.2.10. 1356b; *Anal. pr.* 2.23. 68b35–37.
[222] *Ars rhet.* 2.20.9. 1394a; induction is here strict induction, see Sprute, *Enthymemtheorie*, 136f.; Sieveke, *Aristoteles*, 255f. n. 84.

the one and only inductive similitude does not come until the second dialogue phase and is followed only by the paraenetic argument which builds directly upon it.

(3) Further, in view of Paul's line of argumentation here, we must not forget that Aristotle was convinced that the practical proof that displays the moral character of the orator 'constitutes the most effective means of proof',[223] a circumstance which Paul utilizes at the end of each of the two dialogue phases.

When Otto Michel feels forced to conclude from his analysis of Romans 6 that it is not easy to find 'einen *fortlaufenden Gedankengang* in Röm 6',[224] this is — as with practically all analyses so far — due to the fact that they have all been involved in interpreting the chapter in terms of the theological concept of baptism[225] and not in terms of the argumentative strategy as part of an argument for Paul's thesis of Justification by faith and its consequence in confrontation with Judaizing and/or Jewish synagogual propaganda against the law-free gospel of Paul and other Jewish-Hellenistic Christians.[225a] If, however, the chapter is interpreted from the point of view of its argumentative force in accordance with contemporary rhetoric, the line of argumentation makes complete sense throughout and Paul is shown to be capable of arguing his case in accordance with the best of Hellenistic argumentative rhet-

---

[223] See above, n. 86. Sprute, *Enthymemtheoric*, 136.

[224] Michel, *Römer*, 213 n. 9; cf. also p. 200; cf. already Lietzmann, *Römer*, 71: 'Von v. 6–23 ist ein einheitlicher Gedankenfortschritt nicht zu ersehen ...'; now also Fitzmyer, *Romans*, 444: 'The following verses, 12–23, are not well integrated into the letter ...'.

[225] E.g. Schlier, *Römerbrief*, 213: 'Der zweite Teil des Kap. 6 (6,15–23) sieht also ebenfalls wie der erste auf die Taufe'; Dinkler, 'Taufaussagen', *passim*; Schnackenburg, 'Adam-Christus-Typologie', *passim*; Gäumann, *Taufe*, *passim*.

[225a] See now Bindemann, *Theologie*, 191ff. who is on the right track when he notices that in this chapter Paul is arguing against his interlocutors for 'freedom from sin' and a new 'life in the service of righteousness': 'von hier aus verbietet sich Libertinismus' (195). This is a correct assessment in spite of his failure to notice the different rhetorical types of proofs applied by Paul in chapter 6 including the *exemplum/similitudo* in vv. 16–18.

Independent of but in concord with the analysis given above Hans Hübner (*Biblische Theologie 2*, 246) now formulates the function of our text as follows: 'Das ganze Kap. 6 ist also die theologische Entgegnung auf den gesetzlich-judenchristlichen Vorwurf, geschrieben somit in Richtung auf *diese* Gruppe innerhalb der römischen Gemeinde'.

oric.[226] Thus Hans Hübner is right in characterizing Paul's letter to the Romans as 'ein *rhetorisches Meisterstück theologischer Argumentation*'.[226a]

---

[226] In an article dealing with the question of Paul's Hellenistic education ('Paulus fra Tarsos. Til spørsmålet om Paulus' hellenistiske utdannelse,' *Dionysos og Apollon. Religion og samfunn i antikkens Hellas* [ed. T. Eide/T. Hägg; SNIA 1; Bergen: Universitetet i Bergen, Klassisk institutt, 1989] 259–82 [A German version will appear in my *New Testament and Textlinguistics*]) I have concluded on the basis of analyses of his employment of genre, use of style, disposition of letters and argumentative strategy that Paul by all likelihood possessed an education of the third grade in the Hellenistic school system. The more detailed analysis in this essay of Paul's argumentative skills fully supports that conclusion. When we strive for a better knowledge of the prerequisites for Paul's writing, general considerations are of little value, only profound analyses of his letters may provide the information needed.

[226a] Hübner, 'Die Rhetorik und die Theologie. Der Römerbrief und die rhetorische Kompetenz des Paulus,' *Die Macht des Wortes*. Aspekte gegenwärtiger Rhetorikforschung (Ars Rhetorica 4; ed. C.J. Classen and H.-J. Müllenbrock; Marburg: Hitzeroth, 1992) 169.

6

Romans 7.7–25 as a Speech-in-Character (προσωποποιία)

Stanley K. Stowers

Speech-in-character (προσωποποιία) is a rhetorical and literary technique in which the speaker or writer produces speech that represents not himself or herself but another person or type of character.[1] Here I intend to show that Paul employs this technique in Romans 7.7–25. I will also describe the characterization in chapter 7 and situate it within the larger context of the letter's rhetoric. I arrived at my conclusion that 7.7–25 was an example of προσωποποιία after studying the ancient rhetorical and grammatical sources. I subsequently discovered that Origen had already reached the same conclusion in the third century. Origen's discussion both provides evidence for 7.7–25 as speech-in-character and illuminates the development of an orthodox Christian reading of the passage.[2]

Cicero, Quintilian and the progymnasmata (elementary rhetorical exercises) of Theon, Hermogenes and Aphthonius provide the best evidence from the rhetorical tradition for προσωποποιία in the early empire.[3] For Theon, probably writing in the first century C.E. προσ-

---

[1] I owe the translation 'Speech-in-Character' to James R. Butts ('The Progymnasmata of Theon: A New Text with Translation and Commentary' [Ph.D.diss., Claremont Graduate School, 1986] 459–60). For discussions of προσωποποιία see the following in addition to Butts: Josef Martin, *Antike Rhetorik* (Munich: C. H. Beck, 1974); George A. Kennedy, *Greek Rhetoric under Christian Emperors* (Princeton: Princeton University Press, 1983) 64; D. L. Clark, *Rhetoric in Greco-Roman Education* (New York: Columbia University Press, 1959).

[2] Portions of the following discussion of speech-in-character will appear in my forthcoming book from Yale University Press, *A Re-reading of Romans: Justice, Jews and Gentiles*.

[3] The standard critical edition for Theon has been Leonard Spengel, *Rhetores Graeci* (Leipzig: Teubner, 1854; repr. Frankfurt am Main: Minerva, 1966); for Hermogenes, Hugo Rabe, *Hermogenis Opera* (Leipzig: Teubner, 1913; repr. Stuttgart, 1969) 1–27; for Aphthonius, Hugo Rabe, *Aphthonii Progymnasmata* (Leipzig: Teubner, 1926).

ωποποιία consists both of cases where one invents the ἦθος (i.e. character by means of words) of a known person (πρόσωπον) and also of cases where one invents both the ἦθος and the person. In the latter case, the invented person is a type such as a husband, a general, or a farmer. The later writers, Hermogenes and Aphthonius, employ the term ἠθοποιία to mean approximately what Theon does by προσωποποιία.[4] In all of these writers, ἦθος means using words to portray a person's character 'including presentation of moral choice embodied in words and arguments'.[5] Cicero, Quintilian, Theon, the grammarians, Origen, and perhaps the *Rhetorica ad Herennium* seem to follow a common tradition somewhat different than the tradition followed by Hermogenes, Aphthonius, and the later rhetorical writings.[6]

On general grounds even before observing Paul's specific use of προσωποποιία, the level of education reflected in the letters makes it likely that Paul received instruction in the subject. Paul's Greek educational level is roughly equivalent to that of someone who had primary instruction with a *grammaticus* or a 'teacher of letters' and then had studied letter writing and some elementary rhetorical exercises.[7] Προσωποποιία was important at two points in the kind of education Paul had. First, as I shall discuss in connection with the grammarians, learn-

---

[4]   Butts, 'Progymnasmata', 457–59; Kennedy, *Greek Rhetoric*, 64.

[5]   Kennedy, *Greek Rhetoric*, 64.

[6]   This tradition defines προσωποποιία like Theon and includes the invention of both ethos and person under the figure. The most likely common sources for the tradition represented by Theon are Aristarchus and the Alexandrian grammarians. For Cicero and Quintilian, see Quint. *Inst. Orat.* 9.2.29–32. On the grammarians and Origen, see my discussion below.

[7]   On Paul's educational level, see Abraham J. Malherbe, *Social Aspects of Early Christianity* (Baton Rouge and London: Louisiana State University Press, 1977) 29–59. For education in antiquity, H.-I. Marrou, *Histoire de l'éducation dans l'antiquité* (6th ed.; Paris: Edition du Seuil, 1965); M. L. Clarke, *Higher Education in the Ancient World* (London: Routledge & K. Paul, 1971); S. F. Bonner, *Education in Ancient Rome* (Berkeley: University of California Press, 1977); Antonio Quacquarelli, *Scuola e cultura dei primi secoli cristiani* (Brescia: Edipuglia, 1974). The preceding accounts of education must be modified with the cautions about diversity, dual educational tracks and social status of A. D. Booth ('Elementary and Secondary Education in the Roman Empire,' *Florilegium* 1 [1979] 1–14) and Robert Kaster (*Guardians of Language: The Grammarian and Society in Late Antiquity* [Berkeley: University of California Press, 1988]; 'Notes on "Primary" and "Secondary" Schools in Late Antiquity,' *TAPA* 113 [1983] 323–46). Kaster and Booth concentrate on a period later than Paul's but are nevertheless important.

ing how to read ancient Greek texts involved the identification of characters and persons. Second, προσωποποιία was one of the elementary exercises closely related to learning prose and poetic composition.[8] Theon and Nicolaus point out that the exercise is also used for training in letter writing.[9] The teacher would ask the student to compose a letter imagining what a certain person would say to a certain addressee on a certain occasion. Ovid's *Heroides* are high literary examples of this exercise. The exercise consists of προσωποποιία since it involves the creation of speech that fits the character of some legendary, historical, or type of person. Paul's ability to read and write letters, even if not in the traditions of high literary culture, makes it almost certain that he had been instructed in προσωποποιία.

The modern form of writing and printing removes one of the most important phases of ancient education from the elementary curriculum and reflects our great distance from the oral culture of the Greco-Roman world. Ancient students unlike moderns had to learn how to identify and interpret all of the basic units of sense beyond the letters of the alphabet.[10] Greek and Latin books and writing had virtually no punctuation, sense units, or meaningful textual arrangement. Lines of letters not even broken into words extended from margin to margin. The elementary teacher taught his pupils to impose the interpretive conventions of formal oral speech upon the written texts.[11] First came the identification of words and syllables in the text. Then came instruction in other sense units. Whether the text was poetry or prose, conventions of rhythm, inflection and emphasis were taught as the means of interpretation. Quintilian speaks of teaching boys when to take a breath, when to place a sense pause into a line, how to indicate where units of sense begin and end, how to modulate the voice, to speed or slacken one's reading (1.7.1). Above all, he says, the number one rule is

---

[8]   Clark, *Rhetoric*, 201, 208–9.

[9]   Theon 2.115.22; Joseph Felton, *Nicolai Sophistae Progymnasmata* (Leipzig: Teubner, 1913) 66–67.

[10]   I do not mean that units of sense were present 'in the text' for readers in any simple way. 'Identifying' and 'interpreting' are processes where the reader creates meaning, although the nature of ancient education tended to make reading highly dependent on tradition.

[11]   Marrou, *Histoire*, chap. 7, esp. 165–66.

that the students practice these things so as to understand what they read (1.7.2). The widely influential grammar book from the second century B.C.E. by Dionysius Thrax outlines this process and papyri from Egypt show how students put marks in texts trying to find word divisions and other units of sense.[12]

The identification of the speaking voice and characters formed another aspect of this elementary education in reading. In every passage the student had to ask, 'who is speaking'. Homer, for example, was the favorite text for elementary instruction although many others were also used. Sometimes Homer speaks in the authorial voice; sometimes one character or another speaks but often without the poet specifically indicating that such-and-such has begun to speak except by keeping the words in character with the speaker. The problem of identifying speakers occurs in most types of literature, being especially acute in drama, philosophical dialogue, and narratives that have speeches and dialogue. In the Greek translations of the Hebrew Bible, the Psalms and the Song of Solomon provided special difficulties in identifying speakers and characters that ancient interpreters discuss in terms derived from Greek grammarians and elementary education. Quintilian complains about the excessive dramatization taught by some elementary teachers when giving instruction in the identification of προσωποποιία.

> Neither is it good, like some teachers, to indicate speech-in-character (*prosopopoeia*) in the manner of a comic actor, even though one ought to make use of some modulation of voice [when reading] in order to distinguish speech-in-character from where the poet is speaking in his own person (*persona*).[13] (1.7.3.)

Comic actors interpreted their characters by means of exaggerated par-odies of the character's speech. Quintilian wants to avoid this but nevertheless recognizes that speakers and readers must distinguish characters. This passage forms part of Quintilian's discussion of the most basic aspects of reading. In order to read ancient texts at all, Paul must necessarily have known how to identify instances of προσωποποιία.

---

[12] Dionysius Thrax, *Ars Grammatica*, ed. Gustav Uhlig (Leipzig: Teubner, 1883) esp. 1–5; PBerlin 13839.

[13] My translation.

The grammarian scholars who wrote about the interpretation of texts discuss προσωποποιία in connection with the exegesis of difficult passages. The great Alexandrian scholar, Aristarchus of Byzantium, developed the principle of judging a passage by τὸ πρόσωπον τὸ λέγον (the character speaking) for exegesis and textual criticism.[14] Earlier grammarians had emended many passages in the homeric epics, the 'Bible of the Greeks', that they considered too immoral for Homer to have authored. Aristarchus restored many of these by emphasizing that words spoken by persons in the narrative represented their views and not necessarily Homer's. Thus grammarians developed a technical vocabulary and principles for talking about προσωποποιία that may have influenced the rhetorical tradition represented by Theon. Thus one solution to contradictions and anomalies in the text was by distinguishing characters (λύσις ἐκ προσώπου).[15] Sometimes, for example, Homer speaks from his own character (ἐξ ἰδίου προσώπου) and at other times from a certain heroic character (ἐξ ἡρωϊκοῦ προσώπου). Instances where the poet or a speaker seem to contradict themselves or speak out of character may mean that the words have been attributed to the wrong person. Thus the grammarians speak much about the appropriateness of words to the person (ἁρμόζειν τῷ προσώπῳ). The reader and critic determine who is speaking by certain criteria of appropriateness. Do the words fit the moral habits and inner dispositions (ἤθη, ἦθος) of a particular person or type of person? Do the words reflect the individual's peculiar history (ἰδίωμα)? Are the words worthy of a particular station in life (ἄξιον)? Does the subject matter fit the person? Above all, the reader must look carefully for change of speaker (ἐναλλαγή, μεταβολή) often signaled by dissonance in relation to preceding speech (διαφωνία). The discussions of the grammarians reveal not only the use of a powerful analytical tool but also the degree to which an understanding of προσωποποιία was essential to ancient reading and why it had such a basic place in the schools.

Paul would also have received instruction in προσωποποιία when he learned to write and compose letters. Theon's elementary exercises

---

[14] Adolf Roemer, *Die Homerexegese Aristarchs in ihren Grundzügen* (Paderborn: E. Belzner, 1924) 223, 253–64.

[15] Hans Dachs, *Die λυσις εκ του προσωπου* (Erlangen: Junge, 1913).

represent the kind of information a teacher would have provided for his students. Theon defines speech-in-character as 'introducing into the discourse' a character (πρόσωπον) with 'words appropriate both to the character and the subject matter' (2.115.10–11). He then gives examples of both the προσωποποιία of types and of known figures; words that a husband would say to his wife as he was about to set off on a journey or a general to troops before battle, in the first instance, and words of Cyrus advancing to Massagetae or Darius to Datis after the defeat at Marathon, in the second. One must consider both the speaker's character and to whom the words are addressed. Regarding appropriateness one need consider such things as the character's age (young and old speak differently), social status (e.g. slave or free), gender, vocation, ethnicity (e.g. Laconians speak concisely and lucidly, Attics fluently) and moral-psychological disposition (e.g. someone in love versus someone with self-mastery [σωφρονεῖν])

The author should take into account the occasion, but as the last example shows, the rhetoricians construe occasion broadly. Thus moral and psychological states count as occasions. Indeed portrayals of such states appear frequently since προσωποποιία served as a technique for moral instruction and exhortation.[16] Some of the sources emphasize speech-in-character's power not only to portray moral habits but also to depict and elicit emotion. The *ad Herennium* notes its effectiveness in appeals to pity (4.53.66). Speaking explicitly of *prosopopoeia* with forensic examples in view, Quintilian writes (6.1.25–26):

> The bare facts are no doubt moving in themselves: but when we pretend that the persons concerned themselves are speaking, the personal note adds to the emotional effect. For then the judge seems no longer to be listening to a voice bewailing another's ills, but to hear the voice and feelings of the unhappy victims, men whose appearance alone would call forth his tears ... and as their plea would awaken yet greater pity if they urged it with their own lips, so it is rendered to some extent more effective when it is, as it were, put into their mouth by their advocate: we may draw a

---

[16] Theon and Quintilian emphasize various types of exhortation in and by means of speech-in-character (Theon 2.115. 20–21; 116.23–118.5; Quint. 9.2.30).

parallel from the stage, where the actor's voice and delivery produce greater emotional effect when he is speaking in an assumed role than when he speaks in his own character.[17]

The reference to the stage and to pitiful characterizations aptly fits προσωποποιία since such scenes from Greek tragedy provided models for its use. Aphthonius, who gives a model speech, has the words that Niobe might have uttered after the children were murdered. Like the speaker in Rom 7.24, Niobe cries out concerning her wretchedness. This 'tragic outcry' was in part made famous by Medea.[18] Aphthonius also suggests the examples of Achilles' speech over the fallen Patroclus and the words of Hecuba at Troy's destruction. Hermogenes provides the example of what Andromache might say to Hector. Both Hermogenes and Aphthonius divide speech-in-character into the emotional, the moral and the combined, depending upon what aspect of personality the author wants to emphasize.

Such examples show why προσωποποιία was often in the first person singular, the classic models being examples of tragic self-reflection. Speech-in-character, however, could take the form of monologue, soliloquy, address, and dialogue or sometimes a combination of these. Thus Quintilian explains:

A bolder form of figure, which in Cicero's opinion demands greater effort, is *fictiones personarum*, or προσωποποιία. This is a device which lends wonderful variety and animation to oratory. By this means we display the inner thoughts of our adversaries as though they were talking with themselves. ... Or without sacrifice of credibility we may introduce conversations between ourselves and others, or of others among themselves, and put words of advice, reproach, complaint, praise or pity into the mouths of appropriate persons. ... It is also convenient at times to pretend

---

[17] Translation by H. E. Butler, *The Institutio Oratoria of Quintilian* (LCL; Cambridge, Mass.: Harvard University Press, 1921).

[18] Euripides frg. 841 (*Tragicorum Graecorum Fragmenta*, ed. August Nauck [Leipzig: Teubner, 1889; repr. Hildesheim: Olms, 1964]); Plutarch, *Mor.* 33F cf. 446A; Seneca, *Medea* 992–3; Ovid, *Metamorph.* 7.18; Epictetus, *Diss.* 2.17.18 cf. 26; Plautus, *Trin.* 657; Aristophanes, *Thes.* 1039.

that we have before our eyes the images of things, persons or utterances ....[19] (9.2.30–33)

This variety of forms persuades me that not only the first person speech of Romans 7 but also the apostrophes in 2.1–16 and 2.17–29 and the dialogue in 3.1–9 and 3.27–4.2 ought to be considered types of προσωποποιία.[20] Quintilian places all these kinds of speech involving imaginary speakers, interlocutors, or addressees under προσωποποιία although he recognizes that some authorities do not. He points out (9.2.31–32) that some call imaginary discussions within larger discourses dialogue (διάλογος, sermocinatio). And although his definition and examples include address to imaginary persons, he follows the section on speech-in-character with a discussion of 'apostrophe' as if it were a separate category (9.2.38–39). According to Quintilian's categories, almost all of the dialogical techniques characteristic of the so-called diatribe would be types of προσωποποιία.

Quintilian further points out that the device may be introduced in a variety of different ways, with or without explicitly identifying the imaginary speaker:

> We may also introduce some imaginary person without identifying him, as when we say, 'Here someone says,' or 'Someone will say'. Or the words may be inserted without the introduction of any speaker at all, as in, 'Here the Dolphian host fought, here fierce Achilles held forth'. This involves a mixture of figures, since added to προσωποποιία is ellipse, which here consists in omitting any indication of the one speaking.[21] (9.2.37)

Quintilian's example represents the words of some Trojan surveying the scene after the Greeks had departed.[22] Emporius, a fifth-century orator who compiled earlier materials, wrote a work on *ethopoeia* that gives examples of three ways to begin a characterization.[23] First, one

---

[19] Translation by Butler, *Quintilian.*
[20] Various other passages with objections and false conclusions might also be investigated in light of speech-in-character.
[21] My translation.
[22] Compare Vergil, *Aen.* 2.29.
[23] Emporii Oratoris, *De ethopoeia* in *Rhet. Lat. Min.* ed. K. Halm (Leipzig: Teubner, 1863) 561–63.

may begin with the character starting to speak about herself or himself in the first person ('I have truly deserved it, and I will not try to minimize ...'). Second, the speech may begin as an apostrophe with the author addressing the fictional character ('Oh you of such great fame ...'). Third, if one wants to emphasize the occasion, one should begin by introducing the circumstances (e.g. 'These solemn rites ...' or 'During the war with Argolis ...'). Such examples of speech-in-character without explicitly named speakers provided the difficult texts over which the grammarians worried and, as I shall show, about which ancient exegetes of Romans discussed.

Hermogenes and Aphthonius recommend that the imaginary character refer to his or her present misery, past happiness before the current plight, and wretched future prospects. Both handbooks assume that figures reflecting upon their tragic plights provide the classic models for προσωποποιία. Models of barbarian women hold some place in the examples with the significance of Hecuba and Niobe, both Phrygians. Libanius' models of ἠθοποιία include Niobe with her children and two of Medea, upon marrying Jason and about to kill her children.[24] Hecuba, Niobe, and especially Medea, came to epitomize the Greek stereotype of barbarian psychology and character.[25] One can understand the choice of these three for such scenes of tragic emotion by realizing that barbarians were supposed to be more passionate and less self-controlled than Greeks, and women than men. These women form the antithesis to the Greek male ideal. Theon and Quintilian (*Inst.* 11.1.41) explicitly include foreign ethnicity as categories for προσωποποιία and Theon adds some emphasis to this category by discussing Herodotus' abilities at producing characterizations of barbarian speech (2.115.7–14).

Celsus' polemic against Christianity, *The True Discourse*, extensively employed προσωποποιία. Origen's reply to Celsus includes a critique of his προσωποποιία that I find helpful in understanding the tech-

---

[24] *Libanii Opera*, ed. Richardus Foerster (Leipzig: Teubner, 1903) 3.373–437. Libanius emphasizes the Medea example by placing Medea about to slay her children first of all the examples.

[25] Edith Hall, *Inventing the Barbarian: Greek Self-Definition through Tragedy* (Oxford: Clarendon, 1989) 125, 107–110, 168. Hall points out that the ancestry of Hecuba and Niobe varied in early sources.

nique and the criteria for its intelligible use. Celsus employed a number of different characters and forms of προσωποποιία in his polemic. In one instance he seems to have imitated a child having his first lesson with an orator (*c. Cels.* 1.28).[26] Twice Celsus introduces general types of people; the person who has difficulty seeking God and the fleshly person, suggesting that Christians are like these (6.66; 7.36.17). Most importantly, however, Celsus employs an imaginary Jew through major portions of the work, who first addresses himself to Jesus, then carries on a dialogue with Jesus that Origen explicitly describes as προσωποποιία, and then in another portion of the work Celsus has the (or a ?) Jew speak to caricatured Christians.[27] In all, Origen explicitly refers to Celsus' προσωποποιία using either the noun or the verb some twenty-six times.

Origen complains that Celsus does not create characterizations that fit the persons being described and that he fails to keep his characterizations consistent (1.28.1). Not only must characterizations fit the person or type but each time the character speaks or is reintroduced into the discourse, what the person says must be consistent with what the person said before or what was said about the person. In 1.43, Origen criticizes Celsus for ideas and words that might be appropriate to Epicureans, Peripatetics, or Democritus — that is, to skeptical philosophers — but not to a Jew. Origen himself then uses speech-in-character to address an imaginary Jew. Elsewhere Origen points out Celsus' ignorance of Judaism when Celsus has the imaginary Jew speak as if there were only one prophet who foretold. Origen says that such words might fit Samaritans or Sadducees who hold only to the books of Moses but not the typical Jew that Celsus wants to portray (1.49). In another place, Origen also points out that the imaginary Jew's words are fitting for address to imaginary Gentile Christians but not to the Jewish Christian audience that Celsus depicts (2.1).

---

[26] It is unclear whether this child represents an independent person or whether Origen means that Celsus represented Jesus or the Jew as if they were beginning students.

[27] According to Karl Pichler (*Streit um das Christentum: Die Angriff des Kelsos und die Antwort des Origenes* [Frankfurt am Main: P. Lang, 1980] 124–33), the fragments from Celsus in 1.28–71 come from the Jew's first speech and those in 2.1–79 from the second speech, while from 3.1 Celsus speaks in his own person.

Most of 7.36–37 constitutes an extended critique of Celsus' προσ-ωποποιία. Origen first cites a passage from the *True Discourse* where imaginary Christians speak and Celsus then replies to them in his own person. Origen next levels some criticisms:

> It is a virtue in a writer who puts words into the mouth of someone else to preserve consistency in the meaning (βούλημα) and character (ἦθος) of the person to whom the words are attributed; and it is a fault when anyone attributes to the mouth of the speaker words which are inappropriate (μὴ ἁρμόζειν). Equally blameworthy are those who, in putting words into the mouth of a person, attribute philosophy which the author has learnt to barbarians and illiterate people or slaves, who have never heard philosophical arguments and have never given a proper account of them.[28]

Origen then notes that people praise Homer for the aptness and consistency of his characterizations but that Aristophanes ridiculed Euripides for giving barbarian women and slave girls philosophical sounding lines (cf. Aristophanes, *Acharnians* 393ff.). Theon makes the same compar-ison and refers to Euripides attributing inappropriately philosophical lines to Hecuba (2.60.27–32). Others in antiquity also criticized Homer for inconsistency in characterization (Ps Plutarch, *De Vita Homeri* 66B). Origen's discussion makes clear that ancient readers read with stricter and more stereotyped ideas about characterization. Certain attributes were deemed consistently true of men, women, barbarians, and so forth. If we are to take Paul's characterizations seriously we must read with close attention to their form and consistency.

Finally, Origen's understanding of divine προσωποποιία in Scripture can help us understand the relation of the technique to an author's adaptability in speaking and use of the authorial voice. Celsus charged the Scriptures with crudeness and bad theology for attributing to God passions like love and anger (4.71). Origen replied that God sometimes spoke from his own person in Scripture but when addressing the weak,

---

[28] Trans. by Henry Chadwick, *Origen: Contra Celsum* (Cambridge: Cambridge University Press, 1965).

used προσωποποιία appropriate to their fleshly level of understanding (4.71): God spoke in fleshly terms to the fleshly. Origen's doctrine of revelation through the logos here fits with what moralists and rhetoricians said about the authorial adaptability of speakers and writers.[29] In light of Origen and the general rhetorical attitude toward adaptability to various personae, we should perhaps take more seriously the implications of Paul's claim of adaptability toward Jews, Gentiles, and the weak (1 Cor 9.19-22).

Προσωποποιία in Romans 7.7-25

I will attempt the difficult task of imagining a reading possible for readers in Paul's time. Thus I will not make Christian assumptions and readings that can only be documented later than Paul.[30] We cannot presuppose the introspective Christian conscience of late antiquity or the middle ages. Nor can we assume the much later Christian stereotypes of the legalistic Jew who attempts the impossible task of keeping the law. The picture of Paul the Pharisee who attempted that impossible task clearly comes from reading the narratives of his conversion in Acts through the lens of later Christian constructions of Judaism and the law.[31] Types and assumptions for reading will have to be those that readers in Paul's time could have made.

The section begins in v. 7 with an abrupt change in voice following a rhetorical question that serves as a transition from Paul's authorial voice that has previously addressed the readers explicitly described by the letter in 6.1-7.6. This constitutes what the grammarians and rhetoricians described as change of voice (ἐναλλαγή or μεταβολή). These ancient readers would next look for διαφωνία, a difference in characterization from the authorial voice. The speaker in 7.7-25 speaks with great personal pathos of coming under the law at some point, learning about his desire and sin, and being unable to do what he wants to do

---

[29] Clarence E. Glad, 'Adaptability in Epicurean and Early Christian Psychagogy: Philodemus and Paul' (Ph.D. diss., Brown University, 1992).

[30] Later Christian assumptions and readings, of course, should not be excluded beforehand as possibilities.

[31] Paula Fredriksen, 'Paul and Augustine: Conversion Narratives, Orthodox Traditions, and the Retrospective Self,' *JTS* 37 (1986) 3-34.

because of enslavement to sin and flesh. If one asks whether Paul gives his readers any clues at all elsewhere in the letter that this might be his autobiography, the answer is clearly 'no'. Nor does this picture even fit with what he says about himself in other letters.[32] The passage seems to present a distinctive and coherent ethos with a particular life situation. Like the handbooks recommend, the person speaks of his 'happy' past before he learned about the law (7.7b–8 and esp. 9), his present misery, and his future plight (7.24). Since this tragic characterization also centers on self-reflection and takes the form primarily of a monologue, the passage fits the classic models of speech-in-character. The text portrays emotion, moral-psychological disposition, 'inner thoughts', and 'complaint' (Quint. 9.2.30–33).

In accord with a form of the technique discussed in the handbooks, Paul's authorial voice does not explicitly introduce the person. In comparison with the preceding context in chapters 6 and 7 where Paul's voice clearly addresses 'brothers', the addressee(s) of the voice in 7.7–25 is either ambiguous or only Paul. The explicit audience of the letter addressed in its prescript disappears as it does in 1.18 – 4.23, which I have elsewhere argued is also dominated by προσωποποιία.[33] At one point, again in accordance with προσωποποιία, dialogue appears between the speaker in 7.7–25 and Paul. The characterization of 7.7–25 reads like someone personally witnessing to 'when we were in the flesh, our sinful passions worked in our bodily parts through the law' (7.5) after the false conclusion and its rejection in 7.7a, 'What shall we say? Is the law sin? By no means!' The identity of the speaker at 7.7a is unclear. Perhaps it is Paul; perhaps the person characterized in what follows; perhaps an anonymous objector.

A textual variant generally ignored because it does not fit traditional ways of reading Romans, indicates that Paul addresses the person of 7.7–25 as a conclusion to the passage. Earlier and better witnesses give very strong support to reading σε ('you', singular) in 8.2 rather than με

---

[32] The position of Krister Stendahl is still entirely persuasive ('The Apostle Paul and the Introspective Conscience of the West,' *HTR* 56 [1963] 199–215; repr. in *Paul Among Jews and Gentiles* [Philadelphia: Fortress, 1976]).

[33] See especially my forthcoming book on Romans.

('me').[34] The 'me' became the standard reading and is the reading of most English translations even though the Nestle-Aland critical Greek text reads 'you' singular.[35] This contradictory state of affairs came about because the προσωποποιία in 7.7 – 8.2 (the imaginary speaker in 7.7b–25 plus Paul's address to him in 8.1–2 and 7.25a) became unintelligible to later readers far removed from Paul's historical and rhetorical context. The imaginary dialogue was lost. But in light of ancient προσωποποιία and the sense of the passage, the 'you' fits well indeed. The character's speech ends when Paul addresses him with words of encouragement.

I must conclude that in a formal way, the passages fits very well with what ancient authorities said about speech-in-character and ancient examples of its use. In order to make a fuller case, I will have to discuss the nature, content and rhetorical function of the characterization in chapter 7. At this point, however, it will prove useful to look at Origen's discussion of the passage.[36]

Origen and Others on 7.7–25

Several fragmentary sources have survived for Origen's commentary on 7.7–25.[37] Greek fragments from the *Philocalia* and the *Catenae* show that Rufinus' Latin translation has rather drastically abbreviated the section and not without distortion.[38] Jerome's *Epistle* 121 also depends on Origen's commentary and can be used but only with great caution. Origen says that Paul does not speak of himself alone in 7.7–8 but of every person. He then gives his famous interpretation of the passage as

---

[34] Σε is supported by Sinaiticus B F G 1506*.1739*.a b sy(p); Tert Ambst; με by A D byzantine majority lat sy(h) sa; Cl.

[35] The RSV, NIV, TEV, and KJV use 'me'. The *Jerusalem Bible* chooses 'you'.

[36] Portions of the following discussion of Origen and Nilus on Romans 7 will appear in my forthcoming book on Romans.

[37] C. P. Hammond Bammel, 'Philocalia ix, Jerome, Epistle 121, and Origen's Exposition of Romans vii,' *JTS* 32 (1981) 50–81; *Der Römerbrieftext des Rufin und seine Origenes-Übersetzung* (AGLB 10; Freiburg: Herder, 1985).

[38] On the abbreviation, see Hammond Bammel (*Römerbrieftext*). *The Philocalia of Origen*, ed. J. A. Robinson (Cambridge: Cambridge University Press, 1893); for the catenae, A. Ramsbotham, 'The Commentary of Origen on the Epistle to the Romans,' *JTS* 13 (1912) 209–24, 357–68; 14 (1913) 10–22.

a reference to the time in childhood before rational accountability when the natural law teaches right and wrong to each individual. Origen could have and conceivably may have referred to προσωποποιία here. The fragments make it difficult to be certain of what Origen thought about the rhetoric of 7.7–13 although the principles he lays out in his discussion of 7.14–25 would seem to apply to 7.7–13. Clearly, for Origen the speaker of 7.7–25 does not speak autobiographically of Paul. Among other objections to an autobiographical interpretation, Origen points out correctly that Jews do not speak of a time in their life when they live 'without the law' as 7.9 would indicate on this reading (*Com. Rom.* 6.8 [1082]).

The Greek fragments, Rufinus, and Jerome agree that Origen's main topics for vv. 14–25 were the identity of the speaker(s) and the type of experience described.[39] He begins by pointing to the contradiction between what the person speaking says of himself and the way Paul describes himself elsewhere. The Greek fragments have examples of Paul speaking in his own persona from 1 Cor 6.20; Gal 3.13, and 2.20 in words that contradict the self-description in chapter 7. Rufinus in addition has 2 Cor 10.3; Rom 8.11; and 1 Cor 6.19. Jerome has Acts 9.15; 1 Cor 6.19; and 2 Cor 13.3. I suspect that Jerome has added the texts from Acts and 2 Corinthians but the other sources may have abbreviated. Origen goes on to say that the reader faces contradiction 'unless we should say that the discourse has different characterizations (προσωποποιίαι) and the sections conform to various qualities of characters (πρόσωπα)'.[40]

Origen's key to understanding the content of the προσωποποιία of 7.7–25 is his conception of moral progress. Technical Stoic language and philosophical koine regarding moral psychology and ethics occur

---

[39] Rufinus *Com. Rom.* 6.9 (1085AB); catena xli; Jerome *Ep.* 121.34.14–22.

[40] Hammond Bammel is mistaken in saying that Origen is guarded and tentative about προσωποποιία in chapter 7 because of the expression εἰ μή που εἴπωμεν and Origen saying that the words are 'appropriate' for the characters speaking ('Origen's Exposition', 68). The first expression is due to the condition set up with the preceding section so that Origen speaks of a contradiction 'unless'. In the second case, she does not understand that ἁρμόζειν is a technical term used by the rhetoricians and grammarians to indicate the criteria for προσωποποιία.

densely throughout the chapter. Origen wants to see in the chapter persons speaking who represent different stages. According to the *Catenae* (41.4–5), Origen places all of the character types represented in the section under the category of the unwise who act against their own intentions and purposes — the famous problem of ἀκρασία, lack of self-mastery, or weakness of the will. If Origen had not been so intent on seeing degrees and types of moral progress or lack thereof, he might have described the whole text more simply as a characterization of the ἀκρατής. The catenist understood προσωποποιία and has selected the fragments that introduce the characterizations, for instance, 'the present discourse is appropriate to be said by ... ' (41.6–7); 'These words are appropriate for one to say who ...' (42.1).

According to the *Catena* fragment, verse 14 is said by 'those who have learned concerning the law that it is divine and seen that its commandments are good, but nevertheless do not understand how they fall under sin since they are sold under sin and fleshly' (41.6–7). Origen probably distinguishes the person represented by vv. 14–15 from the characterization of vv. 17–25 because the former seems to be in a state in which he recognizes the good but does not understand the evil powers of the passions and desires, whereas the latter well understands the battle within. The person in v. 14 has just learned about the law.[41] According to Rufinus, Origen referred to 1 Cor 9.22 in order to explain Paul's προσωποποιία (*Com. Rom.* 6.9 [1086A]). Paul adapts himself to the condition of the weak by speaking the words of the weak.

The Catena extract on 7.15 (42) 'fits the words' of

those who wrestle with their desires but who fall due to the weakness of their reason, and those who are conquered by anger and fear and who do what they do not want and what they hate. And also when having been overcome by the elation of reason we are conquered by that which seems to be good but is not truly,

---

[41] According to Rufinus (*Com. Rom.* 6.9 [1085AB]), 14a is spoken with apostolic authority but 14b by one sold under sin. This contradicts the Greek fragments which make no such distinction. Hammond Bammel ('Origen's Exposition', 68) thinks that both may have come from Origen but that Rufinus and the catenist selected from different parts of his discussion. I think it more likely that Rufinus has tried to improve on Origen.

we agree with the law that it is good but we act according to [the demands] of pleasure.

Origen recognizes that Paul is discussing lack of self-mastery (ἀκρασία) and explains the state with technical Stoic concepts. Here Rufinus agrees rather closely with the Greek although he is unable to convey Origen's technical language.[42]

According to extract 43, Paul depicts in vv. 22–23

those who have not yet strengthened their habituation toward that which is best. Just as if a soldier having defeated enemies parades captives, so in regard to the characters set forth, the law of their [bodily] parts wages war against the law of their mind, taking captive the wretched soul and parading it before the law [of sin in their bodily parts].[43]

Origen seems to have read vv. 17–25 as coming from the mouth of the same imaginary character who represents the new convert. Paul interjects the cry of thanksgiving in 25a but otherwise the words represent the person newly come to Christ who has not yet overcome his former habits (*Com. Rom.* 6.9 [1089A–1091B]; Catena 44).[44] Again the Greek fragments show that Origen understands the passage to be discussing ἀκρασία, but here for the situation of the new Christian.[45]

Origen shows us how and why an ancient reader would have understood 7.7–25 as προσωποποιία. He reads the text just as grammar school teachers taught their pupils, and he employs the technical vocabulary that philological scholars and rhetoricians used in exegesis.[46] He employs the criteria of appropriateness and discusses change of

---

[42] Hammond Bammel, 'Origen's Exposition', 69.

[43] The brackets enclose a difficult reading not found in the Munich codex.

[44] Rufinus and the Greek cannot be fully reconciled on vv. 17–25 but Origen's basic approach is clear. Hammond Bammel ('Origen's Exposition', 69–72) seems to assimilate Origen's clear approach to the passage though speech-in-character to Jerome's western theology of human frailty seen also in Ambrose, Augustine, and Ambrosiaster on Romans 7.

[45] Here I would point to Origen's talk of human ἀσθένεια explained in terms of constraints against reason and compulsion toward the opposite (*Cat.* 44).

[46] On Origen and the philologians, see the excellent discussion of Bernard Neuschäfer, *Origenes als Philologe* (Basel: F. Reinhardt, 1987) 263–76.

speaker, characterization, and authorial versus imaginary persona. Origen assumes as patently obvious that the general subject of the characterization is ἀκρασία, failure of self-mastery. But he does not try to historically imagine what this might mean for Paul the Jewish missionary to Gentiles living before the destruction of the temple. Instead, he sees types, ranging from the person who has just come to accountability under the natural law of reason, to the ἀκρατής not understanding the causes of his condition, to the new convert who knows his condition but still struggles for self-mastery. In other words, Origen not surprisingly adapts the characterization to the pedagogical progress emphasized in the philosophically informed Christianity of his own time. Only this last phase of interpretation would not also fit readers in Paul's own time.

Origen is not the only ancient interpreter of Romans to read chapter 7 as speech-in-character. Rufinus and Jerome, at least at the time when they write the texts cited above, seem to accept Origen's approach. Nilus of Ancyra follows the terminology of the later rhetorical tradition describing the 'I' in chapter 7 as ἠθοποιία. This shows that his judgment came independently of Origen. In a letter to a certain Olympius, who in Nilus' view seriously misread chapter 7, Nilus writes:

> God forbid! The divine apostle does not say concerning himself that 'I see another law in my members taking me captive through sin'. Rather these things are uttered by a person (ἐκ προσώπου) representing those who are troubled by fleshly passions. ...[47]

In a subsequent letter, Nilus adds:

> It is easy to grasp that the apostle is employing characterization (ἠθοποιία) when a voice says, 'But I was once living without the law'. And truly there is never any time when a person has respite without the law of Moses; or from a young age he was closely brought up in the law by Gamaliel. Moreover, the person (τὸ πρόσωπον) is to be understood as belonging to those who have lived outside the law of Moses.[48]

---

[47] *Letter* 1.152 (PG 79, 1.145).
[48] *Letter* 1.153 (PG 79, 1.145).

Nilus understands the passage as a speech-in-character but in the terminology of a different rhetorical tradition from Origen's. Apparently Nilus understood 7.7–24 to depict one person; someone not a native to the law who came under the law but who is nevertheless mastered by passions and desires.

The Characterization in 7.7–25

If Origen correctly recognized in 7.7–25 a person or persons lacking self-mastery but imposed an anachronistic Christian interpretation on top of his fundamentally sound reading, how can we imagine a reading closer to what Paul's readers might have read? Here I will offer only some preliminary suggestions toward answering this question. It has become a cliche in literary studies to say that one must first understand the typical linguistic and cultural codes in order to grasp the particularity of a text, extrinsic genre precedes intrinsic genre. Paul's readers would have to grasp culturally shared codes, discourses, generic conceptions and intertextual connections in order to grasp Paul's 'unique' meaning.

I have already pointed to similarities between Romans 7 and tragic monologues by barbarian women. On the scale of self-mastery in Greco-Roman culture, barbarian women had the least of it. Their frequent depiction in literature and moral instruction represents a type on the scale of a central cultural value. I find convincing the arguments of scholars who have presented evidence that 7.15, 19–20 quotes a virtually proverbial saying about ἀκρασία that was widely recognized as the medean saying.[49] The classic text from Euripides's *Medea* (1077–80) was re-echoed in numerous Medeas written in antiquity and endlessly discussed by moralists and philosophers.

Galen, for example, explicitly makes the connection of Medea, barbarian psychology and ἀκρασία in the following passage after citing her words about doing what she does not want to do:

---

[49] H. Hommel, 'Das 7. Kapitel des Römerbriefs im Licht Antiker Überlieferung,' *ThV* 8 (1961–62) 90–116; Gerd Theissen, *Psychological Aspects of Pauline Theology* (Philadelphia: Fortress, 1987) 211–19. I have added to the evidence and reassessed the arguments in my forthcoming book on Romans.

Of course she knows the magnitude of the evils she is going to do, being instructed by reason; but she says that her anger overpowers her reason, and therefore she is forcibly led by anger to do the deed. … Euripides has made Medea an example of barbarians and uneducated persons, in whom anger is stronger than reason; but among Greeks and educated people … reason prevails over anger.[50]

Like sin, which Paul explains by passions (τὰ παθήματα in 7.5) and desire (ἐπιθυμία in 7.7–8), in the example of Medea, passion like an outside force overpowers her rational will to do good. She is the type of the extreme moral other, furthest removed from the ideal of the Greek male.

I am convinced that echoes of this medean myth would have been a component of a likely reading of Romans 7 by Paul's contemporaries. Paul, however, is a Jew so that other Jewish cultural codes come to the fore even if echoing larger Greco-Roman themes. That which corresponds to the barbarian in Paul's sub-culture is the Gentile. Romans 7 also echoes the type of the Gentile as constructed widely in Jewish literature of the second temple period. This conception of the Gentile links Greek psychology of reason and the passions with a critique of polytheism. Because Gentiles have rejected the one true God and worship idols they live by a degenerate *politeia* characterized by failure to control their passions and desires.[51] Thus all manner of vice and sexual immorality characterizes Gentile life.

Paul clearly works with this conception of Gentiles. In 1 Thess 4.4–5 he writes, 'let each man know how to obtain his own wife in holiness and honor, not in the passion of desire (ἐν πάθει ἐπιθυμίας) as the Gentiles who do not know God'.[52] Most importantly, the very text introducing the letter's discussion of the gospel's power to save Jews

---

[50] *Hippoc. et. Plat.* 189.20–190.1. Trans. by P. DeLacy, *Galen on the Doctrines of Hippocrates and Plato* (Berlin: Akademie, 1978).

[51] E.g. *Ep. Arist.* 152; *Sib. Or.* 3.591–99; Philo, *Sacr. Abel* 15, *Virt.* 179–82; Josephus, *C. Apion.* 2.193; O. Larry Yarbrough, *'Not Like the Gentiles': Marriage Rules in the Letters of Paul* (SBLDS 80; Atlanta: Scholars Press, 1985).

[52] Trans. by Yarbrough, *'Not Like the Gentiles'*, 7.

199

and Gentiles encodes this conception of the Jewish other. The story of
1.18–32 narrates how the non-Jewish peoples refused to worship the
true God and turned to idols. God therefore punished them by allowing their enslavements to 'the desires (ἐπιθυμίαι) of their hearts' (1.24),
'dishonorable passions' (1.26), and 'a base mind' (1.28). Because of this
bondage to passion and desire, a mind-boggling list of vices characterizes the life of these polytheistic peoples. Paul says nothing comparable
of Jews. The passage that readers have traditionally made bear this
weight, 2.17–29, does not generalize about Jews but depicts a particular Jewish teacher of the law who instructs Gentiles in the decalogue.[53]

Romans 7 plays on a tradition in which Jewish writers held out the
law epitomized by the tenth commandment of the decalogue as the
solution to Gentile enslavement to passion and desire. Philo and 4
Maccabees explain the moral purpose of the law as the mastery of
passion and desire by reason and treat the tenth commandment, 'thou
shall not desire', as the focus of this program. Philo makes desire
(ἐπιθυμία) the most severe of the passions and the cause of every war
and social catastrophe among Greeks and barbarians (*Dec.* 142, 151–
3). Gentiles who heed the law will immediately gain self-mastery of
their passions and desires (*Virt.* 179–82; *Spec. Leg.* 4.92–132). The
person speaking in 7.7–25 also cites the tenth commandment as a
general prohibition of desire (ἐπιθυμία). Only when this person heard
this commandment did he recognize his bondage to passion and his
sinful state. But knowing the law only told him of his desperate condition; it did not enable him to overcome the passions of the flesh and to
do right. Origen and other ancient exegetes recognized that this could
not depict Paul or other Jews if law here really does mean the law of
Moses. Rather, the person must be a Gentile who has come to know
the decalogue. Instead of envisioning Gentiles attracted to Judaism in
Paul's time, Origen handles the problem by first introducing the idea
of natural law and then by seeing a new convert to Christianity rather
than a Gentile attracted to Judaism in vv. 17–24. The characterization
is certainly not of Paul, who describes himself as 'blameless with regard

---

[53] I devote a chapter to this passage in my forthcoming book. See also my *The Diatribe and Paul's Letter to the Romans* (SBLDS 57; Chico, CA: Scholars Press, 1981) chap. 2.

to righteousness under the law' (Phil 3.6) and speaks of himself and Peter as 'Jews and not Gentile sinners' (Gal 2.15). Paul might admit to the normal human frailty and sinfulness that Jews took for granted but that is far from the figure in Romans 7 'sold under sin' and so enslaved to passions and desire that he cannot do the good.

Recognizing that the passage echoes the types of the barbarian and the Gentile who lack self-mastery still does not reveal what the text means within the context of its discourse in Romans. The traditional ways of reading Romans overlook the evidence that Paul is addressing Gentiles in chapter 6 — the immediate context for our passage.[54] For the first time since the letter's prescript which explicitly describes the readers as Gentiles who believe in Christ (1.6, 13–15 cf. 11.13; 15.14–18), Paul addresses his audience explicitly and personally in chapter 6. Before baptism into Christ, the readers described here were ruled and enslaved by sin, obeying its passions (6.12–14, 16–18, 20–22). At crucial junctures in the chapter Paul stops using the 'we' to include himself with his audience and underlines their past: e.g. 'you who were once slaves of sin have become obedient' and 'just as you once gave your bodily parts in service to impurity and increasing lawlessness' and 'the things of which you are now ashamed' (vv. 17, 19, 20). In nearly the same breath, Paul begins to speak of the same 'brethren' having once been bound to the law but now being free (7.1–6) and speaks of the law having aroused their passions in this past life (7.5).

The description of the readers' past life in chapter 6 is the picture of the Gentile in chapter 1. The readers like the Gentiles in chapter 1 were enslaved to desires (6.12) and passions (7.6). Both texts describe the result of bondage to these powers as impurity and shameful deeds (1.24, 28; 6.19, 21). But the readers here were also under the law. And yet instead of freeing these Gentiles from their passions as Philo, Josephus, or 4 Maccabees would have it, the law only made their bondage worse. Here we have the dilemma dramatized in chapter 7 and introduced in chapter 1. Since the Gentiles refused to worship and honor God, God punished them by ordaining their enslavement to

---

[54] The only scholar whom I have noticed to recognize this is Francis Watson (*Paul, Judaism and the Gentiles* [Cambridge: Cambridge University Press, 1986] 224 n. 22) who says that Romans 6 is ostensibly addressed to Gentiles.

passions and desires. No wonder Paul argues that his readers cannot become righteous by doing works from the law (3.20–21, 27–31; 4.5). Paul opposes Jews like Philo who claimed that Gentiles could gain mastery of their passions and desires through following appropriate teachings from the law. According to Paul, God himself ordained that the Gentiles be punished by enslavement to their passions (1.24, 26, 28) and in Paul's view, only God's plan through Christ can liberate them. The readers Paul depicts in chapter 6 and the προσωποποιία of chapter 7 are Gentiles who had associated themselves with Judaism before coming to Christ, so-called Godfearers. Paul's gospel (2.16) taught that Gentiles could not free themselves from passion and desire through works of the law. Indeed the law only made things worse for these people since it gave them a knowledge of the good at the same time as it revealed their ἀκρασία. Rather Gentiles are made right with God solely through the redemption in Jesus Christ. Thus after the speaker in chapter 7 depicts the dilemma of Gentiles who know the law, Paul in chapter 8 describes how the Gentile can be free from the mind of the flesh and be given a new mind through the Spirit of Jesus Christ. The readers, then, will have replaced their old minds (1.21, 22, 28) corrupted as a result of idolatry with new minds (8.6–7). In this way they can actually 'fulfill the just requirements of the law' (8.4).

Rom 7.7–25 and Paul's address to this imaginary person in 7.25a and 8.1–2 fits extremely well with what the Greco-Roman rhetoricians and grammarians described as προσωποποιία or ἠθοποιία and I have translated as speech-in-character. Paul would have learned to recognize προσωποποιία in his elementary schooling and later have received instruction in its composition. Origen, the most brilliant exegete of the ancient church, and other interpreters recognized that chapter 7 contained speech-in-character. While viewing 7.7–25 as speech-in-character does not settle the exegesis of the passage, it does preclude some readings and suggests others. I have proposed that the characterization echoes broader cultural types from Greek, Latin and Jewish literature that fit remarkably well the προσωποποιία and the characterization of the letter's audience constructed in chapters 1 and 6.1–7.6.

7

The Quest for Honor and the Unity of the Community in Romans 12 and in the Orations of Dio Chrysostom[1]

Halvor Moxnes

The new community Paul envisages in Romans 12 is one in which one does not seek one's own honor. Rather, one associates with the lowly and indeed gives honor to others, thereby overcoming potential threats to the community. On such a reading, Paul's argument in the chapter belongs squarely within the context of the Hellenistic discussion of the quest for honor as a threat to the unity of the polis.

The dual thesis I have just outlined is based on the presuppositions that Paul's exhortations about arrogance and the quest for honor (12.3, 9–10, 16) form not just another theme, but are of structural importance in the chapter, and that the quest for honor is related to the issue of unity as discussed in the letter as a whole. I shall address these presuppositions in a discussion of Romans 12 and 13 in the second part of the paper. The first part is devoted to a presentation of the role of honor within the Hellenistic city as it is described and criticized in the orations of Dio Chrysostom.

The perspective I shall try to apply to Paul is to see him as formulating some of the criticisms and dilemmas of the 'honor culture' within the Hellenistic city as seen from the position of marginal groups in these cities. Thus, Hellenistic concepts about honor and status are not just part of Paul's general 'background'. Rather, he participated in a discussion of their role and influence in community formation and community life.

[1] Quotations from Dio Chrysostom, *Orationes*, are taken from the Loeb Classical Library edition, Bible quotations from the RSV. I am grateful to the editor for his extremely valuable criticism of this paper, far beyond his editorial responsibility.

The Hellenistic City as an Honor Culture

Competition for honor among members of the elite was a major characteristic of life in the Hellenistic city. Honor and status in exchange for munificence towards the city, towards the 'common good', was a central feature in city culture and city life.[2] Attitudes towards honor and status, seen within their social and political context, point towards central elements in Hellenistic conceptions about city and community.

The system of honor and status has been studied from various angles. Archaeological studies have focused on statues, altars, buildings, etc. and epigraphy on inscriptions on buildings and statue bases. Likewise, in art history the use of art to create symbols of power has recently come into focus.[3] Taken together these approaches provide an impressive picture of civic honors and of the central position of beneficence within the social, political, and economic life of Greco-Roman cities.

But art, archaeology, and epigraphy present only one side of the picture. According to C. P. Jones, inscriptions 'tend naturally to mention those aspects of city life which were thought good examples for posterity: generous benefactors, grateful populaces, civic harmony'.[4] Jones contrasts this with a picture of life in the first century drawn from a different angle, in the speeches of Dio Chrysostom. Of Dio's language in his speech against the riot in Prusa (*Or.* 46) he says that it 'anticipates the language of Christian bishops, since they too were more concerned with the vices than the virtues of their hearers'.

I shall attempt to present the dilemmas and the conflicts within the honor-beneficence system. The speeches of Dio Chrysostom provide a good starting point. His criticism of those who seek honor is contrasted

---

[2] P. Veyne, *Bread and Circuses: Historical Sociology and Political Pluralism* (London: Penguin, 1990). Veyne combines a sociological and a historical approach and thereby succeeds to show how evergetism was of structural importance in ancient Greek and Roman societies, in contrast to its peripheral role in modern societies.

[3] See N. Hannestad, *Roman Art and Imperial Policy* (Aarhus: Aarhus University Press, 1988), and very successfully, P. Zanker, *The Power of Images in the Age of Augustus* (Ann Arbor: University of Michigan Press, 1988).

[4] *The Roman World of Dio Chrysostom* (Cambridge, Mass.: Harvard University Press, 1978) 25.

with his vision of the ideal Hellenistic city and of the relations between its citizens. The discussion of Dio helps to identify a plausible social and intellectual context for some of the admonitions of Paul the Christian who wrote about 40–50 years earlier than Dio. Paul too criticizes those who lay claims to honor, and his advice is set within the context of his concept of the Christian community and of its position within the Greco-Roman city.

Dio Chrysostom

Dio Chrysostom was born in Prusa in Northwestern Asia Minor around 40 C.E. and he died about 110 C.E. He belonged to a prominent family well known for its benefactions to the city. Dio continued this tradition and was also able to procure benefits for the city from the Roman emperors since he enjoyed a privileged position with several of them. Thus, Dio was a typical example of a number of Greek philosophers who belonged to the city elites and who wielded influence not only in the city, but also vis-à-vis the emperors and local Roman authorities.[5]

From an early age Dio had direct contact with several emperors and members of the imperial family. Thus, he was in a position to act as a broker, that is, a patron to his city who was also a mediator between the city and the emperor. In this role he was clearly dependent upon the emperor and had to move within the limits set by him, a fact that became clearly visible when he was exiled by Domitian. Dio's situation was not an individual trait; his role reflects the growing dependency upon the emperor on the part of the Hellenistic cities.

Dio's teacher was probably the famous Stoic, Musonius Rufus, and the strongest influence upon him remained Stoic philosophy. In his early period he might have been close to the Sophists, and in a period when he was exiled from Rome and Prusa by the emperor Domitian, he sounded more like a Cynic.[6]

---

[5]   For a study of the role of the Sophists, including Dio, see G. W. Bowersock, *Greek Sophists in the Roman Empire* (Oxford: Clarendon, 1969) 43–58.

[6]   Jones, *Roman World,* 9–12, 49–50. A. A. Long considers Dio to be a Cynic (*Hellenistic Philosophy* [New York: Scribner, 1974] 234). For discussion see especially J. L. Moles, 'The Career and Conversion of Dio Chrysostom,' *JHS* 98 (1978) 79–100.

In his criticism of the system of honors in the Hellenistic cities, Dio provides much information about how the system worked and what the different types of honors were, statues, proclamations, seats of honor, etc. (*Or.* 44). The normal way to obtain honors was by being a benefactor (εὐεργέτης) and by undertaking public services (λειτουργίαι). There was a certain pressure from the city upon wealthy citizens to do this (cf. *Or.* 66). Obviously, such honors could only be obtained by the rich because they were 'bought' at a high price.[7] This was taken for granted by Dio and was the point of departure for much of his criticism of the system.

Dio's criticism of the quest for honor is primarily directed against members of his own social group, the city elite and those who tried to enter that group. His criticism takes two different forms, a radical one from his 'Cynic' period during his exile (83–96 C.E.) and a moderate one from periods before and after the exile when he was himself actively engaged in politics.

It is this combination of elements that makes Dio Chrysostom so interesting to us. A member of the elite in an Hellenistic city, with his close ties to Rome, he was at the same time in a dependent position vis-à-vis the emperors. He knew well how to operate the system of benefactions and honors, but he viewed them from a perspective influenced by Stoic philosophy. He traveled extensively in the cities of Asia Minor and from time to time he stayed in Rome — areas of special importance to the first urban Christians. Living one generation after Paul, his first speeches probably date from around 70 C.E. However, the sociopolitical climate of the cities of the Eastern empire remained quite similar during this period.[8]

Moles rejects the idea that Dio underwent a 'conversion' from being a sophist to a more philosophical position. He holds that there were in all periods a synthetic character to Dio's philosophy, combining elements from various schools, but agrees that Dio's Cynicism became more pronounced during his exile. K. Blomqvist (*Myth and Moral Message in Dio Chrysostom* (Ph.D. diss., Lund, 1989, 223–39) agrees that it is exaggerated to speak of a conversion, but emphasizes that there is a development in Dio's outlook during his exile, in that he developed a deeper social concern.

[7] Cf. Veyne, *Bread and Circuses*, 117–31.

[8] For the issue of changes and developments, see A. H. M. Jones, *The Greek City from Alexander to Justinian* (Oxford, 1940) 179–82.

206

Dio and Rome

Dio's concern to create concord in the city and to do away with dissension caused by competition had a larger political context than just the city itself, namely the situation of the Hellenistic cities in Asia Minor under Roman rule. As already mentioned, the growing dependence of these cities upon the emperor and upon the Roman government influenced Dio's advice on city life.[9] In the early speech to the Rhodians he reminds them that their ancestors had political freedom, which was taken away by the Romans (*Or.* 31.161). Obviously, Dio wanted the Rhodians to accept Roman hegemony and to accept that they could not win prominence by waging wars, making alliances etc. They could still be admired and make themselves prominent, but in a different way: 'there is left for you, I think, the privilege of assuming the leadership of yourselves, of administering your city. ...' (*Or.* 31.162)

Dio follows a similar line of thought in *Or.* 44. The city wanted his assistance to procure for them from the emperor the status of a free city. Knowing that this was a privilege hard to obtain from the Roman government, he said that it rested, 'at the pleasure of those who have control and authority'. Dio downplays its importance and stresses instead the 'inner freedom' that it was possible to maintain under Roman rule: 'the true independence, the kind which men actually achieve, both the individual and the state obtain, each from its own self, if they administer their own affairs in a high-minded and not in a servile and easy-going manner' (*Or.* 44.12). An early speech from 75 C.E. (*Or.* 46) expresses sentiments that are familiar in his post-exilic works.[10] With an elitist attitude he argues that the strength of a city consists not in violent public protest (by the masses) but in wisdom and justice (*Or.* 46.2). He especially emphasizes that it is folly to antagonize the Roman proconsul (*Or.* 46.14).

In another speech (*Or.* 48.9), Dio summarizes his arguments in a typical fashion: 'Do you imagine there is any advantage in market or theatre or gymnasia or colonnades or wealth for men who are at variance? These are not the things which make a city beautiful, but rather

---

[9]   Moles, 'Conversion', 93–96.
[10] Moles, 'Conversion', 93.

self-control, friendship, mutual trust'. The virtue of σωφροσύνη (self-control) was an important aspect of concord in the city (cf. *Or.* 39.2–3). For Dio the real conflict, one that he frequently returned to in his speeches, was between strife in the city on the one hand and self-control, friendship, and mutual trust on the other.[11] It was an aristocratic ideal that aimed at keeping government in the hands of the elite under a benign Roman rule.

'The Autonomous Man' Versus 'Popularity Seekers'

It was in speeches made during his exile that Dio was most critical of political life in the Greek cities and of the destructive effect of competition for honors upon politics as well as upon social relations. *Or.* 66 is a particularly illuminating example. It was probably written towards the end of both his exile and the reign of the emperor Domitian.[12]

In this speech Dio wants to prove that the passion for public reputation and honors is actually more degrading and has graver consequences than two other vices that were regarded by most as being more serious: the desires for pleasure (including sex) and wealth. His criticism is not only directed at those who seek honor for themselves, but also at the cities and citizens who encourage this passion for fame: 'Among men in general each speaks well of this type of malady, deeming it advantageous for himself. Furthermore, by official act virtually all the states have devised lures of every kind for the simpletons — crowns and front seats and public proclamations' (*Or* 66.2). Dio's criticism of the quest for honor is actually aimed at the political system itself, which worked through an interlocking arrangement of benefices and public honors and offices.[13]

Dio proceeds to show that the results for those who crave honor have been disastrous. First of all, the costs are enormous and have often driven men into poverty (*Or.* 66.2–6). But the worst result is not the loss of fortune, but of peace of mind (*Or.* 66.11–22). When people at all times try to please others they are completely at their mercy. Dio compares it to being put on trial for one's life every day. And worst of

---

[11] E.g. *Or.* 36.31; 38.10–11; 39.3, 8; 41.8; 45.8.
[12] Jones, *Roman World,* 135.
[13] Veyne, *Bread and Circuses,* 117–31.

all, it is not before competent judges, but only 'foolish men' (*Or.* 66.18).

It is in his presentation of an alternative to the quest for popularity that the Cynic influence upon Dio becomes most obvious. According to Dio the popularity one seeks is only a fleeting and uncertain phenomenon. Measured against 'the good' such craving for reputation does not bring one any closer to the goal. Rather, it leads away from it. In contrast to the politician who seeks popularity, Dio's ideal is a man who keeps out of all political activity in order to protect his own personal freedom and peace. Moreover, there is a strong element of contempt for others in this attitude: 'Unless you bring yourself to look with scorn upon all others, you will never end your state of wretchedness; instead, you will always lead a pitiable, yes, a painful existence, being at the mercy of all who wish to hurt you ...' (*Or.* 66.24).

This ideal of the quiet life is also developed in other speeches of Dio's. In *Or.* 67 his ideal is the philosopher, the man with self-control (σώφρων) who obeys the Delphic command: 'Know thyself.' He examines everything in the light of truth and consequently 'he will bid farewell to honors and to words of censure and of praise uttered by foolish persons, whether they chance to be many or whether they be few but powerful and wealthy. Instead, what is called popular opinion he will regard as no better than a shadow ...' (*Or.* 67.3).

Dio's description of the wise man contains well-known Stoic elements. But there is a sharpening of attitude. The city with its requirements of public responsibilities has disappeared. The consequences of Dio's drastic criticism of public life governed by the quest for reputation was a withdrawal from public life. In some cases (*Or.* 73) it appears as an aristocratic ideal of the 'quiet life' advocated by the Epicureans.[14] But his criticism not only of the quest for reputation but also of wealth in speeches from this period reflects a more Cynic attitude.[15]

Honors within the Ideal City: Friendship and Goodwill

Dio's extreme scepticism towards 'popularity seekers' in *Or.* 66 reflects

---

[14] E.g. *Or.* 10; Moles, 'Conversion', 94–95.
[15] See G. J. D. Aalders, *Political Thought in Hellenistic Times* (Amsterdam: Hakkert, 1975) 39–44.

a period in his career marked by a forced withdrawal from political life. Both before and after his exile Dio was actively engaged in politics. By the favors of the emperor Trajan Dio returned to Prusa after his exile and he also led a successful embassy to Trajan to win favors for his city. These were high points in his public career. *Or.* 44 was spoken on one of these occasions in response to honors offered to him by the city. The tone of this speech is totally different from that of *Or.* 66. Dio is grateful for the honors that had been awarded to his family and proposed for himself. He now declines, however, to accept the new honors that the city wants to bestow upon him, and justifies his decision by explaining what 'true honor' consists in.

Dio's respectful attitude is expressed first in his addressing the assembly in a conventional, flattering way: 'no honors (are) greater than those you bestow, no praise more splendid than praise from you'. Then he introduces his refusal of these honors: 'Indeed, you may rest assured that I find all my honors, both those that you now propose and any others there may be, contained in your goodwill and friendship, and I need naught else' (*Or.* 44.1, 2). He proceeds to say that when one is loved by one's own fellow citizens one does not need 'statues or proclamations or seats of honor' (that is, relatively common honors), not even 'a portrait statue of beaten gold set up in the most distinguished shrines' (an exceptional honor).

Dio here sets up an alternative to the external expressions of honor consisting in statues, portraits, seats of honor, etc. and it is his reasoning behind this alternative system that is of most interest to us. However, we must also ask whether behind these lofty motives to reject honors there are also some more mundane ones. First, it belonged to the etiquette of rhetoric that benefactors should decline or moderate the rewards they were offered.[16] Von Arnim suggests another motive based on the social conventions of honors as a reward for benefactions to the city.[17] A decision by the city to grant Dio honors entailed expec-

---

[16] Jones, *Roman World,* 105. Similarly Plutarch, *Praecepta gerendae reipublicae* 820C–D, representing a common feeling; C. P. Jones, *Plutarch and Rome* (Oxford: Clarendon, 1971) 116.

[17] H. von Arnim, *Leben und Werke des Dio von Prusa* (Berlin, 1898) 316.

tations of further acts of benefaction, expectations that he might not wish to fulfil. However, Dio appears to recognize that through past honors he has already incurred a debt to the city when he says: 'I feel that I myself owe you the thanks for these honors, and I pray the gods I may be able to discharge the debts' (*Or.* 44.4).

Even if Dio wants to limit his obligations, he recognizes that he is involved in a reciprocal relationship with the city based on an exchange of honor for service. But the structure of that relationship and the content of the honors are very different from that portrayed in *Or.* 66. In his speech to his fellow Prusians he is concerned to show his love for his home city. As an example he tells how he has declined an invitation by the emperor (probably Nerva) to come to Rome and asked instead to be allowed to remain in Prusa (*Or.* 44.1, 6, 12). In this way Dio sets himself up as an example of a man who loves his country, displaying a virtue of the highest rank.

This concern for the city is set within the context of the ever present competition between Greek cities. Dio exhorts his fellow citizens to strive to preserve a prominent position for Prusa among the cities of the Greek world. In the same speech (*Or.* 44) he also presents his vision of an ideal city. That is a city in which men compete not for δόξα, by which Dio means 'vain glory', the popularity of the masses, but for ἀρετή (moral virtue) and εὐδοκία (good repute) from fellow citizens and friends. Dio urges love for the city and encourages competition for promotion of the good of the city (*Or.* 44.8).

Moreover, such competition must be without envy and jealousy, character traits that were often regarded as sources of strife and evil in the city (*Or.* 44.9). Dio struck a popular note when he put forth unity and harmony as important goals. These also had practical implications — if the city could settle its own affairs without internal conflict it was more secure against interventions from the Roman governor or from the emperor.[18] The ultimate goal was the promotion of the good of the city. It was this expression of a 'public spirit' that ought to motivate generosity towards the city instead of a desire for popularity.[19]

---

[18] Jones, *Roman World*, 19–20.
[19] A. R. R. Sheppard, 'Homonoia in the Greek cities of the Roman empire,' *AnSoc* 17 (1986) 241–51.

Thus Dio turns away attention from the outward expressions of honor, emphasizing instead the ideal inner character of the citizens of Prusa. The expression of this character in public life was of vital importance if they were to function together as a unity. Therefore, in *Or.* 44 the alternative to the politician who seeks honor for himself is not (as in *Or.* 66) the aloof philosopher-aristocrat who keeps out of politics to protect his freedom, but the man who serves out of concern for the city and who is rewarded by the spirit of mutual love and friendship (*Or.* 44.2).

Such 'good men' can only be formed through the pursuit of philosophy (*Or.* 44.10–11). Thus there is a need for education. Moreover, Dio sees a correspondence between the individual and the city, between self-control on the side of the individual and self-government on the part of the city. This is a typical Stoic perspective[20] and Dio links qualities like temperance and devotion to the task of rearing and educating children to the communal goal: 'making your city truly Hellenic, free from turmoil, and stable ... refraining from discord and confusion and conflict with one another' (*Or.* 44.10).

In summary, in *Or.* 44 Dio presents his picture of the ideal city in continuity with, but also transcending the actual system of benefactions and honors as practised in his hometown Prusa. He develops a consistent picture of community life based on friendship and goodwill. In this community the driving forces would not be envy and competition for popularity among the masses, but a philosophical and aristocratic ideal — competition among the free, educated, and wise men to develop a good character and love of their city in order to promote its welfare. His ideals for the community of citizens corresponded to his views on the natural laws of the universe as a whole. Dio combined a Stoic theory of the harmonious whole under the guidance of Providence with what is apparently a more Pythagorean concept of concord through balance between opposing groups.[21]

Or. 44 probably reflects the situation of harmony that Dio enjoyed with Prusa at the time. However, he soon met with difficulties and got

---

[20] Long, *Hellenistic Philosophy*, 191.
[21] Sheppard, 'Homonoia', 239; cf. *Or.* 36.29–32; 38.11–12; 40.35–39.

deeply involved in the type of conflicts that he was himself arguing against. Therefore, in other speeches he returns to strong attacks upon self-serving leaders and citizens seeking honor. The philosopher is needed to give judgment and to speak the truth. In *Or.* 77/78, probably from the period before the exile, Dio presents the picture of a philosopher who is actively engaged on behalf of his fellow citizens. The wise man will honor virtue and moderation and he will also try to lead others by his teaching (*Or.* 77/78.38). In an important passage that summarizes the character of such a man, Dio says that he is 'not arousing strife or greed or contentions and jealousies and base desires for gain, but reminding men of sobriety and righteousness and promoting concord ...' (*Or.* 77/78.39).

Of course this is the role that Dio saw for himself. Not only did he represent the ideal citizen who served his city, but as a philosopher he was also actively engaged in educating its citizens: 'I shall not hesitate to exhort (παρακαλῶ) our young men on behalf of these things both in private and in public whenever there is opportunity' (*Or.* 44.10). This was a role that he undertook also in other cities. In his speech at Rhodes, for instance, he starts by announcing that he will set right not 'private matters', but matters of common interest. Therefore, he supposes that 'you will perhaps be vexed that I, who am neither a citizen nor have been invited to come here, yet venture to offer advice ...' (*Or.* 31.1). In several instances Dio describes his activity as an orator as a divine mission, and casts himself in the role of the great philosophers of old, in particular Socrates.[22]

Paul of Tarsus

Paul and Rome

Paul the Christian missionary moved within the same city milieu of Asia Minor a few decades before Dio. He grew up in Tarsus, the scene of one of Dio's speeches, and probably received a Hellenistic education there. In contrast to Dio's speeches Paul's letters do not tell us much about public life of the cities he visited. Rather, he concentrates upon

---

[22] *Or.* 3.1–2, 30–41; 32.12–13; 33.4–5; see Moles, 'Conversion', 96–100.

the internal problems of the small Christian groups that were being formed and sometimes upon their relations to the larger community that surrounded them. There is nothing strange in this; it probably reflects the peripheral position of these groups within the city, as well as Paul's own situation. As a visitor or 'resident alien' in various cities in Asia Minor and Greece he often experienced precarious situations provoked by his preaching.

It is actually more remarkable that Paul is so concerned with questions directly relating to the ethos of the city, viz. honor (and shame). This is true both of his Corinthian correspondence and of his letter to the Romans. I shall now show how much Paul actually continued a Hellenistic type of discourse about honor, and in what ways he modified it by means of specifically Christian ideas.

The passage chosen for a closer study is Rom 12.3–16 where Paul warns against the quest for honor within Christian groups. Rom 12.17–21, a section on how Christians ought to respond to ill-treatment from non-Christians, serves as a bridge to chapter 13. Rom 13.1–7 provides the larger context for Paul's discussion of the quest for honor in chapter 12, as it situates his addressees within the honor culture of Roman society.[23] Rom 13.1–7 represents a remarkable contrast to 12.3–16. It is like coming out from the 'inner room' of the transformed, from the cult room and its atmosphere of 'brotherly love' into the forum with its official buildings, temples, offices for the governors, tax-collectors, statues, and altars for the emperors. Not internal, but external relations are in focus here. This was a situation on which the small, newly founded Christian communities had no influence. Instead, they had to adapt to it.

Paul's vocabulary in Romans 13 is the one used to describe state and city officials in the Hellenistic period,[24] and to a large extent his exhortations formulate a common Hellenistic ideal of a just and honorable

---

[23] For a review of the enormous discussion on Romans 13, see V. Riekkinen, *Römer 13: Aufzeichnung und Weiterführung der exegetischen Diskussion* (Annales Academiae Scientiarum Fennicae. Diss. Hum. Litt. 23; Helsinki, 1980).

[24] See the important studies by A. Strobel, 'Zum Verständnis von Röm 13,' *ZNW* 47 (1956) 67–93; 'Furcht, wem Furcht gebührt,' *ZNW* 55 (1964) 58–62, and W. C. van Unnik, 'Lob und Strafe durch die Obrigkeit. Hellenistisches zu Röm 13.3–4,' *Jesus and Paulus. Festschrift für W. G. Kümmel* (ed. E. E. Ellis; Göttingen: Vandenhoeck & Ruprecht, 1975) 334–43.

man. Of the terms used, ἐξουσία (13.1, 2, 3) probably refers to offices within the administration of the Roman Empire, whereas ἄρχοντες (13.3) and λειτουργοί (13.6) probably indicate city offices. The reference to the sword in 13.4 points towards high officials with important jurisdiction — maybe capital jurisdiction. This was originally reserved for the emperor, but from the time of Augustus onward it could be delegated to the governors.

Paul's addressees are clearly people with a subordinate position within society. The primary thrust of his argument is that they shall be 'subjects' (ὑποτασσέσθω; 13.1, 5). As subjects, they are supposed to pay their taxes and to give honor (τιμήν; 13.7): 'Pay all of them their dues, taxes to whom taxes are due, revenue to whom revenue is due, respect to whom respect is due, honor to whom honor is due.' There is no criticism of the honor claimed by the authorities here.

But the subjects too could receive honor. This was possible in the form of praise from their superiors: 'for rulers are not a terror to good conduct, but to bad. Would you have no fear of him who is in authority? Then do what is good and you will receive his praise' (ἔπαινον; 13.3).

Here the subject person is viewed directly in his relation to his superiors — the authorities. There is no mention of the competition for honor among the members of the elite. Paul betrays that he knows the system of munificence and reward. To 'do good' so that one receives 'praise' from the authorities probably refers to more than an ordinary, quiet life. 'Praise' here probably is used as a technical term referring to a specific form of public recognition, granted either by the city or by a person of authority. And the reason for such recognition usually was an act of 'common good' towards the city. We can hardly deduce from this passage alone that some Christians were public benefactors,[25] but it does show that Paul knew his social practice.

Paul's general attitude is that the members of the Christian communities should not risk conflict with society.[26] This accounts for his acceptance of the existing structures and of his exhortation that each

---

[25] Contra B. W. Winter, 'The Public Honouring of Christian Benefactors,' *JSNT* 34 (1988) 93–94.

[26] Cf. 1 Thess 4.10–12; see A.J. Malherbe, *Paul and the Thessalonians* (Philadelphia: Fortress, 1987) 95–107.

individual should remain within his or her place (cf. 1 Cor 7.17–24). However, there may be a certain reserve in this acceptance. At least Paul's exhortations to be obedient to the 'powers that be' is followed by a return to the attitudes that are specific for the Christian community: 'Owe no one anything, except to love one another' (13.8).

When Paul addresses the recipients of his letter not as actual or potential holders of offices, but as 'subjects', this description may correspond to historical conjectures about the social composition of the early Christian groups in Rome. Peter Lampe has suggested that several members were traveling tradespeople, many were of Oriental origin and probably about two-thirds were slaves or freedmen (and women).[27] Thus most Christians belonged to the *humiliores* rather than to more socially elevated groups.

But first of all Paul's exhortations reveal him as a missionary who took care to keep within the given structures of the Roman Empire. He regards the Roman emperor and his officials as benign power holders. And he presupposes the system of honor based on power or beneficence that formed the structural basis of society. It is from the perspective of this general acceptance of the norms of society at large that Paul's specific exhortation against the quest for honor within Christian groups should be seen.

Rom 12.1–2: Transformation and New Identity

In his book *Paul the Convert*[28] Alan F. Segal has shown how studies of conversion as a social phenomenon can contribute to a better understanding of Paul and his apostolate. Paul's dramatic calling through a vision of the risen Christ gave him a totally new perspective upon the Law and Jewish history and identity. This implied a full reevaluation of his former identity and of Jewish history and necessitated the creation of a new identity and of new social structures. His letters, including Romans, must be read as attempts to do just this not only for himself, but as a collective enterprise. Beyond and behind the individual topics that he discusses lies a larger purpose, that of creating a 'new world' for

---

[27] 'The Roman Christians of Romans 16,' *The Romans Debate*, rev. version (ed. K. P. Donfried; Edinburgh: T&T Clark, 1991) 216–30.
[28] New Haven: Yale University Press, 1990.

his readers, of building a 'space' for their new existence.[29]

Rom 12.1–2 reads as a passage of 'collective conversion', Paul's effort to create a new 'symbolic world'. It is generally recognized that this passage serves as an introduction to and as a headline for the parenetic section of the letter, in a typically Pauline way introduced with παρακαλῶ.

It is a passage characterized by a vocabulary of transformation and renewal: the believers are to present themselves (their bodies) as holy sacrifices, they must not be like 'this world', but instead be transformed by a renewal of their mind. The expression μεταμορφοῦσθε τῇ ἀνακαινώσει τοῦ νοὸς points towards a dramatic change. The sacrifice of believers in v. 1 parallels the sacrifice and death of Christ, unto which the Christians are baptized (Romans 6). Similarities in vocabulary and motifs between chapters 12 and 6 suggest that it is the consequences of baptism that Paul has in mind.[30]

The use of cultic language together with criticism of false reliance upon sacrifice in an ethical context is well known especially in sapiental literature.[31] Moreover, Paul's terminology is not only cultic and sacrificial. It is 'the mind', νοῦς, that must be transformed and renewed. With this emphasis upon the intellectual aspect of human existence Paul comes close to the Stoic notion of *animus transfiguratus*, 'the sudden transformation of the mind that marks the origin of the wise man'.[32] Even if Paul does not make the transformed mind the only source of ethics, it is surprising that he does not here speak of the Spirit as the source of insight into the will of God.[33] It is the intellectual aspect of the 'transformed life' that provides a transition to the following sections in Romans 12.

[29] See T. Engberg-Pedersen, 'Stoicism in Philippians' (below pp. 272–73).
[30] M. Thompson, *Clothed with Christ: The Example and Teaching of Jesus in Romans 12.1–15.13*, JSNTSup 59 (1991) 79–81.
[31] Sir 34.21–35.13; see W. T. Wilson, *Love without Pretense: Romans 12.9–21 and Hellenistic-Jewish Wisdom Literature* (WUNT 46; Tübingen: Mohr-Siebeck, 1991) 137.
[32] H. D. Betz, 'Christianity as religion: Paul's attempt at definition in Romans,' *JR* 71 (1991) 338–39. See e.g. Seneca, *Epistulae Morales* 6.1–2; 94.48. This intellectual aspect is found also within Hellenistic-Jewish wisdom literature, see Wilson, *Love without Pretense*, 138.
[33] H. D. Betz, 'Das Problem der Grundlagen der paulinischen Ethik (Röm 12,1–2),' *ZTK* 85 (1988) 209–18.

217

The rest of the chapter, 12.3–21, spells out this transformed life in what appears to be a more mundane fashion. While Paul in 12.1–2 urges his readers to become totally 'renewed' and freed from 'this world', he phrases his alternative in the form of a reworking of traditional rhetoric.[34]

Most often Rom 12.3–21 is divided into two subsections, one that deals with the church as the body of Christ (12.3–8), and another that focuses upon love as the governing principle of Christian life (12.9–21).[35] Recently, W. T. Wilson has studied Romans 12 in the light of four Hellenistic Jewish sapiental discourses,[36] in terms of the structure and function of the various parts. According to this analysis, 12.1–2 is the programmatic statement, 12.3–8 the descriptive section and 12.9–21 the prescriptive section.

I intend here to focus on one major aspect of Paul's exhortations, viz. that of the quest for honor within the community (addressed especially in 12.3 and 16) viewed in contrast to Paul's acceptance of the system of honor in the city in chapter 13. This perspective makes it relevant to look at the different types of relations addressed in the exhortations.

A. J. M. Wedderburn finds that Paul's emphasis upon 'the renewed mind' in 12.2 helps to recognize a pattern in the parenesis in chapters 12–13.[37] The first section, 12.3–16, deals with 'how such a renewed mind should think' and forms a ring composition with vv. 3 and 16 as parallel arguments. The next section, 12.17–13.7 (8–10) deals with the Christians' response to evil, while 13.11–14 returns to the theme of the renewal of the Christians. This analysis focuses too much upon intellectual terminology and does not pay sufficient attention to Paul's project in this passage — to create the social world of his addressees and to make this construction effective in their lives. Still, Wedderburn

---

[34] W. A. Meeks emphasizes this double aspect of Paul's ethics. He argues for a totally new identity, but at the same time makes use of traditional material (*The Moral World of the First Christians* [Philadelphia: Westminster, 1986] 13).

[35] See J. D. G. Dunn, *Romans 9–16* (Dallas: Word Books, 1988) 718–36; 736–57.

[36] LXX Proverbs 3.11-35; Sir 6.18–37; *Ps-Phocylides* 70–96; *T. Napht.*2.2–3.5; see *Love without Pretense*, 126–46.

[37] *The Reason for Romans* (Edinburgh: T&T Clark, 1991) 76–77.

has pointed in the right direction with his observation that 12.3 and 16 form parallel arguments, and by making a division between 12.16 and 17. In 12.3–16 Paul is concerned with relations within the community,[38] whereas in 12.17–21 he speaks of relations to 'all' (12.17–18) including enemies (12.20), and finally in 13.1–7 of relations to civil authorities.

Rom 12.3–16: Control of Ambition in the Community

Paul's exhortations in Rom 12.3–16 are bound together by a thematic unity — his concern for the social relations within the community of believers.[39] He introduces himself as a teacher, who like Dio, admonishes not only the young men, but 'everyone', and, herein surpassing Dio, he claims for himself an authority based on χάρις (12.3; cf. 1.5). His introductory exhortation in 12.3 serves as a key to the passage: 'I bid every one among you not to think of himself more highly (ὑπερφρονεῖν) than he ought to think (φρονεῖν), but to think with sober judgment (σωφρονεῖν), each according to the measure of faith which God has assigned him.' This exhortation introduces Paul's interpretation of the fable of the body (12.4–5) and its subsequent exemplification in the exhortation to the charismatics of the community (12.6–8). Moreover, in the following section, 12.9–16, v. 16 parallels and expands upon v. 3: 'Live in harmony among yourselves; do not cherish proud thoughts (μὴ τὰ ὑψηλὰ φρονοῦντες), but associate with the lowly. Be not wise in your own estimation.'[40] Also the exhortation to love in v. 9 and its consequences in v. 10: 'love one another with brotherly affection, outdo one another in showing honor', belong to the same context of unity in the community.[41]

Paul's main recommendations in this passage — that no haughty thoughts that produce conflict should be allowed and that the goal

---

[38] Thompson, *Clothed with Christ*, 90, against the more common division into 12.9–13 and 14–21 to be found, e.g., in Dunn, *Romans 9–16*, 738.
[39] K. Berger, 'Hellenistische Gattungen im Neuen Testament,' *ANRW* 25.2 (1984) 1076, although he sees 12.3–21 as a unity.
[40] Translation from Dunn, *Romans 9–16*, 737.
[41] Wilson, *Love without Pretense*, 163.

should instead be unity based on love and humility, recur in several of his letters, for instance, Phil. 2.2–4 and 1 Cor 4.6–13.[42]

Paul's arguments against ambition beyond a sound measure point to what he sees as the sources of conflict in Christian communities. In Rom 12.3–16 he develops a picture of the ideal community of believers. I have suggested that this passage is best understood as an elaboration of the Hellenistic discussion of concord versus conflict in the city that we found many examples of in the speeches of the Dio Chrysostom.[43] Dio considered the competition for honor to be a major source of conflict.

Not to be haughty but to show proper judgment and to keep within one's proper confines was for centuries a much discussed theme in classical Greek and Hellenistic philosophy, above all related to the issue of conflict within the polis. A brief survey of the development of and changes in the meaning of σωφρονεῖν, based on the study by Helen North, will clarify some of the implicit presuppositions for Paul's usage.[44] At first, σωφροσύνη was understood to have a dynamic nature. It was a matter of control over strong passions that were considered to be dangerous if they were allowed a free reign. What passions were considered most dangerous, however, shifted between different periods. Likewise whether the emphasis was upon the public or the individual realm changed over time. A common element in Greek thought, however, was the desire to reach harmony, balance, 'the right measure', and to avoid excess and strife.[45] In classical Greek, σωφροσύνη was above all related to the political scene. Solon (sixth century B.C.E.) emphasized the 'middle way' in politics as a way to balance conflicts. Σωφροσύνη represented this virtue and was associated with increased rights for the hoplites, while excess, hybris, was regarded as the characteristic vice of tyrants.

---

[42] For Phil 2.2–4 see Engberg-Pedersen, 'Stoicism in Philippians,' (below p. 276).

[43] See above, n. 11. For the parallels between Dio and Romans 12, esp. v. 16, see G. Mussies, *Dio Chrysostom and the New Testament* (SCHNT 2; Leiden: Brill, 1972) 149–50.

[44] *Sophrosyne: Self-knowledge and Self-restraint in Greek Literature* (Ithaca, New York: Cornell University Press, 1966).

[45] *Sophrosyne*, 258.

According to Helen North, σωφροσύνη became more directly related in the Hellenistic period to the individual's exercise of self-control, especially in the area of desire and appetite (e.g. related to food, drink, sex). North suggests that 'the strong emphasis on sophrosyne in all the popular philosophies of the imperial age reflects social conditions of the kind that also produced satire and diatribe and the denunciations of pagan luxury, greed and sexual immorality by early Christian moralists'.[46] The popular and philosophic implications of sophrosyne made it easier to integrate this cardinal virtue into a Christian moral universe. We noticed, however, that Dio used σωφροσύνη in a 'political' sense related to community life (*Or.* 39.2).

In the New Testament σωφροσύνη is used in several ways. One usage follows most closely the popular usage of the day, as control or mastery of appetites and desires. This is often found in the Pastorals (1 Tim 2.9; 3.2; Tit 1.8; 2.2, 5, 6). More germane to the genuine Pauline letters is the emphasis upon 'holiness' and 'purity' as a contrast to 'lusts, desires'. North regards this as a Christian version of the contrast between sophrosyne and pathos in Hellenistic thought.[47]

In Rom 12.3, however, Paul uses σωφρονεῖν (of the virtue that consists in keeping within set measures) in a more classical (i.e. political) sense, as an antithesis to hybris.[48] The context of 12.3 supports this communal meaning. The image of the body and its members (12.4–5) that is applied to the various charismatic gifts suggests that the contrast between σωφρονεῖν and ὑπερφρονεῖν (that is, hybris), is here applied to the relations between members of the community.

But what is the concrete issue that Paul is addressing? What are the general attitudes associated with σωφροσύνη or σωφρονεῖν? And whom in the particular situation would he consequently be taken to address, those of 'superior' status or those of 'inferior' status? Paul gives his exhortation and advice so to speak in shorthand with only brief references in 12.4–8 to the fable of the body and to the various charismatic gifts. In order to better understand his exhortation not to be haughty

---

[46] *Sophrosyne*, 229.
[47] *Sophrosyne*, 319.
[48] North, *Sophrosyne*, 317; Luck, *TDNT* 7.1102.

we may look to his discussion of hybris and related topics in other letters, in particular his Corinthian correspondence.[49]

In *Enmity in Corinth: Social Conventions in Paul's Relations with the Corinthians*, Peter Marshall has investigated the social effect of hybris and he provides a plausible context for Paul's use of the concept.[50] Marshall finds that hybris preserved the same meaning within classical Greek and Hellenistic philosophy and literature with little fluctuations throughout the centuries: 'Thus hybris is conceived of as arrogance or insolence born out of an ignorance of one's true self. The hybristic person's failure to think mortal thoughts leads to an arrogant violation of limits, of both human and divine law. It is primarily a social concept which indicates the breach of one's assigned status and thus results in dishonour and shame. It is most commonly caused by undue pride in strength and wealth, both of which are given by the gods.'[51]

That hybris was a temptation especially to those in power was a well-known topos in antiquity, and hybris was often associated with tyrants. Thus Dio Chrysostom urges the good king to act with sophrosyne, the antithesis of hybris (*Or.* 3.80). In Greek philosophy hybris was prim-arily a nonreligious concept that occurred most often in moral and social contexts. As the antithesis of sophrosyne it indicates behavior that oversteps the bounds or limits set by the notion of the mean.

Thus it appears that Paul's exhortation 'not to think too highly' is directed not to an individual character trait, but to a total system of relations between individuals of unequal status. Paul appears to be completely at home with the Hellenistic discussion of sophrosyne, since he plays with the root φρονεῖν in various combinations. There are four main elements in his exhortation:

(1) The first exhortation in 12.3b is directed against hybris: 'I bid every one of you not to think of himself more highly (ὑπερφρονεῖν) than he ought to think (φρονεῖν).' This is repeated in v. 16b and c: 'do not cherish proud thoughts (μὴ τὰ ὑψηλὰ φρονοῦντες) but associate with the lowly. Be not wise (φρόνιμοι) in your own estimation.'

---

[49]   E.g. 1 Cor 1–3; 2 Cor 10–13; see Wilson, *Love Without Pretense*, 181–82.
[50]   WUNT 2.R. 23 (Tübingen: Mohr-Siebeck, 1987) 178–218.
[51]   *Enmity*, 193–94.

(2) In contrast to hybris the desirable behavior (12.3b) is σωφρονεῖν, 'thinking with sober judgment'. From its context it is clear that Paul's exhortation refers primarily to behavior within social relations. It is further illuminated by 12.16b, where the contrast to hybris is to 'associate with the lowly'. This exhortation has its main frame of reference in Paul's use of the fable of the body and its members in 12.4–8.

(3) The element of 'the mean' or 'due measure' is introduced in 12.3c: 'each according to the measure (μέτρον) of faith which God has assigned to him'.

(4) Finally the exhortation to concord, which is threatened by hybris, introduces 12.16: 'live in harmony among yourselves (τὸ αὐτὸ εἰς ἀλλήλους φρονοῦντες)'.

Brotherly Love in the Community of Believers

In Romans 12 Paul apparently uses a pattern of Hellenistic exhortation about the 'proper' life in the polis. This was a type of exhortation that was suitable for his concern to create unity between believers from various ethnic and social groups in the face of the threats of disunity. But although Paul uses a common and well-known pattern it is in significant ways adapted to his purpose. Its purpose is to serve the building of unity not within the Hellenistic polis, but within and between communities of Christian believers. Consequently, Paul introduces four elements of a specifically Christian character: (a) 'faith assigned by God' (v. 3); (b) being one body 'in Christ' (v. 5); (c) 'brotherly love' (v. 10); and (d) 'associate with the lowly' (v. 16). While sharing many elements with the Hellenistic 'ideal community', Paul's vision of community clearly reflects a Christian symbolic universe.

(a) μέτρον πίστεως

Paul's particular perspective is introduced in v. 3c, where the right 'measure' is described as 'the measure of faith which God has assigned to him'. The terms 'faith' and 'God' here clearly signal that the measure that must not be transgressed is not identical with tradition or social consensus, but rooted in God's acts of giving gifts to the community. But it remains for the rest of Paul's argument to spell out the consequences of this statement.

(b) ἕν σῶμά ἐσμεν ἐν Χριστῷ.

This is brought out more clearly in Paul's application of the fable of the body and its members (12.4–8). Compared to the version given in 1 Cor 12.12–26 it occurs here in a very abbreviated form. The passage in 1 Corinthians is closer to the famous fable ascribed to Menenius Agrippa and much used in Stoic literature.[52] In a strife between senators and plebeians in Rome in which the plebeians threatened with mutiny, the senators realized that 'no hope was left save in harmony (*concordia civium*) between the citizens'.[53] Menenius Agrippa was therefore sent to the plebeians to make peace. He told them a fable of the disastrous effects of a conflict between the various members of the body. The purpose of the fable was to make the plebeians repent and to realize that strife was dangerous to all. Thus, the fable was used by the most powerful group with the aim of restoring harmony.

In 1 Cor 12.12–26 Paul uses the same fable in a context of conflict caused by various charismatic gifts in the Christian community. The conflict is described as one between 'honorable' and 'less honorable' members (12.22–24). In 1 Corinthians 12 the conflict is brought out into the open and discussed. In Romans 12, however, the conflict is treated in a much more general way and alluded to rather than confronted. In line with Paul's less polemical style in Romans he does not bring out the polemics and the accusations in the fable. Rather, he refers to it in such a way as to present what he wants to see as the common basis for unity, without directly raising the issue of conflict.

First he describes the body: 'For as in one body we have many members, and all members do not have the same function', and then he proceeds: 'so we, though many, are one body in Christ, and individually members of one another' (12.4–5). The first line of thought speaks of the various *functions* which the members have. In contrast to this the unity of the body is described in a different language when Paul speaks of a unity 'in Christ'. This is an expression of identity which is not dependent upon one's place in the differentiation of gifts, but simply based on the more fundamental fact of 'being in Christ'. It

---

[52] Cf. Liv. 2.32.
[53] Liv. 2.32.7.

is this type of language that E. P. Sanders has described as 'language of participation'.[54]

(c) φιλαδελφία

Being true to one's charisma (12.6) means performing it within the limits that are set by each one being 'members one of another' (12.5b), that is without hybris. Thus it appears that in line with his argument in 1 Corinthians 12 Paul directs his exhortations more against those who became haughty and ambitious as a result of possessing the charisms of leadership than against envy from those who were subjected to leadership by others. This gives a plausible reading to vv. 9–10, with its 'headline' in v. 9a:[55] 'let love (ἀγάπη) be genuine', being explained in v. 10: 'love one another with brotherly affection, outdo one another in showing honor'.

In v. 10 Paul addresses once more the members of the community in their relations to 'each other'. This relationship is defined not in terms of different functions. Instead he speaks of them as 'brothers' — as members of the closest kinship group. This is expressed in his use of a double set of terms for 'love': φιλαδελφία and φιλόστοργοι, both of which are derived from a family situation. This corresponds with his addressing his readers as 'brothers' in 12.1–2.

In what way ought these 'brothers' to behave towards each other when it comes to showing honor? The most plausible translation of τῇ τιμῇ ἀλλήλους προηγούμενοι is 'in regard to honor prefer the others to yourselves'.[56] This translation is recommended by a parallel in Phil 2.3: 'in humility count others better than yourselves (ἀλλήλους ἡγούμενοι ὑπερέχοντας ἑαυτῶν)', as well as by 12.16. Likewise, in 1 Cor 12.24–25 Paul relates God's giving more honor to those who have less as an example to the community that 'the members may have the same care for one another'.

---

[54] *Paul and Palestinian Judaism* (London: SCM, 1977) 453–63.

[55] W. T. Wilson (*Love without Pretense*, 150–55) speaks of 12.9 as 'the thematic statement' of 12.9–21.

[56] C. E. B. Cranfield, *The Epistle to the Romans* (Edinburgh: T&T Clark, 1979) 2.632–33. Dunn (*Romans 9–16*, 741) takes προηγούμενοι in the sense 'go before, lead the way' and translates: 'show the way to one another in respect'.

Some of the old versions and some patristic writers translate προ-ηγούμενοι in the sense 'surpass' or 'anticipate' one another.[57] This may represent a more Hellenistic thought about a competition without envy and jealousy among 'good men', similar to the one that Dio Chrysostom urges in *Or.* 44.8.

(d) τοῖς ταπεινοῖς συναπαγόμενοι

In 12.16 Paul admonishes his readers about life in the community with a terminology that parallels v. 3 in its use of φρονεῖν: (a) τὸ αὐτὸ εἰς ἀλλήλους φρονοῦντες; (b) μὴ τὰ ὑψηλὰ φρονοῦντες ἀλλὰ τοῖς ταπεινοῖς συναπαγόμενοι; (c) μὴ γίνεσθε φρόνιμοι παρ' ἑαυτοῖς. 'To be of the same mind' expresses the motif of the unity of the community that is of central importance to Paul in his argument in Romans (cf. 15.5).[58] His use of ἀλλήλους once more (cf. vv. 5, 10) creates the atmosphere of the close and immediate relations of communitas. Paul is thinking of the unity of mind and purpose on the part of the 'members of the body' and the 'brothers'.

V. 16b is a parallel to v. 3a: 'do not think too highly', but it goes beyond v. 3. It does not speak of keeping within one's limits (that is, within the structures of the different charisms), but introduces an element of antistructure in that it places ὑψηλὰ in antithesis to τοῖς ταπεινοῖς. The alternative to 'thinking too highly' is not to 'keep within one's measures', as it is in v. 3, but rather a total reversal: a break with one's own position and an association with οἱ ταπεινοί, the lowly ones.[59] This contrast between the proud and mighty on the one hand and the low and humble on the other is a common motif in Jewish and early Christian exhortations.[60] Maybe Paul alludes to a specifically theological perspective also with his warning not to be wise in one's own estimation (v. 16c). This is a modified quotation of the first part of LXX Prov 3.7; the second part of the verse contrasts this attitude with the fear of God.[61]

---

[57] I.a. Vulgate and John Chrysostom; see Cranfield, *The Epistle to the Romans,* 632.

[58] Wilson, *Love without Pretense,* 179–80.

[59] τοῖς ταπεινοῖς can also be neuter, but in the New Testament it is regularly used of persons, e.g. Luke 1.52; 2 Cor 7.6; see Thompson, *Clothed with Christ,* 106.

[60] See Wilson, *Love without Pretense,* 181–82.

[61] *Love without Pretense,* 182–83.

The contrast between 'highly' and 'lowly' in this statement is even more striking since ταπεινός has preserved its original meaning of 'lowly, humble' (that which is of low status).[62] It refers to somebody or something that lacks honor, but instead has shame, similar to the foolish, the weak, the despised that was chosen by God (1 Cor 1.27–28). This association between the strong and the humble and low, based on the fact that they are each 'one among the others', demands a break with 'thinking high thoughts', with being φρόνιμοι παρ' ἑαυτοῖς. This requires an act of setting oneself in the same place as the lowly and humble. In Phil 2.3–8 Paul develops this link between the reversal of positions and the acceptance of an attitude of humility: 'Do nothing from selfishness or conceit, but in humility count others better than yourselves.' In Philippians, too, the danger to be avoided is that of strife and 'vainglory'. Instead one must accept a position of humiliation.

The addressees of Paul's admonitions seem to be those who have some status, so that seeking out the lowly will imply a break with the status that they have hitherto enjoyed. Paul's admonitions in Rom 12.3–16 presuppose that desires to seek honor, to compete with others, and to go beyond given measures are present among his readers. He encounters these temptations with traditional Hellenistic arguments, but he adds some specific Christian interpretations. It appears that the Christological argument of participation 'in Christ' (12.5) is the most important one. Thus, the example of Christ lies behind the exhortations not to seek honor for oneself but to identify instead with the lowly.[63] A comparison with Phil 2.1–11 supports this suggestion.[64] This passage combines many of the same motifs that are found in Romans 12 — the unity of mind, brotherly love, not to seek vain glory for oneself, but instead to give more glory to the others, seeking the humble. And much more directly than in Romans 12, Paul emphasizes that this is possible in an act of imitation of Christ, who lived this way.

---

[62] Later 'lowly' became a Christian ideal and virtue (cf. Eph 4.2f.; Col 3.12; 1 Pet 3.8) and thus the social contrast was lost.

[63] Thompson, *Clothed with Christ*, 106–7.

[64] See Engberg-Pedersen, 'Stoicism in Philippians' (below, p. 276).

Thus, Paul has used well-known ideas about control of ambition and honor and applied them within the Christian community. But it is more than a system of checks and balances. The image of the body as applied to the community takes on a new meaning. Paul does not address the *polis* as such, but only a small part within it. In social terms, within the city the Christians were hardly yet recognized as a 'body', but Paul addresses them as such 'in Christ'. Moreover, Paul combines an attitude not to claim honor with an identification with the lowly, in clear distinction from a Hellenistic self-understanding. The result is a distinctive community ethos, primarily addressed to internal relations within groups of Christians.

This emphasis upon concord in internal relations among Christians in one city corresponds to Paul's overall purpose in his letter to the Romans. A major concern was to bring Jews who believed in Jesus as the Messiah to accept fellowship with non-circumcized believers. This is the main point of his interpretation of the Abraham story in Romans 4, in a direct follow-up of his major exposition of justification by faith (3.21–26). Significantly, Paul contrasts justification by faith (3.21–26) with human hybris, in the form of boasting (καύχησις; 3.27; 4.2).[65] 'Boasting' is the attitude of the Jews who, on the basis of their knowledge of the Mosaic law (2.17), make unjustified claims to privileges vis-à-vis God as well as human beings (that is, non-Jews). But boasting was not just a Jewish attitude. In Rom 11.17–22 Paul encounters claims to superiority from non-Jewish believers who compared themselves to non-believing Jews.

In his response to this Paul emphasizes that Jews and non-Jews share the same position — they have all sinned and have no justification to boast and they are all saved in the same way by the power and mercy of God. Furthermore, Paul uses this premise as an argument for unity between Jews and non-Jews in the Christian community.[66] This is a concern of utmost importance to Paul in his letter to the Romans and

---

[65] H. Moxnes, 'Honour and Righteousness in Romans,' *JSNT* 32 (1988) 61–77, esp. 68–75.

[66] See H. Moxnes, *Theology in Conflict* (NovTSup 53; Leiden: Brill, 1980) 78–102; A. F. Segal, *Paul the Convert*, 254–67.

it dominates his arguments in chapters 1–4 and 9–11. Thus, the common view that there are strong links between Romans 1–11 and 12–15 is supported by the parallel between Paul's concern for unity and criticism of the quest for honor in both parts of the letter.

Paul and Dio Chrysostom

Both Paul and Dio, from different positions within Hellenistic society, witness to the all-pervasive character of Greco-Roman culture as an honor culture. That was a given framework within which they and their audiences lived. A philosopher or a preacher of a new religion addressing the human and moral situation of his hearers could not avoid confronting this fundamental aspect of city life. They also show that without doubt the honor system was more than a 'cultural' element in the modern sense of the word, it expressed the very character of the political system, it was power made visible. This explains Paul's acceptance of the honor system with the emperor at the top, followed by his representatives and city officials. He himself and his addressees were in a dependent situation in this respect. To a certain degree that was also true of Dio and his audience. Although he addressed the city elite, he knew well from his own experience that they were dependent upon the emperor and his representatives.

Their criticism of the honor culture therefore had certain given limits, it could only be expressed within the area of self-determination for the group in question. Here there is a major difference between Dio, who addresses the citizen body as such, and Paul, who speaks to much smaller numbers in their capacity as belonging to groups of Christians. Still, the goals are rather similar — the common good of the city or the group, unity and harmony instead of strife, the necessity to constrain one's own ambitions and pride in order to reach these goals.

Since Dio himself belonged to the elite, he could more easily criticize the self-seeking competition for offices and honors. Dio's orations can also be viewed in the context of the problem of financing civic institutions and the desire to encourage benefactions as the most important way to preserve cities as viable social and economic entities. It was Dio's vision that by education and good examples a citizen body could be formed that put the pride of the city before their own. His criticism in his most positive period did not attempt to abolish the honor system, but to reveal its inner nature, and to show that the external signs of honor were in themselves unimportant.

Paul's addressees had a much smaller social area that they controlled. It was limited to their interaction when they met as groups of believers. Consequently, the idea of the ideal city, in philosophic discussions applied to the community of citizens, is in Paul's argument applied to members of the Christian community. But still the powers of an honor culture were at play. In one sense, Paul's criticism is more radical than that of Dio. It is not by education but by a transformation that the believers can break with this culture. Moreover, based on a Hellenistic-Jewish tradition of the reversal motif, association with humble people is put up as an ideal. Still, this is a transformation, not a total break with the honor culture. It is the honor of others, not one's own, that is put in the center.

We do not meet with the Cynic aspects found in Dio's radical criticism in Paul, but rather Stoic ideals of harmony and concord. His exhortation to live in unity and not to cause strife by seeking honor may have a double purpose — to form a community life that was formed after the example of Christ, and to avoid conflicts with neighbors and authorities (12.17–21; 13.1–7). But at the same time this other purpose also had a positive aspect vis-à-vis the outside world. Paul encouraged participation in city life as obedient, but not as ruling citizens.

8

Determinism and Free Will in Paul: The Argument of
1 Corinthians 8 and 9
Abraham J. Malherbe

In this paper I shall examine Paul's argument on determinism and free will in 1 Corinthians 9. This passage has been worked on intensively in recent years, and scholars have frequently agreed on problems they see in the text if not on their proffered solutions.

A perceived roughness in the transition between chapters 8 and 9 has contributed to the description of chapter 9 as a digression from Paul's discussion of idol meat. The digression has then been thought explanatory, particularly of 8.13. Alternatively, 9.1 has been regarded as a transition from a discussion of the Corinthians' *exousia* (ἐξουσία) to eat idol meat to one of Paul's *exousia* to receive financial support, the latter having been occasioned by concerns in the Corinthian church which caused Paul to defend his practice of not accepting financial support from the Corinthians. The view that the present position of chapter 9 in the letter is due to a redactor further separates the chapter, and thus Paul's argument in it, from chapter 8. Opposition to such radical surgery, however, has not meant that the use of *exousia* in 8.9 as well as 9.4, 5, 6, 12, 18 has been regarded as important evidence that the two chapters belong together.[1]

I wish to thank Wayne Meeks and the editor for their valiant efforts to sharpen my argument.

[1] In addition to the commentaries, see F. S. Jones, *'Freiheit' in den Briefen des Apostels Paulus: Eine historische, exegetische und religionsgeschichtliche Studie* (GTA 34; Göttingen: Vandenhoeck & Ruprecht, 1987) 28–42; S. Vollenweider, *Freiheit als neue Schöpfung: Eine Untersuchung zur Eleutheria bei Paulus und in seiner Umwelt* (FRLANT 147; Göttingen: Vandenhoeck & Ruprecht, 1984) 199–201.

The apparent lack of coherence within chapter 9 has also drawn attention. Commentators have been unable to explain why Paul introduces freedom into his discussion in 9.1. Scholars have seen freedom as a standard theme of the wandering Cynic preachers, referring to Epictetus (*Diss.* 3.22.48), but have not made much of the observation. Not many have followed Johannes Weiss, who was unable to make much sense of Paul's reference to freedom here, and suggested therefore that it originated as a gloss. For the most part, scholars have tried to determine the nature of the freedom Paul had in mind (from the Law, from financial dependence, to eat idol meat, or as a description of social status?). But the relationship between Paul's freedom (9.1) and the discussion of *exousia* that follows has been left unclear. This lack of clarity even led Joachim Jeremias to discover an elaborate chiasm in chapter 9 which further disjointed Paul's discussion of freedom and authority.[2]

The spate of recent scholarship on the text, as illuminating and suggestive as it is on certain details, has not yielded clarity on how Paul's argument within chapter 9 coheres and whether or how that argument connects with what he says in chapter 8. I propose that chapter 9 is part of an argument that begins as early as 8.1 and continues to 9.23 (actually to 11.1), and that the argument is made intelligible by examining it in light of the popular philosophic deliberations on the theme of the sage's independence, particularly as it related to determinism and free will. This involves the notion of *exousia*, which can be translated 'permission', 'right', and 'power', or 'authority'. Furthermore, since Paul quotes Stoic slogans some of the Corinthians had introduced into the discussion, his own adoption of Stoic categories was deliberate, and he expected that his argument would be followed.[3]

A note of caution is in order at this point. My attempt to trace Paul's argument does not imply that I think the issue between Paul and some of the Corinthians was in the first place philosophical. The issue was,

---

[2] J. Weiss, *Der erste Korintherbrief* (KEK; Göttingen: Vandenhoeck & Ruprecht, 1910) 231–32; J. Jeremias, 'Chiasmus in den Paulusbriefen,' in his *Abba: Studien zur neutestamentlichen Theologie und Zeitgeschichte* (Göttingen: Vandenhoeck & Ruprecht, 1966) 276–90.

[3] Others, particularly Jones and Vollenweider, have brought the philosophers into the discussion, but have not succeeded in demonstrating how an awareness of the philosophic issues lends coherence to the Pauline text.

rather, one of behavior, which Paul wanted to influence. In attempting to do so, he worked out the implications of the claims they made to justify this behavior. These claims were made in the form of popular philosophical slogans, and Paul's strategy was to work out the implications of these claims, thus laying a theoretical base for the practical direction he gave. Constraints of space require that I concentrate on one theoretical dimension of these chapters.

The Corinthians' Knowledge and Their Claim to Exousia

Paul begins his discussion of the problem of idol meat by relativizing the knowledge the Corinthians claimed for themselves (8.1–6). He contrasts this vaunted knowledge (8.7, 11) and those who have it (8.10) with the weak consciences of some in the church (8.7, 10, 12) and the weak who have such consciences (8.9, 11). Paul thus understood that at the heart of the problem caused by the self-assertive Corinthians was their insistence on their cognitive superiority.

This would seem rather obvious, but it has not sufficiently been appreciated that Paul's description of some Corinthians as weak further defines the issue. I do not think that weakness here describes their social status, as Gerd Theissen has argued, but that it is rather to be understood in light of the moral philosophers' description of some people as weak.[4] Philosophers of all sorts described certain persons as morally and intellectually weak, as has been pointed out recently, but here I want to draw attention to only those features of that description

---

[4] G. Theissen, *The Social Setting of Pauline Christianity: Essays on Corinth* (Philadelphia: Fortress, 1982) 70–73, 121–43. I am not at this point claiming that those who refused to eat idol meat were not socially impotent (the 'weak') according to Theissen's interpretation of 1.26–28. They very likely were, and their intellectual 'weakness' may indeed have been congruent with their social status. But in this paper I confine myself to the philosophical (sc. theological) argument and do so consciously at the expense of the social dimension of the issue. The limit set for this paper permits no more. Furthermore, Paul does not here use 'weakness' in connection with other possible social indicators, as he does in 1.26–28, but with γνῶσις and συνείδησις, which shows that his argument has in view matters cognitive rather than social. For a more sympathetic treatment of Theissen, see D. B. Martin, *Slavery as Salvation: The Metaphor of Slavery in Pauline Christianity* (New Haven: Yale University Press, 1990) 118–24.

that are relevant to my immediate argument, and to concentrate on the Stoics.[5]

The weak were generally identified by philosophers as people who found it difficult to live up to the demands of the virtuous life. Weakness was frequently described as a condition that accompanies moral illness and as a condition or disposition of the self-indulgent (Diogenes Laertius 7.115; Cicero, *Tusc. Disp.* 4.29, 42). By way of contrast, the person who takes up the philosophic life purifies his governing principle (his ἡγεμονικόν [Epictetus, *Diss.* 3.22.19–22, 93–96]). Bad habits and false beliefs were said to twist weak minds (Cicero, *Leg.* 1.29), and both received considerable attention. Intellectual immaturity was described as intellectual weakness (Cicero, *De fin.* 5.43). According to the Stoic theory of cognition, it is because of our weakness that we give our assent (*synkatathesis, adsensio*) to false judgments (*SVF* 1.67; 3.177; Plutarch, *Adv. Colot.* 1122C; Cicero, *Tusc. Disp.* 4.15), and wrong conduct is due to the slackness and weakness of the soul (*SVF* 3.471, 473).[6] An effort to help the weak better themselves recognizes the hold on them of their habits and past associations, for weak minds fear the unfamiliar (Seneca, *Ep.* 50.9). Knowing their own weakness, the weak are not to expose themselves to those things by which they may be seduced (Seneca, *Ep.* 116.5), and they are to avoid the crowd, for their own judgment can easily be turned aside by the crowd (Seneca, *Ep.* 7.1; *De otio* 1.1; cf. *Ep.* 44.1).

What Paul says about the weak in chapter 8 has much in common with the moralists' views of the weak, for example, that the conscience of the weak is not pure but still defiled (v. 7). Paul associates weakness with cognition, and he recognizes the importance of habituation for their condition. A closer examination of these elements and of his psychagogic instructions in light of the philosophers' comments on

[5] See A. J. Malherbe, "'Pastoral Care' in the Thessalonian Church,' *NTS* 36 (1990) 375–91; S. K. Stowers, 'Paul on the Use and Abuse of Reason,' *Greeks, Romans, and Christians: Essays in Honor of Abraham J. Malherbe* (ed. D. L. Balch *et al.;* Minneapolis: Fortress, 1990) 253–86: C. E. Glad, 'Adaptability and Early Christian Psychagogy: Philodemus and Paul' (Ph. D. diss., Brown University, 1992).

[6] See W. Görler, 'Ἀσθενὴς συγκατάθεσις. Zur stoischen Erkenntnistheorie,' *WJA* N. F. 3 (1977) 83–92, for details of the argument that is, perhaps, overly simplified in what follows.

how the weak should be treated would be rewarding, but that cannot now detain us. We turn to the main thread of his argument — the notion of freedom.

It is likely that those Corinthians who claimed knowledge for them-selves were the same ones who called others in the congregation weak.[7] Paul himself uses the term to describe certain persons in Thessalonica (1 Thess 5.14) and uses the term again in Romans 14. But in 1 Corinthians 8 he picks up the term from those who use it pejor-atively. He corrects them, and in the process works out the implica-tions of the claims they make for themselves and about others. What is important for us to note is that it is in the context of his concern for the weak that Paul introduces the Corinthians' proud claim that they have *exousia* (ἐξουσία ὑμῶν αὕτη, 'this right of yours', 8.9) into his argument. The fact that he introduces it with a warning demon-strates the significance he attaches to it in his criticism of their atti-tudes. That this claim of the Corinthians is similar to the etymologically related πάντα μοι ἔξεστιν ('I have the right to do all things') of 6.12 — which was a well-known philosophic slogan — has frequently been observed, but the full implications of the philosophic notions embodied in the slogan for Paul's argument have yet to be drawn.[8] In other words, the Corinthians' claim to have knowledge is inextricably tied to their assertion of their *exousia*. In this they are similar to Stoics who held that it is the person who is free who has *exousia*, freedom being defined as 'the knowledge of what is allowable and what is forbidden, and slavery as ignorance of what is permissible (ἔξεστιν) and what is not' (Dio Chrysostom, *Or.* 14.18).

The *exousia* of the wise man was one of the Stoic paradoxes. The wise man, Stoics said, 'alone is free and bad men are slaves, for freedom is the right to act independently (ἐξουσία αὐτοπραγίας), and slavery is the deprivation of independent action (στέρησις αὐτοπραγίας)'

---

[7]   They may have done so in response to a charge by the scrupulous non-eaters that they were idolators. On the other hand, see Stowers, 'Paul on the Use and Abuse of Reason', 276, 279.

[8]   On 6.12, see S. K. Stowers, 'A "Debate" over Freedom: 1 Corinthians 6.12–20,' *Christian Teaching: Studies in Honor of LeMoine G. Lewis* (ed. E. Ferguson; Abilene, TX: Abilene Christian University Press, 1981) 59–71.

(Diogenes Laertius 7.121). The wise man alone is free and has received from divine law the power of independent action, and *exousia* is defined as the power of decision that conforms to (natural) law (*SVF* 3.544; cf. Epictetus, *Diss.* 4.1.145–46, 156–58). This means that we have *exousia* over ourselves in matters of good and evil (Epictetus, *Diss.* 4.12.8–9), for no one has *exousia* over someone else's judgments (Epictetus, *Diss.* 1.29.11, 50–52). Controlling someone's body or possessions does not mean that one has *exousia* over him (Epictetus, *Diss.* 1.9.15; 25.2), but the person who exercises *exousia* over those externals we desire to avoid is our master (Epictetus, *Diss.* 2.2.26; cf. 13.14; 4.7.10; *Ench.* 14.2).

So, as in the view of the weak, so in the matter of *exousia* we again find ourselves in the midst of Stoic cognitive theory when Paul discusses the very ordinary but difficult issue as to whether it was permissible for the Corinthians to eat meat offered to idols. Only the educated, Stoics said, are free (Epictetus, *Diss.* 3.1.23, 25). One is set free by learning the things that are one's own, and that knowledge is the power to deal with external impressions (χρῆσις φαντασιῶν [Epictetus, *Diss.* 3.24.67–70; 4.1.81–83]).[9] External things are obstacles or hindrances (Epictetus, *Diss.* 1.1.9, 28; 4.4.15; 7.10; *Ench.* 1), and it is important that dealing with the external impressions takes place without any hindrance or compulsion whatever, otherwise one would be under the *exousia* of whoever or whatever exercises such force (Epictetus, *Diss.* 3.24.67–70; 4.1.59, 81–83; 10.8). The ability to choose or reject — namely, the ability to make correct use of the external impressions — is a divine gift, and the person who cares for it will never be thwarted or hindered (Epictetus, *Diss.* 1.1.12). Training (ἄσκησις) is needed to distinguish between those things

---

[9] On the intellectual requirement of this χρῆσις φαντασιῶν, see Epictetus, *Diss.* 1.20. The philosopher must interpret the will of nature to follow it (*Diss.* 1.17.16), and must become a σχολαστικός if he desires to examine the decisions of his own will (*Diss.* 1.11.39–40). The study of those decisions takes a long time (*Diss.* 1.11.40; 20.13; 3.9.11), and defending them requires expertise in Stoic logic (*Diss.* 1.7.1–4). Philosophers exercise their pupils in theory as well as the difficulties of life (*Diss.* 1.26.3), and the two are organically connected (*Diss.* 3.10.10). See A. Bonhoeffer, *Epictet und die Stoa* (Stuttgart: Ferdinand Enke, 1890) 6ff.; and, for ongoing education, B. L. Hijmans, *Askesis: Notes on Epictetus' Educational System* (Assen: van Gorcum, 1959) esp. 33–41. See further, n. 24 below.

that are not one's own and therefore are hindrances, and those things which are one's own and therefore not hindrances. The latter are our proper concern and no one else has *exousia* over them or can hinder them (Epictetus, *Diss.* 4.1.81–82; cf. 2.13.7–8). If someone does not make the distinction properly, he will be hindered, but if he does make it properly, no one will ever be able to compel (ἀναγκάζει) him or hinder him, and he will do no-thing against his will (ἄκων [Epictetus, *Ench.* 1]).

Stoics and writers susceptible to Stoic influence cautioned against the misappropriation of this notion of *exousia.* Epictetus warned that no one has *exousia* to do wrong with impunity (Epictetus, *Diss.* 4.1.119), and Musonius Rufus cautioned that a tyrant could not for long justify his actions by saying ἔξεστίν μοι ('it is permissible for me') rather than καθήκει μοι ('it is fitting for me'; Fragment 31). Dio Chrysostom reflects his uneasiness with the declaration that the person who has the power to do whatever he wishes is free, and corrects it by arguing that it is not permissible (οὐκ ἔξεστιν) to do mean and unprofitable things (*Or* 14.13–16). And, when Epictetus says that the philosopher's consciousness of his commission to reform others affords him the *exousia* to censure them (Epictetus, *Diss.* 3.22.94), he betrays a view of *exousia* that is not entirely self-centered.

Paul's response to the question of idol food is informed by such views as these. He accepts his readers' philosophic slogans and engages them on that level, but not without his own peculiar twists, as he had also done in 6.12–20.[10] After introducing the subject by focusing on the meat eaters' claim to knowledge (8.1–6), he picks up their description of the non-eaters as weak and grants the assumption implicit in such a description that the latter lack knowledge. Paul is addressing those who claim that they have knowledge, and he does not deny that claim, nor does he deny their claim to *exousia.* Indeed, it is essential to his later argument that they are acknowledged to have *exousia.*

Paul introduces the issue in terms recalling the philosophers' description of the weak as persons with limited cognitive faculties (8.7) and then argues that neither eating nor drinking affects our standing before God (8.8). Eating and drinking are what a Stoic would have described as externals — things that should be regarded as ἀδιάφορα.

---

[10] For Paul's method, cf. *Rhetorica ad Herennium* 4.54–56.

The second part of Paul's reply is more pointed and ironic. Now he introduces the *exousia* of those with knowledge and cautions lest this vaunted *exousia* of theirs become a stumbling block. This part of his response extends from 8.9–13 and is bracketed by πρόσκομμα in v. 9 and σκάνδαλον in v. 13, which form an *inclusio*. Herein lies the irony — that the *exousia* of those with knowledge should be treated as a hindrance to the weak. The Stoics, whose slogans the meat eaters were using, were concerned lest the free person, a friend of God, who had *exousia* and made rational use of what had been given him, valued the externals, which are potential impediments and hindrances (cf. Epictetus, *Diss.* 4.3.9–12). What the Corinthians — the ones with knowledge — should have regarded as externals or things indifferent, they rather insisted upon on the grounds of their *exousia*, and this insistence became an impediment to the weak, whose consciences they thus defiled (v. 7) and wounded (v. 12), and whom they caused to stumble (v. 9) and destroyed (v. 11)! The *ad hominem* nature of the argument is clear — Paul uses the Stoic definitions of the Corinthians but then introduces the notion of impediment (also a Stoic concern) to bring them up short. He had already adopted this manner of argument in 6.12–20, and would do so again.

In the second bracket of the *inclusio* (v. 13) Paul personalizes the argument by referring to his preparedness to forego eating meat and so not be a stumbling block to the weak, thus setting up the ensuing presentation of himself as an *exemplum* of not insisting on his own *exousia*.

Paul's Freedom and Exousia

It may be useful to state explicitly at this point what I have assumed in my interpretation so far. If Paul knew that the meat eating Corinthians were proud of their own knowledge and *exousia* and looked down on the weak, and that they described themselves and the others in Stoic terms, it is reasonable to assume that he expected his readers to be able to follow his argument, in which he used Stoic notions.

The idea of freedom was integrally related to that of *exousia* and is implicit in 8.9–13. It becomes explicit in chapter 9, and Paul's mentioning of his freedom in 9.1 and repetition of it in 9.19 should cause neither surprise nor consternation as it has done. According to the

Stoics, one's freedom is inextricable from one's *exousia*, and Paul also argues from freedom (9.1) to *exousia* (9.3 and following). That the two are related in his mind also appears from 10.23, 29, where he again works with Stoic ideas.

The introduction to Paul's exemplary self-presentation consists of four rhetorical questions and an *ad hominem* application to his readers (9.1–2). The form of the questions, with οὐ ('not'), anticipates an affirmative answer. He is free, is an apostle, has seen the Lord, and the Corinthians are his work in the Lord. The first three questions are bound up together — Paul's freedom is a corollary to his apostleship, which derives from his having seen the Lord (cf. Gal 1.12–27; 1 Cor 15.8). So, while Paul does retain the Stoic category, he changes its meaning. The Stoic's freedom was the result of his training; Paul's freedom derived from his encounter with Christ. Paul elsewhere makes similar adjustments to popular philosophic terminology he uses. Thus, in 2 Cor 3.17 it is his encounter with the Lord and the Spirit that provides freedom and the παρρησία with which he carries out his ministry (3.12).[11] Such modification of important philosophic terminology is also found in 1 Thess 2.2, where παρρησία is not grounded in Paul's own effort to obtain freedom, as it was with the Stoics, but is attributed to God's agency.[12] So, while the outline of Paul's argument in 1 Corinthians 8 and 9 and the terminology he uses may be the same as that of the Stoics, his self-understanding is not.

The fourth question lodges the argument in the concrete situation in Corinth. Paul is not defending himself but is applying his self-assertions to his readers. 'If I am not an apostle to others' (v. 2) is hypothetical; the stress is on the second member of the antithesis: he *is* an apostle to them, for they are the seal of his apostleship (v. 3). The reason he so intones the obvious is to strengthen the basis on which he can construct the remainder of his argument.

Vv. 3–12 are the next stage of his argument. By referring to this section as ἡ ἐμὴ ἀπολογία τοῖς ἐμὲ ἀνακρίνουσιν ('my defense to

---

[11] See D. E. Fredrickson, 'Paul's Bold Speech in the Argument of 2 Corinthians 2.14–7.16' (Ph. D. diss., Yale University, 1990).

[12] See A. J. Malherbe, 'Exhortation in 1 Thessalonians,' in *Paul and the Popular Philosophers* (Minneapolis: Fortress, 1989) 58–60.

those who would question me'), Paul is not indicating that there were
people who were bringing specific charges against him which required a
self-defense.[13] His defense is not against such charges but has in view
the anticipated reactions of his readers to his warning in 8.9 that their
exousia not become a πρόσκομμα ('stumbling-block') to the weak.
That Paul expected his readers to react in such a way appears from
10.23, 29, 32, where the same issues turn up again.[14] Paul expected
that his instructions not to insist on their *exousia* on the ground that it
would be an impediment to the weak would meet with the retort that
he was asking them willingly to submit to a limitation of their freedom.
That is why Paul provides a self-presentation in terms of his own
freedom. He has introduced freedom in vv. 1–2 and will return to it in
vv. 13–18, but first he must make the case beyond any doubt for his
own *exousia*.

Compared with the philosophers whose traditions the Corinthians
and Paul used, Paul was notoriously loath to speak of his own *exousia*.[15]
He was equally hesitant to allow others the exercize of their *exousia* lest
they paradoxically become enslaved to it (see 6.12: ἀλλ' οὐκ ἐξουσιασθήσομαι, 'I shall not be placed under authority'). Paul does not
attempt here to secure his *exousia*; his discussion rather drives to the
conclusion in vv. 11–12, where he applies it to the Corinthians' insistence on their own *exousia*.

---

[13] Contra most commentators, I read τοῖς ἀνακρίνουσιν as conative: Paul's ἀπολογία
anticipates a retort to the advice he is giving (probably in response to a request for
direction, see 7.1).

[14] I read vv. 29b–30 as the interjections of an interlocutor. For the problematic
nature of these verses and the various solutions proposed, see W. L. Willis, *Idol Meat in
Corinth: The Pauline Argument in 1 Corinthians 8 and 10* (SBLDS 68; Chico, CA:
Scholars Press, 1985) 246–50; G. D. Fee, *The First Epistle to the Corinthians* (NICNT;
Grand Rapids: Eerdmans, 1987) 486 n. 52. C. A. Pierce (*Conscience in the New Testament* [SBT 15; Chicago: Allenson, 1955] 77–78) and the REV take it in the way I do.
Read thus, the interlocutor here objects to Paul's qualification (vv. 24–29a) of the earlier
interjection (v. 23) by claiming *exousia*, and the concomitant notion of freedom (γάρ in
v. 29b is exclamatory, 'What!' [BAGD 1.f.]). The problem with this interpretation lies in
οὖν in v. 31, but is mitigated if one takes οὖν as introducing the inference of the advice
Paul had given in vv. 23–29a, particularly v. 26.

[15] The references to his or his readers' *exousia* are concentrated in the Corinthian
correspondence, particularly in the section of 1 Corinthians in which he addresses attitudes expressed in popular philosophical slogans (1 Cor 6.12; 7.4, 37; 8.9; 9.4, 5, 6, 12,
18; 10.12; see also 2 Cor 10.8; 13.10; 2 Thess 3.9).

In vv. 3–12 a series of arguments, teeming with rhetorical questions, confirm that Paul did have *exousia* to demand financial support. First, customary apostolic rights within the Christian community are adduced (vv. 4–5), then the common rhetorical examples of the soldier, vinedresser, and shepherd are introduced to show that the practice of providing financial support is self-evidently right (v. 7),[16] and, finally, the Law is claimed to say the same thing (vv. 8–10): The farmer has a right to share in the results of his labor.

Paul makes the application to the Corinthians in vv. 11–12, where he advances his own practice as an example of forgoing one's *exousia*, thus rounding off the discussion begun in 8.8–9. A rhetorical question, which continues the bucolic metaphor and has proverbial force (cf. Rom 15.27; see Gal 6.6), establishes Paul's right to financial support from the Corinthians (v. 11). The conclusion to this part of the argument is rhetorical and *ad hominem* (v. 12): 'If others share in your *exousia*, do not we the more? Yet we have not made use of this *exousia*, but endure all things lest we place any impediment (ἐγκοπήν) in the way of the gospel of Christ.'[17]

---

[16] For a similar set of these examples, see 2 Tim 2.4–6, substituting the athlete for the shepherd, and for this *lex scholastica*, cf. Pliny, *Ep.* 2.20.9; Quintilian, *Inst. Orat.* 4.5.3.

[17] This translation of τῆς ὑμῶν ἐξουσίας ('in your *exousia*') has in its favor that it would form the second bracket of an *inclusio* which begins with ἡ ἐξουσία ὑμῶν αὕτη ('this *exousia* of yours') in 8.9 (see also πρόσκομμα in 8.9 and ἐγκοπή in 9.12), and that it appears to be the obvious meaning. However, εἰ ἄλλοι τῆς ὑμῶν ἐξουσίας μετέχουσιν could also mean 'if others share in *exousia* over you', especially since discussions of *exousia* very frequently are concerned with the exercise of authority over others or over things (e.g. Epictetus, *Diss.* 1.25.2: ὧν ἐξουσίαν οἱ ἄλλοι ἔχουσιν; cf. 9.15; 4.1.82; 10.30, etc.), a concern Paul has already expressed in 6.12: οὐκ ἐγὼ ἐξουσιασθήσομαι ὑπό τινος ('I shall not be placed under the authority of anything' [or 'anyone']). If 9.12a were read thus, Paul would ironically be saying that while the Corinthians insisted on their own *exousia*, they placed themselves in a position where others (including Paul!) had *exousia* over them! Paul could have arrived at this by reasoning along the lines of Epictetus (*Diss.* 2.2.26), who held that if we care for externals, the person who has *exousia* over those externals will be our master and we his slave. Paul assumed that the Corinthians placed value on the matter of financial support to which he had *exousia*, but he considered financial support an external, and he therefore had *exousia* over them. In 8.8–9, when he introduced the issue of their *exousia*, he had also warned that their insistence on eating idol food, another external, would result in their becoming an impediment to the weak. Paul himself, though, did not make use of that *exousia* in order not to be an impediment, thus being able to offer himself as a model for the advice given in chapter 8.

Necessity and Paul's Free Choice

Paul is only halfway through his argument at this point. Why does he go on? Vv. 13 and 14 seem completely repetitive, and vv. 15–18 seem to some commentators to be superfluous in the context.[18] Is this then just another instance of Paul not leaving well enough alone? In fact, however, in vv. 13–18 Paul comes to the heart of his argument.

Instead of saying in v. 12 that he had not been an impediment to the weak, as one would have expected him to say (cf. 8.9, 13), and which would have nicely concluded his exemplary self-portrayal, Paul says his goal was not to let his *exousia* be an impediment to *the gospel*. Once more he adduces a self-evident example in support of his contention (v. 13) and then reaches the culmination of the series of warrants for his claim to financial support, namely a command of the Lord that those who proclaim the gospel should live by the gospel (v. 14). This word of the Lord is introduced to highlight Paul's claim that he had not made use of any of these rights (οὐ κέχρημαι οὐδενὶ τούτων, v. 15, alluding to vv. 4–6). The same claim is made at the end of this section (μὴ καταχρήσασθαι τῇ ἐξουσίᾳ μου ἐν τῷ εὐαγγελίῳ, v. 18), thus forming an *inclusio*. The section thus enclosed deals with the preaching of the gospel; εὐαγγέλιον and εὐαγγελίζεσθαι occur eight times in vv. 13–18 and once, to round off the discussion, in v. 23. By way of contrast, *exousia* occurs only in v. 18.

Superficially viewed, it may appear that Paul is changing subjects; in actuality, however, he is now focusing on what was at the heart of the Stoics' and his own thinking on *exousia*: freedom of choice. This is, then, not an appendix to, but the culmination of Paul's discussion of the problem of *exousia* already introduced in 8.9. Freedom has been the subtext all along; now it begins to emerge as Paul deals with compulsion and voluntarism as they relate to his preaching of the gospel, and then it becomes explicit as he introduces the final section of the argument in v. 19.

---

[18] E.g., E. Käsemann, 'A Pauline Version of the "Amor Fati",' in his *New Testament Questions of Today* (Philadelphia: Fortress, 1969) 218: these verses 'seem to be totally superfluous, because the design of the whole is quite clear even without them'.

There is a strong strain of determinism in Paul's argument here. The Lord has commanded, necessity is laid upon Paul, he can act unwillingly, and he is charged with a commission. This raises the question whether Paul did not understand himself to be in the prophetic tradition, according to which the prophet is commissioned by God, even against his own wishes. My claim that Paul's argument is conducted with the aid of Stoic notions of determinism and free will does not mean that I think Paul saw himself as a Stoic philosopher, particularly with respect to his place in the cosmic order of things. Paul thought of his call or conversion as analogous to that of a prophet like Jeremiah. The initiative was God's, and Paul's understanding of his call could well be understood as part of his Jewishness, as the discussions of his conversion or call have clearly shown. My interest is not to contest that view of Paul's self-understanding, but to make another point.[19]

In 1 Corinthians 9 Paul makes use of Greek philosophic terminology as he discusses the compulsion under which he is to preach the gospel. He does so, not because he is a Greek philosopher, but partly because the practical issue that he is addressing was raised in philosophic terms. When he discusses his call in Gal 1.10–17, he does so in clearly prophetic terms, presumably because it was the appropriate manner in which to do so in that context. It is easier to identify the traditions — Greek and Jewish — that Paul uses and to observe how they are made to function than it is to press beyond their use in argumentation to Paul's actual apostolic self-understanding. The latter is not our interest right now; nevertheless, I do not think that Paul's reason for arguing in the manner he does here is due entirely to the exigencies of the moment. The sense that I have of his letters to the Corinthians is that the means of persuasion he employs in them is less a matter of strategy he picks up or lets drop at will than a mode of intellectual engagement prompted by the Corinthians, but no less genuine and self-revealing for that. To think of Paul as either Jewish or Greek is not only superficial but wrong. If one

[19] For discussion, see H. D. Betz, *Galatians: A Commentary on Paul's Letter to the Churches in Galatia* (Hermeneia; Philadelphia: Fortress, 1979) 64–71; A. F. Segal, *Paul the Convert: The Apostolate and Apostasy of Saul the Pharisee* (New Haven: Yale University Press, 1990) 3–8.

simply cannot work without labels, that of eclectic may be applied to him but only if that label were not taken to describe him as though he indiscriminately collected thoughts from hither and yon.[20] For the moment, however, I pursue my argument that Paul's thought in 1 Corinthians 9 has affinities with that of some Stoics, and I shall comment briefly on Stoic determinism and free will in order to illuminate Paul's reasoning in vv. 13–18.[21]

According to the Stoics, the world, frequently compared to a city, is governed by divine wisdom and providence (Cicero, *De nat. deor.* 2.78–80; Dio Chrys., *Or.* 36.27–32, 37). Of interest to us is the concern of the Stoic with his proper place (τάξις) in the cosmic scheme of things (Epictetus, *Diss.* 3.1.19–20; 24.95). As a citizen of the universe one is required to remain in the station to which he is appointed (Epictetus, *Diss.* 1.9.24) and to hold to God, who administers the world providentially (Epictetus, *Diss.* 1.9.7; 4.1.98). That is the only guarantee one has of security, and the responsibility to do so lies in oneself. According to Epictetus, the training that has to do with security is engaged in only by those who are already advancing (προκόπτοντες) to wisdom but have not yet attained the state of performing perfect actions (Epictetus, *Diss.* 3.2.1, 5; 4.10.13).

This view of an ordered universe accentuated for Stoics the problem of individual freedom. Through one's participation in the Logos, which determines the harmony of the universe, one's freedom is limited by universal law with its implications of causality and determinism. The problem of human freedom, as seen by them, lay in their conviction that on the one hand one is a free agent, but on the other, since one is

---

[20] For a more positive and realistic understanding of the phenomenon, see *The Question of 'Eclecticism': Studies in Later Greek Philosophy* (ed. J. M. Dillon & A. A. Long; Berkeley: University of California Press, 1988).

[21] The subject is discussed with great frequency; e.g., by A. A. Long, 'Freedom and Determinism in the Stoic Theory of Human action,' in his *Problems in Stoicism* (London: Athlone, 1971) 173–99; C. Stough, 'Stoic Determinism and Moral Responsibility,' *The Stoics* (ed. J. M. Rist; Berkeley: University of California Press, 1978) 203–31; esp. T. Engberg-Pedersen, *The Stoic Theory of Oikeiosis: Moral Development and Social Interaction in Early Stoic Philosophy* (Studies in Hellenistic Civilization 2; Aarhus: Aarhus University Press, 1990) 207–34. The simplified account that follows focuses on those aspects of the discussion that appear to me to illuminate Paul's argument.

in the world, one is subject to cosmic law. While as rational beings we are free, there is only one natural law which absolutely orders and preserves this natural order.

The Stoics sought to solve the problem by distinguishing clearly between what is in our power and what is not. The confidence that we are not passive in relation to the universe and its law was expressed in the conviction that the soul is more powerful than Fortune. Freedom comes, they said, not to the person over whom Fortune has slight power, but to the one over whom it has no power at all (Seneca, *Ep.* 110.20). Such confidence is possible when we understand that Fortune does not bestow good or evil on us, but only the raw material of good and evil — the sources or things which, in our keeping, will develop into good or evil (Seneca, *Ep.* 98.2). To be free is not to be a slave to any circumstance or necessity (*necessitas*) or chance, but to compel Fortune to engage us on equal terms (Seneca, *Ep.* 51.9). What this implies is seen from the Stoic understanding that only the wise man is free (Diogenes Laertius 7.121). He is not compelled by necessity (ἀνάγκη) but performs virtuous actions willingly (ἑκών) and not unwillingly (ἄκων [Philo, *Quod omnis prob.* 60]). He cannot escape necessities (Seneca, *Ep.* 37.3), for example, death. But it can be said that he does escape them when he does nothing unwillingly — that is, when he wills to do what necessity is about to force on him (Seneca, *Ep.* 54.7). What is bound to be a necessity if one rebels is not really a necessity if one desires it (Seneca, *Ep.* 61.3).

The pantheistic piety of the Stoics gave a religious coloring to this aligning of individual will with universal law. The classic example of this was the often quoted prayer of Cleanthes (Seneca, *Ep.* 107.11):

Lead me, O Master of the lofty heavens,
My Father, whithersoever thou shalt wish.
I shall not falter, but obey with speed.
And though I would not, I shall go, and suffer,
In sin and sorrow what I might have done
In noble virtue. Aye, the willing soul
Fate leads, but the unwilling drags along.[22]

---

[22] See also Seneca, *De vita beata* 15.5–6; Epictetus, *Diss.* 2.23.42; 3.22.95; 4.4.34; *Ench.* 53; Marcus Aurelius 10.28.

Man must attend uncomplainingly upon God under whose guidance everything progresses (Seneca, *Ep.* 107.9; cf. *De vita beata* 15.4–5). The free man is a friend of God, and obeys him willingly (ἑκών [Epictetus, *Diss.* 4.3.9]). He can then say to God, 'I am one mind with you ... lead me where you will' (Epictetus, *Diss.* 2.16.42; 19.26).[23] He does nothing under compulsion, suffers nothing against his will, nor is he God's slave, but gives his free assent to God (Seneca, *De prov.* 5.6).

As we have seen, freedom is possible only through the correct use of reason. God gave freedom of the will to the mind to liberate it from necessity (Philo, *Quod deus immut.* 47–48). Every good man lives sensibly (φρονίμως) and will have *exousia* to do all things and live as he pleases (Philo, *Quod omnis prob.* 59). Wisdom is the only real freedom, the very service of philosophy being to make us free (Seneca, *Epp.* 37, 4; 8.7).[24]

Of more direct relevance to our present inquiry is how those philosophers who set out to reform others saw themselves in relation to the determined order of things. A few examples will suffice. Epictetus begins his description of the ideal Cynic by cautioning that the task could not be undertaken without God.[25] In this great city, the world, God assigns each and everything its place, and nothing should be attempted without God (*Diss.* 3.22.2–8, 53; cf. 21.12). Everything else in Epictetus' description then assumes that the philosopher would act in conformity with the divine will. Further, when Epictetus speaks of such philo-

[23] See also Epictetus, *Diss.* 1.12.17; Marcus Aurelius 9.1., and W. Theiler, 'Tacitus und die antike Schicksalslehre,' in *Phyllobolia für Peter von der Mühll* (Basel, 1946) 35–90, esp. 85ff.

[24] In this context, philosophy is primarily conceived of as logic and physics. To live rationally and use impressions rationally is to live according to nature (Epictetus, *Diss.* 3.1.25–26), and that requires a knowledge of physics, for life according to nature must be based upon the system and government of the entire world (Cicero, *De fin.* 3.72–73). Logic provides a method by which assent can correctly be given and by which truth can be defended. It makes possible the correct χρῆσις φαντασιῶν by which freedom comes (Epictetus, *Diss.* 3.24.57ff.; *SVF* 2.974–1007), and, since the best use of the impressions rests on one's προαίρεσις, he is free to whom everything happens κατὰ προαίρεσιν (Epictetus, *Diss.* 1.12.9; cf. 1.30.4; 3.22.103).

[25] Not enough attention has been given to the function of such affirmations, which were frequently made, for example, to distance the ideal from popular misconceptions, as is done in Epictetus, *Diss.* 3.22.2–8 (contrast 9–10); 23 (contrast 50); cf. 21.11 in context.

sophic prototypes as Odysseus and Heracles, the same point is made —
they did nothing but follow the role the Divine assigned to them
(Epictetus, *Diss.* 3.24.13–21; cf. Dio Chrys., *Or.* 1.55, 57). So, too,
Dio Chrysostom claimed that he himself had not chosen his philosophic role as an act of his own volition, but by the will of some deity,
for when divine providence works for people the gods provide both
counselors and words that are appropriate and profitable to listeners
(Dio Chrys., *Or.* 32.12).[26] It is this Stoic language of a divine commission that has appeared to some scholars to constitute the closest parallel
to Paul's idea of apostleship.[27]

When such Stoic moral reformers affirmed their place in the divine
scheme of things, they did not thereby sacrifice their free will. Epictetus
may serve as an example. Although he affirms the necessity of a divine
commission,[28] he assumes at every step that the ideal Cynic has the
freedom of will to align himself with the divine will.[29] This is, then, a
particular application of the general Stoic understanding.

Before returning to Paul, it will be useful to situate the Cynics in this
discussion of determinism and free will, for they will come to the fore
below. Cynics had much in common with Stoics, and Epictetus could
use the ideal Cynic, the representative of the stark life of commitment
to virtue, to describe his essentially Stoic philosophic ideal. But when it
came to providence and free will, Stoics and Cynics were poles apart.
There were differences among Stoics as there were among Cynics, but
in broad outline and for our present purposes the following generaliza-

[26] See E. Wilmes, 'Beiträge zur Alexandrinerrede (or. 32) des Dion Chrysostomos'
(Diss. Bonn, 1970) 8–13, for apt comment.

[27] The problem is infinitely more complex than one might suspect from comments
by *Neutestamentler* who draw a comparison between the ideal Stoic-Cynic (*sic*) sage and
the Christian apostle. See A. J. Malherbe, *Paul and the Popular Philosophers* (Minneapolis:
Fortress, 1989) 13 n. 10, and for much of value on the motivation to undertake the
philosophic life, see J. L. Moles, '"Honestius quam ambitiosius"? An Exploration of the
Cynic's Attitude to Moral Corruption in His Fellow Men,' *JHS* 103 (1983) 103–23.

[28] E.g., Epictetus, *Diss.* 3.22.13, 19–20.

[29] M. Billerbeck (*Epiktet: Vom Kynismus* [Philosophia Antiqua 34; Leiden: Brill,
1978]) identifies the major Stoic elements in Epictetus's description of the ideal Cynic.
For an attempt to distinguish between Stoics and Cynics on determinism and free will,
see A. J. Malherbe, 'Pseudo Heraclitus, Epistle 4: The Divinization of the Wise Man,'
JAC 21 (1978) 56–58.

tion will hold. Cynics rejected the Stoic attempt to make free will conform to necessity or providence. Oenomaus of Gadara, for one, inveighed against all attempts to do so (*ap.* Eusebius, *Praep. Ev.* 6.7 255b–260d).[30] He rejects the notion that he must will what necessity forces him to will even if he should be unwilling to do so. The Cynic is fully aware of the difference between choice and compulsion, and insists that we are masters of our own will, and that we cannot be virtuous unwillingly or without choosing to be so.

Oenomaus debates in a philosophical manner, but most Cynics approached the matter otherwise. They rejected tortuous doctrine and intellectual speculation and chose the 'short cut to happiness', the practical life of virtue, which most people regard as disgraceful (ps. Crates, *Epp.* 6, 13, 16; ps. Diogenes, *Ep.* 12).[31] In contrast to the Stoics, for whom security lay in the intellectual endeavor by which they aligned themselves with divine providence, the Cynics insisted that their security lay in the toilsome free life (ps. Crates, *Ep.* 13; ps. Diogenes, *Ep.* 30). Cynics looked to the same philosophic prototypes as the Stoics, but interpreted them as illustrating the importance of exercizing one's own free will (Dio Chrys., *Or.* 8.28–33; Lucian, *Vit. auct.* 8), and they scoffed at the Stoic heroes who did nothing without God (ps. Crates, *Ep.* 19). The practical life the Cynics chose placed the highest value on the exercize of free will. They lived under no compulsion, but freely chose a life scorned by others (ps. Lucian, *Cyn.* 13–15), symbolized by the humble attire they assumed when they adopted that life (Dio Chrys., *Or.* 19).[32]

The important point to note about the Cynics is that their adoption of their garb and their unconventional life was not merely a means by which to set themselves apart from the majority of people and thus draw attention, or to fly in the face of convention thus 'falsifying the currency' (e.g., Diogenes Laertius 6.71; Julian, *Or.* 6 188A). It did all

---

[30] For a useful discussion, see J. Hammerstaedt, *Die Orakelkritik des Kynikers Oenomaus* (Beiträge zur klassischen Philologie 188; Frankfurt: Athenäum, 1988); also, D. Amand, *Fatalisme et liberté dans l'antiquité grecque* (Louvain: Bibliothèque de l'Université, 1945) 127–34.

[31] V. Emeljanow, 'The Cynic Short Cut to Virtue,' *Mnemosyne* N. S. 18/2 (1965) 182–84.

[32] See Malherbe, *Paul and the Popular Philosophers,* 104.

that, but more importantly it reflected their self-understanding as persons who made a free choice to live simply, according to nature, and to demonstrate that choice in their manner of life as they urged others to accept their message.

It is in the context of such discussions of determinism and free will that 1 Cor 9.15–18 becomes fully intelligible. Paul makes it clear that refraining from financial support is a matter of καύχημα ('boast') to him (v. 15) which, he understands, sets him apart from other preachers (cf. 2 Cor 11.10–12). In this respect, Paul was like the Cynics. As their humble attire was disdained by the masses and set them apart, so Paul's manual labor, which enabled him to forgo financial support, was also esteemed low in his society and set him apart.[33] Preaching the gospel, however, is not a καύχημα to him, for ἀνάγκη ('necessity') is laid upon him to do so. Woe to him if he does not preach! Here he differs from Stoic and Cynic alike, for neither countenanced the idea of acting under compulsion. The Stoic only willed himself to conform and the Cynic put even greater emphasis on personal decision, while Paul acknowledged constraint.

But then Paul considers the alternative ways in which it was possible to conform to the necessity laid upon him in a manner reminiscent of contemporary discussions of determinism and free will. Preach he must, but he could either preach ἑκών ('willingly') or ἄκων ('unwillingly'), which were alternatives Stoics considered when arguing about the way the sage retained his freedom in an ordered universe.[34] If Paul were to preach unwillingly (εἰ δὲ ἄκων is hypothetical) he nevertheless has been entrusted with an οἰκονομία ('stewardship').[35] Such terms of house-

---

[33] See R. F. Hock, *The Social Context of Paul's Ministry: Tentmaking and Apostleship* (Philadelphia: Fortress, 1980) 35–36; H. Schulz-Falkenthal, 'Zum Arbeitsethos der Kyniker,' *Wissenschaftliche Zeitschrift der Martin-Luther Universität Halle-Wittenberg, Gesellschaftsreihe* 29 (1980) 6, 91–101.

[34] See Seneca, *De prov.* 5.4, 6; *De vita beata* 15.5–7; *Ep.* 96.2; Epictetus, *Diss.* 4.1.89; Marcus Aurelius 10.28.

[35] My interpretation differs from that of most commentators, who take εἰ δὲ ἄκων as a real condition, interpreting it in light of ἀνάγκη. See the alternatives discussed by Fee, *The First Epistle to the Corinthians*, 419–20. This would mean that (unlike the other apostles) Paul had no right to financial support. Thus: J. Dupont, 'The Conversion of Paul, and Its Influence on His Understanding of Salvation by Faith,' *Apostolic History and the Gospel: Biblical and Historical Essays Presented to F. F. Bruce on His 60th Birth* (ed.

hold management were used by Stoics in their description of the ordered universe as a city or a house.[36] Thus, οἰκονομία referred to the organization of the universe to which we must conform.[37] It was also used of management within that universe, *oeconomia* being a special instance of statecraft.[38] Especially in view is the wise man, who alone is οἰκονομικός and has the οἰκονομία of the household.[39] Significant for our purpose is that Epictetus begins his description of the ideal philosopher with the warning that no one assumes the position of οἰκονόμος in this divine household without being assigned by the Master (Epictetus, *Diss.* 3.22.3). So, by saying that he has an οἰκονομία entrusted to him and that he must therefore preach, Paul is working with Stoic terminology and ideas. He, too, has been assigned a place in the divine economy.

As we have seen, however, Stoics exercized their free will in the manner in which they conducted themselves within the providential scheme of things. So does Paul. He willingly does what necessity has laid upon him, thus exercizing his freedom, the topic that has engaged him throughout this long argument. That it is his freedom of action that predominates in his thinking and not compulsion, is evident from vv. 18–19. There he provides the grounds for forgoing his *exousia* — his freedom did not compel him to insist on his *exousia*, but allowed him to forgo it.

Paul's discussion is practical, and he applies the philosophic categories to the practice that exemplified his freedom, namely his refusal to accept financial support. All the warrants for his *exousia* that he has adduced had to do with earning rewards.[40] Paul attaches his assertion of

W. W. Gasque & R. P. Martin; Grand Rapids: Eerdmans, 1970) 192. In addition to the difficulties inherent in the Pauline text itself, confessional loyalties have complicated attempts to understand Paul's argument (see esp. Käsemann, 'A Pauline Version of the Amor Fati'). My major objection to the current majority interpretation is that it does not do justice to the coherence of Paul's argument, which already begins in chapter 8, and that it in particular does not grasp the significance of the philosophical debates for that argument.

[36] For references, see Billerbeck, *Epiktet*, 49 (on Epictetus, *Diss.* 3.22.4), and *SVF* 2.1127–31.

[37] Plutarch, *De Stoic. repugn.* 1049F–1050B; cf. 1050C (= *SVF* 2.937).

[38] Philo, *Quaest. et solut. in Genesin* 4.165 (= *SVF* 3.624).

[39] *SVF* 3.623; Philo, *De Iosepho* 38.

[40] The soldier, vinedresser, and shepherd (v. 7), the farmer (vv. 10–11), and the temple functionaries (v. 13).

his free will in v. 17 to that preceding list of warrants. In addressing the issue at hand, he uses and modifies Stoic ideas on the problem of how to harmonize their free will with their view of cosmic determinism. Paul's argument seems to run as follows. Although he has necessity laid upon him to preach the gospel, he does so willingly and has a reward. Were he to preach unwillingly, he would nevertheless have to preach, for he has been entrusted with an οἰκονομία. What is the reward that accrues to him from his voluntary preaching? Paradoxically, his free decision not to receive pay for his preaching, but to offer the gospel free of charge. The point of this tortured mixture of philosophical and commercial language is to make the case that by exercising his free will in the manner in which he preached, he did not make full use of his *exousia*.[41]

For Paul, the gospel does not provide a freedom to be exercized without regard to others. Insisting on one's *exousia* can in fact be an impediment to the gospel itself (v. 12). The manner in which Paul labors in the gospel, however, is without compulsion; his free offer of the gospel is the practice of someone who is himself free. In this he approximates the Cynics, whose practical life — not philosophic speculation — demonstrated their freedom. This similarity to a strain of Cynicism that asserted its free decision to adopt a humbling life in order to benefit others will be explored below.

Paul's Freedom to Adapt

Paul reaches the conclusion of his argument in vv. 19–22, which is not a general statement of principle but an integral part, indeed, the culmination of his argument about how the non-eaters should be treated. He

---

[41] On the commercial language, see esp. R. F. Hock, 'Paul's Tentmaking and the Problem of His Social Class,' *JBL* 97 (1978) 555–64; P. Marshall, *Enmity in Corinth: Social Conventions in Paul's Relations with the Corinthians* (WUNT 2. Reihe 23; Tübingen: Mohr-Siebeck, 1987) 295–306, both of whom are aware of the philosophical dimension of Paul's argument, but neither quite does justice to it. It is noteworthy that, although Paul certainly does here have in mind his manual labor, which enabled him to forgo his apostolic rights, and that the Corinthians would have recognized that he was alluding to it (cf. 4.12), he never explicitly mentions it. Paul is, after all, not now concerned with that practice and its attendant problems, but with another practice, the eating of meat offered to idols. He therefore alludes to his manual labor only to the extent that language belonging to that sphere of life coincides with that of the philosophical argument he conducts.

is still speaking about freedom and now explains (γάρ, 'for') the practical consequences of his freedom (ὤν is circumstantial) for the manner in which he preaches the gospel. Paradoxically, Paul, who is free from all things, made himself a slave for all people. His 'slavery' has as its goal the benefit of others (cf. Gal 5.13), and that goal is given specificity in vv. 19–22 — his 'slavish' life is that of the missionary who wishes to gain (κερδαίνειν, vv. 19, 20, 21, 22) and save (σῴζειν, v. 22) people.

Paul's 'slavish' freedom takes the form of accommodation to others in order to save them. His willingness to forgo his rights thus has the exact opposite result to the meat eaters' insistence on theirs. Paul wants to save people; they destroy the weak (8.9). Paul goes still further by identifying himself with the weak, as he does when he omits the ὡς ('as') before ἀσθενής ('weak', v. 22) that he uses with Ἰουδαῖος ('Jew') and ὑπὸ νόμον ('under Law', v. 20) and with ἄνομος ('without law', v. 21).

What Paul means by this identification with the weak receives clarification from 2.1–3. Rather than preach to the Corinthians with persuasive words of wisdom, he resolved to know only the crucified Christ. He had preached ἐν ἀσθενείᾳ ('in weakness') and with much fear and trembling (cf. 2 Cor 7.15; Phil 2.12; Eph 6.5). Weakness here should probably be understood in its cognitive sense: 1 Cor 2.1–3 is Paul's exemplary application of 1.17–25, where he also contrasts destruction and salvation (1.17), wisdom with preaching the crucified Christ to Jews and Greeks (1.18–24), and declares that the weakness of God (!) is mightier than human beings (1.25). In his missionary preaching, Paul had preached a message with no claim to human intellectual superiority, either as to its content or in the way he proclaimed it. Paul himself was weak while through the preaching he saved those who were now insisting on the rights they thought accrued to them from their intellectual superiority.

Only v. 19a in this section sounds Stoic, but the Stoics would roundly reject v. 19b — Paul's claim that, free from all things, he made himself a slave to all people (cf. Gal 5.13).[42] Paul has more in common with

---

[42] Stoics were open to the charge that they made the will a slave of fate (see Plotinus, *Enn.* 3.1.2, 15–17). Chrysippus attempted a compromise (Cicero, *De fato* 39), which Cynics found unacceptable (e.g., Oenomaeus, *ap.* Eusebius, *Praep. Ev.* 6.7 255c [still a half-slave]; cf. Lucian, *Iupp. conf.* 7), despite the insistence of someone like Seneca (*De prov.* 5.6): 'I am under no compulsion, I suffer nothing against my will, nor am I God's slave, but I give my assent to him.'

the Cynics, if not precisely in the way he claims his paradoxical slavery. In 2 Cor 10.3–6 Paul exhibits knowledge of a tradition that goes back to Antisthenes. In two speeches, Antisthenes contrasted Ajax and Odysseus, representing Ajax as strong and uncompromising and Odysseus as inventive and adaptable.[43] Odysseus, thus perceived, was to become the prototype of one kind of Cynic in later centuries, when Cynics interpreted their ancient heroes in a manner agreeable to their own self-understanding.

In his speeches, Antisthenes has Ajax accuse Odysseus of being underhanded, willing to suffer ill-treatment, even allowing himself to be flogged, if he might thereby gain (κερδαίνειν) something. Odysseus replies that he intimately knows the enemies' condition and that he strives night and day to save (σῴζειν) all people, possessing as his only weapons the slavish rags (δουλοπρεπῆ ὅπλα) he wears. This picture of Odysseus would continue to be used by philosophers as they explained why they undertook the thankless task of speaking to people in order to improve them. For example, Dio Chrysostom, Paul's younger contemporary, when introducing himself, justifies his preaching by quoting Homer, *Odyssey* 4.244–46, which refers to Odysseus, who 'subdues his body with injurious blows, casts around his shoulders sorry rags, in guise a slave ...' (Dio Chrys., *Or.* 33.15; cf. 1 Cor 9.27).

Many Cynics rejected this view of the philosopher's willingness to be humiliated as he sought to benefit people, and scorned the policy of adapting speech to particular circumstances. The point to be made, however, is that this way of describing a philosopher's mien and demeanor was one among others at the time Paul wrote 1 Corinthians. That Paul should here express himself in the manner of the moderate Cynic is not surprising, for he does so elsewhere (e.g., 1 Thess 2.1–12; 2 Cor 10.3–6). We have to stop here, but it is not irrelevant to note

---

[43] See *Socraticorum reliquiae*, ed. G. Giannantoni (Rome: Edizioni dell' Ateneo) 2.339–43 (1983), 3.231.37 (1985); H. D. Rankin, *Antisthenes Sokratikos* (Amsterdam: Hakkert, 1986) 155–71; Malherbe, *Paul and the Popular Philosophers*, 98–101. For the moral philosophers' recognition of the need to adapt to the conditions and circumstances of the persons they addressed, see A. J. Malherbe, *Moral Exhortation: A Greco-Roman Sourcebook* (Library of Early Christianity 4; Philadelphia: Westminster, 1986) 50–55, 65–67.

that in the verses that follow (vv. 24–27), Paul again makes use of a Cynic tradition that has also been thought to go back to Antisthenes.[44] Nevertheless, Paul differs from those Cynics with whom he has much in common. They did not quite call themselves slaves, rather, the *manner* in which they chose to present themselves appeared servile to others. Paul goes beyond even these Cynics when he claims the paradox that his freedom was expressed in his voluntarily enslaving of *himself* for the benefit of others.

Paul clearly resonated to that quality of independent action he observed in his unkempt contemporaries, and it is striking how often it finds a place in his descriptions of his own ministry.[45] It does so here, when he wants to stress his freedom while preaching at God's behest. Stoics, too, found room for voluntary action within a predetermined order, but Paul's use of Cynic traditions at the culmination of his argument shows where he wants to place the emphasis — on the side of freedom. Unlike the Stoics, who required philosophical training, especially in logic, when considering how one exercizes freedom of choice, Paul, like the Cynics, places a premium on action, unconventional and contemptible, as a means of benefiting his hearers. That is ultimately his argument to those Corinthians who insisted on their right to eat meat offered to idols.

Conclusion

I have proposed that Paul conducts a sustained argument in 1 Corinthians 8–9 and that an appreciation of the philosophic dimension of the issues he addresses allows us to make sense of those elements in the text that otherwise appear disjointed.

The transition between the two chapters is not abrupt. Basic to the problem he takes up is the notion of personal freedom, an issue that occupies him much in this section of the letter (6.12; 7.4, 36, 37, 39; 10.27, 29) as well as elsewhere (e.g., Rom 7.15–20; 9.16; 2 Cor 8.3, 7,

---

[44] H. Funke, 'Antisthenes bei Paulus,' *Hermes* 98 (1970) 459–71.
[45] See Malherbe, *Paul and the Popular Philosophers*, 35–48, 119.

17; Gal 5.17; Philemon 14).[46] The discussion of his *exousia* in chapter 9 is grounded in his assertion of his freedom in 9.1, which in turn is called forth by the meat eaters' insistence on their freedom and its attendant *exousia*, without any regard for the weak. Paul's clarification of the freedom with which he forgoes his right while under compulsion to preach culminates the argument on freedom and introduces his final exemplary statement on his own conduct as he adapted himself to Jews and Gentiles and identified with the weak.

In this long argument, Paul shows that he is familiar with the philosophic slogans of the Corinthians and with the assumptions underlying those slogans. He draws out the philosophical as well as practical consequences of the Corinthians' and his own philosophical claims, and does so with some sophistication. The philosophic traditions are for him not merely a pile of *topoi* or slogans from which he can draw in order to lay a pseudo-intellectual veneer over a wooden argument. Neither does he, conversely, use these traditions in a manner that shows him to be captive to any one school of thought. What is clearest of all is that the philosophic traditions do not constitute a 'background' against which Paul is to be viewed. Paul is rather to be seen as working within a milieu in which issues that engaged him and his converts were already widely discussed. As his readers appropriated some elements from that discussion to describe their Christian existence, so did Paul, and his mode of self-expression, although in this instance triggered by the Corinthians, was as natural to him as any other that he employed.[47]

---

[46] See P. W. Gooch, *Partial Knowledge: Philosophical Studies in Paul* (Notre Dame: University of Notre Dame Press, 1987) esp. 85–101.

[47] It is of interest to note that another Pharisee, later in the first century, said of the Pharisees that they too affirmed that some things were the work of fate but that room as left for free will (Josephus, *J. W.* 2.162–63; *Ant.* 13.172; 18.13). 'Josephus is able to draw on Stoic terminology, by now to some extent common currency ... In Josephus, there is no evidence of serious immersion in Stoic philosophy; he seeks merely to express his own beliefs in terms intelligible in Greek' (T. Rajak, *Josephus, the Historian and His Society* [Philadelpha: Fortress, 1983] 100). Stoicism, in my judgment, is more integral to Paul than this assessment claims is the case with Josephus.

9

Stoicism in Philippians

Troels Engberg-Pedersen

Introduction: Paul the Spermologos

The last fifteen years of scholarly research on Paul have seen the break-down of the traditional monolithic contrasts — between Paul and Judaism (taken as one simple block)[1] and between Paul and Hellenism (again taken as one simple block).[2] Concomitantly, the attempt to reduce Paul's thought, within the letters themselves, to simple 'core' formulations has broken down.[3] Paul was in fact a *spermologos* (cf. Acts 17.18), in the sense that he picked up scraps of knowledge from everywhere, and the enormous variety of what he is saying and doing in and by his letters should never be allowed to disappear from view.

Here, then, begins the interpreter's slow, painstaking task of bring-ing it all into some kind of order. Several approaches and types of material are relevant. But none must be allowed to take over. In this essay I shall attempt to demonstrate how Paul makes use of certain ideas derived from Stoic ethics as part of his own thinking in his letter

---

[1] Following on E. P. Sanders's pioneering work, *Paul and Palestinian Judaism* (London: SCM, 1977), one of the most impressive works in this line from recent years is that of Alan F. Segal, *Paul the Convert: The Apostolate and Apostasy of Saul the Pharisee* (New Haven: Yale University Press, 1990).

[2] This trend is represented by Hans Dieter Betz (*Galatians: A Commentary on Paul's Letter to the Churches in Galatia* (Hermeneia; Philadelphia: Fortress, 1979); Abraham J. Malherbe (*Paul and the Popular Philosophers* [Minneapolis: Fortress, 1988]); and the Malherbe Festschrift, *Greeks, Romans, and Christians* (ed. D. L. Balch, E. Ferguson and W. A. Meeks; Minneapolis: Fortress, 1990). The 8 volumes of The Library of Early Christianity edited by Wayne A. Meeks (Philadelphia: Westminster, 1986–7) represent a similar attempt to take down fences.

[3] This, in my opinion, is one lesson that has been learned in the currently running annual sessions of the SBL Pauline Theology Group.

to the Philippians. The suggestion is not, of course, that Paul was a Stoic philosopher. There are other important clusters of ideas in that letter which from the outset have nothing whatever to do with Stoicism. And Paul was not a philosopher, but an apostle of Christ. The interesting project, however, is to see how Paul the *spermologos* brings together this disparate thought material. I shall argue that the fusion is total. There certainly remain elements in his thought which have no counterpart in Stoicism. But where he does use Stoic ideas, there is no friction whatever. What is more, I shall end by diagnosing a certain tension in Paul's thought. But the tension is not between Christian and Stoic ideas. On the contrary, as we shall see, it is where Paul is at his most Stoic that he is also at his most Christian.

The Issue: The Meaning of Philippians

I begin by setting aside certain traditional questions concerning the letter, work on which has often prevented scholars from moving on towards a more comprehensive discussion of its meaning.

One such issue concerns the integrity of the letter. It is still not unusual to find scholars insisting that what we have is not a single, complete letter deriving directly from Paul, but rather two or three letters or letter fragments that have been put together by some other hand.[4] I shall not enter into this question here, only register my belief

---

[4] But the tide is turning. For a thorough discussion and overview, see David E. Garland (himself a unitarian), 'The Composition and Unity of Philippians: Some Neglected Literary Factors,' *NovT* 27 (1985) 141–73. The attempt by another unitarian, Duane F. Watson, to argue for unity through rhetorical analysis is less successful; see 'A Rhetorical Analysis of Philippians and its Implications for the Unity Question,' *NovT* 30 (1988) 57–88, esp. 84–88. Apparently, rhetorical analysis is incapable of providing incontrovertible proof either for or against, which is not surprising when one is dealing with such a creative writer as Paul. Another formal approach, in terms of a comparison with Hellenistic 'family letters', is adopted by Loveday Alexander in 'Hellenistic Letter-Forms and the Structure of Philippians,' *JSNT* 37 (1989) 87–101. It proves more genuinely illuminating, but as Alexander herself recognizes (pp. 97, 99), it too can only supplement a thematic analysis. The (by now) traditional German analytic approach is well summarized and argued for by Wolfgang Schenk in 'Der Philipperbrief in der neuren Forschung (1945–1985),' ANRW II.25.4 (ed. W. Haase; Berlin: Walter de Gruyter, 1987) 3280–3313, esp. 3280–86. Compare also Schenk, *Die Philipperbriefe des Paulus: Kommentar* (Stuttgart: W. Kohlhammer, 1984) *passim*.

that there are a number of critical observations, both of method and content, that can be effectively marshaled against the attempt to dismember the text as it stands.[5] The reading I shall present presupposes the integrity of the letter. Scholars who are disinclined to take that view may see the following analysis as an example of how one might read the letter *if* its integrity could be sufficiently established.

Another traditional issue concerns the letter situation.[6] Where was the letter written? What was the situation in Philippi (as far as Paul would know of it) with regard to any opponents (1.28; 3.2, 18), to Philippian suffering (1.29), to the roles of Epaphroditus (2.26–27) and Euodia and Syntyche (4.2–3) and so forth? Since the meaning of the letter will obviously reflect the exact situation addressed in it, these questions remain important, even though some of them may in the end prove unanswerable. However, analysis of the letter must not stick to these questions alone. For there is far more to the meaning of the letter than could be established even by answering those questions to everybody's satisfaction.

In particular, scholars have gradually come to realize that in addition to the manifest meaning of Paul's statements as importing information and responding to the particularities of the letter situation at the level of direct communication, these statements have a number of functions that are more indirect, but no less important for that. Thus, for example, when scholars analyze the Pauline letters from a sociological perspective, they focus on the social issues underlying the questions that

---

[5] Concerning the crucial question regarding the exact meaning of the transition in 3.1–2, note that what Paul says he will repeat is *the whole set* of ideas that forms the content of 1.12–2.18, (a) using Paul's own example (1.12–26, cf. 3.4–16), as a model for (b) the desired reaction of joy and steadfastness on the part of the Philippians, (c) in the face of any supposed suffering they may have undergone. If this is right, then Paul is saying in 3.1b that he is now breaking up the smooth progression of letter topics in order to repeat the essential message of 1.12–2.18, culminating in the injunction to steadfastness (4.1, repeating 1.27). In other words, Paul himself says that he is going to do what analytics who assign the body of chapter 3 to a different letter than that of 1.12–2.18 say he cannot do! (The suggestion of seeing 1.12–2.18 as a close parallel with chapter 3 is markedly strengthened by the similarity of 1.21 with 3.7–11.)

[6] For a good overview of the various issues and positions, see Wolfgang Schenk, 'Der Philipperbrief in der neueren Forschung', 3289–99. A more recent discussion is C. L. Mearns, 'The Identity of Paul's Opponents at Philippi,' *NTS* 33 (1987) 194–204.

Paul is directly addressing, and they consider the social functions of Paul's answers in addition to their more manifest intention. Another functional perspective is the rhetorical one, which asks about the role played by the means of expression in shaping the response of the addressees. Here what the investigator is looking for may not only be formal or stylistic features of the letters. It may also include metaphors, stock motifs whose various connotations are presumed to be well known to the addressees, and also such a phenomenon as the stance adopted by the writer in relation to his addressees. In either case, however, the point is that such functional aspects of Paul's statements are also part of the meaning of these statements simply because Paul is engaged in a specific communicative act between particular people. In fact, the meaning of a Pauline letter should be construed as a sort of conglomerate resulting from the interaction in it of *all* the different types of 'saying and doing' that are active in Paul's statements.

Is it possible to identify this conglomerate a little more clearly by finding a term for it that captures the many different elements of meaning that seem intuitively to go into a Pauline letter? One suggestion has been presented with some success by Abraham J. Malherbe with regard to 1 Thessalonians.[7] His claim is that this early Pauline letter should be seen as a piece of 'exhortation' or *paraklêsis*. A comparable suggestion has been made by Wayne A. Meeks when he argues that the Pauline letters are best seen as an exercise in community-formation.[8] On such a view the task will be to consider exactly what kind of community is being formed and how it is done. Note that these suggestions represent only two specific possibilities out of many others, and are not intrinsically wedded to the general, conglomerate reading of the meaning of a Pauline letter that I suggested.

In this essay, however, I shall consider the interplay between the Stoicizing motifs in Philippians and certain other central motifs on the

---

[7]   See in particular Malherbe, *Paul and the Thessalonians* (Philadelphia: Fortress, 1987).
[8]   This view underlies important parts of Meeks's *The First Urban Christians: The Social World of the Apostle Paul* (New Haven: Yale University Press, 1983). It is further developed in Meeks, *The Moral World of the First Christians* (Library of Early Christianity 6; Philadelphia: Westminster, 1986).

heuristic basis that this letter too is in fact best seen as a piece of *paraklēsis* and that it aims at forming a community of a special kind. By concentrating on the interplay between a few motifs only, I give up from the start any attempt to cover the full meaning of the letter. On the other hand, by looking at the Stoicizing material contained in the letter within the broadly rhetorical context that I have just sketched, I obtain an analytical framework that will not prejudge the results of the analysis. In particular, we should not decide beforehand that for the purpose of determining the overall meaning of the letter one must recognize that there are theological sections or motifs in the letter which have a special status vis-à-vis, and should be kept distinct from, the ethical or parenetic sections or motifs. That is not so, at least not initially. On the contrary, just as we should look dispassionately at the way Paul mixes motifs from different traditions in his own thinking, so we should be on the lookout for indications concerning the interplay between all the elements that make up the letter meaning, including those traditionally set apart as 'theology' and 'parenesis'. They all have a community-forming role and we want to identify their interplay and to grasp how together they contribute to the community-forming function of the letter.

My procedure will be to identify a few clusters of ideas (including the Stoicizing one) that seem to define the main contours of the comprehensive self-understanding that Paul apparently wants to impart to his readers as part of his community-forming enterprise. And the issue to be discussed is whether they cohere in more detail or not and what the overall picture of Christian self-understanding looks like that results from their interplay.

Basic Structures in the Overall Picture Paul is Drawing

One structural cluster of ideas is set out in the thanksgiving section at the beginning of the letter (1.3–11). In its essence it tells a temporal story reaching from the 'first day' when the Philippians came to share in the gospel with Paul to the present time (v. 5) and from now to the 'day of Christ' (vv. 6, 9–10). Paul particularly emphasizes the latter time span. He declares his confidence that 'he who started (ἐνάρξασθαι) good work in you will bring it to completion (ἐπιτελέσειν) until (ἄχρι) the day of Christ' (v. 6), where ἄχρι spells out particularly clearly the idea of a progression 'onward towards' the day of Christ. And he formulates his prayer that 'your love may grow ever richer (μᾶλλον καὶ μᾶλλον περισσεύειν) ... so that you may be flawless and without blame toward (εἰς) the day of Christ' (vv. 9–10). The same overall framework is also used later in the letter, in 2.12–18: the Philippians were always (πάντοτε) obedient and must now (νῦν) work on their salvation (vv. 12, 14) in order to become (ἵνα γένησθε) faultless and the like (v. 15) ... as something that Paul may then boast of on the 'day of Christ' (v. 16). And we shall see it at work in chapter 3. Obviously Paul wants the Philippians to see everything else within that temporal framework, and no wonder, since it both appears to be constitutive of his whole apocalyptic worldview and also an exceedingly forceful tool for bringing his readers' experiences and understanding into order.

Having noticed the ideas of the 'first day' of the Philippians' engagement with the gospel and the (final) 'day of Christ' to which they should be looking, we might feel inclined to stop. We have identified (with very little difficulty) a specimen of understanding that is characteristically Christian and in fact basic to early Christianity. Is this not also the basic structural cluster on which Paul hangs everything else in the letter, as it were *the* pillar of the Christian self-understanding that he is trying to impart to his readers? Not quite. At least, it is not the only one. There are two more such structural clusters, both of which make their first appearance in the thanksgiving section too. Here I shall mention only the Stoicizing one. (The other cluster is centered on what I shall call the *koinônia* motif. I return to this below.)

1. It is noteworthy that both in 1.6 and 1.9–10 Paul brings in certain terms that come from an altogether different semantic field than the day of Christ story: good work (ἔργον ἀγαθόν, v. 6), insight (ἐπίγνωσις) and all manner of perception (πᾶσα αἴσθησις, v. 9), weighing what things really matter (δοκιμάζειν τὰ διαφέροντα, v. 10). These are 'Greek' terms in the sense that they were originally developed as terms with a sharply defined meaning in Greek philosophy.⁹ By Paul's time they had come to belong to ordinary discourse at a

---

⁹ The term δοκιμάζειν was not in fact of philosophical origin; it was political. Compare the helpful analysis of the δοκιμ-root by Walter Grundmann in *TWNT* 2 (Stuttgart: W. Kohlhammer, 1935) s.v. δόκιμος κτλ, 258–64. Of particular interest is

certain level. However, scholars usually recognize the affinity of the term τὰ διαφέροντα with its converse, the ἀδιάφορα, which was distinctly Stoic. But again, is what we are witnessing in Paul not rather so-called 'Popularphilosophie'?[10]

2. If we read on in the letter looking for similar terms, we meet the following in chapter 1: progress (προκοπή) in 1.12 and 1.25 is originally Stoic. Joy (χαρά), which turns up in 1.25 together with προκοπή and is a key term in Philippians from its first occurrence (1.18), is of course not unusual. Still, it was a technical term in Stoic ethics with a particular emphasis of its own.

3. Moving on to chapter 3 note that Paul again brings in his own example, as he did in 1.12–26, as a model for the Philippians. He does it by going back, in effect, to the idea he had employed in the thanksgiving of starting out from 'the first day'. Now, however, he is focusing on his own 'first day' and how it has structured his life onward towards Christ. Here we again come across a cluster of 'Greek' terms closely similar to those we met in the thanksgiving section: knowledge (γνῶσις, 3.8, cf. v. 10), grasping (λαμβάνειν, καταλαμβάνειν, v. 12), being perfect (τετελειοῦσθαι, v. 12, cf. v. 15), striving for (διώκειν, vv. 12–14) and goal (σκοπός, v. 14). Some of these are just general philosophical terms, others have more specifically Stoic connotations (διώκειν, σκοπός, and καταλαμβάνειν — to the extent that it reflects Stoic κατάληψις).[11] But again they seem to belong to ordinary language at a

the whole cluster of terms similar to those in our text that make their appearance in three passages in Romans: 1.28 (which even uses the Stoic technical term καθήκοντα), 2.18–21, and 12.2.

[10] One should be very cautious about using this concept. It does capture an important idea (about how originally technical philosophy may, in diluted forms, become part of the general consciousness), but in Pauline scholarship it is far too often used as legitimation for not taking Paul's use of the various moral terms seriously at all. This is a constant practice in the commentaries — to note the contacts with 'Hellenistic moral philosophy' in the sense of 'popular philosophy' and then rush on to point out the difference (usually in the singular!), e.g. J. Gnilka, *Der Philipperbrief* (HTKNT 10/3; 3rd ed.; Freiburg: Herder, 1980) pp. 51–52 (on 1.9–10: '... Dabei wird der Unterschied ... deutlich ...') or pp. 174–76 (on 4.11: '... das Wesentliche ..., die Kluft, die zwischen dem Apostel und zeitgenössicher Moralphilosophie trotz terminologischen Anschlusses klafft').

[11] As far as I know, nobody has seen the possibility of connecting καταλαμβάνειν here with κατάληψις, which was a key term in the Stoic theory of knowledge indicating

certain level rather than being used in a technical Stoic sense.

4. Finally there is 4.10–20, in which Paul combines the idea of his *chara* (v. 10) with that of his self-sufficiency (*autarkeia*, v. 12). The latter is originally philosophic and specifically Cynic and Stoic; but by Paul's time it need not have any philosophical overtones at all.

There are a few more 'Greek' terms and metaphors that we may quickly note.

5. At 1.27 Paul enjoins the Philippians to 'live as citizens (πολιτεύεσθαι) in accordance with the Christ gospel'. This constitutes a kind of summary of the overall message of the letter. And at 3.20 he places 'our citizen body' (πολίτευμα) in heaven.[12]

6. In close conjunction with this he makes much in 1.27–30 of the sports image of fighting together as in the games (συναθλεῖν, v. 27), of not being made to shy or start (as a horse at a sound) by the opponents (v. 28), but instead sharing in Paul's own contest (ἀγών, v. 30). Similarly, God's upward call in Christ Jesus has placed before Christians a

a complete grasp of the truth which cannot be dislodged by reasoning. Admittedly, Paul may well use the term here only in its immediate sense derived from the language of sports (cf. 1 Cor 9.24, which is closely similar). Still, in the context (3.8, 10) Paul has twice spoken of his experience of coming to know Christ (*gnôsis/gnônai*), which means that the cognitive issue has already been raised. But does it make sense to say that Paul has been 'grasped' by Christ in cognitive terms? It does; cf. the closely comparable formulation in Gal 4.9 νῦν δὲ γνόντες θεόν, μᾶλλον δὲ γνωσθέντες ὑπὸ θεοῦ.

[12] Nobody doubts that πολιτεύεσθαι and πολίτευμα are 'Greek' terms and most commentators agree that Paul uses them with their political sense intact. This has been argued for πολιτεύεσθαι, e.g., by Raymond R. Brewer, in 'The Meaning of *Politeuesthe* in Philippians 1 27,' *JBL* 73 (1954) 76–83. Despite its title the paper by Ernest C. Miller, Jr. ('Πολιτεύεσθε in Philippians 1.27: Some Philological and Thematic Observations,' *JSNT* 15 [1982] 86–96) is philologically wholly unsound when it claims (89–90) that the verb itself has a 'particularly Jewish usage' and 'undergoes a change of meaning' with the Christian writers because it is first connected with Torah and next with Christ. πολιτεύεσθαι means to live as one lives in the Greek *polis*, that is, in accordance with some system (of law) or other, no matter whether it is a Greek law, a Jewish one, or Christ. An oft-cited passage in Philo (*Conf. Ling.* 77–78), to which Miller also refers, shows particularly clearly the mixture of political and philosophical (in this case probably Platonic) Greek language that is implied in πολιτεύεσθαι. Here Philo is also very close to Paul's idea in 3.20, when he speaks of the native land (πατρίς) of the souls of all those whom Moses calls wise (οἱ κατὰ Μωυσῆν σοφοί) as 'the heavenly region where their citizenship lies' (τὸν οὐράνιον χῶρον ἐν ᾧ πολιτεύονται). There is a good overview of scholarship on the meaning of πολίτευμα in Phil 3.20 in Andrew T. Lincoln, *Paradise Now and Not Yet* (SNTSMS 43; Cambridge: Cambridge University Press, 1981) 97–101.

sports prize (βραβεῖον, 3.14), which is presumably that of finally becoming full members of the heavenly *politeuma.*

Is all this just a general athletic, political and philosophical veneer, possibly with a slightly Stoic tinge? Or is it something more? If the first, then Paul's use of these terms will belong in the same category as his talk of 'loss' and 'gain' in his account of his conversion (3.7–8) or of 'expenditure', 'income', and a 'rise in the interest of the Philippians' account' when he speaks of their readiness to give (4.15–16). This is all metaphorical language and there is probably little to be gained from bringing in the exact field of technical discourse from which these metaphors are drawn.

The only way to decide about the two possibilities with respect to the Stoicizing terms is to bring in the technical philosophical material. Once we have been reminded of the full, original sense of these ideas, we may ask whether there are elements of meaning in them which are not present on the surface of Paul's text but which do illuminate what Paul says and does when they are brought into play. If that turns out to be the case, we should conclude that the Stoicizing terms are not just another example of a use of metaphorical language that more or less gratuitously embellishes a discourse whose meaning is settled beforehand or elsewhere. On the contrary, they will form an integrated part of the overall meaning of the text.

I shall argue that this is in fact the case and that the terms I have identified above serve as yet another cluster of terms that structure Paul's message in the letter. In addition I shall try to show that by making use of the full Stoic meaning of the Stoicizing terms Paul employs, we shall obtain a clearer grasp of some of the main issues he handles in the letter and his way of tackling them.

The Stoic Ideal Community

We know nothing about how Paul might have become acquainted with ideas in Stoic ethics and politics. Nor do we know which particular brand of Stoicism he might have come across. There were in fact important developments and changes of emphasis, particularly in the area of Stoic ethics and politics, in the 400–500 years between the founder, Zeno (335–263 B.C.E.), and the emperor Marcus Aurelius

(121–80 C.E.). Two such changes that will be directly relevant to our analysis of Paul should be mentioned here. They both pertain to the foundational work in Stoic political thought, Zeno's *Republic*, and to changes in the conception of the ideal community that Stoics sketched, between Zeno himself and the first century B.C.E.

Unfortunately very few indications of the content of Zeno's work have been left to us and these mainly in sources that are hostile to it. Thus in the most substantial report (given by Diogenes Laertius, *Lives of Eminent Philosophers* 7.32–34) we hear that Zeno was criticized by some (even some Stoics, it appears, 7.34) for declaring the 'allround education' (ἐγκύκλιος παιδεία) useless, for claiming that 'all people who are not morally good (σπουδαῖοι) are hostile to each other, enemies, slaves and aliens to one another (even parents to children, brothers to brothers, friends to friends)', whereas 'only the morally good are citizens, friends, kindred, free.' He also decreed a community of women and declared that 'no temples, lawcourts, or gymnasia should be built in the cities', nor need any currency be introduced either for purposes of trade or for traveling abroad.

There has been much discussion about the precise character of Zeno's projected republic.[13] It evidently stands in the tradition of Plato's *Republic* and shares with that the character of being an ideal community or (as Plutarch terms it) 'as it were a dream or mental image of a philosopher's well-ordered constitution'.[14] There can be little doubt, however, that what Zeno envisaged was what has aptly been called an anarcho-syndicalist state,[15] or rather not exactly a state; for the point of abolishing temples, lawcourts, gymnasia, currency and the institution of marriage seems precisely to be that there should no longer *be* a state. Instead, there apparently would be cities of some sort, probably communities at a very low level scattered in a landscape of no very clear

---

[13] Most recently by Andrew Erskine, *The Hellenistic Stoa: Political Thought and Action* (London: Duckworth, 1990) 18–27; and Malcolm Schofield, *The Stoic Idea of the City* (Cambridge: Cambridge University Press, 1991) 3–56.

[14] ὥσπερ ὄναρ ἢ εἴδωλον εὐνομίας φιλοσόφου καὶ πολιτείας, *On the Fortune of Alexander* 329B.

[15] Johnny Christensen, 'Equality of Man and Stoic Social Thought,' *Commentationes Humanarum Litterarum, Helsinki* 75 (1984) 45–54, esp. 51–2. Christensen speaks, rightly, of an anarcho-syndicalist *democracy* as the Stoic ideal model of society.

limits. Of political rule there would be next to nothing, since the 'cities' that instantiate Zeno's conception would be characterized by three concepts that Zeno is known to have highlighted together: *hómonoia* (oneness of mind, unanimity, concord), *philia* (friendship) and *eleutheria* (freedom, *SVF* 1.263).

It is in complete accordance with this when Chrysippus, the 'second founder' of Stoicism (c. 280–207 B.C.E.), declared that only the morally good man is capable of both governing and being governed. In fact, he alone does govern (ἄρχειν), if not actually then at all events dispositionally. And he alone is 'obedient to authority' (πειθάρχικός), since he follows one who governs (is ἀκολουθητικὸς ἄρχοντι, *SVF* 3.615). It does not matter whether he does one thing or the other since the content of what he determines should be done (if he is the one who governs) or decides in obedience to do (if he is the one who is governed) is the very same.

In short, Zeno appears to have envisaged an ideal community where all social institutions, all socially based distinctions between people, possibly also all distinctions based on gender and finally all political distinctions have been abolished. There were to be no hierarchies whatever, no subordination, since the only thing that counted was moral goodness or the lack of it. In this community there would be total freedom, which the Stoics defined as the right to independent action (ἐξουσία αὐτοπραγίας), as opposed to slavery (δουλεία), which is privation of the same (στέρησις αὐτοπραγίας, Diogenes Laertius, *Lives of Eminent Philosophers* 7.121). For the wise man does all things well (πάντα εὖ ποιεῖν τὸν σοφόν) and all things belong to the wise (τῶν σοφῶν πάντα εἶναι, Diogenes Laertius, *Lives of Eminent Philosophers* 7.125).

After Zeno, there are two changes in the conception of the ideal community. First, there is a change away from the strongly Cynic flavor of Zeno's original conception in the direction of removing from it anything that smacked of Cynicism. This change is reflected in the story about the first-century B.C.E. Stoic Athenodorus, who, while in charge of the library in Pergamon, literally excised from Zeno's works 'what the Stoics considered badly said in them' (Diogenes Laertius, *Lives of Eminent Philosophers* 7.34), in fact, most likely some of the points mentioned above. It is also reflected in the way in which the

second-century B.C.E. Stoic Panaetius of Rhodes specifically repudiated the Cynic links, which he found distasteful.[16] This change may be
of minor importance, but it probably is not. For it seems closely connected with the other one, which is of crucial importance.

This is a change in the whole understanding of Zeno's ideal community. In Zeno himself it was probably conceived fairly concretely as a
kind of recipe for social and political innovation, or even revolution, in
the sense that it might more or less directly be put into practice if some
Greek city should decide to do so.[17] For it was in a sense Cynicism writ
large (and backed philosophically), and in Zeno's time Cynics could be
found wherever one looked. So, applying Zeno's idea in practice would
be following the lead of the Cynics, who were precisely practising what
they preached, and doing so in the very same direction of breaking
down conventional hierarchies whether social, political, or gender-based.

In Chrysippus, however, the character of the ideal community changes.
Now it appears as a community of all those people who are morally
good wherever they live on earth. They all belong to that very same
community (so there is only one such community) just by being morally good. This conception was faithfully reflected by Clement of Alexandria in the following definition of the Stoic city: 'The Stoics say that
the universe (οὐρανός) is in the proper sense a city (πόλις), but those
here on earth are no longer cities. They are called so, but are not really.
For a city is something morally good and a people (δῆμος) is some
kind of refined organization or group of people that is governed by law'
(*SVF* 3.327).

On such a conception, the ideal community would probably not
have been understood by Chrysippus as a recipe for direct social and
political action. Rather, Chrysippus will have understood it as a kind of

---

[16] Cf. Cicero *De Officiis* 1.128 and 148. E.g. 128 int.: 'But we should give no heed
to the Cynics (or to some Stoics who are practically Cynics) ...' (LCL translation by W.
Miller; there is no certainty that this comes from Panaetius but there is general agreement
that the likelihood is great.)

[17] Schofield (*The Stoic Idea*, chap. 2) argues, probably rightly, for the recipe interpretation. He does so, however, primarily by comparing Zeno with Plato, thus leaving
out in effect the Cynic dimension in Zeno. This explains why Schofield does not do
justice to that element in Zeno's conception which made it possible to develop it in the
way we find in Chrysippus (see below).

limiting construct, which may then have been put to use in actual social and political practice in a number of ways. It is noteworthy, however, that in his political thought Chrysippus kept those Cynic links (cf. Diogenes Laertius, *Lives of Eminent Philosophers* 7.187–9) that Panaetius repudiated a hundred years later. For this probably means that Chrysippus too maintained the radically antihierarchical content of Zeno's original conception, as is also indicated by the fragment referred to above which states that the morally good man will both govern and be governed. Here the Cynic links served the purpose of doing away with conventional social and political distinctions and so making room for the idea of what remains, an anarchic, radically nonhierarchical community that ran directly counter to all ordinary societies.

This Chrysippean version, then, is an idea of the ideal community which is neither a direct recipe for political practice (as in Zeno), nor the kind of relatively inconsequential 'moral idea' that it appears to have become in Panaetius, who by severing the Cynic links undercut both the idea of genuinely trying to put the ideal into practice and also its original, anticonventional character. It is this Chrysippean conception, as we shall see, that is most directly relevant to Paul.

But how can we be certain that with different conceptions of the ideal community within Stoicism, it is the Chrysippean version that Paul will have been acquainted with? We cannot. Still, it is noteworthy that Cicero and even later Stoics, like Seneca and Epictetus, and non-Stoics, like Plutarch and Galen, went on, in spite of their individual preferences for middle Stoics like Panaetius and Posidonius (c. 135–50 B.C.E.), to consider Chrysippus as *the* Stoic, who was responsible for the basic doctrines that even defined Stoicism (and that non-Stoics would therefore attack).[18] And so it becomes more than likely that the kind of Stoicism that Paul may have heard of is in fact the Chrysippean one. In addition, one should not forget that Paul lived in the eastern Mediterranean area. And here the kind of Stoicism which was more or less heavily influenced by the Roman experience (Seneca and Cicero

---

[18] As do Plutarch (*On Stoic Self-Contradictions*) and Galen (*On the Doctrines of Hippocrates and Plato*).

and also, I would argue, the Greeks, Posidonius and Panaetius, whose thought appears to have incorporated the fact of the Roman political presence) would not have constituted a major influence.

The Stoic ideas about the ideal community belonged to their political thought. As always in Greek philosophy, however, the substructure of political philosophy was ethics. This too is highly relevant to Paul in Philippians. I shall now sketch the essence of Chrysippus' ethical doctrine. I build upon Cicero's *De Finibus* Book 3. The provenance of the Stoic material in this book is unknown, but the material most likely goes back at least to the last representative of early Stoicism, Antipater of Tarsus (early second century B.C.E.). In addition, there is the comprehensive sketch of what appears to be basically Chrysippean ethics in Diogenes Laertius, *Lives of Eminent Philosophers* 7.84–131. And of course there are the fragments as collected by Hans von Arnim in *Stoicorum Veterum Fragmenta*.[19] As we go along I shall refer to Philippians in order to show how, superficially at least, what Paul says fits into the Stoic system. Only later shall I enter into a more thorough comparison of the Stoic conceptions with Paul's own argument.

Elements of Stoic Ethics

1. The central notion in Stoic ethics is that of the *telos*, the 'end' of activity, that which is 'brought about' by activity or may be said to 'inform' activity in the sense that any activity expresses that end, either as a means to it or as something in which it consists.[20] The *telos*, which the Stoics also called the *skopos*,[21] is what one strives for (διώκειν). And so we are already in the middle of Philippians 3 (vv. 12–14).

Aristotle first developed the logical character of 'the end of action', in *Nicomachean Ethics* Book 1 chapter 7.[22] The Stoics took over almost

---

[19] The following account of the Stoic theory is developed in far more detail in my book *The Stoic Theory of Oikeiosis: Moral Development and Social Interaction in Early Stoic Philosophy* (Aarhus: Aarhus University Press, 1990).

[20] Compare Cic. *Fin.* 3.21: 'that good which is the end to which all else is referred'.

[21] There is in fact a technical difference between *telos* and *skopos* in Stoicism; see *The Stoic Theory of Oikeiosis*, 27–28. It is immaterial here.

[22] For further analysis of this chapter, see my book *Aristotle's Theory of Moral Insight* (Oxford: Clarendon, 1983) chap. 1.

everything from that seminal chapter of Aristotle's, including the determination of 'the end of action' as 'the good'. As is well known, however, they parted company with Aristotle when it came to determining the exact content of the good (cf. *Fin.* 3.41–44). Thus whereas for Aristotle material or external 'goods' were in fact good and so had some role to play as parts of the good life, the Stoics insisted that there is only one thing that is good — what they called 'virtue'. The rest, including so-called external goods, are altogether 'indifferent' (ἀδιάφορα) or at most (while still intrinsically indifferent) 'preferable' (προηγμένα, *praeposita* in Cicero, cf. *Fin.* 3.50–54). So here it is very much a question of δοκιμάζειν τὰ διαφέροντα, as Paul has it (1.10), of weighing what genuinely matters.

Again, however, the Stoics were firmly on Aristotelian ground. For Aristotle had shown that in *formal* terms, at least, 'the end of action' was 'self-sufficient' (αὐτάρκης). What that meant for Aristotle is that the *telos* is defined as the state which is such that once a person is in it, he or she will have no need of anything else. The Stoics took this over claiming that the only thing that is in fact good (namely, virtue) and that therefore fills the bill of making up the *telos* is also precisely 'self-sufficient', which is the reason everything else is just 'indifferent' (cf. *Fin.* 3.23–26, 32). Paul adopts the same language in Philippians 4.10–13.

All these determinations in Greek ethics of the end (*telos* and *skopos* as the object of δίωξις; τὸ ἀγαθόν; τὸ αὔταρκες) tend to emphasize its function as something human beings are striving toward in acts that are directed toward bringing it into existence. Since Paul too employs all these terms, it is reasonable to conclude that he saw, and wished his addressees to see, life in this world in terms of such striving. It is immediately obvious that such a picture fits in completely with Paul's strongly future-oriented directedness towards the day of Christ. So it looks as if Paul was situating within his basically Jewish, apocalyptic framework an understanding of the directedness of human life that had borrowed its conceptuality from the Greeks.

2. The next basic point in Stoic ethics concerns their substantive determination of the *telos*. We already know that the *telos* is 'virtue', but how is that to be understood? Virtue, in Stoicism, is a state of mind that is defined as a form of knowledge or understanding. Paul too

characterizes the result of the change he has undergone in terms of understanding (*gnôsis*, Phil 3.8, 10). In Stoicism, this understanding is, in Cicero's words (*Fin.* 3.73), 'knowledge of nature (or the world) and of the life of the Gods and a clear understanding of the fact that man's nature is in accordance with that of the whole'. 'This knowledge alone,' Cicero adds, 'can impart a conception of the power of nature in fostering justice and maintaining friendship and the rest of the affections.' How is knowledge of that kind relevant to 'virtue' viewed as something specifically moral?

Cicero gives two answers earlier in the book, that serve to identify two distinct elements in moral virtue. One is that a person who has reached the true knowledge that Cicero alludes to in the above quotation has transcended the practice of applying his own subjective or local perspective as the basis for describing the world. Thus even his evaluative judgments, which according to the Stoics are genuine judgments and no less descriptive than any other, are no longer based on his perception of himself as a particular individual with whom he stands in a special, favored relationship. Rather, he has given up his individual identity markers as the basis for evaluation, finding instead his identity in what belongs to all human beings, namely, their rationality. There is a certain structure in all this that is closely similar to the one Paul adopts in Philippians 3: of starting out with the individual (an 'I') in order precisely to move beyond it. At first, the I and its self-perception is the locus of evaluation, but gradually (or in Paul's case suddenly) the I realizes that it 'belongs' (a central Stoic term) outside the I in something that it shares with all others.[23]

This feature of Stoic 'knowledge' is the first element that helps to make it morally relevant, something that may qualify as virtue. Moral virtue, on this account, is an attitude that consists in not looking to oneself since one has no special reason for doing that, but rather adopting an objective perspective on oneself and everything that will happen in the world. It is this objective attitude that is the essence of the famous Stoic *convenientia naturae*, the realization, as Cicero had it, that 'man's nature is in accordance with that of the whole'.

---

[23] Cf. *The Stoic Theory of Oikeiosis*, chaps. 3–4, in which *Fin.* 3.16–18 and 20–21 are analyzed in detail.

There is one more element in Stoic 'knowledge', however, one that turns it into justice and so into moral virtue proper (*Fin.* 3.62–71). This element is based on another 'root fact' about human beings, comparable with, but different from the one from which the Stoics began in their earlier development of moral knowledge. There the root fact was that of the individual applying a local perspective to the world and consequently taking the I as the basis of evaluation. Here, however, the starting point is the fact that human beings will unreflectively care for other individuals with whom they stand in a direct, local relationship — family members and associates of various kinds. On the basis of this initial attitude human beings may develop a more comprehensive attitude which will then become part of knowledge proper — the attitude of caring for all human beings just because they are that. Again, the mechanism is that of transcending the local perspective, only here the root fact that delivers the material for this development is a different one. With this element of Stoic knowledge in place we can see why this knowledge qualifies for being moral virtue. That knowledge, then, is what the *telos* of acts consists in. Acts that tend toward realizing the Stoic *telos* are acts that do not consist in looking to oneself but instead caring for all the others.

So the *telos* consists in knowledge of this kind and in acting in ways that reflect that knowledge. Cicero also brings in a term that he uses to identify the 'place' where those people belong who possess and act on this knowledge. It is the 'universe' (*mundus*, Greek κόσμος), of which the Stoics said that 'it is governed by the will of the gods, it is a city (*urbs*) or state (*civitas*) that is as it were shared by human beings and gods, and each of us is a part of that universe' (*Fin.* 3.64). This is of course Chrysippus' 'cosmic city' and it is here that Stoic ethical and political thought meet. If we ask where the 'cosmic city' is to be found, the answer, as we can now see, should be, in people's minds. It is the 'place' created by or made up of people who have the attitudes that go into Stoic virtue. It is very important, however, that it is conceived of as a genuine place or 'social space', no matter how removed it may be from the here and now. For in this way the idea of the 'cosmic city' may function as a model of a concrete place or social space here and now that people may bring into existence by having and acting on those attitudes. That, it seems, is precisely how Chrysippus conceived it

— as opposed to Panaetius where it appears as more of a 'moral ideal'.

Do we meet similar ideas in Philippians? There are plenty. Paul's *gnôsis* is on the one hand very much an individual affair consisting in *his own* directedness towards Christ (3.3–14). On the other hand, Paul has given up his own individual identity markers, finding instead his identity in Christ, but then he also includes a directedness towards the Philippians in that other directedness (1.24–26, also 3.15–21). Further, in the section that introduces the Christ hymn Paul is explicitly talking about an *attitude* (*phronein*, 2.5) that the Philippians should have. Finally, Paul too combines these ethical ideas with the more comprehensive political idea that the Philippians should live together (πολιτεύεσθαι, 1.27) in a manner that reflects the fact that they too are citizens in a *politeuma* that is 'cosmic' (though certainly in a rather more straightforward sense than in Chrysippus — it is in heaven, 3.20).

3.   The third basic point in Stoic ethics concerns their understanding of the relationship between the *telos* or life in the cosmic city and life in the here and now. The essential term here is *prokopê*. As we saw, that term is also used by Paul in Philippians. The Stoic idea is the twofold one that *reaching* the *telos*, completely and finally, is impossible for human beings, but progress toward it *is* possible. The Stoics developed this idea by means of a distinction between acts which may on the whole be proper and good (they are called καθήκοντα, Cicero's *officia*, cf. *Fin.* 3.58–61) and acts which are through and through good (the κατορθώματα, Cicero's *perfectum officium*, *Fin.* 3.61). Paul does not use this specific vocabulary, but the idea itself of striving towards something which one has not yet quite grasped is of course present in Philippians (3.12–16). Also, as we shall see, the idea of having Christ and (to some extent also) Paul himself as models of the totally appropriate behavior is a very important feature of the letter.

4. There is a fourth element in Stoic ethics which, though important, does not carry quite the same structural weight. It will turn out, however, to be highly relevant to Philippians. This is the Stoic understanding of the 'affections' proper, and in particular one of them: *chara* (joy).

The Stoics divided all affections into four sets, depending on whether they were negative or positive, or concerned with the present or the

273

future (*SVF* 3.380, 391, 392). With regard to the future there is either desire or fear, with regard to the present either pleasure or pain. All four, however, are wrong reactions to the outside world (*SVF* 3.387). And so the Stoics also introduced certain twin attitudes which they termed 'good dispositions' (*eupatheiai*, Diogenes Laertius 7.116). Of these there were only three. Corresponding to desire (future, positive) there was *boulêsis* or *voluntas* ('will', defined as the attitude of desiring rationally). Corresponding to fear (future, negative) there was *eulabeia* or *cautio* ('caution', defined as a rational 'deflection' from bad things). Finally, corresponding to pleasure (present, positive) there was *chara* or *gaudium* ('joy', defined as rational and constant elation). There was no *eupatheia* corresponding to pain for the simple reason that the wise man will constantly be moved by *chara* no matter what happens to him. He is, as it were, secure in his grasp of the good. There is an obvious correspondence with Paul in Philippians, where *chara* is one of the terms that bind the whole letter together.

A Third Structural Element in Philippians

Our aim is to better understand Paul's letter to the Philippians. I have now identified two sets of ideas that appear to play an important role in structuring Paul's argument in the letter. The first is the temporal framework set up by his references to the motif of the day of Christ and all that goes with this theme. The second is the Stoicizing one. Here what I have done is basically to list the originally Stoic terms that are scattered throughout the letter and then to remind us of the meaning they originally had. The issue that should concern us now is how these various ideas work together in Paul's argument.

Before I turn to this, however, I need to bring in one more set of ideas that helps to structure that argument. This is a theme that has recently been highlighted in two contributions, by Wayne A. Meeks and Stephen E. Fowl, on understanding the function of the Christ hymn as part of the letter as a whole.[24] In essence the suggestion is that

---

[24] Meeks, 'The Man from Heaven in Paul's Letter to the Philippians,' *The Future of Early Christianity: Essays in Honor of Helmut Koester* (ed. Birger A. Pearson; Minneapolis: Fortress, 1991) 329–36. Fowl, *The Story of Christ in the Ethics of Paul: An Analysis of the*

the Christ story functions as a 'master model' or 'generative image' (Meeks) or an 'exemplar' (Fowl, in a special sense derived from Thomas Kuhn) which 'sets the terms of the thinking and acting expected of the Philippians' (Meeks).[25] As Paul introduces the Christ story it is intended to serve as a model directly for the Philippians (cf. 2.5, 12).[26] What makes it a genuine master model, however, is the way in which it is also made to structure Paul's various descriptions of himself and his relationship with the Philippians as well as theirs with him.[27] It is worth listing some of these uses.

1. Looking back to chapter 1 from the Christ hymn it is clear that Paul has modeled his description of his own attitude both towards his predicament in jail and towards the Philippians on the Christ story. Paul feels certain that Christ will be aggrandized by whatever happens to his (Paul's) body, whether it is life or death (1.20). For him life 'is' Christ (1.21) and dying would be preferable since it would mean being with Christ (1.23). But like Christ (2.6–7), Paul lets his acts be guided by concern for the Philippians (1.24–26; cf. 2.16–17). We may formalize the motif as follows: 'Christ ← Paul' (Paul being directed towards Christ through modeling himself on him). And we may label it the *koinōnia* motif. The term itself is not used in 1.19–26 (but see 1.5, 7–8 and later), but the idea is — that of Paul's being with (σύν) Christ (1.23) and of his directedness towards the Philippians (1.26), which follows from that other directedness.

2. Paul's fate will be his salvation (1.19) through the Philippians' help when they pray for him and provide him (!) with the spirit of Jesus Christ. Similarly, the Philippians' fate will be their salvation (1.28) when they stand fast in the same conflict that Paul was and is in (1.30). Here the point is no longer 'Christ ← Paul', but 'Paul ↔ the Philippians', *together* reflecting the master model of Christ. But again

---

Function of the Hymnic Material in the Pauline Corpus (JSNTSup 36; Sheffield: Sheffield Academic Press, 1990).

[25] Meeks, 'The Man from Heaven', 335. Fowl, *The Story of Christ*, 92–95.

[26] This will hold in spite of Ernst Käsemann's famous counterattack in 'Kritische Analyse von Phil. 2, 5–11,' *ZTK* 47 (1950) 313–60. For a convincing discussion of Käsemann's view, see Fowl, *The Story of Christ*, 79–85.

[27] Cf. Meeks' analysis in 'The Man from Heaven', 333–35.

the underlying theme is that of a complete *koinônia* across time and place, whether with Christ or between the Philippians and Paul.

3. This line is continued in 2.1–2, where Paul explicitly takes up the *koinônia* motif. Here too the master model is implicitly present, when Paul invokes his own affection for the Philippians (2.1) by a term he had earlier used to describe the same affection as that of the deep yearning 'of Christ Jesus himself' (1.8). Gradually, however, Paul moves towards talking of the relationship between the Philippians themselves, that is, 'the Philippians ↔ the Philippians'.[28] But here too what he says is derived from the master model when he argues against selfishness (ἐριθεία, 2.3, like the one that was *not* found in Christ, 2.6–7), against empty self-esteem (κενοδοξία, 2.3 — Christ by contrast emptied himself), and for humility (*tapeinophrosynê*, 2.3, like Christ's 2.7–8) and placing the others above (ὑπέρ) oneself (as Christ did when he became obedient, 2.8). Here the *koinônia* motif is obviously developed as its most explicit.

4. Paul sometimes employs the master model even more directly. Thus in 2.25–30 he almost explicitly invests Epaphroditus with the fate and character of Christ (2.27, 30) and also with that of Paul himself when he describes Epaphroditus as an *apostolos* and *leitourgos* (2.25; cf. 2.17). So here it is both 'Christ ← Epaphroditus' and 'Paul ← Epaphroditus'. But the passage is also full of expressions of affection back and forth between all those involved.

5. Finally, as commentators have realized with increasing clarity, Paul has modeled his account in 3.7–11 of his own conversion on the Christ story of the hymn.[29] So here it is again 'Christ ← Paul'. But what does he use it for? 3.17 provides the answer. The Philippians should become imitators of Christ together with Paul by taking him as a model (*typos*). So here it is both 'Christ ← the Philippians', together with 'Christ ← Paul', and also 'Christ ←(Paul ← the Philippians)'.

---

[28] Commentators have not seen sufficiently clearly how in 2.1–2 Paul gradually moves from appealing to the Philippians to reciprocate his affection for them to an appeal that they have the same kind of affection towards each other. Thus in 2.2 τὸ αὐτό, sc. φρονεῖτε, probably means 'the same, viz. as I do', whereas τὸ ἕν, sc. φρονοῦντες, probably means 'one thing, viz. among *each other*'. Thus Paul almost writes out in the text his own role as a model.

[29] For details see David E. Garland, 'The Composition and Unity', 157–59.

We should conclude that there is a pervasive motif in the letter which turns on the ideal of modeling personal relationships on the Christ story. What comes out of doing this is a special type of *koinônia* since due to its basis in the Christ story it reflects an attitude of interpersonal subordination, of acting for the sake of (ὑπέρ with the genitive) others because one considers them above (ὑπέρ with the accusative) oneself. Viewed in formal terms there is nothing Stoic about this for the obvious reason that the master model that delivers this whole set of personal relationships is provided by a person and his personal fate and attitude. How, then, should we combine this particular set of ideas with the two others I identified? How, if at all, do they work together to formulate Paul's message?[30]

Stoicism in Philippians

What we have are the following three motifs:
1. The motif of the day of Christ (above pp. 260–61).
2. A number of superficially Stoicizing terms (above pp. 261–63) plus their technical background which may or may not be alive in Paul's use of the terms (above, pp. 269–74).
3. The *koinônia* motif (above pp. 274–77).

Our task is to decide the exact interplay of the three clusters of ideas and in particular whether the Stoic technical background is alive or not. We should ask, Would knowledge of Stoicism have helped the Philippians understand better what Paul appears to be saying (there is no way of knowing whether they had such knowledge)? If the answer is positive, we may conclude that Paul's text has partly been shaped by Stoic ideas (even though Paul himself may not have been entirely conscious of this: again we have no means of knowing).

---

[30] I have emphasized the element of subordination in the *koinônia* motif, as Paul bases it on the Christ story, for a special reason. *Koinônia* in the form that Paul *also* expresses, of a genuine affection between the various parties, is eminently Stoic and part of their view of the ideal community. That is also the reason why everything I say in this essay of the Stoic ideal community fits in completely with the present trend towards seeing Philippians as a 'letter of friendship'. (See, e.g. L. Michael White, 'Morality between Two Worlds: A Paradigm of Friendship in Philippians,' *Greeks, Romans, and Christians*, 201–15.) For as we already know, Stoic friendship is precisely found among the wise (and only there), where there is also *homonoia* and *eleutheria* (*SVF* 1.263). However, for reasons that will become clear, I have wanted the element of subordination in Paul's development of the *koinônia* motif to stand out as clearly as possible.

The only way to answer the question is by asking ourselves whether *we* are helped by a knowledge of Stoicism (the rudiments of which I have set forth above) to understand better what Paul appears to be saying. So, at the risk of appearing a little too fanciful, I shall try to imagine what the Philippians might have taken away with them from hearing Paul's letter had they possessed our knowledge of Stoicism. They might have reasoned as follows.

By being Christians we are in the following situation:

(1.1)   There is an end, a *skopos*, of our life (as Christians). It is being in the heavenly *politeuma* to which we already belong. At present, this *politeuma* does not have the form of a particular body of people living in a particular place. Rather, it is constituted by all those people who exhibit a certain mind-set (*phronein/gnôsis* — through having been caught hold of by Christ and modeling themselves on him).

(1.2)   However, as an ideal community (which will in fact become realized at some point in the future) it calls for being realized by us here and now to the extent that this is possible. (Indeed, God has called us to do so.)

(1.3)   We therefore have the task of bringing into existence as far as possible an actual *koinônia* modeled on that *politeuma* — while also knowing that it cannot quite be done in the hear and now.

(2.1)   Now that task may be fulfilled if we come to have the mind-set referred to above (the one modeled for us by Christ and Paul).

(2.2)   That mind-set is one that gives up any subjective claims based on a perception of individual assets for the sake of benefiting others.

(2.3)   It is marked by *chara* in the face of ordinary human adversity and by *autarkeia* in relation to ordinary human goods since neither of these genuinely matters.

(2.4)   Instead, it focuses entirely on the others (whether fellow humans or Christ) and derives its feeling of *chara* and its sense of *autarkeia* precisely from belonging in a *koinônia* with them.

(3.1)   In fact, as Paul reminds us, we are already on our way towards living in the ideal *politeuma*.

(3.2)   For by entering, on our first day, into the *koinônia* of Paul's gospel (as captured in the story of Christ's fate and as expressed in so many other ways throughout Paul's letter), we already gave up all claims based on ourselves.

(3.3)   Therefore, let us move further in the direction of making the ideal *politeuma* real here in Philippi.

In this small story there is nothing (outside the brackets) that could not also have been said by a Stoic. At the same time it is my contention that the story captures the essence of the three motifs that we have identified and consequently (if these are in fact central to the letter) the essence of the message Paul is trying to convey to his addressees. It formulates the logical backbone of the letter. But in that case it is noteworthy that the story also reflects very precisely the basic ideas that went into Stoic moral and political philosophy: the directedness towards an end, the conceptualization of the end as an ideal community, the strategy of using the notion of the end to inform people's understanding and behavior here and now, the exact way in which this application is thought to occur (it creates a certain mind-set with a distinct content). All of this is both centrally Stoic and also sufficiently specific to make it highly unlikely that it is anything *but* Stoic.

If, then, we have managed to construct a story that is both specifically and centrally Stoic and that also captures the essence of the message Paul is trying to convey to his addressees, then we may conclude that there is Stoicism in Philippians not just in an obvious and slightly superficial way but also in such a way that the technical background to the Stoicizing terms used by Paul is kept alive. And so we may also conclude that Paul is actually using Stoicism in his community-forming enterprise, by elaborating the notion of the 'end' of Christian existence in terms of the idea of a Christian 'social space' (the heavenly *politeuma*) based on all the ingredients that went into Chrysippus' 'cosmic city' and by drawing a number of consequences for life here and now from this *rapprochement*.

This is not to say, of course, that there is not more in the Pauline letter than is to be found in Stoicism. There certainly is. Nor am I claiming that, if asked, Paul would himself have allotted the same importance to the Stoic framework that he is in fact relying on as he obviously does to the apocalyptic day of Christ motif that he is more explicitly using to frame the perception of his addressees. Rather, the claim is that in spelling out, as part of his community-forming enterprise, the meaning of that other fundamental motif, Paul employs the Stoic ideas to structure the understanding that he wishes to impart to his addressees. Similarly, he also employs the (entirely un-Stoic) *koinônia-* and Christ as model motifs for the same purpose of spelling out the content of Christian existence. Paul is not just talking in the manner of a Stoic. But he is also doing that (in addition to much else). He is doing it quite importantly (for his overall community-building purpose). And finally, he is doing it in such a way that there is no friction whatever in the resulting picture. Rather, there is a complete fusion.

Complicating the Picture

Or is there? Various features in the letter seem to suggest that if pressed to its very conclusion the analogy with Stoicism will reveal differences that are so fundamental that one can no longer speak of a genuine fusion. These features are specifically Christian (and with a specifically Jewish background) and I want to consider how they may interact with Paul's Stoicizing thought. The aim is to show that there is a tension in Paul's thought and practice in writing the letter, a tension that becomes clear when one compares those elements in it that have a Stoic counterpart with those that do not. This tension cannot, however, be dissolved by separating the two elements. For the two sides of the tension are both important parts of Paul's overall message. Nor will it be possible to locate the Stoicizing ideas on the one side of the tension and the specifically Christian ones on the other. For the tension goes right through Paul's own Christian understanding and practice. In fact, as I shall end by arguing, it is when Paul is at his most Stoic that he is also at his most Christian.

Before considering the two features in the letter that raise this issue, I shall set aside another feature that to my mind does not raise it but has very often been taken to do so. This feature resides in Paul's claims that he has been caught hold of by Christ (3.12), that he has been called by God (3.14), and that he has somehow come to possess (that is, been given) a righteousness that is not his own, but God's (3.9). Does this connected set of ideas not go against the Stoicizing motif of Paul himself striving for the prize and reaching out for it in order to attain it (3.12–14)? Moreover, is Paul not himself precisely pointing to the contrast when he states that he 'strives with a view to grasping (the end), corresponding to the fact that he has (himself) been grasped by Christ Jesus' (3.12)?[31]

This is not the place to go into a thorough discussion of this whole issue. It is an issue that cries out for further investigation, both in view of the quite automatic way in which it is almost always taken as settled, and also in view of the heavy theological ban that rests upon it.[32] I suggest that there is in fact no contrast and for two connected reasons. First, it remains to be proven that there is any idea in Stoicism corresponding to what modern scholars think of when they speak of 'oneself 'striving' and making an 'effort' to reach 'one's own' salvation or righteousness (as opposed to the one given by God). The idea does not appear in the sources. On the contrary, when for example Cicero describes the Stoic change to a proper grasp of the good (*Fin* 3.20–21), one might just as well say that what has happened is that a person has been 'taken hold of' by the idea of the good or 'struck' by it. And when a Stoic 'strives' to unfold that idea in actual practice, the issue remains one of seeing what that earlier insight 'tells one to do'.[33] Secondly, the contrast discovered by scholars quite clearly reflects a modern theological problematic, in particular the contrast between humanism and Christianity.

What, then, is the contrast that Paul is himself drawing in the passages referred to? There are several quite distinct claims involved here. In 3.9 Paul is in fact drawing a contrast, but not between 'himself' (or Promethean man) and God. Rather, the contrast is between a righteousness coming from the law that Paul himself (and other Jews with him) might point to with pride as something *they* had in preference to

---

[31] Note that on this interpretation of the verse Paul will himself be implying that he is using Stoicizing vocabulary here — a point not always realized by scholars who adopt that interpretation.

[32] The best tratment I know of is William A. Beardslee, *Human Achievement and Divine Vocation in the Message of Paul* (Naperville, Ill.: Allenson, 1961). But there is more work to be done.

[33] In fact, the Stoics spoke of 'right acts' (*katorthômata*), which are the acts that flow from that insight, as 'commands' (*prostagmata*) of the law (Plutarch in *SVF* 3.520). But they also claimed that in the case of the wise man who has reached perfection (the τέλεος σοφός), there is no need of either commands, prohibitions, or exhortations (προστάττειν, ἀπαγορεύειν, παραινεῖν, Philo in *SVF* 3.519). Paul, I think, would have agreed.

non-Jews (it is in this sense that it is 'their own' or just 'theirs') and a righteousness which comes from God and through Christ faith in such a way that it is *nobody's* special prerogative. In 3.12, however, Paul is not drawing a contrast at all. Rather, he is claiming that his striving is wholly in line with the change in understanding (3.7–10) that he has undergone — just as a Stoic might say. The direction is right, so he claims, even though he has not yet gone the whole way.[34]

I conclude that there is nothing in this to suggest any friction whatever between the Christian ideas and the Stoicizing one of striving. On the contrary, had Paul felt that there was a contrast of the type formulated by modern scholars, it is very difficult to understand why he should have dared to employ the Stoicizing language. For this, the supposed qualification in 3.12 would not have been sufficient.

The Two Ideas of Judgment and Subordination

The two genuinely un-Stoic features to be found in the letter are part of the day of Christ motif and the *koinônia* motif respectively. The first is the idea of judgment on the day of Christ. It comes in at a number of places in the letter: 1.10–11 (ἵνα ἦτε εἰλικρινεῖς καὶ ἀπρόσκοποι εἰς ἡμέραν Χριστοῦ plus the reference to a καρπὸς δικαιοσύνης), in 1.28 (the Philippians' σωτηρία ... ἀπὸ θεοῦ as opposed to the opponents' ἀπώλεια) and in 2.15–16 (closely comparable with 1.10–11). In 2.12 Paul exhorts the Philippians to work on their own salvation 'with fear and trembling' (μετὰ φόβου καὶ τρόμου), clearly with a view to God's future judgment. In all four passages it is God (as opposed to Christ) who is explicitly brought in as the one who is in charge of the Philippians' fate. Also in all four passages it is the Philippians' fate (as opposed to Paul's) on the day of Christ that is being addressed.[35] The question we should ask is how this emphasis on judgment (by God) and fear and trembling (on the part of the Philippians) may be connected with the Stoicizing theme that Paul brings in so strongly in

---

[34] I suggest that the same idea is expressed in 2.12–13 through the famous γάρ that binds the two verses together. Here too there is no contrast.

[35] In 2.16 Paul does bring himself in, but in order to emphasize his reasons for *boasting* on the day of Christ.

3.12–14, that of striving eagerly and ardently towards the final goal of being in the heavenly *politeuma*, of *wanting* to be there just, it seems, for its own. The issue here is that of 'heteronomy' versus 'autonomy', of doing something for the sake of some other thing that one wants (or in order to avoid something one dislikes) versus doing it just because it is what one wants.

Before considering this issue further I shall spend some time on the second feature I alluded to. This feature is part of the *koinônia* motif — that the *koinônia* is one in which people care for others (cf. 2.4) because they consider them *above* themselves (cf. 2.3). How does this specific feature of subordination relate to the *Stoic* conception of the ideal community, in which, as we saw, there is at most an 'alternating subordination', with the same person shifting between ruling and being ruled? Is there not a crucial difference here between the Stoic and the Christian conceptions?

Discussion of this issue calls for great care and it is important to draw a number of distinctions. A first question is whether there is a clear difference between the Stoic and the Christian conceptions (as the latter is set forth in 2.3–4) in terms of their actual content, that is, the kind of attitude towards oneself and others expressed in either conception and the behavioral consequences of that attitude. The answer, I suggest, is No. On the contrary, the evidence in support of claiming the similarity to be very close is strong. Thus immediately after his introduction of the *urbs* and *civitas* shared by human beings and the gods, Cicero goes on to say, 'it is a natural consequence [of the fact that each of us is a member of that 'universe'] that we prefer the common advantage to our own. For just as the laws set the safety of all above the safety of individuals, so a good, wise and law-abiding man, conscious of his duty as a citizen, takes care of the advantage of all more than that of any single individual or of himself' (*Fin.* 3.64). This is closely similar in content to Paul's exhortation that the Philippians should not look to their own interests but rather to those of the others (2.4) and his recommendation of Timothy as one 'who has a genuine concern for your affairs' (2.20) in contrast with all the others who only 'seek their own interests and not those of Christ Jesus' (2.21).[36]

---

[36] This similarity, I believe, is the central point that underlies Halvor Moxnes' essay on the similarities between Dio Chrysostom and Paul elsewhere in this volume.

It is important to see that the similarity on this point is in fact very close. Thus it is false to claim that the requirement to act for the sake of others is stronger and more radical in Paul (and Christianity in general) than in Stoicism. It cannot be this since it is precisely a central point in Stoicism that the good lies in grasping that the individual has no claim whatever to any advantages just by being an individual or *this* individual — oneself. Nor would it be correct to say that there remains a difference since a Stoic wise man may still allot to himself a proper share of advantages because he deserves them more than any others do. For the Stoic wise man does not care for these things. The degree of self-abnegation is not greater in Paul's Christian than it is in the Stoic wise man. Self-abnegation is precisely part of the Stoic point, which is one reason why Stoic ethics met with such fierce opposition in antiquity itself.

Summarizing on this first question, then, we may say that Paul's exhortation in 2.3–4 does not go beyond the Stoic idea of justice or altruism. On the contrary, the claim that each should look to the intersts of the others fits immediately in with the Stoic picture of alternating subordination in their ideal community.

However, the subordination motif is employed far more widely in Paul's letter than indicated so far. And so the question remains whether in this wider use there is after all an important difference between the Stoics and Paul.

In order to answer this question let us briefly note the many ways in which the issue of subordination, and in general of hierarchy, comes up throughout the letter. Thus in spite of Paul's repeated references to a genuine, reciprocal *koinônia* that exists between himself and the other human beings to whom he refers, he also clearly presupposes, and wishes to maintain, a hierarchical relationship between them. This comes out in a number of ways in his remarks about his relationship with the Philippians in 1.18–2.18, with Timothy in 2.19–24 and with Epaphroditus in 2.25–30, leading to his exhortation that the Philippians should receive Epaphroditus well and 'hold such people in honor' (2.29). It also comes out in his description in chapter 3 of his own conversion as a model for the Philippians (3.17).

The last verse, however, is even more revealing. First, because Paul is careful to counterbalance his status as a model with the more nonhierarchical suggestion that the Philippians should *join* him (συμ-) in following his example (-μιμηταί). And secondly, because he exhorts them to look to those other people who apparently do take Paul as a model. The connection with 2.29 is obvious and the care with which Paul keeps the differences in status clear is impressive.

The conclusion is that in the very many ways in which Paul handles the theme of *koinônia* throughout the letter he also manages to maintain a clear hierarchy. There is God at the top. Then there is Christ, who subordinated himself and became obedient to God. Then there is Paul, who has both subordinated himself to Christ (by giving up all his earlier advantages) and is also to some degree at one with Christ (and so above those further down the scale). Then there are helpers like Timothy and Epaphroditus and other leaders at this level. And finally there are the Philippians — who are at least higher up in the scale than those outside the Christian circle.

Embedded in the way in which Paul builds up this hierarchy is a particular use of the Christ model. As set out in the hymn, this model may function in at least two ways. Thus Christ may be seen as a model of self-abnegating behavior *willingly undertaken* (he emptied himself etc.). That is the way Paul seems to have applied the model to himself, for example, in 1.18–26. But the story given in the hymn may also serve as support for the claim that self-abnegating behavior of the kind displayed by Christ should be adopted *in obedience* to God and to Christ, the lord. And this is the way Paul seems to apply the model to the Philippians in 2.12. This latter use, then, constitutes another strongly subordinating motif, which serves to set up a hierarchy — obedience through application of the model of Christ as *kyrios*.

We should conclude that there is one element in the *koinônia* motif which has the function of creating and maintaining a clear hierarchy. This element is altogether un-Stoic and so it looks as if we have diagnosed an element in Paul's thought which is both important and goes directly against the nonhierarchic character of the Stoic vision of the ideal community.

Before jumping to that conclusion, however, we should remind ourselves of the fact that there are also other elements in Paul's elaboration of the *koinônia* motif which go strongly against merely settling for a hierarchical *koinônia*, most powerfully the image of the self-humiliating

Christ in the first model function identified above, but also Paul's repeated use of συν- as a sign of a genuinely shared fellowship (e.g. in the almost paradoxical συμ-μιμηταί μου γίνεσθε in 3.17 that we noted) and his many expressions of a genuine, emotional fellow-feeling on his own part toward the Philippians. All of this is through and through nonhierarchical in sentiment and it fits immediately into Paul's other use of the subordination motif in 2.1–4 and its analogy in the Stoic conception of the ideal community.

It looks, therefore, as if we have unearthed something that amounts to a real tension in Paul's thought and argumentative practice. On the one hand we find a development of the *koinônia* motif that stresses hierarchy in various dimensions. This corresponds with one use of the Christ as model motif, namely, the idea of Christ as *kyrios* and of obedience to him (and to God). This understanding of the *koinônia* has no Stoic counterpart. On the other side we find a development of the *koinônia* motif which goes in the opposite direction by giving expression to sentiments that are distinctly nonhierarchical and stressing the idea of giving up individual prerogatives. This corresponds with the other use of the Christ as model motif, namely, the idea of Christ himself willingly giving up his status for the sake of human beings. This understanding of the *koinônia* has a clear counterpart in the Stoic conception of alternating subordination in the ideal community. So there appears to be a tension here.

Hierarchy and Its Opposite: A Genuine Tension and How to Understand It

But is the supposed tension in fact real? One might argue as follows. There is no tension. Christ is *kyrios* and he demands obedience. But acting in obedience to Christ as *kyrios* in no way precludes that one may also willingly undertake whatever act is involved. Both ideas are present in the Christ hymn with no apparent tension between them, since Christ is represented as both acting willingly and also, of course, in obedience to God. In any case, to insist on the genuinely non-hierarchical character of the kind of *koinônia* that Paul is envisaging is to leave Paul himself behind. For on his conception, Christ remains *kyrios* (3.20–21), moreover, he does this by acting as *kyrios*, by subjecting (ὑποτάξαι) everything to himself (3.21) and so down to the very word placing human beings where in Stoic terms they will precisely not be — in slavery (δουλεία) defined as subordination (ὑπόταξις) that consists in the lack of independent action (στέρησις αὐτοπραγίας). So one can argue there is no tension.

But I insist that there is. First, note that speaking of Christ as the *kyrios* who subjects everything to himself does not in fact separate Paul from the Stoics. There is evidence that the Stoics too thought of the relationship of human beings to the Gods in the 'cosmic city' as one of subjection. Arius Didymus says (*SVF* 2.528): 'Just as a city may be spoken of in two ways, as the dwellingplace and as the community (σύστημα) made up of those living there together with the citizens, so too the cosmos is, as it were, a city made up (συνεστῶσα) of Gods and human beings, with the Gods having the leadership (ἡγεμονία) and the human beings being in subjection (ὑποτεταγμένοι). But there is fellowship (κοινωνία) between them because they share in reason. …'

Does this passage not go against the nonhierarchical picture of the Stoic conception of the ideal community that I have given? Not at all. Hierarchy there certainly is, between Gods and men, but as the last quoted sentence shows, there is also a genuine *koinônia* in the 'cosmic city' between Gods and men, because they both share in reason. Furthermore, at the level of human beings alone there is nothing but a genuinely nonhierarchical *koinônia* — as we saw in Zeno's and Chrysippus' original elaboration of it. The same, I suggest, is true in Paul's case.

The crucial argument for this claim lies in the following observation. If we ask where in his letter Paul is thinking in hierarchical terms and where not, a consistent pattern emerges, which shows that there is in fact a difference between the two ideas and hence also a tension. Hierarchy is on the agenda where Paul is speaking to his addressees — the Philippians. They should model themselves on Paul and on Christ in obedience to God. And they should recognize the higher status of Timothy, Epaphroditus, and others like these. In short, they should comply. Similarly, returning to the motif of God's judgment which I left hanging, we may recall that this motif too was directed at the Philippians. In fact, all three ideas (of God's judgment, of subordinating oneself in obedience, and of modeling oneself on somebody higher up in the hierarchy) are found together in 2.12 which is very explicitly and pointedly directed at the Philippians.

By contrast, when Paul is speaking of himself, the agenda is no longer hierarchical. Paul never speaks of himself in relation to God's judgment in terms of 'fear and trembling'. Rather, as we noted, he looks forward to the day of Christ as one on which he will have reason to boast of his preaching (1.26; 2.16). And there is absolutely no suggestion that he preaches in order to gain salvation for himself. (On the contrary, woe is him if he does not preach! 1 Cor 9.16.)[37] Nor does he ever in the letter depict himself as one who is just obedient, either to Christ or to God. Rather, he himself reaches toward what lies ahead (3.13), the prize that is to be found in God's upward call in Christ Jesus (3.14). Nor, finally, is he in the least unwilling to model himself on Christ. On the contrary, his desire is to depart and be with Christ since that is far better (1.23). Even in this life his aim is to be found in Christ (3.9), to become as like him as possible (συμ-μορφιζόμενος) by entering into a koinônia with his suffering (that is, by himself coming to suffer like Christ did) in the hope that he may also reach the resurrection, like Christ did (3.10–11). Paul has come to know Christ and he now strives to make this knowledge complete, so that Christ may take over completely. In Paul's own case, then, there is no suggestion of heteronomy. Instead, there are very clear expressions of autonomy on Paul's part. Here there is only an ardent wish to become a full member of the heavenly politeuma.

---

[37] And so we are back to the Stoic theme of freedom; see Abraham J. Malherbe, 'Determinism and Free Will in Paul,' above, pp. 231–55. Johannes Weiss treated the same theme in Die Christliche Freiheit nach der Verkündigung des Apostels Paulus (Göttingen: Vandenhoeck & Ruprecht, 1902). Weiss was far more open to the influence of Stoicism on Paul than scholars have generally been since 1920 and more searching in his quest for the differences. His quotation (p. 34) from Cicero, Paradoxa Stoicorum 34 is highly pertinent to the point I have been making about Paul on freedom and obedience: 'What is freedom? The ability to live as one wishes [potestas vivendi ut velis, that is, ἐξουσία αὐτοπραγίας]. Who then lives as he wishes, if not the one who follows what is right, who rejoices (gaudet) at his duty, ... who does not obey (paret) the laws from fear (propter metum), but follows and cherishes (colit) them because he considers that maximally salutary?' Cf. Paul in Rom 8.15: οὐ γὰρ ἐλάβετε πνεῦμα δουλείας πάλιν εἰς φόβον, ἀλλὰ ἐλάβετε πνεῦμα υἱοθεσίας. And 8.17: κληρονόμοι μὲν θεοῦ, συγκληρονόμοι δὲ Χριστοῦ, εἴπερ συμπάσχομεν ἵνα καὶ συνδοξασθῶμεν.

I conclude that there is a tension. As Paul describes his own relationship with Christ, he is a man who has been struck by an insight that makes him strive to be in a heavenly *politeuma* in which there is no status hierarchy. Instead there will at most be, at the human level, an alternating subordination of the kind that Paul also wishes to see applied here and now in Philippi (2.3–4) and which is also partly prefigured in his own emotional relationship with the Philippians. As against this, there is quite another handling of hierarchical motifs in the letter which is straightforwardly directed towards making the Philippians comply. The tension is there and we shall do well to recognize it.

We should not conclude from this that either the nonhierarchical sentiment or the hierarchical one is the one that captures Paul's understanding of Christian existence to the complete exclusion of the other. Rather, they are both there as part of Paul's overall 'theology'. Still, having come so far, we may perhaps risk the question where Paul is more true to his own Christian insight — in what he says of his addressees or in what he says of himself? The answer should be: in the latter. For whereas we have noticed how Paul makes use of the nonhierarchical motifs too in relation to his addressees, we have not come across a use of truly hierarchical, heteronomous motifs in relation to the apostle himself. If we then add that the nonhierarchical set of motifs is also the one that has its direct counterpart in the Stoic elaboration of the notion of the 'cosmic city', we may further conclude that when Paul is at his most Christian, he is also at his most Stoic. When he develops the idea of a genuine, nonhierarchical *koinônia* and *politeuma* as the *telos* and when he describes himself as the model *prokoptôn*, then he is at the same time at his most Stoic and his most Christian. But when he turns to the language of hierarchy in an attempt to provide structure to the Philippian congregation and when he applies emotional force to the Philippians, then he is dangerously near to compromising his own most basic insight into the character of Christian existence. And that is when he is not arguing like a Stoic.

There is no friction, then, between Stoic and Christian ideas in Paul's thought in the letter. On the contrary, the analysis of Paul's use of Stoic ideas may even help us to diagnose a tension within Paul's own Christian thought which one might otherwise either have overlooked or else tried to explain away.

Conclusion

There remains the master model himself. His crucial importance is clear from every verse of the letter. Nothing at all comparable is to be found in Stoicism. However, I have been concerned with Paul's use of the Christ figure, with how it enters into the set of ideas and concepts that he brings into play in order to reach his aim in the letter. That aim is fundamentally parenetic and the whole letter is, as Paul himself says, a specimen of *paraklêsis* (2.1). The object of the paraklesis is, as we can now see, to bring into existence, as far as possible, in Philippi a preliminary form of the future heavenly *politeuma*. Paul attempts to reach his aim by interweaving with his basic Christian ideas (the apocalyptic framework and the ideas set out in the Christ hymn) a number of equally basic ideas in Stoic ethics and politics. There is tension in the picture that results, but not between the Christian and the Stoic ideas. Rather, it is a tension within Paul's Christian understanding and practice itself.

10

Human Nature and Ethics in Hellenistic Philosophical Traditions and Paul: Some Issues and Problems

David E. Aune

Introduction

After more than a century of debate, there are still wide areas of disagreement on the complex question of whether Paul's views of human nature are explicable on the basis of Jewish tradition alone, or whether he was influenced by Hellenistic conceptions of human nature, perhaps refracted through Hellenistic Judaism. It is obvious that Paul did not simply adopt an existing anthropological model from 'Judaism', 'Hellenistic Judaism', or 'Hellenism' (precise boundaries between these cultural categories did not in fact exist). In part this is because he evinces no concern to develop a consistent view of human nature. Even though he uses a variety of Greek anthropological terms to explain aspects of human behavior in sections of his letters, he often does so on an *ad hoc* basis with the result that there is little overall consistency evident when these passages are compared. Paul was an eclectic who drew upon a variety of anthropological conceptions in a manner subsidiary or tangential to the more immediate concerns he addresses in his extant letters.

In this paper I shall touch a number of problematic issues relating to the theme of human nature and ethics in Paul and his Hellenistic intellectual environment. Since Hellenistic views of human nature were extremely varied and complex and have too often been caricatured by New Testament scholarship, I shall focus on aspects of this issue. I shall then discuss the perspectives on human nature that can be teased out of the Pauline letters — an area that is often oversimplified. Finally, I shall discuss the specific issue of the use of death as a metaphor for the transformed life in both the Hellenistic world and Paul.

Complexities in Hellenistic Views of Human Nature

One widely held assumption is that ancient views of human nature must be either monistic or dualistic, conceptions often linked to the Hebrew or the Greek view of the person. The two most popular Hellenistic philosophies during the third and second centuries B.C.E., however, were Stoicism and Epicureanism, both of which espoused a monistic and hence materialistic view of human nature. Various strands of early Judaism reflected a variety of cultural and religious traditions in which there was no consistent view of human nature,[1] and in which Hellenistic conceptions of human nature were assimilated to various degrees.[2] There were, in fact, *many* monistic and dualistic conceptions of the universe and human nature (the two are often understood homologously). Dualistic models consistently anticipate that plurality will ultimately be resolved into unity.

While it is no longer possible to speak of *the* Pauline view of human nature, neither is it possible to speak of *the* Platonic, *the* Aristotelian, or *the* Stoic conceptions of human nature. Plato's view of human nature, elements of which were drawn from both philosophical and popular traditions, changed radically during his lifetime and were never forced into a single coherent system. The most obvious change was from his view of the ψυχή as a simple substance in the *Phaedo*, to the tripartite division of the ψυχή in the *Republic*. In the *Phaedo* alone the term ψυχή is used with a relatively extensive variety of connotations:[3] (1) the

---

[1]   George W. E. Nickelsburg, Jr., *Resurrection, Immortality, and Eternal Life in Intertestamental Judaism* (HTS 26; Cambridge, Mass.: Harvard University Press, 1972) 170–80.

[2]   For a variety of early Jewish views of death involving the separation of body from spirit, see Wis 8.19–20; 9.15; *Jubilees* 23.30–32; *1 Enoch* 102.5; 103.2–4; 104.3; *T. Asher* 6.5–6; 4 Macc 7.19; 13.17; 16.25; Ps.-Phocylides *Sent.* 105–8. Josephus frequently imported popular Middle Platonic body–soul dualism into his narrative when discussing the beliefs of first-century Palestinian Jews (*J.W.* 2.154; 3.362–88; 7.344–48), including the Zealots (*J.W.* 7.344–48), the Essenes (*J.W.* 2.154), and the Pharisees (*J.W.* 2.163).

[3]   David Gallop, *Plato, Phaedo* (Oxford: Clarendon, 1975) 88–91.

element within us whose good condition constitutes our true well-being; (2) the 'true self' or 'real person' (115b–116a); (3) the intellect, reason or thinking faculty (65b–c; 76c); (4) the 'rational self' in contrast to emotions and physical desires (94b–d); (5) the 'life principle' or 'animating agent' (64c; 72a–d; 105c–d); (6) generic 'soul-stuff' in contrast to individual souls, just as matter may be contrasted to individual bodies (70c–d; 80c–d). These various meanings of ψυχή cannot be understood within a single consistent framework. How can the soul 'bring life' to the body (105c–d), 'rule and be master' of the body (80a; 94b–d), and yet be a 'prisoner' within the body (82e–83a)? According to Plato, the soul wore the body like clothes to be discarded (*Phd.* 87b), the soul is woven through the body (*Tim.* 36e), or a person is a soul using a body (*Alc.* 129c–e). One of the persistent problems with Plato's conception of the soul–body relationship (and one which was attacked by both Stoics and Epicureans) was the assumption that the incorporeal could somehow associate with the corporeal to form a single substance — a human person.

Aristotle's views on the relationship between body, soul, and mind are complex and exhibit at least two phases — a 'Platonic' phase (in which he regarded the soul as a separate substance, as in Plato's *Phaedo*), and a final 'hylomorphic' stage in which he regarded the soul as the form or the realization of a natural body (reflected in the *De Anima*).[4] The *Eudemus* (belonging to the genre of consolation literature) and the *Protrepticus* (an exhortation to pursue the philosophic life) are both products of the 350s, and though extant only in fragments, represent the earliest stage of Aristotle's views on ethics and psychology.[5] According to the *Eudemus*, the soul is a separate substance that existed before entering the body and survives separation from the body. This conflicts with Aristotle's later view in the *De Anima* that only the νοῦς is immortal. The same body–soul dualism is also evident in the *Protrepticus* (Düring, *Protrepticus*, frag. B23: 'man is by nature composed of soul and body'; cf. frags. B59, B107), and the life of the soul is superior to that of the body (Düring, frags. B23, B34, B61). The soul has both a

---

[4]   See the developmental scheme proposed by John M. Rist, *The Mind of Aristotle: A Study in Philosophical Growth* (Toronto: University of Toronto Press, 1989).
[5]   Rist, *Mind of Aristotle*, 165–70.

rational and an irrational part and νοῦς belongs to the rational part (Düring, frags. B23, B60). In the latest stage of Aristotle's psychological theory, he believed that mind or the 'active intellect' (*De An.* 3.5; 430a) was present in the human person, but separate from the soul–body complex (*De An.* 408b), and it alone is divine.[6]

There is no soul–body dualism for Stoics, for the same force directs both physical and mental processes; a person has no irrational faculties. The soul is essentially distinct from the body, but develops its full nature only in conjunction with the birth of the body, with which it is joined. Death is understood as a separation of the soul from the body.[7] While the Old Stoa and Chrysippus believed in the unity of the soul, Posidonius rejected that view in favor of the Platonic tripartite distinction between reason, spirit, and passion. The fundamental distinction is actually bipartite — between the rational and irrational part of the soul.[8] The irrational part was further divided into the part that seeks pleasure and one that seeks power.[9] Posidonius argued that each person has two *daimones* within them, a good and a bad.[10] The δαίμων within is the person's true self.

Despite the many differences that can be registered, there were a number of views of the soul and the body shared by the major Hellenistic philosophical traditions (Platonism, Aristotelianism, Epicureanism, and Stoicism):[11] (a) All distinguished the soul from the body. (b) All regarded the soul as the center of intelligence within the human frame. (c) All thought that the soul was localized or at least centered in a particular part of the human body (typically the chest, head, or brain). (d) All attributed mental and moral qualities to the soul, not the body. (e) All agreed that the soul had both rational and irrational aspects. (f) All (even Epicureans and Stoics) thought that death could

---

6   Rist, *Mind of Aristotle*, 177–82.

7   *SVF* 1.145 (Zeno); 2.792 (Chrysippus: ὁ θάνατός ἐστι ψυχῆς χωρισμὸς ἀπὸ σώματος).

8   Ludwig Edelstein and I. G. Kidd, *Posidonius*, Vol. 1: *The Fragments* (2nd ed.; Cambridge: Cambridge University Press, 1989) frags. 145–46; I. G. Kidd, *Posidonius*, Part II: *Commentary* (2 vols.; Cambridge: Cambridge University Press, 1988) 1.541–44.

9   Edelstein-Kidd, *Fragments*, frags. 31–35, 142, 148, 152, 157.

10   Edelstein-Kidd, frag. 187.

11   Some of these common features are discussed by A. A. Long, 'Soul and Body in Stoicism,' *Phronesis* 27 (1982) 35–36.

be defined as the separation of the soul from the body.[12] (g) All but the Epicureans and the Stoic Panaetius (Cicero *Tusc.* 1.79) believed that the soul continued to exist for at least a limited period of time after separation from the body at death.[13] This is a significant list of common convictions, many of which coincide with popular views widely subscribed to in the Hellenistic and Roman world.

Refutations of proposals that Hellenistic conceptions of human nature influenced Paul's own views have frequently been based on caricatures of '*the* Greek view', often based on an oversimplified understanding of classical sources coupled with a superficial understanding of Hellenistic paradigms of human nature. Thus W. D. Davies has argued that according to 'Hellenistic dualism' the material body was regarded as intrinsically evil, but the term σάρξ was not used in 'the prevailing Hellenistic literature' (whatever that means) for the material as opposed to the ideal.[14] Aside from the problematic use of the phrase 'Hellenistic dualism', which masks the variety of Hellenistic views of human nature, Davies is wrong

---

[12]   (1) Plato and the Old Academy (Pl. *Phd.* 66e, 67d; *Grg.* 524b; *Tim.* 81d–e). (2) Popular Platonism in the second or first century B.C.E. (Ps.–Pl. *Axiochus* 365E). (3) Epicurus and Epicureans (Sext. Emp. *Pyr.* 3.229; Lucr. 3.838f.; although the soul does not survive the separation). (4) Stoics, e.g. Zeno (*SVF* 1.145); Chrysippus (*SVF* 2.790 = Karlheinz Hülser, *Die Fragmente zur Dialektik der Stoiker* [3 vols.; Stuttgart-Bad Cannstatt: Frommann-Holzboog, 1987–88] 427): ὁ θάνατός ἐστι ψυχῆς χωρισμὸς ἀπὸ σώματος; *SVF* 2.604, 792; Epict. *Diss.* 2.1.17. See Matthias Baltes, 'Die Todesproblematik in der griechischen Philosophie,' *Gymnasium* 95 (1988) 97–128, esp. 97–98.

[13]   Epicurus was a monistic materialist who held that the soul like the body is mortal (both are made of atoms), and cannot survive the destruction of the body (Epicurus *Ep. ad Men.* 124–27; Hermann Usener, *Epicurea* [Leipzig: Teubner, 1887] 60–62). Some Stoics held that only the ἡγεμονικόν (one of the eight parts of the soul) survived until the ἐκπύρωσις of the world (Adolf Bonhöffer, *Epictet und die Stoa: Untersuchungen zur stoischen Philosophie* [Stüttgart: Ferdinand Enke, 1890] 107–8; John M. Rist, *Stoic Philosophy* [Cambridge: Cambridge University Press, 1969] 256–57), although middle Stoics, Panaetius and Boethus of Sidon rejected the doctrine of ἐκπύρωσις (Edelstein-Kidd, *Fragments,* frag. 99b; cf. Kidd, *Commentary* 1.407–8). On the varied and complex views of the survival of the soul after death in Stoicism, see Bonhöffer, *Epictet,* 54–67. Those Stoics who contemplated the survival of the ἡγεμονικόν typically refused to consider any change or development of the independent ἡγεμονικόν or soul. The Stoic view that the soul ascends after death to the sky mentioned by Sext. Emp. (*Math.* 1.71–74) may in fact be derived from Posidonius; cf. A. D. Nock, *Essays on Religion in the Ancient World* (2 vols.; Oxford: Clarendon, 1972) 2.870–71. The ascent of the soul after death is also reflected in Cynic letters (cf. Ps.-Heraclitus *Ep.* 5).

[14]   *Paul and Rabbinic Judaism* (rev. ed.; London: SPCK, 1955) 18–19.

on both counts. It was only during the second century C.E. and later that Platonic idealism was radically interpreted to mean that matter was intrinsically evil and spirit intrinsically good,[15] a position that characterized (but was not restricted to) most strands of Gnosticism. Further, while Davies is correct that ψυχή and σάρξ are not used antithetically in *classical* Greek literature,[16] in the tripartite psychology of Marcus Aurelius, the term σάρξ is used interchangeably with σῶμα (2.2, 3.16; 12.3), and σάρξ is also used as a synonym of σῶμα by Epictetus (*Diss.* 2.1.17, 19; 3.7.4, 9), and Philo (*De gig.* 29–31).

The notion that the body was intrinsically evil and a temporary prison for the immortal soul (exaggerated, to be sure), generally considered an Orphic or Pythagorean view adopted by Plato, is primarily associated with the *Phaedo.*[17] Plato's *Timaeus,* however, was even more influential and probably one of the most important philosophical treatises in the Hellenistic and Roman period,[18] particularly after Platonism began to dominate philosophical discussion beginning with the first century B.C.E.[19] In his lengthy discussion of the fashioning of the soul and body of the human person in *Tim.* 69a–92c, Plato observes:

> From both these evils [diseases of the body and soul] the one means of salvation is this — neither to exercise the soul without the body nor the body without the soul, so that they may be evenly matched and sound of health. (*Tim.* 88b; LCL trans.)

Plotinus, who noted that Plato did not say the same thing about the soul everywhere in his writings, alludes to various passages in Plato's *Phaedo, Cratylus,* and *Republic,* and then calls attention to the positive assessment of the soul–body dualism in the *Timaeus:*

---

[15] Albrecht Dihle, *The Theory of Will in Classical Antiquity* (Berkeley: University of California Press, 1982) 66.

[16] Ernest DeWitt Burton, *Spirit, Soul, and Flesh* (Chicago: University of Chicago Press, 1918) 51–52.

[17] This exaggerated view of the antithetical relationship between body and soul in the *Phaedo* has been refuted by Michael A. Grosso (*Death and the Myth of the True Earth in Plato's Phaedo* (Ph.D. diss., Columbia University, 1971).

[18] See the survey of its influence in David T. Runia, *Philo of Alexandria and the Timaeus of Plato* (Leiden: Brill, 1986) 38–57.

[19] H. Dörrie, 'Die Erneuerung des Platonismus im ersten Jahrhundert vor Christus,' in his *Platonica Minora* (München: Wilhelm Fink, 1973) 154–65.

And, though in all these passages he disapproves of the soul's coming to the body, in the *Timaeus* when speaking about this All he praises the universe and calls it a blessed god, and says that the soul was given by the goodness of the Craftsman, so that this All might be intelligent, because it had to be intelligent, and this could not be without the soul. (*Enn.* 4.8.1; LCL trans.)

A similarly positive assessment of the soul–body dualism is found in Aristotle's *Protrepticus* (Düring, *Protrepticus*, frag. B60), an early exoteric work reflecting the 'Platonic' phase of his views of human nature:

In the soul, there is on the one hand reason (which by nature rules and judges in matters concerning ourselves), on the other hand that which follows and whose nature is to be ruled; everything is in perfect order when each part brings its proper excellence to bear; for to attain this excellence is a good.

The materialistic monism of Epicureans and early Stoics meant that they also had a positive attitude toward physical existence in this material world. Posidonius, the eclectic middle Stoic, expressed a view similar to that reflected in the *Timaeus* (perhaps based on his reading of that dialogue):[20] τὸ τέλος is 'to live contemplating the truth and order of absolutely everything (τῶν ὅλων), and contributing to the establishment of it (αὐτήν) as far as possible (in oneself), without being influenced by the irrational part of the soul (ὑπὸ τοῦ ἀλόγου μέρους τῆς ψυχῆς]'.[21] A positive assessment of the relationship between soul and body is reflected in Ps.-Heraclitus *Ep.* 9 (trans. Malherbe),[22] reflecting a more popular view: 'The body, while a slave to the soul, is at the same time its fellow citizen, and it does not irritate the intellect (νοῦς) to dwell with its servants.'

---

[20] Clem. Al. *Strom.* 2.21; Edelstein-Kidd, *Fragments*, frag. 186.

[21] Since Posidonius rejected the notion of parts or divisions of the soul (he preferred the term δύναμις over μέρος; cf. Edelstein-Kidd, *Fragments*, frag. 146), the last part of this quotation ('without being ... soul') is probably an addition by Clement; cf. Kidd, *Commentary* 2.674.

[22] Abraham J. Malherbe, *The Cynic Epistles: A Study Edition* (SBLSBS 12; Missoula: Scholars Press, 1977).

Pauline Perspectives on Human Nature

The problem of the internal coherence and structure of Pauline thought, including a reconstruction of his views of human nature, has continued to challenge New Testament scholarship. Yet this task has proven problematic, in part because theories of the development of Paul's thought based on the reconstructed order of the Pauline letters have not met with general acceptance, and in part because Paul was neither systematic nor completely consistent in his (admittedly random) statements about human nature.[23] Some of the common strategies for dealing with this problem include proposing conceptual frameworks that incorporate much of the evidence for Paul's views of human nature, but then dismissing the intractible passages as survivals of popular conceptions,[24] or to force them willy-nilly to conform to the overall perspective,[25] or to claim that Paul is parroting the views of his opponents in order to refute them.

There is a widespread view among New Testament scholars (due primarily to the influential scholarship of Rudolf Bultmann), that the major Pauline anthropological terms (καρδία, νοῦς, συνείδησις, σῶμα, πνεῦμα, φρήν, and ψυχή) are not ontologically distinct *parts* of the human person (supposedly the Hellenistic view), but rather different *aspects* of human personality viewed from various perspectives (suppos-

---

[23] The problems are summarized in Robert Jewett, *Paul's Anthropological Terms* (AGJU 10; Leiden: Brill, 1971) 1–4 (Jewett's own thesis is that conflict situations are the primary reason for inconsistencies in Paul's anthropology); cf. Hans Dieter Betz, *Galatians* (Hermeneia; Philadelphia: Fortress, 1979) 280, where the right questions are raised, but no suggestions are proposed.

[24] Cf. Joseph A. Fitzmyer (*Paul and His Theology* [2nd ed.; Englewood Cliffs, NJ: Prentice Hall, 1989] 82), who says that the Greek terms Paul used for body, flesh, soul, spirit, mind, and heart, 'do not designate parts of a human being but rather aspects of the person as seen from different perspectives'. Yet in the next sentence he observes: 'A popular, common conception of the human being as made up of two elements is found at times in Paul's writings (1 Cor 5.3; 7.34; 2 Cor 12.2–3).'

[25] This is frequently the strategy adopted by W. David Stacey (*The Pauline View of Man in Relation to Its Judaic and Hellenistic Backgrounds* [London: Macmillan, 1956]). On p. 201, for example, in refuting a view of Pfleiderer on νοῦς in Paul, he says: 'The first objection to this view is that it contradicts the oft-asserted idea that Paul thought of man as a totality.'

edly the view of the Old Testament and Paul).[26] This issue is extremely complex, however, for when Hellenistic writers are concerned with the *function* of the realities represented by the various anthropological terms mentioned above, they are in effect interested in *aspects* of human nature. Thus in many ways the dichotomy between *parts* and *aspects* is a false one.

Paul has more to say about human nature than any other early Christian author, yet he never deals with the subject directly, nor do the fragmentary expressions of his views of human nature exhibit internal consistency. Further, only in Romans 6–8 and Gal 5.13–6.10 does Paul *explicitly* link his views of human nature with Christian ethics. Paul does use a number of dichotomous designations for human nature: (1) σάρξ-πνεῦμα (Rom 1.4; 8.4–6, 27; 1 Cor 5.5: the destruction of the σάρξ [that is, death] will ensure the salvation of the πνεῦμα; 2 Cor 7.1; Gal 3.2–3; 4.29; 5.16–18; Col 2.5). (2) σῶμα-πνεῦμα (Rom 8.10–11, 13; 1 Cor 5.3 [cf. Col 2.5 σῶμα = σάρξ]; 7.34; 12.13; cf. Eph 4.4). (3) νοῦς-σάρξ (Rom 7.22–25; cf. Col 2.18). Only in 1 Thess 5.23, does Paul use the trichotomous designation σῶμα-ψυχή-πνεῦμα,[27] where taken together these three anthropological terms function to encompass the entire person. The presupposition, however, is that the person is constituted of these elements.

Paul distinguishes between the πνεῦμα and the νοῦς in 1 Cor 14.14–19, and advises against allowing the spirit to do what the mind cannot participate in. According to vv. 14–15:

> For if I pray in a tongue, my spirit (τὸ πνεῦμά μου) prays but my mind (ὁ νοῦς μου) is unfruitful. What am I to do? I will pray with the spirit (τῷ πνεύματι) and I will pray with the mind (τῷ νοΐ) also; I will sing with the spirit (τῷ πνεύματι) and I will sing with the mind (τῷ νοΐ) also.

---

[26] Ernst Käsemann, 'On Paul's Anthropology,' *Perspectives on Paul* (Philadelphia: Fortress, 1971) 7: 'The basic insight of Bultmann's interpretation was that the apostle's anthropological termini do not, as in the Greek world, characterize the component parts of the human organism; they apply to existence as a whole, while taking account of its varying orientation and capacity in any given case.'

[27] A. J. Festugière, 'La division *corps-âme-esprit* de I Thess., v. 23, et la philosophie grecque,' *L'Idéal religieux des Grecs et l'Evangile* (2nd ed.; Paris: J. Gabalda, 1981) 195–220.

According to this passage, both the πνεῦμα and the νοῦς are distinguishable faculties within the person that can perform the same activity — praying or singing aloud (*comprehensible* prayer is attributed to the νοῦς, while *incomprehensible* prayer is attributed to the πνεῦμα). These faculties may be coordinated (comprehensible praying or singing means that the νοῦς and the πνεῦμα are functioning properly with the latter somehow subordinate to the former), or uncoordinated (incomprehensible praying or singing means that the πνεῦμα is active, but the νοῦς is on hold, that is, ἄκαρπος). These faculties may be distinguished from each other and both belong to the 'higher' (non-physical) faculties within the human person. Since the term νοῦς is not a major vehicle for expressing Paul's views on aspects of human nature, it appears that he has applied a widespread ancient theory of inspiration (derived from Plato) in which the πνεῦμα temporarily displaces the νοῦς in prophetic utterance (Philo *Heres* 265), in order to differentiate between comprehensible prayer and praying in tongues.[28] Though Reitzenstein argued that Paul and his audience would understand πνεῦμα and νοῦς as synonyms based on the equivalence of the phrases τὸ πνεῦμα τοῦ θεοῦ (1 Cor 2.11, 12, 14), and νοῦς κυρίου or νοῦς Χριστοῦ (1 Cor 2.16),[29] it is obvious that they are not synonymous in 1 Cor 14.14–15. In Rom 7.23–25, Paul distinguishes between his νοῦς which is equated with his ἔσω ἄνθρωπος on the one hand, and his σάρξ, or μέλη, or τὸ σῶμα τοῦ θανάτου on the other. Thus the πνεῦμα-νοῦς contrast in 1 Cor 14.14–15 may be construed as part of a more comprehensive contrast between the πνεῦμα-νοῦς-ἔσω ἄνθρωπος on the one hand and the σάρξ on the other. This inner–outer contrast reflects a split in human nature that cannot be ignored.[30] Yet the νοῦς is not divine, as in many strands of Hellenistic philosophy and Hermetic thought, for it must be renewed or transformed (Rom 12.2; cf. Eph 4.23).

---

[28] The term νοῦς occurs fourteen times in the genuine Pauline letters, although only here and in 1 Cor 2.16, Rom 7.23–25, and Rom 12.2 is its usage relevant for our discussion.

[29] Richard Reitzenstein, *Die hellenistischen Mysterienreligionen* (Darmstadt: Wissenschaftliche Buchgesellschaft, 1966) 337–38.

[30] Samuel Laeuchli, 'Monism and Dualism in the Pauline Anthropology,' *BR* 3 (1958) 15–27, esp. 19.

2 Cor 5.1–10 is an important, though variously interpreted, passage for understanding Paul's views of human nature.[31] Vv. 1–4 are of particular significance:

> For we know that if the earthly tent (οἰκία τοῦ σκήνους) we live in is destroyed, we have a building from God, a house not made with hands, eternal in the heavens. Here indeed we groan, and long to put on our heavenly dwelling (τὸ οἰκητήριον ἡμῶν τὸ ἐξ οὐρανοῦ), so that by putting it on we may not be found naked.

Several observations can be made about this passage:[32] (1) the use of the image of the house (οἰκία) or tent (σκῆνος) as a metaphor for the physical aspect of human existence (the σῶμα, cf. vv. 6–8) occurs frequently in Hellenistic tradition from Plato on,[33] but rarely in early Judaism.[34] (2) Paul distinguishes the real person from the purely physical dimension of human existence, so that this is essentially a pluralis-

[31] Friedrich G. Lang, *2 Korinther 5, 1–10 in der neueren Forschung* (Tübingen: Mohr-Siebeck, 1973).

[32] See Egon Brandenburger, *Fleisch und Geist: Paulus und die dualistische Weisheit* (WMANT 29; Neukirchen-Vluyn: Neukirchener Verlag, 1968) 175–77, where he discusses the close parallel between 2 Cor 5.1–4 and Philo *Heres* 267 (LCL trans.): 'God does not grant as a gift to the lover of virtue that he should dwell in the body as in homeland, but only permits him to sojourn there, as in a foreign country.' See also Cic. *Tusc.* 1.11.24 (LCL trans.): 'souls, on their separation from the body, find their way to heaven as to their dwelling-place (*posse animos, cum e corporibus excesserint, in caelum quasi in domicilium suum pervenire)'*.

[33] Democr. B. 37, B. 187, B. 223 (Diels-Kranz, *Vorsokr.* 2.155, 183, 190); Longinus *Subl.* 32.5; Ps.-Hippocrates *Cord.* 7; *Anat.* 1; Ps.-Plato *Axiochus* 366a; Philo *Quaest. in Gen.* 1.28; *PGM* I.319; IV.448, 1951, 1970, 2141 (here σκῆνος means 'corpse'); Timaeus Locrus *De nat. mundi* 45, 60, 62, 86; *Corpus Hermeticum* 13.12, 15; *Sentences of Sextus* 320 (σκήνωμα); *PGM* 19a.49: 'every limb of this corpse and the spirit of this body (τὸ πνεῦμα τούτου τοῦ σκηνώματος)'; the phrase θνητῷ σκήνει in Achilles Tatius 2.36.3 is an emendation for κάλλει in the mss., and probably incorrect (Ebbe Vilborg, *Achilles Tatius, Leucippe and Clitophon*, Studia Graeca et Latina Gothoburgensia, I and XV [Stockholm: Almqvist & Wiksell, 1955–62], I.46; XV. 62); for this usage in early Christian literature in addition to 2 Pet 1.13f., *Ep. Diog.* 6.8, and *Apoc. Sedrach* 9.2, *s. v.* σκῆνος in *LPGL* 1237. This metaphor occurs frequently in Neopythagorean literature; cf. Holger Thesleff, *The Pythagorean Texts of the Hellenistic Period* (Åbo: Åbo Akademi, 1965) 43.21; 49.9; 70.9; 80.2; 124.18; 143.19; 145.2. Philo (*De somn.* 1.122) speaks of ὁ οἶκος τῆς ψυχῆς, τὸ σῶμα.

[34] See Wis 9.15; *Par. Jer.* 6.6f. (where σκήνωμα is parallel to σαρκικὸς οἶκος).

tic or dualistic appraisal of human nature reflecting neither common Hellenistic nor common early Jewish conceptions, but rather appears to be Paul's own theological construct. (3) Running throughout this passage is an undeniably *negative* evaluation of physical existence in comparison to the positive evaluation of the type of existence possible following death (cf. Rom 8.23). (4) To be 'naked' refers to that state of postmortem existence in which the self is separated from the physical body.[35] (5) The οἰκοδομὴ ἐκ θεοῦ (v. 1) or the οἰκητήριον ἐξ οὐρανοῦ, is a way of referring to the glorified body of the Christian — a form of corporeality in which the dualistic conflict between flesh and spirit is transcended by a monistic form of existence.

In 2 Cor 5.6–9 Paul continues to use the first-person plural (representing the view of Christians generally) of the desirability of being absent from the body and present with the Lord.[36] Dropping the tent metaphor which he used in vv. 1–4, he says that 'while we are at home in the body we are away from the Lord' (v. 6b), and 'we would rather be away from the body and at home with the Lord' (v. 8). Paul does not identify the Christians with their physical frames, but with the separable 'we' (that is, the true person). He does not explicitly label that part of human nature that will be separated from the body upon

---

[35] According to Plato's myth of the Vision of Judgment, told in Pl. *Grg.* 532a–524a (see E. R. Dodds, *Plato, Gorgias* [Oxford: Clarendon, 1959] 372–79), and repeated in Plut. *Consolatio ad Apoll.* 121a–c, people were once judged just before their death, but this resulted in bad decisions, for base souls were sometimes clad with beautiful bodies. Therefore Zeus arranged that people would be judged immediately after death when 'naked' (γυμνός), i.e., when their souls had been divested of their bodies. In Pl. *Cra.* 403b, people are said to fear Pluto ὅτι ἡ ψυχὴ γυμνὴ τοῦ σώματος παρ' ἐκεῖνον ἀπέρχεται. See Hans Dieter Betz, *Lukian von Samosata und das Neue Testament* (TU 76; Berlin: Akademie-Verlag, 1961) 93. Schmithals' view that 'naked' means 'dead', i.e., the absence of being, is simply impossible (*Gnosticism in Corinth* [Nashville: Abingdon, 1971] 264).

[36] This is a disputed passage which some construe as Paul's use of the language of his opponents. Schmithals finds gnostic language throughout this passage (*Gnosticism in Corinth*, 259–75), and Jewett argues that the term σῶμα reflects Paul's use of the anthropological categories of his gnostic opponents (*Paul's Anthropological Terms*, 274–77). The view that 'while we are at home in the body we are away from the Lord' is a slogan of Paul's opponents and therefore does not reflect Paul's own views has most recently been argued by Jerome Murphy-O'Connor, "Being at Home in the Body we are in Exile from the Lord" (2 Cor. 5.6b),' *RB* 93 (1986) 214–21.

death. If pressed, however, Paul probably would have preferred the term πνεῦμα to ψυχή, since the former was used as commonly in Hellenistic Judaism as the latter was among pagans. In Phil 1.21–26, Paul says of the possibility of his own physical death that τὸ ἀποθανεῖν κέρδος, 'to die is gain' (v. 21), and that to 'depart' and be with Christ would be πολλῷ μᾶλλον κρεῖσσον, 'infinitely better'.[37] He refers to τὸ ζῆν ἐν σαρκί, 'life in the flesh' (v. 22), and τὸ ἐπιμένειν [ἐν] τῇ σαρκί, 'remaining in the flesh' (v. 24), as the less preferable alternative, and in both instances σάρξ is used as the equivalent of σῶμα. Obviously it must be Paul's true self that will 'depart and be with Christ', although again he does not label this separable element. In 2 Cor 12.2–3, where not death but an altered state of consciousness is in view, Paul uses the term ἄνθρωπος for the self, the center of consciousness (whether himself or someone else). In the two contrastive states of ἐν σώματι and ἐκτὸς τοῦ σώματος or χωρὶς τοῦ σώματος, he contrasts the body with the self.

The discussion of these passages indicates that Paul did not simply take over (as did such other Jewish authors as Josephus and the author of 4 Maccabees) one particular model of Hellenistic anthropology, and indeed appears to have had no real interest in doing so. Nevertheless, Paul does refer to a variety of dualistic or pluralistic features within the human person that cannot simply be explained using Israelite models.

In ancient Mediterranean world there was a tendency to understand human life as homologous to the life of the cosmos — that is, 'the cosmos becomes the paradigmatic image of human existence'.[38] In Platonism, Stoicism, and Gnosticism, although each conceives of human nature and the cosmos in very different ways, in all three the person is understood as a microcosm of the universe.[39] Since the framework of

---

[37] D. W. Palmer ('"To die is Gain" (Philippians i 21),' *NovT* 17 [1975] 203–218) argues that the Pauline phrase is a commonplace in Greco-Roman literature for those whose life is burdensome.

[38] Mircea Eliade, *The Sacred and the Profane* (New York: Harper & Row, 1959) 165.

[39] E. Schweizer, *TDNT* 7.1028 (for primary and secondary literature); cf. Democritus, frag. 34 (*SVF* 2.153): ἐν τῷ ἀνθρώπῳ μικρῷ κόσμῳ ὄντι. In Gnosticism the three constituents of each person correspond both to human society as a whole (as well as to the visible and invisible cosmos), with its three classes of 'spiritual', 'psychic', and 'fleshly' or 'hylic', as well as to the material and immaterial cosmos.

Pauline thought is largely determined by his apocalyptic worldview (rather than a particular model of the cosmos), there is a tendency in Paul to conceptualize human nature and existence as a microcosmic version of a Christianized form of apocalyptic eschatology — that is, the apocalyptic structure of history becomes paradigmatic for understanding human nature. Just as Paul's Christian form of apocalyptic thought is characterized by a historical or eschatological dualism consisting of the juxtaposition of the old age and the new age, so his view of human nature can similarly reflect a homologous dualistic structure. The death and resurrection of Christ in the past was regarded by Paul as the eschatological event that separated 'this age' (Rom 12.2; 1 Cor 2.6; Gal 1.4) from 'the age to come' (though Paul does not explicitly use the latter term, but cf. 2 Cor 5.17; Gal 6.15), and though the final consummation was still future, for Christians the new age was present. The change in ages thus has microcosmic ramifications for individual existence (2 Cor 5.17), where the microcosmic dualism is experienced in terms of the tension between the 'already' / 'not yet' polarity — the juxtaposition of the indicative and the imperative (e.g. Gal 5.25: 'If we live in the Spirit, let us also walk by the Spirit'). It is at this point that one of the central problems of Pauline ethics become evident. If the flesh has been crucified with Christ (Gal 2.20; 3.24; 6.14; Rom 6.2, 6–7, 22; 8.13), why are the desires of the flesh still a problem for Christians (Gal 5.16–18; Rom 6.12–14; 8.5–8)? Appealing to the 'already' / 'not yet' model does not solve so much as preserve the contradiction.

However, the presence of a macrocosmic paradigm does not necessitate a detailed correspondence between a microcosmic conception of human nature and Paul's conception of the apocalyptic macrocosm. Bultmann not only demythologized the apocalyptic framework of Paul's thought, but also used an existential model as a key for what is essentially an allegorical interpretation of Paul's anthropological terminology as the choice between authentic and inauthentic modes of existence. Ernst Käsemann took Paul's apocalyptic framework seriously, and understood his dualistic use of 'flesh' and 'spirit' (along with other anthropological terms) as cosmic powers rather than as designations for aspects of human nature. Bultmann's existentialist understanding of Pauline anthropological terms (the human person is a free agent responsible for his or her own decisions) and Käsemann's apocalyptic or cosmological understanding (the human person is a victim of supernatural cosmic forces) are not mutually exclusive categories. In some respects this is a chicken-and-egg problem — did Paul's mythological view of eschatological dualism give rise to a homologous view of human nature in which the old and the new are juxtaposed until the eschatological consummation, or did his mythological view of the structure of human nature provide confirmation for his Christian understanding of Jewish apocalyptic eschatology? Neither of these possibilities is quite satisfactory, for the answer is probably more dialectical. It is more likely that Paul linked his Christianized apocalyptic outlook with current conceptions of the human person, since the former is far more unified than the latter.

Paul and the Hellenistic Philosophical 'Practice of Death'

A Platonic view articulated only in the *Phaedo* is that 'those who pursue philosophy aright study nothing but dying and being dead' (64a). The cognate terms ἀποθνῄσκειν and θνῄσκειν are metaphors, since Socrates goes on to say that most people 'do not know in what way the real philosophers desire death, nor in what way they deserve death, nor what kind of a death it is' (64b; LCL trans.). The most important purpose in life is for the soul to withdraw from the concerns of the body; asceticism (broadly defined as various forms of self-denial) is a proleptic anticipation in this life of the liberation which can only be fully experienced following death (*Phd.* 61c–69e; 80c–84b; *Tht.* 176a–b).[40] Plato's Socrates calls this μελέτη θανάτου ('the practising of being in a state of death' or 'the practice of death'; *Phd.* 67e, 81a); in other words, the preparation while in the body for the true life which is possible only when the soul is separated from the body at death.[41] This is reiterated in *Phd.* 81a (LCL trans.):

---

[40] J. C. B. Gosling and C. C. W. Taylor, *The Greeks on Pleasure* (Oxford: Clarendon, 1982) 84–86.

[41] Pl. *Phd.* 61b–c, part of a preliminary statement of Socrates in this dialogue, is also a text of central importance for ancient philosophical discussions of suicide; cf. Arthur J. Droge, '*Mori lucrum*: Paul and Ancient Theories of Suicide,' *NovT* 30 (1988) 263–86.

> If it [the soul] departs pure, dragging with it nothing of the body,
> because it never willingly associated with the body in life, but
> avoided it and gathered itself into itself all along, since this has
> always been its constant study — but this means nothing else
> than that it pursued philosophy rightly and really practiced being
> in a state of death (καὶ τῷ ὄντι τεθνάναι μελετῶσα): or is not
> this the practice of death (μελέτη θανάτου)?

The central theme of the *Phaedo* is the separation of body and soul, a
separation which is complete at death, but which is in process during
life. One must do everything possible in this life to keep the soul
untainted from the body, and the separation of the soul from the body
at death (toward which this process is directed), makes the attainment
of complete knowledge possible. The term 'separation' is used in the
sense of the attainment of freedom — something which biological
death will not automatically confer (81c).[42] Death is therefore both a
biological phenomenon, and more importantly, a way of living in this
world in which the self is transformed. Thus human experience is one
of conflict between the rational element of the soul and the body; while
this conflict can be partially mitigated by the philosophic life, complete
resolution of the conflict is possible only in death, when the soul will
be freed from the negative influences of the body. In short, 'true philosophers practice dying (οἱ ὀρθῶς φιλοσοφοῦντες ἀποθνῄσκειν
μετελῶσι)' (Pl. *Phd.* 67e), a passage alluded to by Cicero (*Tusc.* 1.30.74):
Tota enim philosophorum vita ... commentatio mortis est, 'For the whole
life of the philosopher ... is a preparation for death.'[43] The purpose of
the μελέτη θανάτου, is the unity and integration of the ψυχή, which
in its natural state is dispersed throughout the body and in conflict
with itself (*Phd.* 83a; *Resp.* 443d; *Grg.* 482c), and conflict is also caused
by the passions, desires, and fears of the body (*Phd.* 66c).

The idea of *commentatio mortis* or μελέτη θανάτου was relatively
widespread in antiquity. In Ps.-Plato *Axiochus* 366c (trans. Hershbell),[44]

---

[42] For Plato, a ψυχή may be biologically separated from the body and yet retain its
bodily orientation and material desires (81d–e); cf. Grosso, *Death,* 16.

[43] The context of this allusion is a discussion about suicide.

[44] Jackson P. Hershbell, *Pseudo-Plato, Axiochus* (SBLTT 21; Chico, CA: Scholars
Press, 1981).

Socrates is made to say (a clear allusion to the *Phaedo*), 'my soul has longed for death (θανατᾷ μου ἡ ψυχή)'. Here biological death (perhaps even suicide) is in view. Yet the therapeutic effect of Socrates' consolatory words to Axiochus frees him from the fear of his approaching death and transforms him so that he can say γέγονα καινός, 'I have become a new person' (370e). The *commentatio mortis* is also mentioned in several Cynic letters. In Ps.-Socrates *Ep.* 14.8 (trans. Malherbe), there is a clear allusion to the *Phaedo*:

> For the philosopher does nothing other than to die, since he disdains the demands of the body and is not enslaved by the pleasures of the body; and this is nothing other than the separation of the soul from the body, and death is nothing other again than the separation of the soul from the body.

See also Ps.-Diogenes *Ep.* 39 (trans. Malherbe):

> Take care, also, for your migration from here. And you will take such care, if you practice how to die (μελετήσειας ἀποθνήσκειν), that is, how to separate the soul from the body, while you are still alive. For this, I think, is what the associates of Socrates, too, call death.

A similar view might seem to lie behind the Epicurean motto '*meditare mortem*' (Sen. *Ep.* 26.8; Usener, *Epicurea*, frag. 250), which according to Seneca means that '*Qui mori didicit, servire dedidicit*, 'The one who has learned to die has unlearned slavery' (*Ep.* 26.10).[45] The Epicurean view that the philosopher must μελετᾶν ἀποθνήσκειν, 'practice dying' (Porph. *Abst.* 1.51; Usener, *Epicurea*, frag. 470) can be traced to Epicurus himself (*Ep. ad Men.* 126; Usener, *Epicurea* 61):

---

[45] A recurring theme in Hellenistic moral philosophy was to regard the various stages of life as preparations for death. When a person passed from one stage of life to another (typically conceptualized as childhood, adolescence, adulthood, old age), the previous stage 'died', so that the death that follows old age should not be viewed as abrupt but as part of a lifelong process (Sen. *Ep.* 24.20; 58.22–24; 120.17–18; *Ad. Marc.* 21.6; Philo *De Iosepho* 127–28; Plut. *De E apud Delph.* 392c–d; Marcus Aurelius 9.21; cf. Christian Gnilka, 'Neues Alter, neues Leben,' *JAC* 20 [1977] 9–13).

The one who advises the young person to live well but the old person to die well is simpleminded, not only because life is desirable, but also because to practice living well and to practice dying well are one and the same.

While this is reminiscent of Plato (*Phd.* 64a–69e; 80c–84b), Epicurus cannot have agreed with Plato that death is a positive intellectual and moral development, but rather regarded dying not as something to be feared, but as the appropriate completion of a good life. The *commentatio mortis* also played a role in the dualistic psychology of late Stoics (Sen. *Ep.* 70.17; LCL trans.): 'Would you be free from the restraint of your body? Live in it as if you were about to leave it.' Similarly, Seneca says in *Ep.* 65.16 (LCL trans.):

> For this body of ours is a weight upon the soul and its penance; as the load pressed down the soul is crushed and is in bondage, unless philosophy has come to its assistance and has bid it take fresh courage by contemplating the universe, and has turned it from things earthly to things divine. There it has liberty, there it can roam abroad; meantime it escapes the custody in which it is bound, and renews its life in heaven.

The μελέτη θανάτου is also mentioned in Iambl. *Protrepticus* 3 (ed. Pistelli, 13), which presents itself as Pythagorean teaching:

> The deliverance from evils, which few value, encourages the separation from the body and a focus on the life of the soul itself, which we call 'the practice of death' (μελέτην θανάτου).

Up to this point it appears that the *commentatio mortis* is primarily an intellectual matter which finds concrete expression in ascetic behavior — a turning away from the encumbrances of physical life that impede the life of the soul, or more particularly, the mind. Yet I believe there is also a positive counterpart to the *commentatio mortis* which consists of an intellectual focus on the definite advantages of the mode of living that characterizes postmortem existence. An example is found in Aristotle's *Protrepticus* (Düring, frag. B43; Iambl. *Protrepticus* 9; trans. Düring, *Protrepticus*, 65), in which the focus is not on death itself, but on a traditional feature of Greek afterlife mythology:

Best of all one would see the truth of what we are saying if someone carried us in thought (τῇ διανοίᾳ) to the Isles of the Blest. There there would be need of nothing, no profit from anything; there remain only thought and philosophical speculation (τὸ διανοεῖσθαι καὶ θεωρεῖν), which even now we describe as the free life (ἐλεύθερον βίον). If this is true, would not any of us be rightly ashamed if, when the chance was given us to settle in the Isles of the Blest, he were by his own fault unable to do so?

In this postmortem existence, the conflict between the somatic and noetic modes of existence would be resolved in favor of the latter. In effect this is a type of realized eschatology — that is, the challenge to live in this world in a way approximating postmortem conditions as far as possible. A similar conception is articulated in Pl. *Tht.* 176a–b (LCL trans.):

Therefore one ought to try to escape from here (ἐνθένδε, that is, from this world) to there (ἐκεῖσε, that is, to be ἐν θεοῖς) as quickly as possible. Escape means likeness to God as far as possible, and this likeness means to become just and holy and wise.

Similarly in Ps.-Plato *Axiochus* 366A (trans. Hershbell, 33):

Yet all the while the soul yearns after and is athirst for its native heavenly aither (τὸν οὐράνιον αἰθέρα), always striving for the life there and the divine choral dance. Thus the release from this life is a change from a kind of evil to a good.

This discussion of the Hellenistic philosophical *commentatio mortis* invites comparison with the important role the metaphorical significance of death had in Pauline ethics.[46] Death is certainly the most radical of metaphors for the transformed life, and Paul frequently used

---

[46] This metaphor was also used in Deutero-Pauline literature (Col 2.12–13, 20; 3.1–3; Eph 2.5–6; cf. 1 Pet 2.24) although without the so-called 'eschatological reservation' characteristic of Paul, that is, when Paul speaks of being raised with Christ he uses the future tense (but cf. Rom 6.13), while post-Pauline literature sometimes uses past tenses (e.g., Col 2.12–13; 3.1; Eph 2.5–6). Traces of the metaphor occur also in Ignatius of Antioch; cf. *Rom.* 7.2: 'My desire has been crucified [ἐσταύρωται] and there is in me no fire of love for material things.'

the language and imagery of death and dying to describe a mode of living in which the liberating effects of the death of Jesus are actualized in the present moral experience of Christians. Death as a metaphor for the morally transformed life occurs neither in early Judaism nor in Hellenism apart from the *commentatio mortis* theme. It is therefore possible that Paul's use of the metaphor of death as the basis for ethical behavior,[47] is based, at least in part, on the popular philosophical *commentatio mortis* theme in both its cognitive and behavioral dimensions.

Paul used death as a metaphor of his daily experience in 1 Cor 15.31: 'I die daily [καθ' ἡμέραν ἀποθνήσκω]' (cf. Sen. *Ep.* 24.19: *cotidie morimur*). He also argued that just as a wife is legally obligated to her husband as long as he lives, but is freed from those obligations when he dies, so Christians have been freed from the Torah through the death of Christ (Rom 7.1–6). Paul also connects the metaphor of the continual experience of death with the death of Jesus, as in 2 Cor 4.10–11:

> Always carrying in the body the death [τὴν νέκρωσιν] of Jesus, so that the life of Jesus may also be manifested in our bodies. For while we live we are always being given up to death for Jesus' sake, so that the life of Jesus may be manifested in our mortal flesh.

Here there is no development of the possible ethical implications of metaphorical death. Rather, 'death' functions as an *imitatio Christi* in that the mortal dangers Paul experienced are construed as analogous to those experienced by Christ. Yet in referring to ἡ ζωὴ τοῦ Ἰησοῦ, he doubtless means the resurrection life of Jesus. Similarly in 2 Cor 5.14 Paul links the death of Christ with the death of all believers: 'one died for all; therefore all have died'. Paul refers not only to the death of Christ as metaphorically replicated in the 'death' of the believer, but he also exploits the more shocking metaphor of crucifixion. (This barbaric

---

[47] The 'dying and rising god' model for understanding the ritual experience of those who participated in the ancient mystery cults is seriously flawed, and the link to Romans 6 is tenuous; see Jonathan Z. Smith, 'Dying and Rising Gods,' *The Encyclopedia of Religion* (16 vols.; New York: Macmillan, 1987) 4.521–27, and Walter Burkert, *Ancient Mystery Cults* (Cambridge, Mass.: Harvard University Press, 1987) 99–102.

form of execution, referred to as the *servile supplicium*, is understandably never referred to in a positive sense in connection with treatments of the *commentatio mortis* theme.)[48] Paul, however, exploits this metaphor in a positive way in Gal 2.19–20:

> I through the law died to the law, that I might live to God. I have been crucified with Christ; it is no longer I who live, but Christ lives in me; and the life I now live in the flesh I live by faith in the Son of God, who loved me and gave himself for me.

Here the verb συνεσταύρωμαι is a perfect passive — the agent who performs the action specified by the verb is someone other than Paul. The crucifixion metaphor is important for Paul and appears again in Gal 5.24, where he claims that 'those who belong to Christ Jesus have crucified the flesh with its passions and desires'. Here Christians, the subject of the verb ἐσταύρωσαν, have actively 'crucified' their σάρξ which represents (and hence serves as a metaphor for) their παθήματα and ἐπιθυμίαι. In Gal 6.14 Paul speaks of the cross of Christ, 'by which the world has been crucified to me, and I to the world'. Here the effects of crucifixion are again individualized (as in Gal 2.19–20) because they are explicitly applied only to Paul's own experience. While 'death' and 'crucifixion' are used as metaphors in Galatians (ἀποθνή-σκειν in 2.19, 21; συσταυροῦν in 2.19; σταυροῦν in 5.24; 6.14), the possible *ethical* implications of the resurrection are not developed in this context.

The metaphor of death as the basis for the transformed life permeates Romans 6–8.[49] In Rom 6.2, Paul affirms that 'we died to sin', and bases this view on baptism, understood as a vicarious ritual experience of the death and resurrection of Christ. Though this understanding of baptism is arguably pre-Pauline, the *ethical* implications of this

---

[48] Note the metaphor Plato uses in *Phd* 83d (LCL trans.): 'Each pleasure or pain nails (προσηλοῖ) it (the soul) as with a nail (ἧλον) to the body and rivets it on and makes it corporeal, so that it fancies the things are true which the body says are true.' Here the metaphor of crucifixion is used negatively.

[49] There is an extremely high concentration of terms for death, many used metaphorically, in Romans 5–8: (1) ἀποθνήσκειν (17 times; elsewhere in Romans 6 times in 14.7–15); (2) θάνατος (21 times; elsewhere in Romans only in 1.32); (3) νεκρός (9 times; elsewhere in Romans 7 times); (4) συσταυροῦν (only in Rom 6.6; cf. Gal 2.19).

ritual re-enactment of Christ's death and resurrection were probably a Pauline innovation. Since the person who has died has been freed (δεδικαίωται) from sin (Rom 6.7), in baptism Christians have experienced liberation from the life of bondage by vicariously sharing the death of Christ.

In both the philosophical discussions of the *commentatio mortis* and Paul's discussions of the ethical implications of the death and resurrection of Christians, a certain kind of *knowledge* is critically important for determining behavior. There is a pervasive use of cognitive language in Paul's discussion of how the death of Christ can be appropriated: (1) 'Knowing (γινώσκοντες) that our old self (ὁ παλαιὸς ἄνθρωπος) was crucified' (Rom 6.6). (2) 'If we died with Christ we believe (πιστεύομεν) that we will also live with him, knowing (εἰδότες) that Christ being raised from the dead will never again die' (Rom 6.8–9). (3) 'Consider (λογίζεσθε) yourselves dead to sin but alive to God' (Rom 6.11). (4) In Romans 8, Paul speaks of those who 'set their minds (φρονοῦσιν)' on concerns of the flesh or the Spirit, for 'to set the mind (τὸ φρόνημα) on the flesh is death, but to set the mind (τὸ φρόνημα) on the Spirit is life and peace' (Rom 8.5–6). This use of cognitive language indicates that baptism itself does not produce an automatic transformation of the one baptized. The metaphorical character of Paul's language is clear not only on the basis of these cognitive terms, but also from the simile in Rom 6.13: ὡσεὶ ἐκ νεκρῶν ζῶντας, 'as though alive from the dead'.

There is a phemonenological similarity between the negative and positive cognitive and behavioral aspects of the *commentatio mortis* and Paul's utilization of the language of death and resurrection as bases for Christian ethics. The major difference lies in the fact that for a philosopher the proleptic experience of death was always limited to the anticipation of his own death, whereas in Paul, the death and resurrection of Christ became paradigmatic for individual experience. Certainly the language of 'death' as a radical metaphor for the transformed life was available to Paul in the widespread popular philosophical doctrine of the *commentatio mortis*.

Index of
Jewish and Christian Scriptures

315

318

Index of
Ancient Literature Outside Scripture

Index of
Modern Authors

335